Readers and writers with a difference

Readers and writers with a difference

A HOLISTIC APPROACH TO TEACHING LEARNING DISABLED AND REMEDIAL STUDENTS

Lynn K. Rhodes
School of Education
University of Colorado at Denver

Curt Dudley-Marling
Faculty of Education
York University
Toronto, Ontario, Canada

Heinemann
Portsmouth, NH

Heinemann Educational Books, Inc.
70 Court Street   Portsmouth, NH   03801
Offices and agents throughout the world

We are grateful to the following for permission to reprint previously published material:

For Figure 2−1: From *Pancakes for Breakfast*, copyright © 1978 by Tomie de Paola; copyright © 1978 by Harcourt Brace Jovanovich, Inc. Adapted and reproduced by permission of the publisher.

For Figure 7−1: From Nancie Atwell, "Having a Writing Conference with Yourself," *Livewire* (December 1984). Reprinted by permission of the National Council of Teachers of English.

For Figure 9−2: From J. Gale, *Neat and Scruffy* (Toronto: Ashton Scholastic, 1975), pp. 2−18. Reprinted by permission of Ashton Scholastic Ltd.

For Figure 9−3: From J. E. Richardson, *A Risky Trip* (Beverly Hills, CA: Benziger, 1976), pp. 40−41. Reprinted by permission of Glencoe Publishing Company.

For Figure 10−1: From Taffy E. Raphael, "Teaching Question−Answer Relationships, Revisited," *Reading Teacher* 39 (1986): 519, Figure 2. Reprinted with permission of Taffy E. Raphael and the International Reading Association.

Predictable Trade Books for Young Children: From Lynn K. Rhodes, "I Can Read! Predictable Books as Resources for Reading and Writing Instruction," *Reading Teacher* 34 (1981): 511−18. Reprinted by permission of the International Reading Association.

Predictable Books for Middle-School Children: From Margaret Atwell, "Predictable Books for the Middle School Child," in D. Watson (ed.), *Ideas and Insights: Teaching the English Language Arts K−6* (Urbana, IL: National Council of Teachers of English, forthcoming). Reprinted by permission of Margaret Atwell and the National Council of Teachers of English.

Every effort has been made to contact the copyright holders for permission to reprint borrowed material. We regret any oversights that may have occurred and would be happy to rectify them in future printings of this work.

Library of Congress Cataloging-in-Publication Data

Rhodes, Lynn Knebel.
  Readers and writers with a difference.

  Bibliography: p.
  Includes index.
  1. Learning disabled children—Education—United States.   2. Language arts (Elementary)—United States.
3. Reading (Elementary)—United States.
4. Interdisciplinary approach in education—United States.   I. Dudley-Marling, Curt.   II. Title.
LC4705.R5 1988   371.9′0973   87−23819
ISBN 0−435−08453−4

Front cover photo by Kenyon Shannon.
Designed by Wladislaw Finne.
Printed in the United States of America.
92 91 90 89 88   10 9 8 7 6 5 4 3 2 1

Contents

v

Introduction

Before you begin reading this book, we'd like you to think about what it means to be a holistic teacher, and how the instructional and assessment strategies presented throughout this book should be viewed.

Holistic teachers are concerned with more than reading and writing. Holistic teaching extends to all areas of learning and the curriculum. Holistic education is a philosophy of teaching, not an approach to reading and writing instruction. It is as applicable to science, math, geography, and history as it is to teaching written and oral language. Holistic teachers endeavor to place students' learning within the context of their own experiences. When learning is meaningful, students learn. In fact, in a meaningful environment, it is difficult to stop children from learning.

When learning is not meaningful, artificial rewards must be used to encourage students' efforts. No artificial rewards were needed, however, to help children learn to talk, walk, or want to play with their friends because learning to talk or walk fulfilled important social and emotional needs. Holistic teachers seek to ensure that reading and writing also meet the emotional and social needs of their students.

Holistic teachers do not fragment learning, nor do they divide and subdivide learning into artificial time periods. Just as holistic teachers encourage reading, writing, and oral language across the curriculum, they attempt to integrate all areas of the curriculum. They will be just as likely to take advantage of an opportunity to teach a geography lesson during reading as the other way around.

Holistic teachers are themselves learners, learning with and from their students. At the same time, teachers are students of learning, regularly observing their students as they learn and respond to instruction. As a result, holistic teachers learn about literacy development and modify their instruction according to their students' needs. Teachers also reflect on their own teaching, and on themselves as readers and writers, so that they can share their own literacy experiences with their students.

Holistic teachers respect the learning capabilities of students. They recognize that students will learn what is personally meaningful to them. For this reason, they carefully consider the literacy environment they create with students, striving to mirror the purposes, audiences, and materials of the literate world. They also recognize that students must have plentiful opportunities for reading and writing if they are to become readers and writers.

In this text we present strategies that we believe will encourage the reading and writing development of learning disabled and remedial readers. We focus upon those strategies with which we are personally familiar or which teachers we know have shared with us. You will certainly encounter many other strategies elsewhere. And we have no doubt that you already have or will invent successful strategies worth sharing with others.

The strategies we suggest in the forthcoming chapters should be considered only as models for written language assessment and instruction. It may be that some of them will work for you without adaptation while others may not work at all; in general, most will have to be modified in accordance with teachers' individual styles and the unique needs of each of their students. We hope that teachers will use the strategies presented in this book productively and not prescriptively. Those who use the information presented here as another experience in their continued learning and growth will obtain the greatest benefit from this text. We have not and cannot provide teachers with *the* answers for meeting the needs of their students. What we can do is to help promote their growth as teachers by stimulating their thinking and sharing some of our ideas. We hope that our readers will use our ideas this way, continue to seek the ideas of others, and, more importantly, integrate these ideas into their own experiences with students. We wish our readers the best in their continued growth.

We'd like to conclude this introduction by thanking our colleagues who have contributed to our ongoing learning, especially the many teachers who have talked with us and challenged our thinking about literacy development and instruction and continue to do so.

I

Learning disabled and remedial students: A holistic view

Teachers have always been challenged by students who don't succeed in reading and writing at the same rate as their peers. These students may be labeled learning disabled, dyslexic, underachievers, remedial readers, and the like. When we taught children, we often wondered why some students were placed in remedial classes while others were placed in learning disabilities classes; their reading and writing performance seemed quite similar to us and, in fact, often resembled the performance of normally achieving younger students. No doubt you've wondered and observed the same things.

In this chapter, we'll continue to wonder about these things. To help shed light on a very murky situation, we'll briefly trace the emergence of the field of learning disabilities and compare learning disabled and remedial students. Most importantly, we'll talk about why a holistic view of learning is an essential foundation for reconsidering the reading and writing instruction we offer to students who are not succeeding in learning to read and write, no matter what they are labeled.

LEARNING DISABILITIES THEN AND NOW

Educators have been concerned about children who have serious difficulty learning to read and write, especially learning to read, ever since the systematic teaching of reading and writing began in our schools (Lipa, 1983). Most of our attention has been focused on students whose reading failures could not easily be explained, or traced to obvious physical or sensory difficulties or to low intelligence.

Physicians were among the first to consider these unexplained reading failures. They described children and adults who couldn't read despite normal sensory and

1

intellectual development. For example, Kussmaul (cited in Weiderholt, 1974) identified "word blindness" in adults who couldn't read even though the powers of sight, speech, and intellect remained intact. Later Hinshelwood (1917) described children who suffered from "congenital word blindness."

Gradually, as more and more physicians, psychologists, speech and language specialists, and educators focused their attention on reading failures, a consensus emerged that these reading failures were due to processing problems caused by neurological dysfunction. The label "learning disabilities" (LD) slowly began to replace other terms like "Strauss syndrome," "minimal brain damage," "perceptual handicap," and "dyslexia." Today, of course, learning disability is a widely recognized handicap, and public school classes for learning disabled children are common throughout the Western world. Nonetheless, debate about the nature of learning disabilities continues.

Although most learning disability specialists today subscribe to a neurological view of learning disabilities, direct evidence of neurological damage in people identified as learning disabled is rare. Instead, the assumption of neurological deficits is usually based upon correlational evidence. For example, it's often assumed that those labeled learning disabled are neurologically impaired if their performance on certain tests is like that of persons known to have some sort of brain damage. It's further assumed that neurological impairment is responsible for the students' reading and writing difficulties.

Theories on the causes of learning disabilities are not limited to neurological deficit hypotheses. Diet, vitamin deficiencies, food additives, inner ear problems, vision defects, and heredity have also been identified as possible etiological factors. It's unlikely, however, that a single cause can be identified that will explain all learning disabilities. It's much more likely that a number of conditions act either singly or in combination to influence the diagnosis of a learning disability.

Historically, speculation about the causes of learning disabilities has tended to focus on conditions intrinsic to the student. Recently, however, increased attention has been focused on factors extrinsic to the student that may influence the diagnosis of learning disabilities. Sleeter (1984), for example, asserts that an understanding of the development of the field of learning disabilities depends upon an understanding of the social context within which the field has emerged. She cites the sharp rise in standards for reading achievement during this century, especially as a result of the launching of Sputnik by the Soviet Union and the more recent "back to basics" movement.

While having a positive effect on average reading scores, higher standards in reading achievement and curriculum have also increased the number of reading failures (Sleeter, 1984). Apparently, increased attention to reading instruction hasn't affected all students equally. Sleeter argues that the assumption that learning disabilities are intrinsic to the child serves as a convenient explanation for our most severe reading failures. The child, not the curriculum or standards for achievement, is seen as the problem.

It's our view that neither extrinsic nor intrinsic factors can, by themselves, adequately explain a learning disability. What is more likely is that the diagnosis of a learning disability is the result of factors both extrinsic and intrinsic to the individual student (Kavale & Forness, 1985) that interact and change continually. The nature of the relationship between these factors and how it affects children's learning has not been adequately explained. But it's likely that extrinsic factors such as class size, teacher competence, academic standards, and instructional methods will interact with a variety of learner variables to affect the diagnosis of a learning disability. In any case, teachers can only do something about extrinsic variables in their efforts to help LD students learn to read and write.

WHAT IS (ARE) LEARNING DISABILITIES?

The numerous definitions of learning disabilities proposed over the years share a number of common features. These definitions typically restrict learning disabilities to cases of impaired language or academic development: "A learning disability refers to a retardation, or delayed development in one or more of the processes of speech, language, reading, spelling, writing, or arithmetic" (Kirk, 1962, 253). Some definitions of LD also refer to social deficits, which "become evident in both academic and social situations" (Ontario Ministry of Education, 1980, 4). Many definitions acknowledge neurological factors in explaining learning disabilities (e.g., "...we refer to children as having a psychoneurological learning disability, meaning that behavior has been disturbed as a result of a dysfunction of the brain" [Johnson & Myklebust, 1967]) and often include some reference to processing disorders without specifying the nature of the disorders. Bateman (1965), for example, states that the educational problems of learning disabled students are "...related to basic disorders in the learning processes" (220).

More recent definitions of learning disabilities routinely include exclusion clauses, which describe who may not be labeled learning disabled. The official federal definition of learning disabilities in the United States states: "The term does not include children who have learning problems which are primarily the result of visual, hearing, or motor handicaps, of mental retardation, of emotional disturbance, or of environmental, cultural, or economic disadvantage" (*Federal Register*, 1977).

There has been some confusion about the intent of exclusion clauses. They are not meant to exclude visually and hearing impaired, emotionally disturbed, and culturally different children from the category of learning disabilities but instead, only those children whose learning problems can be adequately explained by other handicaps or environmental influences, including poor teaching. A visually or hearing impaired child may also have a learning disability, and learning disabilities may be especially likely among the economically disadvantaged (Kavale, 1980).

The definition of learning disabilities proposed by the National Joint Committee on Learning Disabilities (NJCLD), one of the most recent, is a representative definition that has received the endorsement of a large number of organizations concerned with the oral and written language problems of children and adults:

> Learning disabilities is a generic term that refers to a heterogeneous group of disorders manifested by significant difficulties in the acquisition and use of listening, speaking, reading, writing, reasoning or mathematical abilities. These disorders are intrinsic to the individual and presumed to be central nervous system dysfunctions. Even through a learning disability may occur concomitantly with other handicapping conditions (e.g., sensory impairment, (mental retardation, social and emotional disturbance) or environmental influences (e.g., cultural differences, insufficient/ inappropriate instruction, psychogenic factors), it is not the direct result of those conditions or influences. (Hammill et al., 1981, 336)

In this definition, a learning disability is considered to be largely an academic problem, presumably of neurological origin, and it avoids the controversy over the nature of processing problems by making no reference at all to processing problems. This definition also includes a strong statement about the intrinsic nature of learning disabilities, which, along with an exclusion clause, is intended to limit the effect of extrinsic or environmental influences on the diagnosis of a learning disability. However, in practice it's difficult to separate intrinsic and extrinsic factors. Intelligence tests are routinely used in the diagnosis of a learning disability, for example, but it's possible for staffing teams to debate endlessly the relative influence of intrinsic and extrinsic factors on IQ test performance. And how can "inappropriate instruction" be defined and separated from how the student currently reads and writes?

Many parents and professionals are frustrated by the apparent vagueness of most accepted definitions of learning disabilities. LD definitions have not been particularly useful for determining eligibility for LD services nor do they help teachers and parents decide what to do for the student instructionally. However, the process by which definitions are adopted is a political one that often involves many compromises. A very specific definition may get the enthusiastic support of some groups but may also arouse considerable opposition. Therefore, definitions of learning disability are necessarily vague although still useful in providing a focus for advocacy, research, and the provision of services.

WHO'S WHO? LEARNING DISABLED AND REMEDIAL STUDENTS

Although identification procedures vary greatly, learning disabilities are most commonly identified in terms of a discrepancy between measures of ability, usually an IQ test, and measures of academic achievement. For example, in many educational jurisdictions students qualify for LD services if they exhibit a "significant" discrepancy between measured IQ and a particular achievement test (e.g., 15 percentile points) and if their learning problems are not *primarily* the result of impaired vision or hearing, emotional disturbance, environmental influences, and so on. Even though it's common to define learning disabilities in terms of a discrepancy, discrepancy criteria vary greatly across jurisdictions (Kavale & Nye, 1981; Mercer, Hughes, & Mercer, 1985; Perlmutter & Parus, 1983) with the result that children identified as LD in one jurisdiction may not be identified as LD in a neighboring jurisdiction.

The practice of operationalizing learning disabilities as a discrepancy has met with some criticism. There has been concern, for example, about the reliability of "difference" scores (Algozzine et al., 1979). There has also been concern that an overreliance on discrepancy criteria might limit learning disabilities solely to academic problems, ignoring children with severe social difficulties. Discrepancy indices also tend to limit learning disabilities to students performing significantly below grade level. Though some exceptionally bright students may be functioning at grade level, they may be experiencing considerable stress from exerting tremendous energy trying to remain organized (Doreen Kronick, personal communication, April 1985). Students like these may be candidates for LD services but, in many jurisdictions, they are effectively excluded from the LD category. In general, critics of discrepancy criteria would be satisfied if discrepancy indices were just one of many criteria used for identifying a learning disability (Cone & Wilson, 1981).

There is increasing evidence that current assessment practices fail to discriminate LD students from other underachievers, especially students who are placed in remedial classes. Researchers have shown that school psychologists and special education teachers aren't able to discriminate reliably between students in the lowest quartile of academic achievement and children identified as learning disabled (see Epps, McGue & Ysseldyke, 1982; Epps, Ysseldyke, and McGue, 1984). Other studies indicate considerable overlap in the characteristics of LD students and underachievers (Ysseldyke, Algozzine, Shinn, & McGue, 1982; Deshler, Schumarker, Warner, Alley, & Clark, 1980) and even between LD and normally achieving students (Dudley-Marling, Kaufman & Tarver, 1981; Harber, 1979, 1982; & Weener, 1981).

Apparently, the only characteristic that separates groups of learning disabled students from underachieving students is the degree of underachievement. Learning disabled students, at least in terms of current identification practices, appear to be a subset of underachievers (McLeod, 1983), as different from each other as they are from normally achieving students (Poplin, 1984a). Algozzine, Ysseldyke, and Shinn (1982) conclude that "learning disabilities is merely a sophisticated term for underachievers" (304).

Remedial readers, another subgroup of underachievers, are so delayed in their reading and writing development that they require special attention, but they have not been labeled learning disabled. As a group of severe underachievers, remedial learners may be especially similar to those students identified as learning disabled. Research suggests that remedial readers might be identified as learning disabled if only they were referred for a learning disability evaluation (see Epps, McGue & Ysseldyke, 1982; Epps, Ysseldyke & McGue, 1984). It is certainly clear that not all teachers have the same criteria for referring students for learning disability placement.

We don't wish to give the impression that we think there are no differences between students who are identified as learning disabled and those who are identified as remedial. Though we see few differences in the reading and writing of underachievers no matter what their label, there are a few students in learning disability programs who clearly have more severe difficulties than those usually found in remedial programs.

However, we agree with Ysseldyke and Algozzine (1983), who assert that the argument over what is and is not a learning disability is fruitless and actually misses the more important point about those labeled learning disabled: "to ponder, argue, quibble, and mix about what to call them and who they are has merely served to sidetrack interest from the bigger, more important question— what do we do with them?" (29). There are children who are failing in school, children in need of our help. Our most important task is to identify effective teaching strategies for these students and not to engage in endless polemics over what to call them.

TEACHING LEARNING DISABLED AND REMEDIAL STUDENTS: A HOLISTIC VIEW

Until recently the debate over the best methods for teaching LD students focused on the effectiveness of the ability training model, which assumes that specific abilities underlie success in learning to read and write. Many teachers have viewed learning disabilities in terms of remediating underlying ability deficits before academic learning can proceed normally. Although there are a number of variants of the ability training model, these programs typically focus on the training of perceptual-motor skills, "psycholinguistic abilities," or both.

Some of the same sort of thinking has influenced remedial instruction. Remedial students, especially younger ones, have been subjected to many of the same perceptual-motor and visual discrimination exercises as learning disabled students, only, in the case of these students, they've been called "readiness" activities.

It has become increasingly obvious, however, that many of the ability deficits assumed to be causally related to reading failure are not uncommon in normally achieving students (see, for example, Hare, 1977). Many professionals have also questioned the adequacy of tests used to identify perceptual-motor and psycholinguistic problems as well as the efficacy of ability training programs (see Arter & Jenkins, 1979, for a review of this literature). While ability training programs may affect students' performance on ability tests, most studies have shown that they have little effect on students' reading and writing performance (Arter & Jenkins, 1979; Kavale & Forness, 1985). Even the widespread practice of attempting to match children's preferred learning modality to teaching methods has been seriously questioned (Arter & Jenkins, 1979; Tarver & Dawson, 1978). All of this has led to a dramatic decline in the popularity of the ability training model during the last decade.

Contemporary approaches to teaching learning disabled students and remedial learners tend to focus directly on the academic area in which the student is having difficulty. Thus, if a student has reading difficulties, instruction focuses on working with sound/letter relationships, word recognition, and/or reading texts as opposed to teaching an underlying ability like perceptual skills. Debate over how to teach reading and writing to LD and remedial students continues, however. The field is now divided between those who teach reading and writing as a sequence of component skills and those whose teaching is based on a holistic or "whole language" theory of reading and writing instruction.

Holistic teaching places teaching and learning in meaningful contexts. The following discussion of memory illustrates differences between holistic teaching and skills-based approaches, which isolate learning from meaningful contexts.

At a recent conference in Toronto a locally well-known speech and language specialist recommended half a dozen tests that could be used to assess auditory-sequential memory, on the presumption that many types of school failure can be traced to memory problems. However, even if auditory-sequential memory could be reliably assessed, which is doubtful, what can be done with the knowledge that a student has performed poorly on tests of auditory-sequential memory? Do you try to "strengthen" the child's auditory memory skills through drill and practice? Or do you teach the child specific strategies to improve memory performance? Neither of these remedial practices is uncommon. However, this discussion begs the more interesting question: memory for what? Is the problem remembering digits? Difficulty repeating sentences? Not following directions? Forgetting items at the grocery store?

"Memory for what?" is an important question because most of us realize, or should realize, that a host of factors affect memory. Isolated memory tasks are rare and, in fact, are probably limited to formal tests of memory and experimental manipulations. Even in these situations subjects are known to confound diagnosticians and psychologists by trying to "make sense" of the task. And making sense, or meaning, is one of the factors that significantly affects memory performance. Would any of us be surprised to discover that a child who was not able to repeat more than five random digits had no difficulty recalling the phone numbers of all of his friends? Not only is meaning an important factor in memory but what's meaningful is intrinsic to the individual. We are more likely to remember what's important to us as individuals. We also know that other factors like background knowledge, mood, fatigue, and purpose affect memory performance.

There are several conclusions that can be drawn from this discussion. First, there is no reason to assess memory using isolated, contrived tasks. Children do not usually remember isolated bits but try to integrate new information into their existing knowledge about the world. It also makes little sense to drill children on memory skills since this is only likely to affect performance on isolated memory tasks that, as we've argued, are rare events in real life. It's not that sequential memory can't be assessed and taught or that children won't exhibit some improvement on tests of sequential memory. It's just that these tasks, because they only superficially resemble how people actually go about remembering, are unlikely to affect children's real-life memory performance. Efforts to improve children's memory performance, if undertaken, should consider all of the factors that affect memory performance in natural settings.

This isn't a book about memory, but these arguments generalize beyond teaching auditory-sequential memory. Human beings don't learn in isolated, contrived settings. They learn in environments that contain a wide variety of factors affecting learning. Piaget has taught us that children actively construct reality by assimilating new information into existing knowledge structures and when necessary, modifying these knowledge structures to accommodate new information. In other words, what children learn and how they learn will be affected by what they already know. In turn, what children know will be affected by what they learn. Learning cannot be understood by focusing only upon the task. Children learn in contexts or situations. Efforts to understand human learning must consider the learner *and* the learning environment. Similarly, since human learning is affected by a variety of learner and context variables, humans must learn in environments where these variables are naturally present.

Holism is a philosophy, a way of viewing the world, which suggests that we can understand our world only by looking at wholes. For example, much has been written about the effects on parents of having a handicapped child. It has been suggested that such parents typically go through a series of stages as they adjust to the presence of a handicapped child. However, focusing on parents in isolation has done little to help us understand the reactions of parents of handicapped children. Not all parents, or even most parents, experience the same reactions. We've learned that if you wish to understand parents of handicapped children you must examine the "whole" family, a system that is affected by a variety of factors, including the personalities of individual family members, religious beliefs, socioeconomic status, culture, and so on (Turnbull, Summers & Brotherson, 1983). Even in medicine we've learned that our understanding of a disease is often incomplete without a consideration of individual diet, life-style, and psychological factors (i.e., holistic medicine). Similar examples can be drawn from other disciplines. If you wish to understand the parts of a system, you need to examine the whole and, if you wish to understand the whole, you need to examine how the parts interact to affect the whole. Little can be learned by studying the parts of a system as isolated objects or events.

Reductionism represents a contrasting view of reality. Reductionism, which in our schools takes the form of behaviorism, suggests that wholes are best understood (and learned) by breaking them down into smaller parts. Behaviorists argue that learning is easier and more efficient when tasks are broken down into subtasks (i.e., task analysis). From a behavioral view, if you wish to teach children how to swim you first teach them how to float, then how to kick, how to stroke, and then you teach them how to put it all together. Learning is additive: the whole is equal to the sum of its parts.

While the behavioral model provides a fairly satisfactory explanation of some forms of learning, like learning to swim, there are difficulties in applying this model to higher forms of human learning such as language. Language can be segmented, and children can learn isolated bits and pieces, but, in our view, what they learn are isolated bits that do not combine to form the whole. Higher forms of human learning are not additive; the whole is not equal to the sum of its parts. The whole is, in fact, different from the sum of its parts. A child who knows the concept "dog" and then learns the concept "cat" has not merely added a new concept to her/his repertoire. Learning the concept cat will, in all probability, affect the child's previous concept of dog (Poplin, 1984b).

A more serious problem is that by teaching reading and writing, or any other higher form of learning, as isolated skills we strip away meaning and make learning more difficult. Poplin (1984b) states:

> By breaking the learning process into sequential instructional objectives we strip from the activity the student's own interpretation from which she/he makes sense of the new information, making learning not less difficult, but more so. (291)

Additionally, much of what children need to learn can be learned only in context. Language learners, for example, must learn to manipulate a variety of language features in accordance with the demands of the environment. In other words, what they say and how they say it depends on factors like setting, audience, relationship to audience, mood, fatigue, and so on. We can learn this only by using language and hearing language used in settings where factors affecting language use are actually present. It makes no sense to first teach children the elements of language, as often happens in schools, and then teach them how to use language in context, for context is a part of language. Context, and how it operates, is a significant part of what children need to learn in order to become effective communicators. Children who learn about language in contrived settings learn only how language works in contrived settings. We'll make the same sort of argument for written language in the next chapter.

We are in the midst of a holistic revolution in our Western cultures (Heshusius, 1982, 1985; Tofler, 1980). This shift from viewing reality in terms of isolated events to a more holistic perspective is apparent in science, philosophy, medicine, and even in education (Poplin, 1984b). Tofler (1980) argues that holism is one of the characteristics that separates the industrial age, the "Second Wave," from the emerging nonindustrial age, the "Third Wave."

> These deep changes in our views of nature, evolution, progress, time, and space begin coming together as we move from a Second Wave culture that emphasized the study of things in isolation from one another to a Third Wave culture that emphasizes contexts, relationships, and wholes. (Tofler, 1980, 301)

As holism emerges as a dominant philosophy in our culture, its effect on our institutions, especially our schools, has been relatively slow. However, even in education the influences of holism are apparent. More and more educators stress teaching the "whole child." Others emphasize the teaching of reading and writing "across the curriculum," and our teacher education programs at universities stress "interdisciplinary study." In other words, we are growing increasingly aware that knowledge and learning cannot be fragmented into isolated pieces.

CONCLUSION

There is still considerable debate over the nature of learning disabilities and it's likely that this debate will continue. However, several conclusions about learning disabilities based upon current identification practices are possible. First, current identification practices, which stress academic underachievement, have produced a heterogeneous population of LD students, students who are as different from each other as they are from normally achieving children. The characteristics of this population of LD students overlap considerably with underachieving students and remedial students, and even normally achieving students. In fact, research indicates that current assessment practices cannot reliably discriminate between LD students and other underachievers. The available evidence indicates that the characteristics of learning disabled children and remedial learners are quite similar. Additionally, LD and remedial learners are likely to be served in similar programs, often using similar teaching methods. For these reasons we feel justified in considering these two groups of children together.

Although we favor holistic approaches to reading and writing instruction with all children, they may be especially valuable for LD and remedial learners. Behavioral approaches to written language instruction subject LD and remedial students to years of meaningless drill and practice. Additionally, the constant barrage of drill and practice focuses on students' deficits or weaknesses. This deficit model, with its constant reminder to students of their inadequacies, has had a devastating effect on the lives of many LD and remedial students (Poplin, 1984a). Finally, drill and practice encourage passivity in learners. The teacher decides what is to be learned and how it is to be learned. Because of the focus on isolated skills, students are unable to take advantage of previous learning.

Holistic approaches, because they take a developmental view of children's reading and writing problems, focus on children's strengths and not children's weaknesses or deficits. And by placing learning in meaningful contexts, holistic approaches encourage children to actively integrate what they are learning into what they have already learned.

In this text we will present a holistic view of reading and writing instruction. It's our view that reading and writing cannot be learned by breaking written language down into fragmented parts. We are firmly committed to holistic approaches because they are consistent with our view of the world and of learning. For us the world can be understood only by examining whole systems, not by analyzing fragmented parts. We also believe that, except in cases of adult interference, children learn holistically. They learn about their world by confronting their world in natural settings and actively trying to making sense of it. They do not make sense of their world by first focusing on isolated, meaningless bits of information.

Reading and writing, like other higher forms of human learning, must be learned in natural contexts. Fragmenting written language into skills and subskills does violence to the very nature of written language. These arguments are explicated in the following chapter, which presents a holistic theory of reading and writing development.

It's our intention to present reading and writing assessment and intervention strategies throughout the rest of this book. While we will be attempting to address a particular audience, teachers of LD and remedial students, the strategies presented here are appropriate for all children, delayed as well as normally achieving readers and writers.

II

Reading and writing as language

Since reading and writing are language, it's vital that teachers of reading and writing understand how children develop language, what it is that children learn as their language develops, and how children use what they know about language to transact meaning. Basic language tenets presented in this chapter should help teachers implement the assessment and intervention strategies presented throughout this text and, perhaps more importantly, help teachers invent their own assessment and intervention strategies as needed.

The first section of this chapter, language as development, presents some basic principles of language learning as they apply to learning to read and write. In subsequent sections we examine the various language cues (i.e., graphophonic, syntactic, semantic, and pragmatic) used by readers and writers and how they use these language cues in the process of transacting meaning. In the final section of this chapter we'll consider reading and writing instruction in light of our discussion of reading and writing as language.

LANGUAGE AS DEVELOPMENT

Reading and writing develop as students experience language in its various expressions—speaking, listening, reading, and writing. And, although children tend to mature as readers and writers later than they do as speakers and listeners, reading, writing, speaking, and listening develop in concert with one another, each contributing to the development of the other. What a child learns from reading a book or listening to a conversation becomes part of the child's linguistic data pool (Harste, Burke & Woodward, 1981), which will contribute to the continued development of other language expressions such as speaking or writing.

13

It's clear that the development of various language expressions doesn't follow a rigid hierarchy in which the mastery of speaking and listening precede the development of reading and writing.

Viewed from a socio-psycholinguistic perspective, written language (reading and writing) and oral language (speaking and listening) not only develop in concert with each other but also in analogous ways. That is, because reading and writing are language, the principles that govern the development of oral language also apply to written language. These language-learning principles form the basis for this book and for decisions about reading and writing evaluation and instruction. In this section we'll discuss seven language-learning principles that contribute to our understanding of how students learn to read and write.

1. *Children learn language by using language.* Children are immersed in talk during their preschool years. They have frequent opportunities to use talk and to hear talk used for a variety of purposes, in a variety of settings. Similarly, children learn to read and write by reading and writing. In other words, children must spend a great deal of time reading and writing in order to become effective readers and writers. Direct reading and writing instruction may be necessary, but it is not a sufficient condition for students to develop into effective readers and writers. Reading and writing instruction must be embedded in an environment in which students have frequent opportunities to use reading and writing and to see reading and writing used for a variety of purposes, in a variety of settings. Frequent reading and writing build on, consolidate, and extend knowledge gained from reading and writing lessons. For some students frequent opportunities to read and write may even be sufficient for literacy, although this is not usually the case for LD and remedial students.

Many of the children who are eventually assigned to LD and remedial classes come to school with relatively few reading and writing experiences. They may not have had opportunities to see reading and writing used and valued by people in their home environments, and have little or no experience in reading and writing for themselves. Other students may have been exposed to rich literacy-learning environments during their preschool years but continue to require frequent demonstrations of the uses of print. In either case, it's our responsibility to provide rich literacy-learning environments in our classrooms. LD and remedial students must see reading and writing demonstrated by others and must have frequent opportunities to engage in reading and writing themselves. They need to read and write whole texts from the time instruction begins and spend more time, rather than less, reading and writing in school. LD and remedial students need to be immersed in written language.

Additionally, like speaking and listening, reading and writing develop together, each building upon the other. Students regularly read and reread as they write (M. A. Atwell, 1980) and much of what writers learn about the craft of writing comes from their reading (F. Smith, 1982b). Therefore, reading and writing instruction shouldn't be separated, nor should writing instruction be postponed until students are able readers.

In summary, adults can promote language development by immersing children in talk and print. In addition, adults, including parents and teachers, can encourage language development by responding meaningfully to children's attempts to use oral and written language.

2. *The focus in language learning is on meaning and social function rather than form.* From infancy, children's language learning is guided by the principle of communicative usefulness (Snow et al., 1984). In other words, children learn language because it works—it helps them fulfill authentic needs. Children master language forms only insofar as it helps them fulfill their intentions. They don't set out to master language forms for their own sake. Parents encourage the development of function over form by responding to the meaning and function of their young children's language, largely ignoring form (Cross, 1984; Lindfors, 1980). When a young child says, "I tersy [thirsty]," most parents respond by giving the child something to drink, not by correcting grammar or pronunciation.

Similarly, the primary focus in learning to read and write must be on meaning and social function rather than on form. In other words, students should use reading and writing to construct meaning for authentic social purposes from the beginning—for entertaining, exploring ideas, informing or being informed, and keeping in touch with other human beings. Students should be encouraged to use reading and writing for their own real purposes even before they control written language conventions like handwriting, spelling, punctuation, and word recognition skills.

Likewise, reading and writing instruction should focus primarily on students' ability to use written language to fulfill personal communicative intentions, and not on the isolated drill of reading and writing forms. Written language forms are important, but only insofar as they help readers and writers fulfill their intentions. A heavy emphasis on forms distracts readers and writers from their authentic purposes, their reasons for reading and writing in the first place. Teachers can help students who focus too much of their attention on written language forms to gain perspective on the place of conventions in reading and writing. When they discuss language forms in instruction, teachers can help students understand the purpose of using standard forms within a social context and within whole meaningful language. Teachers can help students understand, for example, that standard conventions in writing make the job of the students' reading easier.

The social nature of written language indicates that comprehension and composition are enhanced by a community of readers and writers who share what they've read and written. Teachers should facilitate the sharing of texts, knowing the potential for extending each reader's/writer's meaning of text.

Just as in oral language, many reading and writing corrections, or attempts to directly teach skills, are misunderstood or rejected by students. When a child doesn't use the oral language rules of adults we often smile at how "cute" the mistakes are and assume that the child will use correct forms in time. In reading and writing, however, we are much more likely to conclude that the student is slow, has underlying processing difficulties, or worse, is stubborn, careless, lazy, or inattentive. Instead, the student probably isn't using the written language rules taught by teachers for one of two reasons: either her/his own language rules (which we'll say more about) make more sense to her/him than the adult rules you want the student to use, or the student can't integrate or balance all the language cues called for in the language situation.

Some students will spell a word (or words) correctly on a weekly spelling test but spell the same word incorrectly in a composition. This may happen because on the spelling test students need to attend to only one aspect of language (graphophonics), while on the composition, they must consider a number of language cues simultaneously (e.g., graphophonics, syntax, semantics). When students' attention is focused on the construction of meaning, as it should be, they may overlook, at least temporarily, the precise use of conventions such as spelling. Misspellings at this level aren't important anyway since they can be corrected at the editing stage.

3. *Language learning is personally important, concretely based, and free from anxiety.* Children tend to use oral language in situations in which they are comfortable. When the people and the surroundings are familiar, children freely express meaning. Comfort engenders risk-taking. If you've been a parent of small children, you'll recall times when your usually talkative child suddenly stopped talking, unwilling to use language in a new or uncomfortable situation.

Children are also most likely to speak or listen when they deem the situation personally important. As parents, how many times have you encouraged your child to retell something that happened during the day to someone else only to end up telling it yourself? The topic may have been important to you but it certainly wasn't to the child.

Young children's language also tends to focus on people, objects, and events actually present in their immediate physical context. It's only as language develops that children use language to refer to people, objects, events, and experiences outside their immediate realm of reference. This direct connection between environment and language enables children to infer how language represents the world.

As with oral language, children are most likely to learn to read and write in environments in which reading and writing are personally important, concretely based, and free from anxiety. This is especially important for LD and remedial students, for whom written language learning has been a struggle. Students need to feel free to use written language to fulfill personal intentions that reflect their interests and their experiences.

Perhaps nothing we do can totally alleviate the anxiety some of our older students feel toward reading and writing, but this anxiety can certainly be reduced to the point where students are willing to commit personally important thoughts to paper and read about personally relevant issues, events, and experiences. Reading and writing must be internally motivated if literacy is to take root and grow as part of a student's life. Students will be motivated to read and write when the topics they read and write about are personally important to them, reflecting their own experiences and feelings. Sometimes teaching requires that the teacher guide students toward written language that is obviously connected to their experience, while at other times teachers may help students activate their experiences in order to understand the connection between written language and experience. This is discussed in greater detail in chapter 8.

Establishing a community of readers/writers provides the support necessary for students to take risks and fulfill their written language intentions. Even older students can learn to revalue reading and writing (K. Goodman, 1982, 1986b) so that they perceive it as the communication of meaning rather than as yet another opportunity to fail with language forms. Making reading and writing functional and authentic for our students is a must if we ever hope to relieve their anxiety about reading and writing and help them discover that written language can have relevance in their daily lives.

4. *Children learn to use language in an ever-widening variety of contexts and to vary their language according to the context in which it occurs.* Young children rely heavily on physical and situational context in using and understanding oral language. A close connection between context and language, including gestures, tone of voice, etc., provides emerging language learners with the data they need to understand the language around them. Similarly, adults use their knowledge of context in order to understand children, inferring children's meaning from the context in which they use language.

Readers and writers also rely on context to make meaning. The nature of texts, purposes, illustrations, interests, and so on affects the ability of readers and writers to make meaning and determines how they actually go about transacting meaning via a text. For example, students usually do their best reading when they read whole texts and are able to take advantage of an increasing amount of contextual information. As students continue reading texts, they are often able to "figure out" previously uncomprehended words and ideas (Menosky, 1972).

Another example of the influence of context is the ability of students to recognize words in some contexts but not in others. Students are most likely to recognize words in texts that enable them to draw upon their experiences and their knowledge of language to transact meaning. Consequently, students recognize words more effectively when they are embedded in text than when they are presented in isolation (K. Goodman, 1965). Students' word recognition skills aren't absolute; word recognition varies as a function of context. In early miscue research, for example, Y. Goodman (1976) reported that students had more difficulty with words like *circus* when they were used as adjectives (e.g., circus bear, circus balloons) than when they appeared in the more familiar noun position.

Writers also use context to help them convey meaning. Young writers often use drawing to provide contextual support for their compositions. Some students rely on their drawing to get their writing started. Others vacillate between drawing and writing as if working in one medium encouraged greater thought about the other. One young girl drew a Halloween picture, brought it to one of the authors, and proceeded to tell a story based on the picture. At one point, she interrupted her own story, "...and they're saying 'Boo!,'" to say, "But they're not saying it loud enough!" She picked up her black crayon, added "BOO" in large letters, and continued her story, apparently satisfied that the addition of written language to her drawing communicated what the drawing by itself could not. As students' control of various written language conventions increases, they're less likely to depend on drawing to communicate meaning.

Children also learn to vary both the form and the content of their language according to the situation. They usually discover that "locker room" language isn't acceptable at home, and yet the polite ways of talking they use at home may be rejected by their peers. So children not only learn what to say, they learn how to say it, depending on the context. They learn the subtleties of language use by being immersed in language and by being exposed to a wide variety of conversational settings.

Similarly, students must learn to vary their reading and writing strategies as a function of context—purpose, audience, and so on. Writers don't use the same formal style for letters to friends that they do for an English paper. A romance novel doesn't require the same type of reading as a history textbook. Reading and writing aren't a simple matter of "mastery" but rather, of learning to assess the reading and writing context and flexibly apply a variety of strategies.

Students need to experience the variations that textual and situational differences cause, including the differences between expository and narrative texts. They need to learn that texts written for different social purposes, or with linguistic differences, may require different reading responses. They need to experience writing for a wide variety of purposes and a wide variety of audiences, who expect or demand variations in style and conventions. They need to experience the constraints imposed by different situations and to receive support and feedback in these situations. In short, students need to have frequent opportunities to read and write in a variety of contexts, for a variety of purposes.

5. *Knowledge of language rules is largely intuitive. Children abstract rules from the language data around them and employ these rules when using language.* Children induce the rules of language from the linguistic data around them. They learn what to say and how to say it because of their repeated exposure to language in natural, conversational settings. However, children do not simply parrot the language forms and functions they hear adults use. Like adults, their knowledge of language is rule-governed, but the linguistic rules used by children are typically different from those used by adults. One child we know, while on a camping trip in the mountains, jumped up in the middle of the night and announced "all done tent." Another child we know once called all four-legged animals "doggie." A third child now talks about having "runned" to the store. Any parent can cite many similar examples. The key here is that children represent their meanings by producing forms they may never have actually heard before. The child on the camping trip has never heard an adult say "all done tent." She merely used this form, which she based on her own understanding of language, to convey her discomfort. It's also noteworthy that children can demonstrate their awareness of language rules without actually being able to state the rules, although this is also true for most adults. Our knowledge of language is largely intuitive.

The development of written language follows a similar pattern. Children typically induce the rules of written language from repeated exposure to meaningful print in a variety of settings. Their knowledge of these rules only gradually approximates adult forms and, as with oral language, it is largely intuitive.

Knowing that children's early reading and writing efforts are developmental and not simply "mistakes," teachers can use children's reading and writing errors to make inferences about their development. Children's oral reading "errors" have been called miscues (K. Goodman, 1973) to draw our attention to the fact that oral reading errors, even though they may not match the text, provide insights into the rules and strategies children employ when they interact with text.

Young children's "pretend reading" of familiar stories provides evidence of the rule-governed nature of their early written language development. The following excerpt from a child's pretend reading of *Pete's Dragon* (Disney, 1977) contains some interesting examples of her rules about "book language."

TEXT	CHILD'S READING
One day, a boy named Pete walked into a little town by the sea.	One day Pete and Elliott walked down the street near the lake.

The child begins the story by setting the scene, which requires an introduction of both the characters and the place. Though the details of the setting are somewhat different, her reading reveals an understanding of the notion of "setting" in stories.

TEXT	CHILD'S READING
Later, Pete was eating dinner at the lighthouse with Nora and Lampie. Suddenly, there was a bright flash of lightning and a loud crash of thunder. "My goodness!" exclaimed Nora. "It must be a terrible storm. We'd better check the lamp." Nora and Lampie had to be sure the lamp in the lighthouse was lit all the time so ships could find their way to shore.	But when they got home, there was a big clap of thunder. Nora said, "My gracious. It might be a big storm. We got to check the lamp in case it runs out of fire."

The child not only reveals her knowledge of how conversation is used in stories, but also her awareness of the complexity of the language used in stories as compared to the language used in everyday conversation. Compare the complexity of the declarative sentences she uses in this section with the less complex sentences she uses when she constructs the sort of conversation one has in oral language.

The pretend reading of *Pete's Dragon* also reveals the child's hypotheses about particular word meanings. For example, it reveals the child's approximate but incomplete understanding of the workings of a lighthouse lamp. In the text she read, she appears to think that the lamp "runs out of fire." In a later section of the story, her reading reveals more about her understanding of this concept. The text reads, "He [Elliott] blew a great blast of fiery breath upon the wick of the lamp," which she reads as "He blowed a big, big blast of fire on the glass."

Children's invented spellings provide another interesting example of the rule-governed nature of children's written language development. The sample in Figure 2−1 was written for the first three pages of *Pancakes for Breakfast* (dePaola, 1978), a wordless picture book to which a child has decided to add text. (The first page of the book is reproduced with the child's writing to indicate how her writing was done to accompany the pictures. The translation of her writing is as follows: "One morning the little lady. She woke up that cat. She decided to make pancakes.") Note that this child often uses the letter names to represent sounds. She begins "yan" (one) and "yadc" (woke) with *y* because its letter name comes closest to the beginning sound of the word she is attempting to represent. She uses a similar strategy when she spells *she* as "hae" and "hie." Note that the pronunciation of *h* as "aitch" is quite close to the initial sound in *she*. The final *e* in "lade" (lady) is a similar example.

This language-learning principle not only helps us look at students' written language miscues as evidence of development, but it should also help us reconsider written language instruction. Educators often operate on the belief, or at least act as if they believe, that reading and writing rules ought to be made

---

FIGURE 2−1   Writing on *Pancakes for Breakfast* (DePaola 1978)

explicit. But this discussion suggests that it's no more necessary for students to be able to verbalize written language rules in order to learn to read and write than it is for them to be able to verbalize oral language rules in order to learn to speak and listen. Many parts of the curriculum violate this notion, however, especially the worksheets and skills exercises that are so much a part of reading curricula. Some students are able to read and understand text at a particular grade level but unable to pass the skills tests required in the same curriculum because the tests demand explicit knowledge of rules and terminology (Jackson, 1981).

6. *Language learning is largely self-directed.* Children learn oral language by selecting what they need and want to know (Snow et al., 1984) from the language that surrounds them. They listen, question, hypothesize, and try out language in order to learn as well as to communicate. Children, not their parents, control the language-learning process. Parents do very little direct teaching, and even this may be ignored by their children. Nor do parents segment and sequence language to make it easier for their children to learn. There is no oral language scope and sequence for the crib. Parents do intuitively "simplify" language for their youngsters to some extent, but parent-child language continues to be meaning-based, whole, and connected to a supportive context.

Though children largely direct their own language learning, we recognize that parents do play an important role in their children's language learning. Parents demonstrate language use—its enormous importance in life, its functions, and its forms or conventions. Adult language, used by significant adult models, provides children with the data they need to induce language rules. Adults also reward children's language use by responding to their attempts to communicate, by fulfilling their needs as expressed in language, and by answering their questions.

Children also learn about written language by selecting what they want and need to know from the written language data around them. One emerging reader listened to an adult read this page from *Too Much Noise* (McGovern, 1967),

> So Peter let the cow go.
> He let the donkey go.
> He let the sheep go.
> He let the hen go.
> He let the dog go.
> He let the cat go.

and commented, "Everytime you say 'he' and it looks the same!" The adult, picking up on the child's insight that oral and written language have a consistent relationship, drew the child's attention to this relationship in the rest of the passage, e.g., "let the ——— go."

Children also regularly use questions to direct their own learning. Knowledgeable adults can look for patterns in these questions in order to discern what the child is learning about print. As an example, let's look at questions asked by the child whose *Pancakes for Breakfast* writing you saw earlier:

YAN MARE VAE LEDL LADE [One morning the little lady]

Is "morning" two separate words?
Is "little lady". . . is "little" a separate word?

HAE YADC UP VET CAT [She woke up that cat.]

What comes first for "up"—the *u* or the *p*?

HIE DAECA TO MAC PANCAKES [She decided to make pancakes.]

Is "decided" all one word?
Is "pancakes" a whole word?

Four of the five questions this child asked concerned the nature of words. Her understanding of the concept of word is apparent from her questions. Interestingly, we don't directly teach children rules or definitions for "word-ness," though it is an important concept for them to grasp. They learn the concept of word by grappling with all the examples they see in print as they read and by hypothesizing and asking questions about the concept as they write. Through these demonstrations, children reach an intuitive understanding about the nature of "wordness," an understanding that, for most of us, remains intuitive.

Educators need to trust the natural ability of children to learn about print without direct instruction. Too often, however, adults take control of written language learning, deciding what, how, and when students will learn. Reading and writing are guided by "scope and sequence" charts, which prescribe the instruction to be provided to students, often down to the most minute detail. Adults determine, often through task analysis, what the most "simple" bits of language are, undermining the meaning and wholeness of language that students depend on in natural reading and writing settings. Further, students are often denied the use of questions in their learning. One of the first lessons children learn in school is that teachers, not students, ask most of the questions.

As teachers, we need to be careful to allow children to direct their own learning where possible. Certainly this is more difficult in a school situation where there are many children than in a home situation where there are few, but it's not impossible. Students will direct their own learning more frequently if they are given choices, choices about which materials they will use, about what they will do with those materials, about assignments, and so on. They'll also direct their own learning more frequently when their assignments are open-ended, when they are encouraged to ask questions, and when they assume the responsibility for self-correction.

Returning responsibility for learning to children doesn't diminish teachers' role in literacy learning. They simply have a different role to play, analogous to that played by parents in oral language development. Teachers provide children with frequent, meaningful demonstrations of the uses of written language and opportunities to use reading and writing for a variety of their own purposes. This is important for all students, but it's especially important for students who have come from environments where literacy has not been valued. Teachers also respond to the meaning in students' attempts to communicate rather than to the correctness of form. Students' natural efforts to read and write are driven by the communicative context, not by the skills that need to be learned. In turn, teachers' responses (and those of others) should be driven by the students' communicative intent, not by the skills that need to be learned.

Returning responsibility to students doesn't obviate direct teaching, however. And even in teacher-directed lessons, there is room for students to direct their own learning. But as teachers of ineffective readers and writers, we need to direct student attention to some aspects of written language in order to encourage development. First, lessons should be predicated on the teacher's observation of what the student is attempting to do. For example, the child who is attempting to signal the end of sentences by putting periods at the end of each line could be asked to examine the placement of periods in a favorite book. Second, open-ended lessons encourage students to find and/or use information of their own and to ask questions. Third, if lessons all use whole, meaningful text, students may attend to cues in the text and use language systems and strategies other than those that are being highlighted; in fact, they are always encouraged to do so.

Finally, it's important to remember that, although some lessons are teacher-directed, the language knowledge and language strategies being taught must eventually be student-directed. That is, students must come to use the knowledge/strategies independently before they can be said to have truly learned the lessons. Pearson and Gallagher's (1983) model of instruction, adapted in Figure 2–2, is useful in considering how to withdraw the teacher support given to LD and remedial readers as they gradually assume responsibility for using new language knowledge or strategies.

Especially because reading and writing rely on active construction of meaning, this model, which moves from teacher demonstration or teacher-led discovery to use guided by the teacher to independent use, is an important one for the LD and remedial students under consideration in this book. Both teachers and students must leave behind their notion that reading is a passive process of meaning recognition. Direct reading and writing instruction must constantly demonstrate the active meaning-construction processes of reading and writing and ensure that students assume responsibility for constructing meaning for themselves.

7. *Though rate of development is different, the conditions necessary for language learning are similar for all.* Most parents tolerate a fairly wide range of language behaviors in their children. They seem to realize that, although children may exhibit very different patterns of language development, almost all children are effective language users by the time they enter kindergarten.

Certain conditions are particularly favorable for normal language development, however. First, children must be in an environment in which speaking

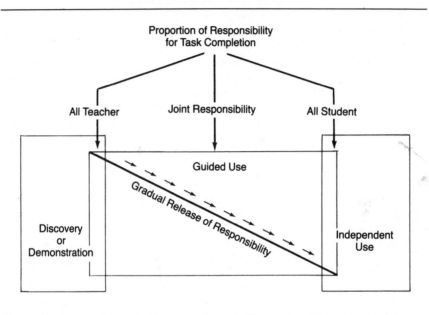

FIGURE 2–2   The Gradual Release of Responsibility Model of Instruction
(Adapted from Pearson & Gallagher 1983)

and listening occur. Second, children must not only be in an enivornment where oral language is used, they must actively participate in the speaking and listening. Third, children must have personal reasons for using oral language. Younger children in families are often relatively late in reaching language milestones compared to their older brothers and sisters, presumably because their needs are often anticipated. One of us has a sister, the fourth-born child, who didn't speak until much later than the norm, not because she lacked the ability, but because her needs were usually met without speaking. Finally, children must receive feedback from others about their communicative competence: significant adults in their environment must ensure that their language works, that it has the intended effect.

Similar conditions are necessary for written language development. First, children require a literate environment in which they can see reading and writing used in functional ways by significant others; and second, they must have opportunities to participate actively in written language use themselves.

Third, students will fully engage in reading and writing only if they discover personal reasons for reading and writing. The environment must provide regular demonstrations of the functional, purposeful, and meaningful nature of reading and writing. Many students, especially those in LD and remedial programs, see no need for reading and writing in their lives, perhaps because this message wasn't instilled at home and hasn't been instilled at school. If we are to succeed with these students, we need to help them discover the power of print in their lives.

Finally, students need feedback from the written language experience about their reading and writing competence. To be sure, written language competence includes the standard use of conventions in writing and the ability to recognize words in reading. But we need to accord developing readers and writers what we accord developing oral language users—opportunity and effort. They need opportunities to use conventions, and at the same time, they require the understanding and patience of informed adults who will allow them to discover the uses of print without having to be overly concerned with forms.

Some feedback about communicative competence comes from fellow readers and writers, including the teacher, but students should also provide themselves with feedback in the process of reading/writing. As students read, they should be asking, "Does this make sense to me?" As students write, they should be asking, "Will this make sense to my readers?" Students who can supply this kind of feedback to themselves can teach themselves much of what they need to know to read and write.

In summary, it's our view that reading and writing development are guided by the same language-learning principles that govern oral language development. Children learn language, oral or written, to fulfil personal, communicative intentions. Children learn best when they are actively involved in their language learning, when they are immersed in language, and when they are exposed to frequent demonstrations of the uses of written language in a variety of contexts. Children must also have frequent opportunities to use written language to fulfill personal intentions in a variety of settings that affect language use. In this way, LD and remedial students will come to see themselves as readers and writers, not merely as people who have difficulty with written language forms. As K. Goodman has written,

> The key to helping readers (and writers) in trouble is to help them revalue themselves as language learners and users, and revalue the (written language) process as an interactive, constructive language process. They must set aside the pathological view of themselves, cast off the labels, and operate to construct meaning through written language using the strengths they have built and used in making sense of oral language. (1982, 88–89)

LANGUAGE AS A SYSTEM

From a holistic perspective, language is a system. Readers and writers simultaneously consider both their knowledge of the world and their knowledge of language when they read and write. They construct meaning based on their knowledge of sound-symbol rules, word ordering rules, the structure of stories, the meanings of words, and so on, and they transact meaning by combining this knowledge with their experience of how language is used in different contexts. The meaning of a particular phrase within a text, for example, can be known only by reference to both the text and the context of the reading (the reader's purposes and experience, etc). Since no readers have precisely the same experience, no two readers will ever construct precisely the same meaning. Reading and writing are thus not simply a matter of knowing about graphophonics *and* syntax *and* semantics *and* pragmatics (rules governing the use of language in context). They also require readers and writers who simultaneously apply their knowledge of all of these components of written language to construct meaning.

In the following sections we consider the various cues of written language—graphophonics, syntax, semantics, and pragmatics—and how readers and writers use these cues to construct meaning. We must say again, however, that we are discussing these cues separately only for the convenience of our readers. It's our view that these cues aren't learned nor should they be taught separately.

GRAPHOPHONIC CUES

Graphophonics refers to the knowledge readers and writers have about the marks on the page—the sound/letter relationships represented there, the white spaces denoting word boundaries, and so on. Graphophonic rules are both enormously complex and largely intuitive, not the result of direct instruction.

Readers and writers "know," for example, which letter combinations in English are permissible (e.g., *la-*, *qu-*, *ee*, etc.) and which are illegal (e.g., *qi*, *lx*, *yl*, etc.) even though they may never have been explicitly taught rules governing English orthography nor could they actually state these rules. Readers and writers also know which letter combinations are permissible, or even likely, in certain positions within a word. For example, we would be very surprised to encounter a word that began "*rv-*" even though this is a permissible letter combination within a word (e.g., *curve*).

Readers and writers use their knowledge of graphophonic rules to construct meaning, but effective readers and writers do not overrely on this aspect of written language. Instead, they combine their knowledge of graphophonics with their knowledge of other language cues and their knowledge of the world to construct meaning.

SYNTACTIC CUES

Syntax refers to the morphological and word-ordering rules that readers and writers share about the structure of language. Of course, no one would disagree that children possess a considerable store of syntactic knowledge before they are exposed to formal reading and writing instruction. Effective readers and writers draw extensively upon their knowledge of syntax in order to construct meaning.

The following exercise illustrates the importance of syntax from the perspective of the reader. To get a feeling for the importance of syntax in language, read the following story (from K. Goodman, 1968) and answer the questions that follow it using complete sentences and the same "language" in which the story is written. As you read and answer the questions, pay attention to the specific cues you use.

THE MARLUP

A marlup was poving his kump. Parmily a narg horped some whev in his kump. "Why did vump horp whev in my frinkle kump?" the marlup jufed the narg. "Er'm muvvily trungy," the narg grupped. "Er heshed vump horpled whev in your kump. Do vump pove your kump frinkle?"

1. What did the narg horp in the marlup's kump?
2. What did the marlup juf the narg?
3. Was the narg trungy?
4. How does the marlup pove his kump?

As you read and answered the questions, you certainly used syntactic cues as well as graphophonic cues. You probably used your knowledge about the meaning of word position, modifiers, and so on, and in addition, you used morphological information such as adding "-s" for plural nouns, "-ed" for past tense verbs, and "-ly" for adverbs. Punctuation (and capitalization) undoubtedly played a major role in your ability to answer the questions because it allowed you to determine where sentence structures began and ended, and helped you to understand that there were characters talking with each other and where the talk took place. In addition, if the function words we take for granted, "the," "a," "in," etc., had been missing, or had been replaced by another "language," you would not have been able to take advantage of many of the syntactic cues in the text.

Even though you were unable to utilize semantic or meaning cues (unless you attempted a partial translation), you were still able to "understand" the language well enough to answer the questions posed to you about the story. The reader's knowledge of syntax is, undoubtedly, an important factor in constructing meaning. However, students' reliance on syntax can sometimes fool us. Although you were able to answer the questions following "The Marlup," you wouldn't claim to have understood the story. Teachers often assume that if students can answer the questions, they've understood what they've read. It may be, however, that students are simply using their knowledge of syntax to answer questions, just as you did.

SEMANTIC CUES

Although there has been considerable debate over the domain of semantics, from our perspective semantics refers to the knowledge shared by readers and writers about the world and how the world is represented by language. Semantics refers not only to vocabulary but also to the concepts represented by that vocabulary and how those concepts are organized into schema, our structured knowledge about the world.

In order to give yourself a sense of the role of semantics in written language, read the following passage (from Glass & Stanley, 1970, 171–72) and then retell the passage to yourself or to someone else.

The concepts underlying biserial correlation lead to such generalizations as triserial or other polyserial correlation. If Y is measured trichotomously, a triserial correlation coefficient can be used to estimate the product-moment correlation between X and the normally distributed Y assumed to underlie the trichotomy. The generalization R_{bis} to polyserial correlation is the work of Jaspen (1946). It has been the authors' experience that often the magnitude of a polyserial correlation coefficient is little different from the value of R_{bis} that would be obtained by coalescing the several categories of Y into just two (as when a trichotomous variable is changed into a dichotomous variable by combining two adjacent categories).

If you reacted as most readers do, you were probably able to pronounce the words of this passage but didn't understand what you had read. Perhaps you think that you didn't understand the passage because you didn't know the meaning of some of the words. Look the words up in the dictionary, study them, read the passage again, and then attempt to retell it once more. You'll find that studying the meanings of individual words doesn't help much. Unless you possess the relevant conceptual background, this passage will never make much sense. You were able to read the passage so that it sounded like language because you used the graphophonic and syntactic cues, but you still didn't understand the passage because you and the author do not share a schema for the topic.

Does this mean that you can't learn something new by reading about it? Well, it depends. Readers can learn new information from reading if they're able to make a connection between what they already know and what the author is telling them. If such a connection cannot be made, then learning will be difficult, if not impossible. In other words, you must have a schema to which the new information can be added or a schema that is changed in some way by the new information.

PRAGMATIC CUES

Pragmatics refers to the rules that govern the use of language in context. Language users may know vocabulary and may know rules for generating gramatically correct sentences, but their choice of topics, vocabulary, and particular grammatical structures depends on the context. For example, the two sentences "The dog bit the man" and "The man was bitten by the dog" have the same meaning but aren't usually interchangeable in conversational settings. Typically, passive sentences are reserved for more formal contexts such as speeches or formal papers. Readers also refer to context in constructing meaning from a text, to decide, for example, whether "It's cold in here," spoken by a man to his butler, is an assertion (It IS cold in here) or a request for action (Shut the window).

There is much more to reading and writing, however, than our knowledge of graphophonics, syntax, semantics, and pragmatics. Written language is an active process by which readers and writers combine their knowledge of the world with their knowledge of language to transact meaning. This is the topic of the following section.

LANGUAGE AS A PROCESS

Reading and writing are transactive processes (Rosenblatt, 1978; Shanklin, 1981) in which people use active strategies for constructing meaning as they interact with print. "Transaction designates...an ongoing process in which the elements or factors are...aspects of a total situation, each conditioned by and conditioning the other" (Rosenblatt, 1978, 17). Reading and writing are transactive processes because they are always used and understood in a context that contributes to their meaning.

> Language comes to life only when functioning in some environment. We do not experience language in isolation—if we did we would not recognize it as language—but always in relation to a scenario, some background of persons and actions and events from which the things are said to derive their meaning. (Halliday, 1978, 28)

Each instance of written language behavior is a complex socio-psycholinguistic event requiring the orchestration of graphophonic, syntactic, and semantic cues within a language context in order to construct meaning (Harste & Burke, 1978). That is, reading and writing require that the language user process graphophonic, syntactic, semantic, and pragmatic cues simultaneously. The various cues interact with each other to facilitate the production or reception of other language cues. Because available cues and processing requirements vary according to the context of use, each composition-comprehension transaction between writer and reader is unique.

Readers and writers are confronted with a myriad of problems as they use print to construct meaning. As readers, we use a variety of problem-solving strategies to make decisions about an author's meaning and to construct meaning for ourselves. As writers, we also use problem-solving strategies to decide what our readers need as we construct meaning for them and for ourselves.

In reading or writing, we use a variety of strategies to process language cues, strategies that are also used in listening, speaking, and other cognitive activities. Readers/writers use these strategies—predicting, confirming, and integrating— as they find them useful, often simultaneously. The strategies help them to orchestrate graphophonic, syntactic, semantic, and pragmatic cues at both focal and global levels.

Predicting is a strategy we use in all aspects of our lives. Before we open our eyes in the morning, we may make global predictions about what we expect to happen that day. We may also make focal predictions about what we expect to see when we open our eyes. We predict our way through the events of our lives, only becoming conscious of our predictions when we are surprised that they are not confirmed. The same thing happens during reading. In reading, we predict what the author will say next and how s/he will say it. We might globally predict the next event in the story at the same time that we make a more focal prediction about the next sentence. We may also predict how the author will use language in the rest of the sentence and what letters are likely to be in the rest of a word.

Our enormous store of knowledge about the world, the structure of language, and print allows us to make predictions with enough confidence that we need only sample the print on the page. We sample only those cues we need to make sense of a text. On the basis of our experience with print, we usually know which cues are significant and need to be considered. When we are on the same wavelength with the author and have shared backgrounds and language, predicting is an easy task. When we do not share the author's background and/or language, predicting is not easy and we find ourselves sampling more cues from the text in an attempt to construct meaning. In other words, when our background knowledge and the text do not match, we are forced to depend more heavily on graphophonic cues.

In writing, we also use prediction strategies that are based on the context of the writing situation and on the text we have produced once we begin writing. Prior to and during writing, we make global predictions about what we need to say and what we don't need to say in order to fulfill our communicative intentions toward our readers. As we write, we continue to make global predictions, but we also make focal predictions about content and language— what we'll say next and precisely how we'll say it. "As in reading, prior text constrains what one may write in upcoming text" (Shanklin, 1981, 81). As we read what we've written, we predict again, this time partly as an outside reader of our own writing and partly as an inside reader, considering other options available to us in composition.

Confirming is another strategy we use regularly in our lives. As we experience life, we monitor whether our experiences make sense. When an experience doesn't make sense, we may dissociate ourselves from the experience; we may rethink the experience; we may seek the experience again, hoping to make sense of it this time; or we may seek outside help in attempting to make sense of the experience. Again, the same is true of reading and writing.

Proficient readers constantly monitor whether they are making sense of the author's cues. In essence, they ask themselves, "Does this make sense?" and when it does they keep reading. When a text doesn't make sense, they have several options. They may decide not to read the text. They may read the text again in hopes that it will provide more cues or that they'll think of something that hadn't occurred to them before. They may continue reading in hopes that the author will provide more cues, or they may rethink what they have read. Or they may look outside the text for help in understanding what they are reading.

In writing, we also use confirmation strategies to monitor whether we are making sense to ourselves and to our potential readers. When we read our own text and think we are making sense, we keep writing. When we don't think we're making sense, we may decide to stop writing, we may revise our text so that it does make sense, we may keep writing in hopes that we'll eventually figure out how to make sense, or we may even orally provide what we did not provide in writing to our readers. At the same time writers consider whether they're making sense to potential readers, they also consider whether they're making sense to the first reader of any piece, the writer her/himself. If it doesn't make sense to me, the thinking goes, it can't possibly make sense to anyone else.

In reading and writing, the strategies of predicting and confirming (or disconfirming) not only help readers/writers process language cues and solve meaning construction problems, they also provide continual feedback. Readers or writers keep a constant check on their own comprehension or composition monitoring until the text has been read or written.

A third strategy we use in our lives and apply to reading and writing is integrating. That is, as we read, we integrate what we already know, believe, and feel with our interpretations of what the author knows, believes, and feels. We choose which information will be remembered or integrated on the basis of whether the information is important for the reading purposes we have established and on the basis of the relationship between our schema and the author's schema. Because all of us approach a text with different backgrounds, beliefs, and feelings, the strategy of integrating renders the reading transaction unique each time a text is read.

As we write, we must keep in mind our potential readers' needs. For example, if we are to persuade our readers to a particular point of view with a piece of writing, we have to think about how what we say and how we say it will be perceived by the readers. Essentially, we have to integrate what it is that we know, believe, and feel with what it is that we perceive our readers know, believe, and feel in order to make decisions about what to write and how to write it. If we can't do that, our attempt to present a particular point of view to our readers is likely to fall flat. We choose which information will be included in the piece of writing on the basis of whether the information is important for the writing purposes we have established and on the basis of the relationship between our own schema and what we perceive to be the readers' schema.

As we have described the strategies used in the reading and writing processes, we have attempted to explicate the parallels between reading and writing. Our description of reading and writing as processes can be graphically represented, as shown in Figure 2–3 (adapted from Y. Goodman & Burke, 1980).

The notion that reading and writing are analogous processes provides an important basis for the evaluation and instructional chapters of this book. It is not only the end products of reading and writing that we are concerned with observing, but also the processes themselves. What students do during reading and writing provides data from which instructional decisions about reading and writing can be made, including how to positively affect reading and writing products. Likewise, we have found that instructional attention to the process of reading/writing, in particular to the strategies of predicting, confirming, and integrating, has a positive impact both on reading and writing and on reading and writing products. If students learn to process language cues and solve meaning construction problems more effectively in the process of reading/ writing, their comprehension and composition improve as well.

FIGURE 2–3   Reading and Writing as Processes (Adapted from Goodman & Burke 1980)

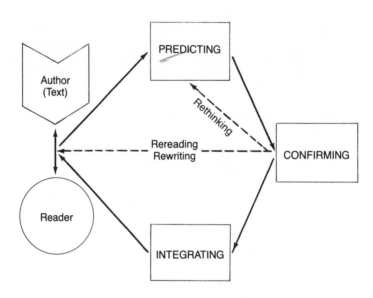

It should be clear from our description of reading and writing that they are clearly defined in our minds as processes involving personal meaning construction with print. Whenever we speak of reading or writing in this book, we are referring to the reading and writing of whole texts for the purpose of communication. We don't think that students doing worksheets are reading any more than we think that students doing handwriting exercises are writing. Reading and writing involve the use of all written language cues, orchestrated by means of language strategies. Nothing else constitutes reading and writing.

TEACHING READING AND WRITING AS LANGUAGE: A CONCLUSION

If the goal of teaching is. . .to support children's learning to "respond to what the child is trying to do" as Frank Smith (1973) would have it, then we would do well to try to understand what children's learning is like, what the child is trying to do. (Lindfors, 1984, 605)

In this chapter, we have focused on how people learn to read and write, on what it is that people learn as they become readers and writers, and on how they use what they know about language in order to transact meaning during reading and writing. We have focused on these things because they are what teaching should support. Without knowing a great deal about how people learn to read and write and how proficient language users read and write, teaching cannot connect to learning, at least in the ways teachers intend for it to connect.

Lindfors (1984) defines literacy teaching as "the instructional activities and sequences (teachers) design with the intention of increasing children's ability to relate language meanings to printed symbols" (602). From what we know about language learning, we can deduce that demonstrating reading and writing to students, helping them "discover" what proficient language users do as readers and writers, and facilitating students' engagement in and sharing of reading and writing constitute the "activities and sequences" that Lindfors refers to as teaching. In essence, that is what children's first language teachers, their parents, did to teach them oral language.

Teaching can only contribute to learning if students attend to what the teacher hopes they will attend to in the lesson. If they do not, it does not mean that they have not learned. Almost always, learning takes place, but it may be learning the teacher has not intended. Thus, although teaching has taken place and learning has taken place, there has been no connection between teaching and learning.

What is taught is often based on prescribed curricula, curricula that do not consider what we know about language learning and use. We know, for instance, that readers and writers must attend to meaning if they are to comprehend and compose, and if they are to provide themselves with feedback during comprehension and composition. We know that readers and writers learn about written language conventions as they observe their use in purposeful and meaningful reading and writing. Students cannot attend to meaning when bits of language are presented in isolation from whole, meaningful text; nor can they efficiently learn about written language conventions when these are presented in isolation from whole, meaningful text. In fact, those students who have learned that reading is the correct recognition of words and that writing is the correct spelling of words make even less sense of these sorts of lessons. At least students who can and do read and write know where isolated language instruction is supposed to lead. With students who are readers/writers, some of this sort of teaching may connect (though we must question why it's necessary with students who are already reading and writing effectively) but with the students who are the subjects of this book, this sort of teaching is not likely to connect to learning in the way the teacher intended.

This book presents numerous teaching strategies that are likely to connect with student learning because they are based on what is known about literacy learning and literate behavior. However, even these teaching suggestions will not connect to learning unless you take into account what your particular students are trying to do in their reading and writing. It is your observations and assessment of what your students are trying to do in their reading and writing, in the light of what you know about language learning, language cues, and language processing, that ought to be the foundation of what you decide to do in the name of teaching.

Teaching reading and writing as language is a professionally demanding task but probably one of the most fulfilling tasks you will ever engage in if your teaching connects with student learning. This is especially true of teaching literacy to learning disabled and remedial students. It is our hope that you will revalue your students' learning abilities, if that is necessary, and use the information in this book to make teaching decisions that connect with the learning of which your students are capable. In turn, you will have the satisfaction of watching your students revalue literacy and become effective readers and writers.

III

An observational approach to assessing reading and writing

Special and remedial education have been dominated by the familiar diagnostic-prescriptive teaching model, in which educational problems are first "diagnosed" and appropriate educational interventions are then "prescribed." In the diagnostic phase, students with school learning problems are singled out for intensive testing of cognitive, linguistic, academic, and social abilities. The results of these tests are then used to produce educational diagnoses (e.g., the student has a reading disability) and to develop specific instructional plans.

The diagnostic-prescriptive teaching model depends heavily on the validity and reliability of the initial assessment. Tests must focus on stable behaviors, and educational plans are useful only if they are based on representative samples of students' behavior. A reading test, for example, is useful only if it accurately and reliably predicts students' actual reading performance in school. It's widely believed that, because of their objectivity and reliability, standardized tests provide the best information on which to base educational decisions. However, the greatest strengths of standardized tests, their objectivity and reliability, are also their most serious weaknesses.

Standardized reading and writing tests focus on measurable written language behaviors that, presumably, cannot be easily influenced by the subjective judgments of teachers. Formal tests of written language are necessarily limited to discrete, measurable reading and writing skills. Therefore, "objective" assessments of reading and writing are likely to focus on measurable skills like word recognition, sound blending, punctuation, and spelling. Other often more important aspects of written language development, such as the writers' ability to consider the needs of audiences or the readers' ability to integrate new knowledge into existing knowledge (D. W. Moore, 1983), are ignored because these abilities cannot be easily measured.

Concern about reliability also restricts the range of reading and writing behaviors sampled by standardized tests. The predictive value of these tests depends on the sampling of relatively stable behaviors. However, because many of the most interesting reading and writing behaviors are not stable, they are excluded from standardized tests of reading and writing achievement. Graves (1983) reports that children's best writing is often followed by several less successful attempts at writing. Even the writing of professional writers varies in quality. Almost all of us occasionally experience writer's block (although few of us ever forget how to spell or punctuate). Our experience also indicates that readers' ability to comprehend what they've read is equally variable, depending on such factors as fatigue, interest, background knowledge, and so on. Standardized tests of written language may sample stable reading and writing behaviors, but real reading and writing are not stable. Too often we let testing theory and not reading and writing theory determine what we assess. If we can't count it or if it isn't stable, we don't assess it. The danger is that if we don't assess it we probably won't teach it either (D. W. Moore, 1983).

Many teachers have attempted to overcome the limitations of standardized tests by replacing, or at least supplementing, them with informal assessment. Many of these informal tests are teacher constructed. For example, teachers may construct their own lists of sight vocabulary words for students to read or their own Independent Reading Inventories. Other informal tests, like the *Reading Miscue Inventory* (Goodman, Watson, & Burke, 1987), are commercially available. Informal tests tend to include more representative samples of reading and writing behavior and are more likely to reflect teachers' own philosophical and instructional approach to reading and writing. However, the validity of formal or informal assessment may be limited by the context within which tests are administered.

When we contrive a reading or writing task, setting the topic and the purposes for reading or writing, what we observe may bear little resemblance to students' natural reading and writing behavior (that is, students reading and writing for their own purposes, on topics of their own choosing). Edelsky and Smith (1984) report dramatic differences between the quality of primary students' journal writing and their writing in response to a researcher's prompt ("Write about your summer"). Similarly, Burke and Harste (1978) report differences in the quality of students' retellings when they retold a story to a friend instead of an adult researcher. These studies confirm our own experience: students' reading and writing behaviors in contrived settings may be very different from their reading and writing performance when they use written language for their own purposes. Contrived procedures for eliciting reading and writing behavior will not result in "best" examples of students' work, and perhaps not even in representative samples. They tell us only how well students read and write when given someone else's purposes and topics.

Another problem with both formal and informal reading and writing assessments is that we typically draw conclusions about students' written language development on the basis of one or two instances of reading and writing behavior. It's unlikely, though, that one or two samples of reading and writing behavior, however thorough, will be representative of students' actual reading and writing ability. Reading and writing are variable, and contextual factors such as topic, audience, interest, and purpose affect students' reading and writing performance. Using formal or informal tests to collect multiple samples of behaviors in a variety of settings would help, but this solution is prohibitively time-consuming.

Educators have worked hard to develop objective, valid, and reliable instruments for identifying learning problems and then to develop remedial programs. Our concern for objective and reliable measurement, however, has limited our focus to narrow, fragmented sets of reading and writing behaviors that often do not relate to what students actually do when they read and write for their own purposes. Tests, even informal tests, contrive settings that do not resemble natural learning environments. We find out about our students' reading and writing performance in response to *our* purposes and on topics of *our* choosing on a narrow set of written language behaviors. We get very good answers to the wrong questions. The questions we should be asking are "What do our students know about reading and writing?" and "What evidence is there that reading and writing development are taking place?"

It's our view that these questions can be addressed only by observing students *as* they read and write and *as* they respond to written language instruction. In this sense, assessment doesn't necessarily precede instruction, as most of us have been taught. Assessment is an integral part of instruction. We assess as we teach, planning and adapting instruction in response to our students' actual reading and writing performance.

Evidence of students' literacy development will come from a variety of sources. We can learn about our students' reading and writing development by observing them in the classroom, the halls, and the cafeteria, on the school bus and the playground, and so on (Y. Goodman, 1978). Evidence will emerge as we observe students choose books and talk about books they've read. Journal writing, in-class writing assignments, notes to friends, and letters to grandma will be among the many important sources of information about students' written language development, as will the observations of regular classroom teachers, parents, and others.

Observing children isn't just a matter of waiting for certain behaviors to occur so that they can be recorded. Observation is a skill, one that teachers must practice frequently over an extended period of time. The following are some guidelines for observing children:

1. Reading and writing should be observed over a period of time in a number of different contexts. For example, contexts for silent reading might include teacher-initiated versus student-initiated reading, reading different types of material (content-area reading, novels, comics, etc.), and reading for different purposes.

2. The setting, as well as students' reading and writing behaviors, must be

thoroughly considered. By setting we mean information about the physical setting, who initiated the activity, the teacher's instructions (if any), and the teacher's approach to teaching reading and writing.

Students' previous instruction is also an important part of the setting. For example, students' oral sharing of what they've read may be limited to rote recall because this was what previous teachers expected. In some cases even the principal's behavior (perhaps following the dictum that only "basic skills" be taught) may be relevant. Any information that can contribute to an understanding of students' reading and writing development should be considered.

3. Teachers should also consider their own behavior as part of students' instructional setting. Teachers may find that their feedback to students' miscues may encourage the belief that reading is a matter of getting the words right. Or teachers may find that students' discussion of their reading and writing is more thoughtful when they increase their "wait time" (the amount of time teachers give students to respond to their prompts or questions).

4. Observations should be regularly summarized and recorded. If someone not acquainted with the child or the setting read the record of the observations would they have a clear picture of what went on? Even if the observations aren't going to be shared with anyone else, they can still be confusing to the teacher who wrote them several weeks or months later if the record of the observation is not sufficiently explicit. Teachers will learn how explicit to make observational records by rereading past records and finding out what's confusing and what they would like to have remembered more about. More is said about recording observations in the following chapter.

5. In many cases it's helpful if observations are supplemented with pictures, audiotapes, or videotapes. Teachers may, for example, tape their students' oral reading and listen to the tape in the car on the way home. Audio- and videotapes and pictures will also be especially helpful for sharing information about students' reading and writing with parents.

6. Observations of students don't have to be unobtrusive. It's fine if students are aware that they are being observed, especially if observation is a routine practice in the classroom. It's helpful to let students know that they are being observed and why ("I just want to see what you do while you're writing."). Observation will affect students' performance only if students are rarely observed in their classrooms.

7. There are times when it's useful to ask students questions to clarify what's been observed. While observing a student's restlessness during silent reading, for example, a teacher might ask, "What's the problem? You seem restless about something."

8. Observation need not be excessively time-consuming. In some cases it may be necessary to sit back and watch students as they read and write, but these observations needn't take more than several minutes. In general, the richest source of information will be close attention to students as they respond to instruction and as they read and write.

In many North American jurisdictions specific tests are often required to determine students' eligibility for LD and remedial programs. Where such practices obtain we recommend that formal tests be supplemented by observation, even when testing is done for purposes of identification and placement. Observational data can be used to confirm or disconfirm the results of more formal assessments. Teachers should be confident about sharing the results of their observations with other professionals. They should remember that the validity of standardized tests depends on how well they predict what students actually do. In other words, if the results of testing conform to teachers' observations, then the test results are valid. Too often educators use the results of standardized tests to confirm teachers' observations (e.g., "My testing indicates that your observations about Johnny's reading problems are correct."). This is ludicrous. In cases where LD and remedial teachers must live with standardized tests, they should make the best of it, but they should also endeavor to keep tests in their proper perspective.

In some jurisdictions LD and remedial teachers are also required to develop specific instructional plans for their students before or shortly after students enter their programs. We believe every effort should be made to resist specific programming until LD and remedial teachers have had an opportunity to observe students in their classroom, at least for several weeks. It's unlikely that any program plans developed solely on the basis of a battery of formal or informal tests will be meaningful or effective. When administrative requirements oblige LD and remedial teachers to develop formal educational plans (e.g., IEPs) based on initial assessments, teachers must do what they're required to do. Then they can modify these plans as they have the opportunity to observe students in their classrooms. But we shouldn't be deluded into thinking that these tests tell us much about our students' written language development. At most, students' performance on these tests may raise our awareness about certain aspects of their reading and writing ability. But again, the dynamic nature of literacy learning and the variability of reading and writing performance make it impossible to understand students' written language development if assessment is based on only a few instances of reading and writing behavior. It's not unlike trying to capture a vacation with a few snapshots.

In this chapter we'll discuss strategies for observing students' reading and writing to discover what they know about reading and writing in order to plan and modify our instruction. We'll also address the interpretation of teacher observations. For the sake of discussion, reading and writing will sometimes be addressed separately although we will consider them together whenever possible. We'll begin with a discussion of emergent reading and writing development.

OBSERVING EARLY READING AND WRITING DEVELOPMENT

When Anne Dudley-Marling was two years old she was once observed carefully making scribbles on a piece of paper with a crayon. When she noticed the presence of an adult she announced that she was writing. Asked what she was writing she said that she was making a grocery list. Although no one would have recognized the marks Anne was making on her paper as writing, she had made an important discovery about writing—"marks" on paper can be used to represent meaning. What she had not learned was how to use various written language conventions to convey her meaning and, therefore, her "writing" was unrecognizable.

Teachers sometimes assume that children who can't read or write text in a standard way know little, if anything, about reading and writing. Therefore, emergent reading and writing assessment tends to focus on "readiness" skills, a collection of perceptual and motor skills presumed to be necessary before written language instruction can begin. What we teach tends to be related to what we assess, so for many emergent readers and writers instruction has focused on these readiness skills, with little exposure to the print of texts. It's our position that the relationship between reading, writing and reading, and writing readiness as it's commonly defined is dubious at best. There's little doubt that reading and writing do require sophisticated perceptual and processing skills. However, any child who can discriminate cartoon characters probably possesses sufficient visual perceptual skills for reading and writing (F. Smith, 1973). In fact, most children come to school already knowing a great deal about print, and, as the example of Anne's grocery list demonstrates, even children as young as two or three years of age typically know something about print (Y. Goodman, 1980; Hiebert, 1978; Reid, Hresko & Hammill, 1981). The goal of early reading and writing assessment is to find out what they know.

Although commercial tests of early reading development are available, these tests are usually designed to provide comparisons of children's reading performance with that of other children. The *Test of Early Reading Ability* (TERA) (Reid, Hresko & Hammill, 1981) assesses children's knowledge of print in a variety of situations. A number of items are designed to measure children's ability to read signs, logos, and other environmental print. For example, one item presents the familiar "golden arches" of McDonald's. Other items assess children's knowledge of letters and words and their ability to read text orally and understand written language read aloud. Although the TERA is norm-referenced, it is probably more valuable as an informal survey of children's knowledge about print. The TERA is also useful as a model for guiding teachers' observations of their students' emergent reading development.

Although tests like the TERA may be useful as models, the best procedure for evaluating students' early reading development is to observe them as they interact with print. Teachers will learn the most about their students' early reading development through their own observations and the observations of parents and others. The following questions can guide teachers' observation and appraisal of their students' early reading development:

1. Does the student enjoy being read to?
2. When the student is being read to what does s/he do? Does s/he ever finish a sentence or anticipate what's coming next? Does s/he follow along with her/his finger? If s/he does follow along with her/his finger, does s/he demonstrate a concept of the voice-print match?

3. Does the student have a favorite book(s)?
4. Does the student ever talk about books that have been read to her/him? Does s/he talk about these books in different situations? For example, does the student talk about a dog s/he has read about when encountering a similar dog in the street?
5. Does the student look at books on her/his own?
6. If the student looks at books by her/himself does s/he point to words and turn the pages front to back?
7. What does the student say, if anything, while looking at books? Does what the student says relate to the book s/he is looking at?
8. Does the student recognize signs (e.g., stop signs), labels (e.g., "Campbell's"), or logos (e.g., "McDonald's" or "Burger King")?
9. Does the student recognize her/her name?
10. Does the student recognize letters? Words? In what contexts?

Of course, these are only some of the questions teachers might ask as they watch emergent readers interact with print. But these kinds of questions will help teachers discover what their students know about books and print. In particular, these questions will help teachers investigate whether students have made the most significant discovery about reading—that print is meaningful.

Similarly, although children's knowledge of the conventions of writing develops slowly, their awareness of the purposes for which writing can be used often develops very early. Like Anne, children usually begin by "scribbling" their meanings. In time, however, they will probably write random letters and numbers to represent their meanings, usually to label objects or write their names. Gradually their writing will take on more and more of the features of conventional written English. Their spellings begin to resemble conventional English spellings and they begin to produce more and more words using various organizational and stylistic conventions.

As with reading, teachers need to be alert to any evidence that students are learning about writing. They can learn about students' developing awareness by observing them as they work with pencils and crayons and by asking students questions about their work. Parents are an especially valuable source of information about children's writing development. Evidence of students' knowledge of writing may start coming from new sources. No doubt there are children somewhere pounding on the keys of a computer keyboard who, when asked what they are doing, will answer that they too are "making a grocery list." Again, almost all school age children will know something about writing. Our task is to find out what that is. Once we have found out what our students know, we will be in a better position to describe their progress and plan instruction.

OBSERVING STUDENTS AS THEY READ

In chapter 2 we discussed the various language systems readers and writers use to construct meaning. Successful readers use graphophonic, semantic, syntactic, and pragmatic cues in order to transact meaning. Readers who rely too heavily on one language system are likely to have difficulty reading. The extent to which students use graphophonic, semantic, syntactic, and pragmatic cues and the degree to which they seek meaning can be ascertained by examining students' oral reading performance, focusing particularly on their deviations from text or miscues. Teachers can then use this information to plan and adapt instruction to the needs of individual students.

Consider the following example. Two students orally read the sentence, "The second little pig made a house of straw." The first student read, "The second little pig made a horse out of streets." The second student read, "The second little pig made a home out of sticks." Some might be tempted to conclude that these two students were demonstrating similar reading abilities. Both students committed two oral reading errors and, in fact, both had difficulty with the same two words—"house" and "straw." However, the reading of the two students differs in an important way: The miscues of the first student result in a construction that makes little sense and significantly changes the meaning of the text, while the second student's miscues do not significantly affect the sentence's meaning.

Kenneth Goodman has coined the more neutral term "miscue" to describe oral reading errors. A miscue is any oral reading response that does not match the text (K. Goodman, 1973). All readers produce miscues when they read, but miscues aren't random. They follow a pattern (K. Goodman, 1973; Hammond, 1982) and give us information about readers' thought processes during reading (K. Goodman, 1973). For example, we may infer that the first student in the above example is focusing on the appearance or sound of words as he reads, while the second student is focusing more on meaning. The pattern of the second student's miscues is more typical of good readers. When good readers produce miscues they err on the side of meaning. Poor readers tend to err on the side of phonics (Hammond, 1982). A careful analysis of students' oral reading miscues will help teachers develop and modify reading instruction as well as help them gain a better understanding of students' in-process reading behaviors, what students do as they read.

Y. Goodman, Watson, and Burke (1987) have published the *Reading Miscue Inventory* (RMI), which involves the intensive examination of a single reading experience. Students are asked to read orally a carefully selected text. Their miscues are then coded and classified according to a detailed taxonomy, e.g., "Is the miscue syntactically appropriate?"; "Was it corrected?"; "Does it change the meaning of the text?"

Although an intensive examination of students' oral reading miscues during a single reading event is possible, in most cases this is unnecessary. The RMI may be most helpful when used as a guide to teachers' informal observations of students as they read orally. Observing students' miscue patterns will enable teachers to discover if students are relying too heavily on one system for reading. They will also be able to observe how students' miscue performance varies as a function of texts or of students' background experience. This may alert teachers to the need to consider certain prereading strategies (see chapter 8) to provide background experiences for students, or in-process reading strategies (see chapter 9) to encourage students to take advantage of graphophonic, syntactic, semantic, and pragmatic cues to construct meaning.

In some cases it will be sufficient to note whether or not students' miscues are corrected and whether the meaning of the text was preserved or disrupted (Bean, 1979). If students' miscues don't change the meaning of the text there is no need for concern. Even proficient readers produce miscues that make sense. There should only be concern if students regularly produce miscues that change the meaning of the text and that are not corrected. If students regularly produce miscues that disrupt the meaning of texts, teachers will want to learn more about the specific nature of their reading problems, specifically: What information is the student using to construct meaning from a text? and, Is s/he relying too heavily on one or more language systems to the exclusion of others? Research indicates, for example, that reading disabled students tend to overrely on graphophonic information (e.g., Cambourne & Rousch, 1982; Hammond, 1982), thereby producing miscues that are more likely to change the meaning of texts (Pflaum & Bryan, 1982). Other poor readers, however, may depend too heavily on their previous knowledge of a story, ignoring graphophonic information.

The following questions for analyzing students' oral reading behavior are adapted from McCormick (1981):

1. How does a student's performance in reading words in texts compare with his/her reading of words in isolation? Students who use all of the contextual clues at their disposal should do better at recognizing words in context.
2. Are there performance differences in first, second, and third readings? Students using contextual information should recognize words better on subsequent readings of the text.
3. When a student substitutes words while reading, do the words look similar, e.g., does s/he read "The third little pig made a hose of bricks" instead of "house of bricks"?, or does s/he substitute words that have roughly the same meaning, e.g., "home of bricks" for "house of bricks"? A student whose substitutions do not disrupt the meaning of the text does not have a problem.
4. When a student substitutes, adds, or omits words while reading, does the resulting text sound like language (Tortelli, 1976)? For example, the child who reads "The second little big made a house of sticks" has produced text that is not grammatical.
5. What strategies does the student use when confronted with an unrecognizable word? Does s/he attempt to sound it out? Skip it? Skip it and then return to it later? The student's strategies will tell the teacher whether the student is trying to read for meaning or merely trying to "get the words right."

AN EXAMPLE OF MISCUE ANALYSIS

For purposes of illustration we include a coded sample of oral reading along with a brief analysis. The reading selection was provided by the child's teacher. The following codes are used:

- A word with another word written atop it indicates a substitution—for example, Victor. *[Visitor written above Victor]*

- A circle around the word indicates an omission—for example, (said) .

- An encircled C indicates a correction—for example, ©said.

- An encircled R indicates a repetition—for example, ®said Victor to Billy.

The student read as follows:

Visitor   Bill
Victor and Billy were brothers.

*   © do   ®*
"Look what you did," (said) Victor to Billy one day. "You broke my plane."

*   mind   Bill*
"I didn't mean to," Billy said.

Visitor pick   the   He
Victor picked up his broken plane. "I told you not to get into my things," he said.

*   want   that Bill*
"I just wanted to see it," Billy said.

"This is my new plane!" Victor said.

© Is tore Bill   his
He took Billy by the arm. "Say you're sorry."

*   © his Bill*
"You can't make me say anything," said Billy.

Victor took something out of his pocket.

"See this roll of tape?" he said. "I'm going to put a line of tape right down the middle of the room!"

*   Bill © want   how*
"What for?" Billy wanted (to) know.

What   © s—
"Wait and see," Victor said.

Then Victor made a line with tape right down the middle of the room.

"Now," Victor said. "This is better."

"How come?" said Billy.

*   watch ore*
"Now you'll know which is your side and which is mine. I don't want you *   my   own*
ever to step over that line. From now on, stay on your side."

This reader produced a fairly large number of miscues. Over half of the miscues sounded or looked like the word in the text. Although most of his miscues sound like language, many do not (e.g., he read "From my on, stay own your side" for "From now on, stay on your side"). Many of his miscues resulted in meaning changes, but few of these were corrected, while miscues that differed from the text in terms of sound and appearance were likely to be corrected. Miscues that didn't look like language and that changed the meaning of the text were often uncorrected. For example, he read "Bill want how" for "Billy wanted to know," indicating that, for this reader, the physical similarity between "know" and "how" was more compelling than meaning. In general, this student appears to be overly dependent on graphophonic information and all too willing to accept miscues that result in serious disruption of meaning.

This example, of course, is based on a brief reading episode. More examples of reading behavior would be necessary before we could make confident judgments about this student's reading abilities. However, even if we had a much longer reading sample for this student, it's still unwise to depend too heavily on a single sample of reading behavior. No matter how lengthy the sample, we need to examine oral reading at a number of different times, with different reading materials, done for different purposes, and so on.

One of the limitations of miscue analysis is that it focuses only on students' oral reading, not their silent reading. "Reader selected miscues" (Watson, 1978a), which we discuss as an instructional strategy in chapter 9, is a useful assessment strategy that partially overcomes this limitation. During regular silent reading periods, students are given bookmarks and instructed to place their bookmarks in the book at any place where they're having trouble and then continue reading. When they've finished reading, students are instructed to select miscues that were particularly troublesome for them, miscues that caused a loss of meaning or distracted them from their reading. Students then write each sentence containing miscues on a bookmark and underline the trouble spots. Knowing the types of words and contexts that cause students difficulty can be very useful for teachers in planning instruction.

Some students may mark no miscues at all because they have not had any difficulty with the text. But if you suspect that this isn't the case, then you'll need to investigate further. You may wish to talk with them about whether they have understood the instructions. Or they're paying so little attention to meaning, they don't know when the meaning they construct doesn't make sense. In these cases it will be helpful to ask students to read the text orally.

The use of cloze exercises, another popular instructional strategy, can also provide insights into students' reading behavior. Students' ability to complete cloze exercises indicates the degree to which they use contextual information to construct meaning and the sources of contextual information they are able to use. For example, a student who completed a cloze sentence as "The girl is to the store" was able to produce a meaningful response in terms of what came before, but not after, the blank. Cloze exercises can also indicate students' ability to use information from adjoining sentences or paragraphs to make predictions about meaning. In general, many of the questions used to analyze students' oral reading miscues apply to their performance on cloze exercises.

We recommend the use of cloze for assessment only when it is also used as an instructional strategy to encourage students to make predictions. As we argued in the introduction to this section, there is no need to contrive tasks for purposes of assessment. It's sufficient to observe students as they read, and in the case of cloze, as they respond to instruction.

It's possible to observe other evidence of reading development as students read silently. Hunt (n.d.) notes that a number of behaviors may be observed during periods of sustained silent reading: 1) increased concentration during sustained silent reading; 2) a reluctance to stop reading when the period has ended; 3) greater spontaneous reaction during silent reading; 4) selection of reading material of increasing difficulty; and 5) greater impatience with disturbances. An increase in any of these behaviors may indicate increased attention to meaning and a greater interest in reading. It may also indicate that students have discovered particular reading materials that interest them. Teachers should be especially alert to this possibility.

OBSERVING THE PRODUCTS OF READING

The most obvious product of students' reading is the experience or meaning they construct as a direct result of their reading experiences. We usually refer to this as reading comprehension. Traditional methods for assessing reading comprehension tend to focus on a narrow set of comprehending behaviors (D. W. Moore, 1983), usually rote recall. Too often it's assumed that, if students can recall the details of a text in a logical order, they've gotten the author's intended meaning or, more likely, the teacher's interpretation of the author's intended meaning. But Johnston (1983) cautions against concluding that readers have comprehended something if they can give only a rote recall of the elements of the text.

Although rote recall is one way to assess reading comprehension, there is obviously more to it than that. No text has a *single* meaning. Several readers can read the same passage and comprehend or experience the text in different ways (Page and Pinnel, 1979b). In fact, the same reader often experiences different meanings on subsequent readings of a text. Those of us who have reread Lewis Carroll's (1960) *Alice's Adventures in Wonderland* as adults construct layers of meaning very different from those we constructed as children. Reading comprehension is dependent on a number of factors that are independent of the text, including readers' background knowledge, their familiarity with the structure of the text, their interests and attitudes, their maturity as readers, their mood, their purposes for reading, and so on. For our purposes, reading comprehension is a matter of establishing connections among ideas in the text, stating them in alternative form, and relating them to the reader's experience.

One way of learning about students' reading comprehension is to listen to students as they orally share what they've read. It's preferable to have students share texts they've read silently, since oral reading may focus students' attention on graphophonic information and may, therefore, interfere with meaning construction (Newman, 1978). We present a number of ways of encouraging students to share orally what they've read in chapter 10. Students' retellings will be most meaningful if the students believe that there is some real reason for them to share what they've read, and that it is not just another occasion for evaluation.

The following questions can guide teachers' interpretation of students' oral sharing of their reading:

1. How much of the material presented in the text did the reader retell (Griffin and Jongsma, 1980)?
2. Did the reader's retelling include information not stated explicitly in the text, that is, information that was inferred (Griffin and Jongsma, 1980)? For example, the statement "The man tried to climb the mountain" implies that he failed unless the text specifies otherwise.
3. Did the retelling include information not stated (implicitly or explicitly) in the text or false information (Griffin & Jongsma, 1980)?
4. Did the reader's retelling reflect the structure of the text? Did the reader retell the text in a logical way? Texts are typically organized in ways characteristic of their genre. For example, fairy tales usually begin "Once upon a time" and follow a standard story structure format. Children as young as five may demonstrate an awareness of basic story structure (Marshall, 1983). Expository texts also use characteristic structures. Intuitive knowledge of text structures can aid reading comprehension and will be reflected in the reader's retellings.
5. Did the reader bring any background experience or knowledge to her/his understanding of the material (Griffin & Jongsma, 1980)? For example, a student's retelling of a story about camping may include some details from the student's own camping experiences.
6. Did the reader use details to relate major topics or did s/he merely state the details (Griffin & Jongsma, 1980)? For example, if a student read a story about the animals of the forest did s/he merely discuss each animal in the forest or did s/he attempt to discuss the relationship of the animals to each other and to the forest?
7. Did you feel that the reader's retelling represented an adequate understanding of the text (Griffin & Jongsma, 1980)? This may seem to be an especially subjective criterion for judging retellings but it's important nonetheless. Again, just stating the information doesn't necessarily mean that the reader really understood what s/he read. You may have to question the reader to get a good sense of this. Questions like "Why do you think the author wrote this book?" and "For whom do you think the author wrote this story?" (Brown, 1981) may be helpful.

These questions aren't meant to be a checklist but are merely guidelines for evaluating students' oral sharing of their reading.

Students' oral sharing of their reading will be affected by what they already know about a topic. You can expect richer sharing, including more background knowledge, on topics with which readers are familiar. If students' background knowledge about a topic is not evident in their sharing of a story, ask them what they already knew about the topic. Relevant background knowledge is not limited to information about the topic itself (computers, for example) but also includes familiarity with the author and the genre (mystery stories, fairy tales).

After students have finished sharing what they've read, it may be helpful to ask some questions to elicit additional information about the reading. Ideally, these questions will come from other students. Teachers should be very careful not to encourage students to believe that this is another test. Teachers should question students to clarify their own understanding of the text, not only for evaluation. Teachers should also be aware that some students may share very little of what they've read or incorporate little personal experience into their retellings because they fear that they're being evaluated. Such students may have learned that it's better to play it safe. For this reason, it's helpful if teachers model sharing by orally sharing their own reading experiences with students from time to time, including how what they've read relates to their own personal experience.

Evidence of students' reading comprehension will not be limited to their oral sharing. Evidence will also appear in their drawings, in projects like plays and pantomimes, and in their response to written instructions (all of which are discussed as instructional strategies in chapter 10). Other evidence may emerge in discussions with parents or other teachers. Teachers should also be alert to students' spontaneous comments about what they've read. For example, a student the teacher believes to be a very poor reader may reveal that he has no difficulty following a recipe or the directions for constructing a model car.

In summary, reading comprehension is a matter of constructing meaning. In fact, reading comprehension *is* reading. The idea that students can read without comprehension makes no sense to us. The goal of observing the products of students' reading is to examine the meanings they construct. Do students make sense of what they've read at all and, if so, what are the meanings they construct? Do they integrate what they've read with their background experiences? Do they use their knowledge of the world (and language) to help them understand what they're reading? The meanings students construct will vary according to their experiences as individuals, but there are obviously limitations to the range of acceptable meanings. In general, problems in this area indicate an overdependence on one language system—e.g., graphophonics—or a reluctance to integrate reading into their own experiences.

OBSERVING READING FLEXIBILITY

Reading flexibility is a matter of adjusting reading rate, comprehension strategies, and effort according to the reader's purposes and the nature of the reading material (Rankin, 1974). Most readers adjust their reading rate and their comprehension strategies according to whether they are reading for pleasure or studying for an exam, for example. Poor readers, especially the learning disabled, may have difficulty adjusting their reading behavior according to their purposes for reading (Alley & Deshler, 1979; Rankin, 1974). Many poor readers may approach all reading material with the same strategies, whether they are reading for pleasure, studying for an exam, or just trying to locate some piece of information in a textbook. This is obviously a very inefficient and frustrating approach to reading.

Although a number of tests that assess reading flexibility have been published, observation of the student's reading behavior is the best approach. Observations of students and personal interviews with them will allow teachers to address questions like: Does the student read at the same speed for all types of material? Does the student vary her/his reading rate according to her/his purposes for reading? Does the student ever use strategies like skimming and scanning as well as reading for detail? If teachers discover that students cannot (or do not) adjust their reading behavior according to these kinds of variables, they may need to employ instructional strategies designed to increase students' reading flexibility.

OBSERVING STUDENTS' WRITING

In this section we'll discuss approaches to evaluating students' writing that tell us what students know about writing and how they go about using written language to make meaning and fulfill communicative intentions.

All too frequently students' writing is evaluated in terms of such features as punctuation, spelling, word usage, and grammar. Students' writing is also frequently evaluated using some formal test that examines students' writing in terms of the presence or absence of these features. However, from our point of view, students' writing should be evaluated in terms of two general questions: Does the writing fulfill its purpose (to report, persuade, elicit some feeling, etc.)? and, What do students know about writing, including writing conventions, that helps them fulfill their intentions?

We suggest some questions below that will help teachers better understand their students' writing and, at the same time, assist them in planning instruction. Most of these questions can only be answered by carefully observing students as they write. Donald Graves (1983) suggests that assessment of students' writing be based on routine examination of their written work, including observing members of the whole class as they write. Graves also recommends about five minutes of "close in" observation of individual students, which involves sitting right next to or in front of students as they write, and suggests that students be told its purpose. Teachers may wish to say something like, "I'm going to watch what you do while you write for a few minutes. It'll help me figure out how to help you better. Just go on with what you're doing as if I'm not here." Again, it's desirable to observe students writing for a variety of purposes and audiences on a variety of topics of their own choosing. It's insufficient to observe only one or two instances of students' writing.

WRITING ASSESSMENT GUIDELINES

The following questions will help teachers evaluate students' writing:

1. Who initiated the writing? The student? The teacher? Perhaps the writing was initiated by the principal or a guest in the classroom. In any case, students are most likely to produce their best writing if they initiate the writing to fulfill their own purposes. Therefore, writing initiated by someone

other than the students should be judged differently from writing initiated by students themselves.

2. Who chose the topic for writing? If the student chose the topic, did s/he have much difficulty choosing a topic? What was the topic s/he chose? Did s/he choose to write on a topic s/he knew much about? Of course, if the student wrote on a topic s/he knew or cared little about, her/his writing would have to be judged cautiously. In some cases students may have to be asked about their interests and their knowledge about writing topics.

3. How much did students write and how much of the writing time did they spend writing? Did they write without prompting? We don't mean to suggest here that students should be expected to write continuously for long periods of time. Good writers often pause to compose their thoughts or review what they have already written, or they just get stuck. But it is worth noting exactly what students do as they write.

4. What, if anything, did students say aloud while they were writing? Did they speak first, then write, or did they speak as they wrote? Did their utterances give you any insight into their writing strategies? For example, we overheard one young writer saying, "No, they'll never understand what this means" as she erased a line of text from her paper. Other writers may indicate that their erasures are motivated mainly by neatness or by spelling miscues.

5. Was there anything about students' body language as they wrote that provides any insights into their feelings about writing? Continual squirming or sighing may be an indication of a student's feelings about writing, or at least about a particular writing assignment.

6. Did students reread and/or revise what they had written? What sorts of revisions did they make? Why? If you don't know why, ask the student. Knowing why students revise their work (or don't revise it) can provide important insights into how students go about writing and why. Some students' revisions may consist primarily of erasures in order to replace unknown spellings with more certain spellings, e.g., substituting "hot" for "warm." Other students may make revisions primarily in the interest of clarity.

7. For what audience was the piece of writing intended? This is important for a number of reasons. First of all, different audiences have different informational needs. Audiences also differ in their relationship to the author. Writing for an audience that already knows a great deal about the topic allows the author to provide less background information. Writing to a friend usually involves a less formal style than, say, writing to an elected representative. Any evaluation of students' writing must not only examine how well the writer considers the needs of her/his audience; the writing must also be judged in terms of the relationship between the writer and the intended audience. Too often writing is evaluated according to absolute standards, as if all writing were formal and all audiences the same. However, the standards for punctuation, grammar, and even spelling are not the same for notes to friends, letters, business memos, and academic papers.

8. For what purpose was the piece written? Knowing why the piece was written puts the teacher in a much better position to judge its effectiveness. In most cases students will have to be asked why they wrote the piece. If the student says, "I wrote it so the student council will vote to do my project," for example, does the piece have the potential to persuade readers? How well a piece of writing fulfills its purpose can only be evaluated in terms of the audience for which it was written. It's also instructive to know if the piece was written only because the teacher asked the student to write it.

   Knowing the purpose for which a piece of writing was written will also enable a teacher to judge the student's use of writing conventions. A piece of writing that reads like a long narrative may be counterproductive if the purpose was to give simple directions for completing a task. On the other hand, a long narrative may be very useful if the writer's purpose was to tell a story. Knowing a student's purpose will help the teacher evaluate the student's use of style and conventions. For some purposes formal English may be an impediment to effective communication (e.g., notes to friends), while in other cases it may be essential.

9. How well does a piece of writing "hang together"? Does it come together as a cohesive whole or does it read like a series of sentences related only by topic. Effective writers, like effective speakers, use a number of conventions to make their language flow. Conjunctions, transitions, pronouns, and so on serve this purpose. For example, rather than stating the names of persons, places, and objects over and over we typically use pronouns and other references (e.g., here/there). Organization is another important factor in how well a piece of writing flows or develops. It's tempting to compare students' writing to some absolute standard—for example, does the story begin with a description of the setting?—but this ignores the writer's purpose and audience. Organization, like other stylistic conventions, should only be judged in terms of how well writers fulfill their communicative intentions for a given audience. We've all read and probably even recounted stories by beginning at the end, not the beginning. In some cases this is an effective means for capturing an audience's attention and, therefore, helps writers realize their intentions.

10. How effectively do students use language structures? How well do students use syntactic rules or rules governing word endings? Do students omit words (verbs, for example) or use only short, simple sentences? Perhaps a writer uses the same sentence structures over and over. What about word endings? Does the writer effectively "mark" plurals, verb tenses, and so on?

11. How effectively do students use words in their writing? Do they use a wide range of words or only a few words; do they repeat the same words or use words inappropriately? A student may continually describe a character she's writing about as "good," either because her vocabulary is limited or because she is uncertain about the spelling of synonyms for "good."

12. How does students' written language compare to their oral language? Significant differences between oral and written language may suggest that the student is still learning about the conventions governing written language. However, it may also indicate that students are unwilling to take risks,

which could be related to their instructional history. It may also indicate that students write without conviction, that is, that they write only to fulfill the expectations of others and not to realize their own intentions.

13. Does the writer's "voice" come through in students' writing? Graves (1983) argues that this is very important. Voice is related to a writer's urge to express her/himself, ownership of the writing, and efforts to put her/himself into the writing. Which of us hasn't "heard" the voice of a friend as we read a letter? Voice is often the difference between the dull, vapid writing done only to please teachers and the writing students do for themselves, which is often full of life and conviction. Students who have learned all the appropriate forms for writing but who write without conviction may have learned how to produce products that satisfy many teachers but have failed to discover writing as an expressive tool.

14. Is students' writing performance fairly consistent? While consistency would seem, on the surface, to be a desirable characteristic, this may not be the case. Each piece of writing produced by students, or adults, will not be equally effective. Graves (1983) has found that children's writing performance is often highly variable, and he argues that variability is, in fact, a desirable quality. It indicates that writers are taking risks in their writing and not just playing it safe.

15. What do writers know about punctuation, capitalization, and spelling? The next section, "Writing Conventions," presents information to help teachers describe students' use of capitalization, punctuation, and spelling.

Much of the information needed to answer these questions about students' writing will come from observing students as they write and from examining the products of their writing. Another important source of information about the students' knowledge of the process of writing comes from asking writers questions before and after they write.

Before writing, ask:

• What are you going to be writing about?
• How are you going to put that down on paper?
• How did you go about choosing that topic?
• What problems do you think you might run into?

After writing, ask:

• How did you go about writing this?
• Did you make any changes?
• What are you going to do next with this piece of writing?
• What do you think of this piece of writing?
• Why do you think it's good/bad? (Graves, 1983)

These "before and after" questions can provide important insights into students' writing strategies and the process of their writing.

An adequate understanding of students' writing will also depend on a consideration of their instructional history. For example, some teachers severely penalize students for spelling errors. Students who have had such teachers may regularly avoid words they aren't sure how to spell. They won't take chances with new words and, therefore, it may only appear that these students have a limited writing vocabulary.

All of the guidelines for evaluating students' writing suggested here should only guide the description of students as they write and the products of their writing. These questions should not be used as a checklist nor are they exhaustive. In addition, it's not necessary or even desirable to attempt to address all these questions when evaluating each piece of writing. These impressions will develop as teachers experience students' writing over time. For initial evaluation, if necessary, teachers should try to address as many of the above questions as possible, but it won't be possible to address all of them. It's worth repeating that even initial evaluation shouldn't be based on a single writing sample. Every effort should be made to collect as many samples of students' writing as possible, including writing produced in the regular classroom and at home. It may be that all of a student's writing was produced for someone else's purposes and on assigned topics. This sort of writing, while contributing some useful information, must still be viewed with considerable caution.

We also recommend that teachers ask students to read what they've written aloud. This will provide an opportunity to ask students additional questions about their writing—"Why did you choose this word here?," for example—and will clarify any confusion that might arise because of poor handwriting or unrecognizable spellings. Students' comments, self-corrections, and oral revisions should also be observed. Spontaneous comments are likely to provide interesting information about students' views of the writing process, while self-corrections and oral revisions will help teachers understand the student's potential in revision and editing.

WRITING CONVENTIONS

It's useful to recall again the role of conventions—capitalization, punctuation, and spelling—in writing. These standardized forms are an important part of the written language code writers use to fulfill communicative intentions. Writers do not (or at least should not be required to) learn forms as an end goal. They learn forms, or conventions, so they can be understood and thus more easily fulfill their intentions. This is an important consideration when evaluating samples of students' writing since the appropriateness of conventional forms depends on the writers' purposes, potential audiences, and so on. What counts for appropriate spelling, for example, depends on the context of the writing. "Thru" may not be an appropriate spelling in a formal paper but certainly is acceptable in a memo or a note. Similarly, rules governing capitalization and punctuation may be suspended or modified in a diary, a journal, or even a letter to a friend. The point here is this: It isn't sufficient just to find out whether or not students "know" the rules of punctuation, spelling, and capitalization.

Writers must also know how to apply these rules flexibly depending upon the context of their writing.

Punctuation and capitalization

It's best to examine spontaneous writing to evaluate students' ability to use rules governing punctuation and capitalization. It may also be helpful to take students back to a piece of writing and ask them to edit generally or to put in periods or capitalization, and then observe what happens. This will reveal what students actually know, not just what they have used from what they know about conventions. In addition, it isn't enough simply to compare children's use of punctuation and capitalization to some absolute standard. Instead, we need to describe how children apply these rules.

When Kara Rhodes was in first grade, each line of her writing often began with a capital letter and ended with a period whether it was the end of a sentence or not. It would be tempting to conclude that Kara didn't know how to use the rules governing punctuation and capitalization. Remember, however, that writers learn about punctuation and spelling by seeing these conventions used by others, that is, by reading. Kara was regularly exposed to reading primers at this stage of her school career. These books are typically written one line at a time, each line beginning with a capital letter and ending with a period. Kara made a reasonable guess about how to use capital letters and periods based on her experience with these books. The goal of assessing children's use of writing conventions isn't merely to check for correct punctuation; it is to note, if students are using punctuation and capitalization at all, how they are using them.

Spelling

In this section we'll consider the developmental nature of children's spelling and then discuss a developmental assessment of spelling.

Many people are frequently frustrated with the English spelling system, which they may perceive as being highly irregular. Why, for example, should there be a *g* in *sign* or an *e* in *gate*? And why is *phone* spelled *p-h-o-n-e* and not *fone*. In fact, the frequency of irregular English spellings is often blamed for children's spelling difficulties, and since the introduction of typesetting, considerable commentary has been devoted to spelling reform. However, English spelling is quite regular and ideally suited for its purpose if we recognize that words with similar meanings tend to have similar spellings. This is indeed a highly desirable feature. We would clearly not want the spelling of words like *sign* and *signal* to be significantly different (e.g., *sine*, *signal*) since this would mask the relationship between words and their derivatives. We would not want our spellings to be related to variations in pronunciation. We would not, for example, want Americans to spell *again a-g-e-n* and Canadians to spell it *a-g-a-i-n* (or *a-g-a-n-e*). We would also not want the spellings of words to change as their pronunciation changed over the course of time. So, although English spellings may not be highly regular in terms of phonetic rules, they are rule governed.

Children demonstrate an early awareness of the regularities of English spelling and even the spelling of learning disabled students tends to be rule governed (e.g., Gerber, 1984). However, young spellers, and many learning disabled and remedial students, tend to overrely on phonetic rules (Gerber, 1984; Read, 1975). In fact, the evidence indicates that children progress from a developing awareness of the phonological rules governing English spelling and an overreliance on these rules to an ability to employ the visual features of standard English spelling. In the process of developing a knowledge of the rules governing English spelling children move along a continuum of spelling development, passing through various points of spelling development in the process.

In the remainder of this section we'll explicate points of spelling development along a continuum and discuss how they can be applied to the assessment of students' spelling. The first point in spelling development is *prephonemic* spelling. A prephonemic speller has learned that letters or letterlike symbols represent language. However, these students use random strings of letters, numbers, and other "markings" to represent words. Prephonemic spellers are not usually reading yet and therefore have not developed the concept (from reading) that there is a regular correspondence between print and oral language.

There's a wide range of writing that is considered prephonemic. The example of prephonemic spelling presented in Figure 3−1 was written by a normally developing three-year-old. This child read what she had written as: "It is green. You put food in it. You take it to picnics" (the answer: a cooler).

A second writing sample (Figure 3−2) was written by a second-grade boy. When he was asked to read what he had written, he "read" Jack and Jill, a nursery rhyme that his Chapter I reading teacher had taught him. Although some of the words do begin with *J* as Jack and Jill should, this may be because his own name begins with *J*.

This writing sample, unlike the earlier piece, contains only conventional letters to represent words. Other prephonemic spellers, especially those who are being taught to read text, may incorporate some correctly spelled words they have learned from their reading lessons. However, most words are represented by random strings of letters.

In contrast to prephonemic spellers, *phonemic spellers*, have discovered phonetic principles of spelling and attempt to capture the sounds of words in their own writing. However, phonemic spellers represent only some of the sounds in words, often only the first and/or last sounds, although they often recognize that they haven't represented all of the sounds. For example, a normally achieving kindergarten student wrote herself a note so that she'd remember to draw a picture of a rainbow the next day. She laboriously sounded out the word *rainbow* like this:

"R...r...r..." and then she wrote "R."

"Ray...ray..." and then she wrote "A."

FIGURE 3–1   Prephonemic Spelling by a Three-Year-Old

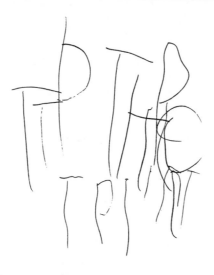

FIGURE 3–2   "Jack and Jill" by a Second-Grade Boy

"Bow...bow...b...b..." and then she wrote "B."

She then looked at what she had written and announced, "It's not long enough!" and promptly added three more letters without sounding them out, ending up with what's shown as Figure 3–3.

Phonemic spellers represent more and more letter sounds until they represent all of the sounds in a word, when they become *letter name* spellers. Letter name spellings represent all of the sounds of words but do so on the basis of letter names. For example, letter name spellers may spell *baby* as "BABE" or *letter* as "LETR." Once you catch on to the letter naming strategy, most spellings are

---

FIGURE 3–3   "Rainbow" by a Kindergarten Student

---

fairly transparent, but can you guess what word the child who wrote "YET" was trying to represent? It turns out that the child was trying to represent the sounds in *went*. Why did the child use *Y* to represent the letter sound /w/? Well, *Y* is the letter name that comes closest to representing the sound /w/. Similarly, many letter name spellers use the letter name "H" to represent the sound /sh/ and /ch/. (See page 20 for examples.)

Readers may wish to try to decipher a child's note to the tooth fairy explaining how she lost her tooth:

TOH FARE MY TOH WET DON EAE JAAN

BAT SO CAN I HAVE SAM MANE

[Tooth fairy, my tooth went down the drain
but so can I have some money?]

It is interesting to note that this child's spelling of *drain* as "JAAN" is further evidence of her reliance on a letter name strategy. Although drain is spelled with an initial *dr-* most speakers pronounce it "j-rain." Most of us cannot even hear this oddity in pronunciation, but young children do and often represent the /dr/ sound with the letter *J* or the letter *G*.

Even older students can sometimes be letter name spellers, especially learning disabled and remedial learners. For example, a fourteen-year-old boy wrote this entry in his journal:

I said after schooh to hip Mer Shagr part up sham hares.

[I stayed after school to help Mr. ———— put up some chairs.]

It's worth noting, however, that this student, like other students, does not rely exclusively upon a letter naming strategy. For example, he does represent the /k/ sound in "school" with the appropriate *ch*. But when he is uncertain, he reverts to the letter naming strategy.

As students learn to read they may notice differences between their own and conventional spelling. At this point students begin to incorporate some of the visual features of standard English orthography into their own spelling. These students are *transitional spellers*. Although transitional spellers have begun to employ many of the visual features of standard English spelling, they may overgeneralize these features. They may, for example, spell *eat* "eet," *altar* "alter," *business* "busyness," and so on.

Students become *correct* spellers when they begin to employ regularly the visual features of standard English spelling. This doesn't mean that students are correct spellers only if they can spell all words correctly, only that they regularly spell words correctly.

A final word about these various points or stages in spelling development. Spelling stages are not discrete, and you may not observe students' progress through all of the stages. They merely serve to describe children's progress along a continuum of spelling development. Children may also revert to earlier strategies when they attempt to spell less familiar words. The fourteen-year-old boy in one of the above examples demonstrated an awareness of many of the features of standard English orthography (e.g., "said," "schooh") but relied on a letter naming strategy when he was uncertain.

Observing spelling development

Temple, Nathan, and Burris (1982) present instructional strategies appropriate for students at various points in their spelling development. Therefore, it's useful to determine the approximate point of students' spelling development in order to decide how to respond to students' spelling. This can be accomplished by rating each spelling "error," or miscue, according to its developmental level:

1 = Prephonemic
2 = Phonemic
3 = Letter name
4 = Transitional
5 = Correct

These ratings can be applied to students' spellings and then averaged to obtain a *rough* estimate of a student's developmental spelling level.

The following example is from an eight-year-old LD student's written spellings of a word list (from J. W. Beers, 1980).

WORD	STUDENT'S SPELLING	RATING
hat	hat	5
back	bik	2
stack	sak	2
sap	sip	2
bed	bed	5
step	sep	2
wreck	rik	2

speck	pek	2
lip	lep	3
stick	sik	2
pit	pit	5
lid	led	3
gate	gate	5
lake	lak	3
spade	pad	3
drape	gap	3
week	wek	3
seat	sete	4
creek	kek	2
streak	set	2
ride	ride	5
light	lite	4
tribe	cib	3
dike	dik	3

This student's average rating is approximately a 3 indicating that, in general, she is using a predominantly letter name strategy. Although this example uses student responses to a list of spelling words, it's much better to evaluate students' spelling within the context of their spontaneous writing. The only time you should need to resort to spelling lists for purposes of evaluation is if students play it so safe in their writing (i.e., attempting only words they know how to spell) that there is no spelling data to observe. Also, it's best to evaluate students' spelling only after they've had the opportunity to edit their work.

It's also useful to observe students as they spell words. Be willing to ask them how they decided on a particular spelling. This will provide additional insights into students' orthographic knowledge.

SAMPLE EVALUATION OF TWO WRITING SAMPLES

In this section we present two writing samples and sample evaluations. The first writing sample is by a thirteen-year-old girl who was referred to a reading clinic because of difficulties in reading and writing. She wrote the piece in response to a request from a teacher to write a story on anything she wished to write about.

Writing sample A

Love is like a game of football
if you play the game right you both can win!
Summer was nice and fun. It's nice to be with your friend's, and in joy your salf. It's time to play and a time to go places. I alwas have fun in the summer. My friends and I do new thing and go new place. Sometimes I go out of town, its nice to go on vacasn and to get out of the house.

This piece of writing was on a topic chosen by the student but it was initiated by a teacher. The student first said she would write a love poem and then, with encouragement, she produced more writing. Since the first sentence is topically unrelated to the rest of what she wrote, it may be that the teacher's encouragement sent her off in an entirely new direction. Overall, she wrote fairly quickly and without much hesitation. She did make several erasures as she wrote, which she said were to correct her spelling or to improve her handwriting, a noticeable focus on forms. None of her corrections affected the meaning or structure of the story.

The topics of love and summer are of interest to this student, and she has written about them before. However, she does not rely on her personal experience in her writing. In fact, it's clear that she doesn't understand love or football, or perhaps both. Her paragraphs are reasonably well organized and her sentences follow in logical order, but she repeats herself frequently and does not fully develop any of her ideas. She makes fairly extensive use of conjunctions and pronouns to achieve some degree of cohesion, at least at the sentence level, but she does not make use of transitions across sentences or paragraphs.

Her use of punctuation and capitalization indicate that she has a fairly good grasp of the rules governing these conventions, but her use of apostrophes with plural nouns shows some confusion about the rules for marking plurals. She uses appropriate, yet simple syntax, although she does omit ''to'' between ''go'' and ''new'' in line 5. She has spelled most of the words in her paragraph correctly but has produced a few spelling miscues, e.g., ''salf'' for *self*, ''alwas'' for *always*, ''vacasn'' for *vacation*, and ''in joy'' for *enjoy*. These errors indicate that she is a transitional speller; that is, her spelling miscues, while not correct, employ many of the features of standard English spelling.

Perhaps the most obvious characteristic of this writing sample is its lifelessness. It conveys no conviction or urge to express, nor does it reflect the student's knowledge of language or her own personal experiences. Her erasures indicate more concern with producing accurate forms than in communicating anything that is of real interest to her. This is probably to be expected, however, given the purpose and audience for the writing. She might have produced a more effective piece of writing (and we could have learned more about her as a writer) if she had been asked to revise and/or edit her writing.

Writing sample B

The following piece of writing is excerpted from a longer report written by Mary, a sixteen-year-old learning disabled student. It's noteworthy that Mary has been a reluctant writer and has never before produced writing of such length or conviction.

My dream is to work with handicapped people I want to help them and know there troubles and care for them Because if no one will love them how will. I think they are very smart but they just need more help then others. You have to have the time to learn and understand them. In this picture is a guy name Michael he is 14 and he is telling me about him. But what I've listen to what he says and does is that he is very smart and a great person. I have interview him on tape and I want you to listen to him and tell me that he is a very smart boy. I hope my dream comes true and then one day I'll know that they are great people and learn to love, live and laugh with them. You may think this is crazy and you don't have a disability in thing then I'll be honest with you. That you have a disability and face it. But it don't mean your dumb because I know I have a disability in some things.

The report from which this excerpt is taken was written after Mary had completed writing a summary of a book on dyslexia. She initiated the writing and chose the topic. Mary typed the composition herself, so some of her misspellings may be typographical errors, and it was written at home, so we don't know how long it took her to write it or how much editing, if any, she did.

The attention of most teachers and parents is probably drawn immediately to the problems Mary has with writing conventions. She has omitted a couple of periods at the ends of sentences and misspelled a number of words, usually homophones (e.g., their/there). A couple of times she has failed to mark the past tense of verbs ("I have interview him"), and many of her sentences are awkward or even ungrammatical, e.g., "But what I've listen to what he says and does . . . ." So-called run-on sentences are also common in her writing.

But these observations overlook important strengths in Mary's writing and indicate only that she may need help in revising and editing her work, although this is uncertain until we've had more opportunity to observe her as she writes. It is clear that in this piece, Mary has made a marvelous breakthrough in her writing, a breakthrough not always achieved in the writing of many "good" students. She has discovered that writing can be used to express and share her feelings with others. In her interview of a handicapped adolescent, she attempts to persuade and move her audience, and her writing is full of life. Mary cares about what she has written. She has a reason to edit and improve her writing because she has something she wants to share. She has also done an adequate job of organizing her writing; her ideas are well developed and she uses pronouns and conjunctions effectively to give her writing some degree of cohesion.

Readers will note that we haven't attempted to answer all the questions about writing we posed earlier. It isn't necessary, or even possible, to address all these questions when describing a single sample of a student's writing. They can only be addressed by observing students' writing over a period of time. In some cases not all of the questions will be relevant for some students, e.g., students who are not yet fluent writers.

OBSERVING STUDENTS' PERCEPTIONS
OF READING AND WRITING

Assessing students' perceptions of reading and writing can provide an additional source of information about students' reading and writing behavior. For example, if students' truly believe (of course, we can never know for sure exactly what they believe) that reading is a matter of sounding out words, we need to confront this belief. Such information about students' beliefs may surface during reading and writing conferences, class discussions, or individual or group reading or writing activities. Many teachers also find individually administered informal reading and writing interviews helpful.

A number of reading and writing interviews have been proposed. Here we include a relatively brief reading and writing interview used in the Chapter I "Instructional Assistance Project" of the Denver Public Schools.

READING AND WRITING INTERVIEW

A. 1. When you are reading and you come to something that you don't know, what do you do?
   2. Do you like to read? Why or why not?
   3. Do you think you are a good reader? Why or why not?
   4. Name your favorite books. Where did you read each of them?
B. 1. When you are writing, what kinds of troubles or problems do you have? What do you do about them?
   2. Do you ever make changes when you are writing? If so, what things get changed?
   3. Do you like to write? Why or why not?
   4. Do you think you are a good writer? Why or why not?

This interview can give teachers some information about how students feel about themselves as readers and writers as well as indicating the strategies students are conscious of and prefer (or at least say they prefer) when they encounter difficulty in reading or writing. It may also uncover their misconceptions about reading and writing. It's common for students to think that they aren't good readers because they sometimes reread sections of text or because they don't always remember everything they've read. But, of course, these behaviors are also typical of good readers. The reading and writing interview can also be useful in groups, perhaps to help students confront their beliefs about written language.

CONCLUSION

We stated earlier that the diagnostic-prescriptive teaching model continues to be very popular in special and remedial education. It's still common for teachers to make judgments about students' abilities and to develop instructional plans based on a battery of formal or informal tests. However, this model is inadequate in dealing with reading and writing development. The development of written language in children and adolescents is in a constant state of change and cannot be described by static measures. Teachers need to attend regularly to their students' reading and writing performance, and continually evaluate what their students know and what sort of instructional support they need. Assessment must not be thought of as something that precedes teaching but as something that is an integral part of teaching. Human learning is dynamic and, therefore, teaching must also be dynamic, responding to the ever-changing knowledge and needs of learners. This can only happen if teachers are alert to students' performance and respond accordingly.

The key to ongoing evaluation is observation. Teachers must become skilled observers of reading and writing development if they are to influence students' literacy development effectively. They must learn to observe students as they read and write and as they respond to reading and writing instruction. Continuous observation of students as readers and writers will enable special education and remedial teachers to discover what their students know about written language and, most importantly, how students use this knowledge to make meaning and to fulfill their communicative intentions. Of course, evidence of students' reading and writing development will be readily available only if students read and write often.

IV

Planning instruction

In the previous chapter we discussed guidelines for observing and assessing children's literacy development. Assessing literacy development is a matter of observing children reading and writing in a variety of situations, recording these observations, and making judgments about children's ability to use written language. These observations, however, are useful only if they actually influence instruction on a daily basis. It's possible for teachers to observe children's literacy development regularly and yet fail to use this information effectively when planning instruction, often because they don't see the relevance of the information they've collected.

Making effective use of the information gathered from observational assessment may be difficult for some teachers, especially for those trained and practiced in behavioral approaches to teaching reading and writing. What do you do, for example, about writers whose writing is lifeless or readers who are more concerned with "getting the words right" than with constructing meaning?

In this chapter we'll discuss using assessment information to plan and adapt instruction to the ever-changing needs of developing readers and writers. We'll address the problems in writing goals or objectives that are consistent with the principles of holism.

WRITTEN GOALS OR OBJECTIVES

Written goals or objectives are a good idea. They help guide instruction and encourage accountability, reassuring parents and administrators that students are receiving instruction tailored to their individual needs. Goals or objectives are also something most good teachers have always included in their teaching, even those not compelled to write them by law. Teachers must have some sense of the reading and writing development of their students if they are to be effective. They should have a good idea of what their students know about reading and writing and what kinds of experiences and feedback they should provide for them to encourage continued literacy development. Most importantly, however, producing goals and objectives encourages reflection about individual students, a process that facilitates the planning of literacy programs for individual LD and remedial students.

Written goals can provide teachers with a focus for instruction that is responsive to students' ever-changing needs. For example, through observation and record-keeping, a teacher may become aware that a student rarely writes more than a few words at a time. As a result, the teacher establishes a primary goal for this student: to increase writing fluency. Making a written record of this goal will influence the teacher to provide activities that encourage the student to write, and write often. However, if written goals or objectives are going to be useful, they must be referred to often and revised on the basis of ongoing observation. They must not be written and forgotten, something that happens all too often with Individual Education Plans (IEPs) (Dudley-Marling, 1985).

Ongoing evaluation aids teachers in adapting instructional strategies in accordance with changing student needs. If the student who usually writes very little begins to produce a large amount of writing, the teacher may decide, as a result of more recent observations, to have the student focus on writing for different purposes and audiences. At some point the teacher may also identify revising and editing as areas needing attention. The key is that the teacher is always aware of a student's current level of reading and writing development, alert to evidence of continued development, and knowledgeable about the student's course of development in reading and writing. This awareness forms the basis for revising teaching and learning goals.

Setting goals is a good idea, but only if they actually influence instruction. The problem for those whose teaching is based on the philosophy of holism is the behavioral nature of the goals or objectives written for most LD and remedial students.

BEHAVIORAL OBJECTIVES

Special education and remedial teachers are well acquainted with behavioral objectives. In Canada and the United States, LD and remedial teachers are typically required to develop specific educational plans for each student in the program. Many of these educational plans include specific, measurable, short- and long-term goals or objectives. But writing measurable instructional objectives results in fragmented, behavioral objectives.

"Johnny will pronounce the first one hundred words from the Dolch Word List with 80 percent accuracy by Jan. 1" is a representative short-term, behavioral objective. The expected student performance is stated precisely and is measurable. It's clear what you and Johnny will have to do to show that this objective has been met: you will show Johnny the first one hundred words of the

Dolch List and, if he pronounces 80 percent of the words correctly, the goal has been achieved.

Through task analysis teachers identify component parts of the learning process and teach those isolated tasks using appropriate reinforcement (Astman, 1984). Mastery of the task is defined in terms of learning those individual subskills thought to make up the task. It follows that writing behavioral objectives for reading and writing is a matter of identifying the component parts of the task of written language. Reading, then, may be defined in terms of sight vocabulary or mastering a finite set of letter-sound correspondences. Once these words or correspondences have been learned to the point of automaticity, it's assumed that students can read.

But, of course, reading is not merely a matter of pronouncing words nor is writing simply a matter of spelling, punctuation, and sentence structure. Reading and writing are systems for constructing meaning and fulfilling intentions. Readers and writers use their world knowledge and their knowledge of language, as well as their knowledge of written language conventions, to make meaning. Reading and writing are different from the sum of their parts and, in any case, the "parts" cannot be removed from the context of the whole without destroying the integrity of written language.

For example, a women may be able to pronounce the French words on bilingual Canadian Government forms, but if she cannot construct meaning from the French, she is not reading French. She is merely making what for her are meaningless sounds. Of course, an ardent behaviorist might argue that she should now focus on learning the meanings of the French words, and that this process could be task-analyzed and appropriate goals or objectives written, and so on. But again the meaning of a text is not the sum of the meanings of the individual words. Readers construct meaning based on a whole range of cognitive and socio-linguistic factors including, but certainly not restricted to, the meanings of individual words. Readers can only learn how this multitude of cognitive, social, and linguistic factors interact to affect meaning if they encounter words and word meanings within the context of whole texts and within meaningful, communicative contexts. Similar arguments can be made for writing. This still might not deter an especially ardent behaviorist, but we doubt that anything we say could.

Behavioral objectives are well motivated. They presume to ensure maximally efficient instruction by focusing on well-defined, easily achievable "building blocks" of learning. But they depend on a technology that does not exist. Precise descriptions of cognitive, social, and linguistic behavior, including reading and writing, are not possible and probably not desirable. Higher forms of human learning are not reducible to their component parts.

In addition, behavioral objectives trivialize learning, seriously underestimate the potential of learners, including students identified as learning disabled and remedial, and strip away the meaningfulness of what is presented to students. By stripping meaning from reading and writing, behaviorists deprive students of their most powerful vehicle and motivator for learning—making sense of their world. Certainly many students can learn the content of behavioral objectives that have been written for them, but what they learn in this way has little value for them in their lives outside of school. Poplin (1983) captures our feelings about behavioral objectives best when she states, "Anything you can put into a computer or analyze into behavioral objectives is not worth teaching" (10).

The problem for us is to provide alternatives to behavioral goals or objectives for teachers committed to holistic approaches to literacy learning but justifiably concerned with accountability and with fulfilling their legal responsibilities.

A HOLISTIC APPROACH TO PLANNING INSTRUCTION

As we've said, we do think that developing written goals and objectives and a detailed instructional plan for students, especially students who are struggling to become literate, is a good idea. However, we object to behavioral approaches to describing written language behavior and developing reading and writing objectives. As an alternative, we suggest a four-step approach for planning written language instruction: 1) developing concise summaries of current reading and writing performance, 2) developing learner objectives, 3) developing teaching goals, and 4) providing ongoing evaluation of student learning.

DEVELOPING SUMMARY STATEMENTS

For purposes of discussion, we'll talk about planning instruction for students new to your program. The first step in planning instruction tailored to the needs of an individual student is to write concise summaries of the student's current reading and writing development, based on the observations you've made, from which learner objectives can be produced. These summaries are a collection of brief statements that describe what the student does as a reader and writer— statements of effective and ineffective processes and products. Some examples of summary statements are presented in Figure 4–1.

Ideally, these summary statements will be developed only as teachers have the opportunity to work with the student over several weeks, observing the student as s/he reads and writes and as s/he responds to reading and writing instruction. If teachers are compelled to develop an instructional plan after only initial evaluation sessions with a student, they should remember that the behaviors they have observed may not be representative. More reliable information about students' reading and writing performance will come only from daily observation of the students' reading and writing during instructional time.

No doubt some of our readers will be uncomfortable with terms like "usually," "typically," and "seldom," which we used in our examples of summary statements. Those trained to write behavioral objectives have been taught that general terms like "typically" are imprecise and antithetical to good teaching practices. After all, how do you measure "typically"? How will you know if the student has progressed? Many would probably be tempted to translate the kind of general summary statements we're proposing into more precise, behavioral-

---

FIGURE 4–1   Examples of Summary Statements

John's reading miscues are typically graphophonically similar but do not make sense.

John's reading miscues are seldom corrected.

When John comes to a word he doesn't know, he often asks the teacher or another student to tell him the word.

John's oral retellings consist mostly of the random recall of a few facts.

John's oral retellings do not include any references to his own personal experiences with the topic of the text.

John rarely writes more than one or two sentences at a time.

John does not usually use capital letters or punctuation to mark sentence boundaries in his writing.

John's background knowledge does not include information about "classical" literature, i.e., common fairy tales, folktales, and tall tales.

John's spelling depends heavily upon a letter-naming strategy, including those words he frequently sees during reading.

John doesn't initiate the reading or writing of texts outside of school; he does choose to read (but not write) during school "choice time."

When John chooses books to read, he frequently selects those recommended by classmates or previously read by the teacher.

Though John reads and writes far less than his classmates in the same length of time, he concentrates on the reading and writing for the established period of time.

John does not revise or edit as he writes.

---

sounding objectives. What's wrong, for example, with stating that "John's reading miscues do not make sense 76 percent of the time"?

This kind of quasi-behavioral statement would be very misleading. Students' reading and writing performances are variable and context dependent. A student may depend heavily on the sound and appearance of words when she reads her history book at school but focus much more on meaning when she is reading a Nancy Drew story or *Anne of Green Gables*. So statements like "76 percent of her/his miscues do not make sense" imply a false precision. At other times, in other contexts, many more of her miscues may make sense.

As we noted earlier, reading miscue performance (and all other reading and writing performance) will depend on a host of factors, including the text, students' background knowledge, their interest, and so on. The use of general descriptive statements is a recognition of reality, because reading and writing performance, like all higher forms of human learning, are variable and context dependent, and can only be described generally.

DEVELOPING LEARNER OBJECTIVES

Once you've described your individual student's current reading and writing performance, the next step in instructional planning is to think about how you want that reading and writing performance to change. Learner objectives refer to what teachers hope will happen as a result of their teaching interactions with students. They encourage teachers to be aware of learning milestones, which indicate the effectiveness of their teaching efforts. Written learner objectives also facilitate communication with administrators and parents, who may be particularly anxious for evidence of literacy development.

Of course, the overriding objective of written language instruction is that students develop into lifelong readers and writers. This is the ultimate test of a reading and writing program. If students achieve a series of learner objectives but fail to use reading and writing in and out of school for their own purposes, the reading and writing program has not succeeded. Examples of learner objectives, based on the preceding summary statements, are presented in Figure 4–2.

Remember that the learner objectives you establish should be based on the summaries of a student's reading and writing behavior that you have prepared and on what you know about the course of reading and writing development. Your knowledge about development may preclude writing a learner objective for some summary statements. For example, because the teacher knows that fluent writing development precedes the development of the conventional use of

---

FIGURE 4–2   Examples of Learner Objectives

John will balance his use of the language systems more consistently while reading.

John will correct oral reading miscues that don't make sense more frequently.

John will rely on independent strategies when he comes to words he doesn't know.

John's oral retellings will include important information from the texts he has read, organized in a logical fashion.

John will make connections between what he reads and his own life, first at the teacher's initiation and then on his own.

John's writing will increase in length and fluency.

John will experience a variety of classical literature.

John will use features of standard English in his spelling; he will begin to use correct spellings of the words he sees most frequently while reading.

John will initiate the reading and writing of texts outside of school; he will occasionally choose to write during school "choice time."

John will add information to his writing drafts when appropriate.

capitalization and punctuation, no learner objective was written to correspond with the summary statement on capitalization and punctuation. In other cases, the learner objective should take into account the usual course of development. Developmentally, students learn to add information in revision before they learn to subtract or reorganize information. Thus, the objective written for John regarding revision takes that into account.

The summaries of effective reading and writing (e.g., "he concentrates on the reading and writing...") do not require a corresponding learner objective unless you feel that you need to do something as a teacher to maintain or expand the behavior.

DEVELOPING TEACHING GOALS

The next step in instructional planning is to develop teaching goals—the general steps a teacher takes to encourage the student's literacy development toward the learner objective. In other words, what will you do to help the student move from the current description of reading and writing performance in the summary statement to the learner objectives you have established?

Teaching goals will include general statements about instructional strategies, suggested materials and resources, and so on. These goals represent an overall plan or a road map for literacy instruction. Some examples of teaching goals are presented in Figure 4–3. Again, they are related to the summary statements and learner objectives presented earlier.

As with learner objectives, it's sufficient to indicate just some of the teaching strategies and resources that will be used with students. It's unreasonable to be expected to indicate all of the instructional strategies that will be used. It's also important to remember that teaching goals will change all the time in response to students' ongoing development. Teaching goals will always include the provision of a literate environment for students, including the establishment of plentiful opportunities for reading and writing.

ONGOING EVALUATION

As we said earlier, developing individual goals or objectives does not make sense unless these goals and objectives are routinely reexamined and revised in light of a student's daily reading and writing instruction. Thus, ongoing evaluation is a necessity in instructional planning if instruction is to meet the needs of students and respond to what they are currently trying to learn and do.

In order to conduct ongoing evaluation, teachers must routinely record their observations of students' reading and writing performance. This needn't take more than a few minutes each day. Teachers can jot a quick note whenever they observe something new about students' reading or writing, and they should be prepared to make a few notes after conferencing with students. Graves (1983) suggests several ways for teachers to make regular notes in students' writing folders. Another possibility for recording observations is to write each student's name on a yellow "Post-it" note before school and then put the Post-it notes on

---

FIGURE 4–3   Examples of Teaching Goals

The teacher will help John discover meaning-based strategies for figuring out words.

The teacher will help John identify miscues that don't make sense and discover strategies for self-correcting those miscues.

When John asks for help with words, the teacher will refer him to the chart of meaning-based strategies for figuring out words that he has generated.

The teacher will encourage John to participate in oral storytelling based on well-structured stories he has read.

The teacher will use prereading strategies with John to encourage him to activate his background knowledge prior to reading.

The teacher will schedule daily writing time in a journal for the entire class.

The teacher will construct a thematic unit featuring classical literature for the entire class.

The teacher will encourage John to think about how words look in print so that he begins to access visual information he has from reading.

The teacher will talk with John's parents about establishing an inviting literacy environment for John at home. The teacher will also establish a literacy environment at school that encourages more person-to-person writing, such as message boards or mailboxes.

The teacher will arrange for others to conference with John about what he has written so that he learns what information can be added to his writing. The teacher will help John learn how to add information to his writing.

---

a clipboard. Before the day or the week is through, write something on each student's note. At the end of the day/week, transfer each note to the notebook pages devoted to that particular student and review the note in light of the others already there from past observations. You could use index cards in the same way. It isn't usually necessary to make a detailed record of your observations, but do write enough so that you'll be able to understand the details and significance of your own notes days or weeks later.

As we have said before, assessment and instruction are inseparable. Teachers must also be prepared to spend a routine amount of time reviewing not only observational notes but also learner objectives and teaching goals, and then revising as needed. Evidence that learning is taking place will not be limited to the stated learner objectives. Teachers must be alert to any evidence that learning is taking place, and their alertness improves with consistent and continual review of notes, summaries, and objectives. One way to make certain that you continually review student needs and developmental progress is to schedule a daily review of a certain number of the students you see for instruction.

Careful record-keeping and close monitoring of goals or objectives is the only way teachers can respond flexibly to the needs and development of individual students. It isn't enough for teachers to do all they can and hope for the best; that is a "shotgun" approach to teaching reading and writing. It fails to consider students as people with individual needs and developmental rates and is contrary to the basic principles of special and remedial education. Careful record-keeping is also important for communicating with parents, who deserve a detailed account of their child's literacy development.

THE INDIVIDUAL EDUCATION PLAN: A NOTE TO SPECIAL EDUCATORS

As any special educator in the United States is well aware, the main components of the individual education plan (IEP) include statements indicating students' current level of functioning, short- and long-term instructional objectives, and some indication and how short- and long-term objectives will be evaluated. The format we've presented for developing written instructional plans was designed to be as IEP-like as possible. Our format includes statements of current reading and writing performance, and long-term goals or objectives. The evaluation of progress toward objectives is based upon ongoing observation. Our format does not include short-term objectives for learners because we feel that short-term learner objectives are inconsistent with the basic principles of holism.

It's easy enough to state that some isolated skill (e.g., "John will pronounce all of the letters of the alphabet") will be learned by such and such a date, but more meaningful types of learning just don't work this way. It's not possible to predict the rate or precise course of higher forms of learning, including oral and written language, with any certainty.

A teacher we know described the early writing development of one of her students for us. In September she observed that the student's writing was limited to several lines of unintelligible scribbling, which looked like cursive writing, written alternately right to left and then left to right. A few weeks later the teacher observed that the student began to write cursivelike lines only from left to right. After several more weeks, she noticed that letters were beginning to appear in the student's writing and, finally, that the student's name appeared among the letters. Certainly this student's writing showed developmental progress similar to other children's, but the rate of development and precise course could not have been predicted.

Short-term behavioral objectives also imply that teachers are technicians. Presumably, task analysis and appropriate reinforcement techniques allow teachers to influence the rate and course of learning with a high level of success. Anyone who have observed the cognitive development of young students knows that the rate of students' cognitive development is often uneven and unpredictable. It would make no sense to state that we expected a two-year-old to begin using adjectives within a month, and it makes no more sense to us to make similar short-term predictions for students' reading and writing development. We have set aside expectations of a gradual and incremental learning curve; we have observed that many students do not reveal their progress toward literacy in this way.

We have also made some compromises to make our planning format IEP-like. We aren't entirely comfortable with the format we've presented for writing learner objectives. There is a risk that teachers will unduly focus their attention on these objectives and not respond to what students are trying to do or notice other development that may come about as a result of their teaching efforts. For example, Allen and Hansen (1986) talk about a boy who shared a piece of writing about whales that had only three lines of information. A teacher who had written learner objectives like the ones for John about increasing the length of writing and adding information to writing might have responded to the boy's writing by calling attention to these things. In this case, the boy's friends asked him what he wanted to do next and he replied, "Write one on seals. This was the first time I used the card catalogue and I want to use it again tomorrow before I forget" (689). Obviously, the teacher needs to set aside her learner objectives in such a case and respond to the student's initiative even though it may have nothing to do with established learner objectives.

In general, we are confident that the format we have presented for planning instruction satisfies the basic components of the IEP and, more importantly, satisfies the spirit of the IEP, which holds that all students placed in special and remedial education programs should have individualized education plans tailored to their needs as learners. However, in some cases special education teachers (and even remedial teachers) may feel that they are compelled to write short- and long-term behavioral objectives even though they are uncomfortable with behavioral approaches to teaching reading and writing.

In this case, teachers should probably try to shape their goals and objectives into a behavioral format. For example, they might state something like "Johnny will write a story with thirty words by June 1" or "Mary will spontaneously correct 80 percent of any reading miscues that don't make sense by March 1." Given the conditional nature of these goals, they aren't very meaningful, but they will likely satisfy those administrators who insist on behavioral goals and objectives.

CONCLUSION

In this chapter we've presented a set of procedures for translating the results of assessment into instructional plans. We've recommended that teachers begin by summarizing the results of assessment with brief summary statements and then develop learner objectives. Teachers may then establish goals to help the student develop as a reader and writer in the direction of the learner objectives. Finally, and most importantly, teachers must routinely evaluate student progress, modifying learner objectives and teacher goals as needed.

We've also made every effort to assist special educators by making the format for planning instruction IEP-like, yet faithful to our views on reading and writing development. However, it's worth restating that the key to instructional planning is observation—observing children as they read and write and as they respond to reading and writing instruction. This careful observation of students' reading and writing development will enable teachers to modify and adapt their instructional plans as their students progress. Teachers who do this will provide students with literacy experiences tailored to their dynamic and ever-changing needs.

V

Designing environments for literacy development

Much is known about the environments in which children learn to talk. In general, parents provide frequent and authentic opportunities for their children to talk and to hear others talk. We also know something about the nature of early literacy environments—the kinds of environments common to children who learn to read before they come to school. In these environments, children are exposed to a wide range of reading materials, are read to frequently, often see others reading and writing, have easy access to writing materials, have adults who respond to their intentions when they try to read or write, and have parents and siblings who are willing to answer their questions about reading and writing (Forester, 1977; Teale, 1978). Early literacy environments immerse children in print, providing frequent demonstrations of the uses of reading and writing, and frequent opportunities to engage in reading and writing. Also, parents and siblings tend to respond to the functions and not the forms of children's early literacy attempts.

The remarkable similarity between language-learning environments and early literacy learning environments is inescapable. In both oral and written language-learning environments, children have frequent opportunities to use language and to hear or see language being used in meaningful, communicative contexts. The development of both oral and written language is also facilitated by adults who recognize and respond to children's meanings and intentions.

Most teachers readily accept the important role of the home environment in children's oral and written language development. Most of us would agree that parents who model literate behaviors are especially likely to encourage reading and writing development in their children. But what about the influence of the classroom environment, an environment over which teachers have direct control? What role does the literacy learning environment of the classroom play in students' reading and writing development, and more importantly, what kinds of environments are most likely to promote literacy development?

As we stated in chapter 1, we believe that reading and writing failures cannot be adequately explained simply by pointing to disabilities or problems intrinsic to the child. Learning to read and write is a matter of an interaction between students and their learning environments. Just as certain home environments are likely to foster literacy development, certain classroom environments are much more likely to foster literacy development than others, especially for learning disabled and remedial readers. Literate classroom environments will encourage students to learn *how* to read and write as well as *to* read and write. Charlotte Huck (1976) states that readers are "children who *can* read, *will* read, and will *want* to read" (590, emphasis added). The same can be said of writers.

The purpose of this chapter is to discuss the important features of a classroom environment that is supportive of literacy learning and use. Specifically, we'll talk about the importance of immersing students in print and demonstrating the uses of print, opportunities for reading and reading, and purposes and audiences for students' reading and writing. In addition, we'll address the types of reading and writing materials conducive to literacy development and discuss thematic units as a curricular vehicle that supports literacy development.

IMMERSION AND DEMONSTRATION

In order for reading and writing to be used in functional ways in a classroom, students must be surrounded with print that invites them to read and write often and demonstrates that reading and writing are purposeful and worthwhile. A literate classroom environment could, for example, contain both reading and writing centers.

A reading center is a quiet, comfortable place, often set off from the rest of the classroom and crammed with books and other reading materials, where students can go and read (Huck, 1976; Shuman, 1982). Shuman (1982) recommends that the reading area also include collections of taped stories and a tape recorder. Taped stories can be purchased or teachers can tape their own.

If space permits, a writing center might also be set off from the rest of the room. Writing centers can contain a variety of writing surfaces, writing implements, and bookbinding materials. Today, many writing centers might also contain one or more microcomputers for word processing.

Smaller special education or remedial classrooms can be conceived and arranged as complete reading and writing centers. In addition to providing opportunities and physical space for reading and writing, reading and writing centers show students that their teachers consider reading and writing important.

There are many other ways to surround students with print. Classroom walls can be covered with prominent displays of children's written work or the written work of others. One teacher we know copied poems onto large sheets of cardboard, illustrated them, and then displayed the poems in her room, often a half dozen or more poems at any one time. Some readers may be skeptical about the chances of interesting many students in poetry this way, so it's worth noting that the classroom we've described here is a learning disabilities resource room in the core of a large American city used by mostly minority students. This same classroom also displays posters advertising children's books, a written schedule of the activities for the upcoming month, the daily lunch menu, and a chart listing the poems each child has learned to read independently. A bulletin board features each student's picture and an accompanying autobiography. Written notices to students frequently appear on the blackboard. Everywhere in this classroom students are encouraged to read print and are reminded that print can be meaningful and important to them personally.

Of course, it is not enough to surround students with print—they must also observe demonstrations (F. Smith, 1981) of authentic uses of print. LD and remedial students must observe others who are effective language users reading and writing, including the teacher.

One way teachers can demonstrate the functional and enjoyable uses of reading is to read to students regularly. Like early readers whose parents or siblings read to them often (Forester, 1977; Teale, 1978), school-age students also benefit from being read to frequently. Reading to our students helps them understand the nature and purposes of reading and familiarizes them with the patterns of written language (Bass, Jurenka & Zirzow, 1981). Reading to students can also interest them in different types of literature and in different authors and encourage them to discover the joys of reading good literature. Students' reading vocabulary, their reading comprehension, their reading interests, and the quality of their oral language have been shown to be positively affected by having someone read to them (Huck, 1979; McCormick, 1977). Secondary level students also enjoy being read to and will benefit from this experience. There is reason to believe that students from lower socioeconomic groups and from lower ranges of reading achievement (e.g., LD and remedial readers) may benefit the most from being read to (McCormick, 1977). Reading to students is also an excellent vehicle for broadening students' experiences and may be an especially effective way to assist students who may not have background experiences teachers feel are important.

Another way teachers can demonstrate the functional aspects of literacy is to write to and with their students. Writing to students provides them with opportunities to read and demonstrates the various purposes of written language. Teachers could routinely send notes to their students, thereby giving students authentic reasons for reading while illustrating one or more of the purposes of written language. Teachers could also write with their students, not merely through "parallel writing" but literally collaborating with them on some writing project—a letter, a report, a class diary, or a language experience story, for example. However, this will be effective only if it involves true collaboration and does not become yet another instance of a teacher-dominated activity.

OPPORTUNITIES FOR READING AND WRITING

Development in reading and writing can only take place in environments where students regularly engage in reading and writing, where there are frequent opportunities for students to read and write whole, meaningful texts. There is considerable evidence, however, that many students do relatively little reading and writing in their classrooms, and the situation may be even worse for learning disabled and remedial students (for example, see Allington, 1980). Students may spend as little as six minutes a day actually reading (Allington, 1980); and even secondary students have few opportunities to write anything longer than a paragraph (Applebee, Lehr & Auten, 1981). Students who do poorly in school may have even fewer opportunities to read and write (Allington, 1980; Miramontes, Cheng & Trueba, 1984; R. D. Morris, 1979).

One reason for this situation is the all too frequent emphasis on isolated skills, often to the exclusion of the reading and writing of whole texts. It is not that LD and remedial students have less instructional time that is devoted to reading and writing, but that the time is spent on drilling isolated skills rather than on reading and writing whole texts to fulfill personal, communicative intentions. Poor readers may also be given relatively few opportunities to engage in silent reading (Allington, 1980). This situation has been exacerbated by the recent "back to basics" movement. Taylor (1983) argues convincingly that "making sense," not skill mastery, ought to be the "basic" of reading and writing instruction.

An issue related to that of opportunities to read and write is the amount of time students spend reading easy text—materials that they do not need to struggle with as they construct meaning. Good readers spend the majority of their time reading easy material while poor readers often struggle to read the texts used for instruction (Gambrell & Sokolski, 1983). All readers, not just good ones, need to have plentiful opportunities to easily construct meaning for themselves if they are to become better readers. Reading easy material helps students consolidate their fledgling reading strategies; they can self-correct and teach themselves if the material is easy enough for them to maintain their focus on making sense.

Teachers of learning disabled and remedial learners must make every effort to provide their students with frequent and sufficiently easy opportunities to read and write, to make sense of text. They should also work with regular classroom teachers in their role as consultants to ensure frequent reading and writing in students' regular classrooms. Although the effort to increase students' opportunities to read and write needs to be deliberate, the occasions for encouraging reading and writing are frequent and arise naturally during the day—in response to students' questions, their personal needs, or their interests. For example, some current event may reveal intense student interest in space. Teachers can take advantage of this opportunity to encourage a discussion about space and potential writing topics related to space, and about reading as a means of finding out more about space or of resolving points of contention that have arisen during the discussion. Here, opportunities for reading and writing emerge naturally, initiated by students and their concerns.

Natural opportunities for reading and writing that are inspired by students' interests and concerns are especially important, since students are more likely to read and write if they see written language as a means of fulfilling their own intentions. Students read and write because they need to and want to. The teacher often creates the opportunity, providing students with the time, materials, and space necessary for them to read and write whole meaningful text. Over time, students should take a greater role in initiating their own reading and writing opportunities in and out of school.

Too often we depend on a system of extrinsic rewards to increase student engagement in reading and writing. This may have some positive and necessary short-term effect on reading and writing frequency in the classroom, but it's unlikely to affect students' long-term views of themselves as readers and writers or their development into lifelong readers and writers.

Opportunities for reading and writing should permeate the day, i.e., there should be reading and writing "across the curriculum." Daily opportunities for reading and writing can be provided at any time during the day and in any academic subject. For example, Radebough (1981) provides a list of children's books that can be used to learn math concepts. Nonacademic subjects also provide opportunities for reading and writing. For example, art teachers might encourage students to write text to accompany their projects, or they might read condensed biographies of artists and craftspersons to their students. Physical education teachers might display collections of paperback books on sports and sports figures in the locker rooms.

Although most special education and remedial reading and writing teachers will not be directly involved in teaching content-area subjects, art, music, or physical education, they may be able to influence other teachers to increase student involvement in reading and writing. They can let these teachers know that students need to read and write frequently and to see reading and writing as functional in their lives in order to become better readers and writers. They can give regular classroom teachers and specialists ideas for expanding student opportunities for reading and writing. Special education and remedial teachers can use the Individual Education Plan, or its equivalent, to encourage more reading and writing in the regular classroom. They can also let other teachers know how these increased opportunities to engage in reading and writing can benefit their other students, even above average readers. The prereading strategies we discuss in chapter 8 can be used to help all students, not just learning disabled and remedial students, deal with texts in a more meaningful way. Finally, they can work with principals to show them how their involvement in promoting reading and writing across the curriculum can reduce the number of reading failures in their schools without detracting from performance in other areas.

Some readers may feel that increasing the amount of reading and writing in content-area classes increases the chances of failure for learning disabled and remedial students. Until recently, most of us concerned with the education of learning disabled and remedial students have argued that we should adapt the curriculum in content-area classes so that less information is presented through text. Perhaps it would be better to think of textbooks as summaries of instruction instead of the principal source of information (Stansell & DeFord, 1981). Increasing students' background knowledge prior to the reading of a text through a variety of alternative modes of presentation will make reading much easier for LD and remedial students (and, in fact, all students). Alternative presentations can include films, field trips, film strips, class discussion, guest speakers, experiments, observations, simulations, and so on. Allowing students to choose from alternative reading and writing assignments is also helpful. For example, some students may find historical novels an easier guide to history than history textbooks.

Although content-area teachers are in a particularly favorable position to demonstrate the value of reading and writing as tools for learning, some may be reluctant to make adaptations to accommodate the individual needs of LD and remedial students. These teachers may be much more flexible, however, if LD and remedial teachers express a willingness to work closely with them to help them modify their teaching practices and select a wider variety of materials.

LD and remedial teachers can also solicit the input of content-area teachers to supplement what goes on in the regular classroom program. History teachers may suggest historical novels for the resource room that will provide students with an alternative or supplementary view of material presented in history class. In addition, volunteers can produce taped versions of content-area reading assignments for students to read along with in the resource room or at home.

The manner in which teachers respond to students' reading and writing will also affect the frequency and the quality of students' engagement in written language activities. Some students' experiences have shown them that reading orally or putting pen to paper are invitations for criticism. When they have endeavored to read or write, they have frequently been reminded that they don't do it well. It's no wonder that many learning disabled and remedial students are reluctant readers and writers. Teachers would be well advised to respond to the meaning of children's reading and writing efforts, especially for less fluent readers and writers. This does not mean that teachers should ignore what they regard as errors, but that they should follow their students' progress and develop strategies that will foster continued reading and writing development.

INTEGRATING READING, WRITING, LISTENING, AND SPEAKING

A literate environment not only provides students with lots of opportunities to use written language, it also encourages the use of oral language. Oral language can help students activate relevant background knowledge before they read and integrate what they have read with what they already know. Talking can also help students at different stages of writing. Class discussions may encourage reading and writing. Interest in knowing more about the history of their town, for example, may emerge during a discussion of some local event. In the same way, reading and writing may stimulate lots of talk. The key is to surround LD and remedial students with all modes of language. It is also important to remember that there is no reason to separate oral and written language. It is far better to view them as part and parcel of the same process: students' attempts to fulfill communicative intentions.

A major premise of this book is that reading and writing should be taught together as complimentary language modes, a view that is supported by recent research. Reading is an important factor in the development of writing, and much of what we learn about writing we learn through reading (F. Smith, 1983). Children's writing typically includes some of the features of their reading texts (DeFord, 1981; Eckoff, 1983), and a relationship has been noted between students' exposure to children's literature and their writing ability (Maya, 1979).

Some teachers believe that writing instruction should be delayed until students have become readers. But this would be analogous to not allowing children to talk until they had first mastered listening. Writing is an important influence in students' reading development (Shanahan, 1980; Vacca, 1981). Students not only learn to read by reading and to write by writing, they also learn to read by writing and to write by reading (DeFord, 1981; K. Goodman & Y. Goodman, 1983; Maya, 1979). Smith (1983) states:

> To become writers children must read like writers. To read like writers they must see themselves as writers. Children will read stories, poems, and letters differently when they see these texts as things they themselves could produce; they will write vicariously with the authors. (565)

PURPOSES AND AUDIENCES FOR READING AND WRITING

It might be a useful exercise for you to stop reading for a few moments and write down everything you have read or written in the last twenty-four hours. Write down everything, including grocery lists, signs, labels, notes, and so on. When you've finished, go back and try to identify why you did your reading and writing. Did you write something down so you wouldn't forget it or read something to get information?

There are lots of reasons people read and write. We don't read for the sake of reading nor do we write for the sake of writing. We do these things with some purpose in mind. These purposes are varied and include the creation and use of records (Stubbs, 1982), the creation and appreciation of art (Applebee, Lehr & Auten, 1981), the exploration of ideas (Shaugnessy, 1977), communication (Feldman, 1977), and personal uses such as journals and diaries (Applebee, Lehr & Auten, 1981).

Now consider the different purposes for which children read and write in their classrooms. Perhaps you should also write these down. It should be apparent that in school, most students read and write for a limited number of purposes compared to the wide range of purposes for which most of us read and write in our daily lives.

The most common purposes for writing in school are to record information (e.g., notetaking), recount events, and recall information. Most often, writing is done only for the sake of writing—to practice the forms or conventions of written language. Too few students discover that writing is also a way to explore their ideas and feelings or create art forms.

The purposes for reading in school are similarly limited. Most students are encouraged to believe that reading, even of narrative material, is done solely to get information. Like writing, most reading is done for the sake of reading—to practice reading skills. Teachers don't consciously encourage their students to read only for these purposes, but their actions demonstrate to children that reading is a matter of getting the facts and the skills exercises right (see Rosenblatt, 1978; F. Smith, 1981). Isn't most of the reading students do in many classrooms followed by exercises to see what they remember or by isolated skills work? Such exercises demonstrate to children that these are the purposes for reading. Teachers must consciously endeavor to demonstrate other reading and writing purposes that students will see as a natural part of their everyday lives.

Shuman (1982) recommends that students and teachers keep "Reading Activity Logs" as a means of demonstrating the various purposes of reading. As an introductory activity, Shuman suggests that teachers generate a discussion leading to class definitions of reading. Teachers can ask students why they read, what they do when they read, and what they read (Page & Pinnel, 1979a). Students are then given a length of time (a week, for example) during which to keep track of all their reading activities. At the conclusion of this week, students can share what they've read and why. For teachers of learning disabled and remedial readers who work with children individually or in very small groups, we recommend persuading regular classroom teachers to try this activity in their classrooms with poor readers present. It may be particularly useful for learning disabled and remedial readers to hear what good readers think about reading. "Writing Activity Logs" can be handled in a similar manner.

Occasions for stressing the purposes of written language can occur quite naturally within the classroom context (N. E. Taylor & Vawter, 1978). For example, at various times during the day children can be asked to record their observations. A lesson on current events might influence some children to write a persuasive letter to a public official. A center containing paper and other material for making greeting cards will invite students to keep in touch with friends and relatives through writing. Activities like these will encourage students to discover the value of reading and writing in their daily lives. In general, students who have real reasons for reading and writing will do more reading and writing (Toth, 1982).

Related to the restricted range of purposes for which students typically read and write in their classrooms are the audiences for whom they read and write. Most of children's oral reading and writing is directed to only one audience— the teacher. However, teachers are odd audiences since they usually initiate the reading or writing and often provide extensive feedback only on the use of forms. For students, the purpose of reading or writing is to please the teacher, not to fulfill their own personal intentions. LD and remedial students should be encouraged to write for a variety of audiences—each other, pen pals, children in other classes, authors of children's literature, and especially, themselves. Graves (1983) recounts how one class wrote regularly to the residents of a nursing home. Electronic mail can also be used effectively to give children access to a variety of audiences. Teachers could also provide students with standard memo forms (such as those shown in Figure 5–1) to encourage them to write more frequently to their teachers and classmates for real purposes.

Writing for different audiences—for oneself, a government official, a friend, or someone who can send some desired item or material—will also affect the purposes for which students write. And of course, having frequent opportunities to write for different purposes will help children learn how to vary the content and form of their writing.

Oral reading should also be directed to other audiences besides teachers, audiences who will not feel compelled to provide instant feedback. Students can read to brothers and sisters, younger children, and so on. Most importantly, they should be encouraged to read silently, with only themselves as an audience.

FIGURE 5–1   Memos Written on Standard Forms

READING AND WRITING MATERIALS

The availability of a variety of reading and writing materials invites students to read and write. A variety of reading materials encourages students to read for different purposes. A variety of writing materials, and the time to use them, encourages students to write frequently for different purposes. The kinds of materials teachers select also play an important role in demonstrating the purposes of reading and writing to students. Books and workbooks filled with drills of written language skills demonstrate to students that reading is dull, meaningless, and uninteresting (F. Smith, 1981).

Establishing classroom writing centers filled with a variety of writing implements and writing surfaces—chalk, magic markers, print sets, crayons, paint brushes, pencils, pens; paper of different types and sizes, cardboard, chalk-boards, T-shirts, and so on—encourages students to write often and for purposes that mirror those of people outside of school. In some classrooms, students write on walls covered with large sheets of brown paper. In others, they use notepads and student-designed stationery. Message boards and mail boxes also offer invitations to write.

Different types of materials can also affect the purposes for which students write. Pen and lined paper seem to encourage more formal kinds of writing, smaller pieces of paper lend themselves better to lists or informal notes, tagboard strips may encourage labeling, and so on. Typewriters and word processors are also valuable additions to a writing center. We have observed young children asking a myriad of questions about the alphabet when using a typewriter. And many teachers have told us about their students' sudden change in attitude toward drafting, revision, and editing and the increase in the length of their writing when they use a word processor.

Writing centers can also include bookbinding materials and instructions on how to use them. Gonzales (1980) recommends establishing author centers that include writing materials, bookbinding materials, and dictionaries, with areas set aside where students can work on rough drafts, revising, editing, illustrating, and bookbinding.

The teacher's choice of materials will also affect the frequency of students' engagement in reading, their attitudes toward reading, reading performance (Rhodes, 1979), and even the quality of their writing. For example, the overuse of basal readers written in a simplified or stilted style can influence students to produce simplified or stilted writing (DeFord, 1981; Eckoff, 1983). "Exposure to literature is probably the best experience future writers can have. Books can help our students to explore, to feel, and to expand their imaginations" (Wilcox, 1977, 549).

The following questions are helpful to keep in mind as you select reading materials for learning disabled and remedial learners:

1. *Were the materials written for authentic communicative purposes?* Were the materials written to communicate a feeling, idea, information, or story, or were they written to teach or reinforce reading skills? Materials written for authentic

communicative purposes are far more likely to invite repeated reading and the real construction of meaning.

2. *Do the materials use natural language?* Reading materials should use language that is both natural and familiar to students (Gourley, 1984). It is much more difficult for students, especially learning disabled and remedial learners, to construct meaning from texts that use unnatural language (e.g., "The fat cat sat on the mat" or "See Spot run. Run, Spot, run."). Texts that use unnatural language make it very difficult for readers to use their knowledge of syntax and semantics while they read (Rhodes, 1979).

3. *Are the materials relevant to the background experience of students?* Students' experiences are an important factor in the selection of reading materials. If there is a serious mismatch between the information presented in a text and the background knowledge of the reader, it will be very difficult for the reader to construct meaning. A book may be the greatest children's book ever written, but if it doesn't match children's experiences, it may not be appropriate for them (Huck, 1976). However, this should not be taken to extremes. Books can also be a vehicle for broadening students' backgrounds and beliefs when a teacher develops students' background knowledge and/or helps them understand how their experiences "match" a text.

4. *Do the materials invite lengthy engagement in reading?* Classroom environments should include some materials that invite lengthy engagement either because the text itself is lengthy or because the students like the text well enough to read it repeatedly. However, this is not an essential characteristic for all reading materials. Some excellent reading materials are naturally brief and may be read only once.

5. *Do the materials encourage divergent responses?* Some reading materials, especially worksheets, encourage only convergent responses. Reading materials that encourage a wider range of responses, that enable students to share and extend the meaning they have constructed from text, are more desirable.

6. *What can the student learn about the world as a result of using the materials?* It isn't necessary, or even desirable, that all reading material teach some value or provide information about the world. However, much of what students read in school is unrelated to everyday life, especially for those students who are least likely to find anything of value to them in the classroom (Duggins & Finn, 1976). Therefore, students may find little reason to read. Materials related to the world outside of school are likely to teach students something about their world and thus invite reading (see Singer, McNeil & Furse, 1984).

7. *Are the materials representative of out-of-school materials?* Materials that mirror out-of-school reading materials are more likely to match and catch student interest and demonstrate that reading is meaningful and purposeful. Materials that do not resemble out-of-school reading materials may encourage the belief that reading is something useful only in the classroom.

8. *Are the materials predictable?* Reading materials that support the prediction of certain features of text are especially valuable for readers who aren't yet fluent or don't use effective reading strategies.

PREDICTABLE BOOKS

Books are predictable when they enable students to quickly and easily predict what the author is going to say and how the author is going to say it based upon their knowledge of the world. The following text characteristics, adapted from Rhodes (1981) and Atwell (1987), increase the likelihood that readers will be able to take advantage of the different types of knowledge they bring to the reading of a text:

- *A good match between text content and reader's life experiences and concepts.* Authors like Judy Blume are so popular because adolescents can easily identify with the characters and events in her books. The good match between the content of the text and students' experiences renders the books highly predictable.
- *Rhythmical, repetitive, or cumulative patterns.* The author repeats words, phrases, or themes in a pattern that can be discerned after only a few pages (McClure, 1985), or the author uses a pattern of successive addition. Bill Martin's (1970) *Brown Bear, Brown Bear, What Do You See?* is an example of a repetitive pattern: "Brown Bear, brown bear, what do you see? I see a redbird looking at me. Redbird, redbird what do you see? I see a yellow duck looking at me." *I Know an Old Lady* (Bonne & Mills, 1961) is an example of a cumulative pattern.
- *Familiar stories or story lines.* Any text that is highly familiar to a student fits this category. Familiarity may arise from hearing or reading the text or a version of it repeatedly, or from experiencing it in other forms, such as an oral story, song, movie, or TV show. Examples include *The Three Little Pigs*, *Star Wars*, and *That Was Then; This Is Now*.
- *Familiar sequences.* Eric Carle's (1969) *The Very Hungry Caterpillar* combines repetition with two familiar sequences, the days of the week and numbers: "On Monday he ate through one apple. But he was still hungry. On Tuesday he ate through two pears. But he was still hungry."
- *Series books.* Children and adolescents frequently get "hooked" on a character or character type and will read every book that features the character (type). Examples include Lois Lenski's *The Little Farm* (Lenski, 1942), *Cowboy Small* (Lenski, 1949), *Policeman Small* (Lenski, 1962), as well as James Marshall's books featuring George and Martha and C. S. Lewis's *Chronicles of Narnia*. It also includes the ever-popular Hardy Boys and Nancy Drew Mysteries and the *Anne of Green Gables* series.
- *A good match between the text and illustrations.* Good children's literature frequently contains effective and attractive illustrations. One benefit of these illustrations is that they allow readers to more easily predict meaning. For example, Mercer Mayer's (1975) *Just for You* features attractive illustrations that correspond closely to the text.
- *Guessing books.* These texts actually invite the reader to make choices, to become actively involved in the stories. *Choose Your Own Adventure* books are written in this manner for both older and younger students. Joke or riddle books and the *Encyclopedia Brown* series also invite this sort of interaction.

Predictable books foster reading fluency in students, helping overcome the habit of many learning disabled and remedial students of sounding out every word (McClure, 1985) by encouraging students to use their knowledge of the world and of language in responding to the book (Rhodes, 1981). In additional, students use the predictable aspects of books to develop word recognition knowledge (Bridge, 1979) while they are reading instead of before reading. Predictable books can also be a valuable resource for children learning to write, since children frequently emulate the style, format, and conventions of authors they have read (Rhodes, 1981). Predictable books may be especially useful for students whose oral language is delayed (Rhodes & Shannon, 1982) and for students using nonstandard dialects (Tompkins & McGee, 1983).

The back of this book contains two extensive lists of predictable books—one for use with younger or lower-level readers and one for use with adolescents. However, teachers should remember that these books are only potentially predictable; it's only through knowing and observing a student's reading of a book that they can determine whether that book is truly predictable for that student.

TEXTBOOKS

Texts published specifically for use in school, some of which may also be predictable, are another valuable source of reading material for developing readers. Too often, however, teachers are overly concerned with readability levels, which are determined by readability formulas. Textbooks, especially basal reading series, are chosen for their apparent simplicity (i.e., readability) rather than for their potential interest and predictability. Teachers should be very cautious about readability formulas that consider a restricted range of factors such as word difficulty and sentence length. Many texts that use controlled vocabulary and shorter sentences to achieve lower readability levels, especially some of the high interest-low vocabulary books and programmed readers written for the poorest readers, are often choppy, disjointed, and difficult to read (Gourley, 1984; Mason, 1981; Rhodes, 1979). The National Council of Teachers of English and the International Reading Association have issued a joint statement questioning the use and validity of readability formulas (K. Goodman, 1986). The predictability of a text for a particular student is far more important in the selection of texts than the readability level of the text.

A few basal reading series meet many of the selection criteria we outlined earlier. Basal readers that include good children's literature may be worth using as one source of reading material. Teachers who don't feel confident about judging what children's literature is good can consider our criteria along with outside sources such as university classes on children's literature and the advice of librarians and their colleagues. In general, teachers should avoid "Dick and Jane" type readers that employ unnatural language and are not predictable (Gourley, 1984; Rhodes, 1979).

Since basal readers feature predominantly narrative texts, every effort should be made to encourage students to read expository texts as well, both nonfiction tradebooks and textbooks used in classes such as social studies and science. Expository texts make up a significant portion of what many of us read outside of school.

One way to adapt published-for-school texts is to create skinny books (Watson, in press). Teachers can cut out good and useful portions of old texts on particular topics or on themes being studied and bind them individually into "skinny books." For example, if some students are interested in reading about space, teachers may use a variety of sources including old magazines and textbooks containing articles, sections, or chapters on space, cut them out, and bind them using colored construction paper into small books with titles, authors, and so on. Because skinny books are short they have the advantage of being less intimidating to many students.

TRADE BOOKS AND PAPERBACKS

Trade books (library books), including paperbacks, are being used increasingly for reading instruction. Trade books are especially likely to invite students to read because they are usually attractively packaged and written to be read, not to teach reading. Trade books are also useful for teaching content-area subjects because they may be more up-to-date than textbooks (Huck, 1976). And because tradebooks are available that match the interests and background knowledge of any child, they are often more predictable than published-for-school books. The importance of trade books is illustrated by indications that children who have access to a well-equipped library read many more books than students who do not enjoy such access.

Trade books should have a prominent place within the classroom. Classroom collections of trade books should change regularly and should include multiple copies of books so that several children can read the same book at the same time. Paperback book purchases make sizeable classroom trade book collections and multiple copies affordable, and some students may actually prefer the paperback editions of books (Huck, 1976). Daniel Fader's (1976) "Hooked on Books" program, which depends heavily on the use of paperback books, has been used very successfully with extremely reluctant adolescent readers.

For teachers who are unfamiliar with children's literature, a number of resources are available. First of all, most universities offer courses on children's and adolescent literature, and since special educators' training rarely includes such courses, they may benefit from additional coursework in this area. If courses on children's literature are unavailable or inconvenient, school librarians are usually familiar with a wide array of children's and adolescent literature and can offer suggestions. There are also a number of anthologies of children's literature, such as Charlotte Huck's *Children's Literature* (1976), which are excellent resources for selecting and using children's literature. Journals such as *Reading Teacher*, *Language Arts*, and the *English Journal* regularly feature reviews of children's and adolescent literature. In addition parents and students themselves may prove to be useful resources for recommending titles of books that will likely appeal to the students in special and remedial programs.

Big books

Big books are often trade books, sometimes well-known children's stories, which have been enlarged for the school market. These books are ideal for teachers reading to groups of young children since the large text makes it easy for children to follow along. The novelty of Big Books may also be a special invitation for some children to read. Most publishers market packages that include Big Books, a number of conventionally sized copies of the book, and a tape-recording of the story. Students can watch the teacher read while they listen to the story and then have the freedom to read their own copies or listen to the tape while reading along in their own books. Because Big Books are often expensive and relatively few titles are available, many teachers have produced their own.

Song and wordless picture books

Song picture books and wordless picture books are two additional examples of commercially produced books that can be helpful in encouraging reading. Song picture books are particularly useful for some reluctant readers. Lamme (1979) presents a nice list of song picture books that includes lullabies, hymns, nursery rhymes, folk songs, and so on. Song books are also found in the lists of predictable books at the end of this book. Older students may find record jackets and song charts particularly motivating.

Wordless picture books are another vehicle for getting children interested in books. Although wordless picture books are usually associated with younger readers, McGee and Tompkins (1983) describe their use with older readers and provide a list of wordless picture books with special appeal for older readers. Wordless picture books can be used to encourage prediction skills and writing fluency in both younger and older readers. They can also be used to generate language experience stories and repeated reading.

STUDENT-PUBLISHED BOOKS AND NONBOOK MATERIALS

A literate environment need not depend only on commercially produced books. Student-produced books and a wide variety of nonbook materials also contribute to an environment designed to support literacy development.

Students' own compositions, including language experience dictations, are one of the most useful sources of reading material. Compositions written by students are predictable because they are based on students' own experiences and language structures. Encouraging children to read their own compositions can result in better comprehension of materials written by others (Maya, 1979).

The audience for children's compositions is not, of course, limited to the children who authored them. It is increasingly popular for children to write and bind their own books, which are then placed in the classroom or schoolwide library where other students can check them out. From the standpoint of reading, this provides students with a rich source of interesting reading material. From the standpoint of writing, it provides students with feedback on the effectiveness of their own writing.

Classrooms can include a wide variety of nonbook materials to invite reading. Nonbook materials may be especially attractive to many students, and these materials are usually inexpensive and sometimes free (Shuman, 1982). Think about using bus, air, and rail schedules; store catalogues; newspapers (particularly the supermarket and classified sections); telephone directories; driver's license manuals; cookbooks; real estate catalogues; and labels from cans and empty food boxes (Shuman, 1982). Everyday materials such as signs, advertisements, directions, recipes, posters, letters, magazines, and comics (Schoof, 1978) are also useful additions to reading centers. Publications such as the *National Enquirer*, because they are eye-catching and likely to appeal to the interests of teenagers, have been used successfully with unmotivated readers (LaSasso, 1983).

Many reluctant readers may also be attracted to shorter, less formidable reading materials such as jokes and jingles. Moe and Hopkins (1978) present a list of 150 short items including jokes, jingles, limericks, poems, proverbs, puns, puzzles, and riddles, which can be read quickly. Newsom (1979) recommends the use of popular song lyrics and articles about rock singers and musicians to interest unmotivated readers.

A literate classroom environment can include anything that children and adolescents are likely to read. The key is whether the materials are likely to interest students, not whether they interest teachers or parents or are judged by adults to be fine literature. A case certainly can be made for not including materials that feature gratuitous sex or violence, but adults should generally let students' interests be their guide when they select reading materials, especially while students can still be characterized as reluctant readers.

INTEGRATING LANGUAGE AND THE CONTENT AREAS: THEMATIC UNITS

One way to integrate reading, writing, and oral language with the rest of the curriculum and thus provide real purposes and audiences for language is through the use of thematic units. Teachers using thematic units relate instruction in a variety of academic areas to a theme, a problem, an area of interest, or a topic (Hittleman, 1983).

Thematic units increase students' opportunities for reading and writing by inviting them to read and write in order to explore their interest in a topic. They treat reading and writing as functional skills to be used rather than as school subjects to be learned. Thematic units take advantage of students' natural curiosity and experience (Moss, 1984) while expanding their knowledge and experiences.

Thematic units may be especially advantageous for LD and remedial students because they have the potential to bring more continuity to pull-out programs. Once a topic has been established, students understand the continuing nature of its study and begin to look forward to and plan for the unit. Students often become excited about learning more about the topic and take control of the direction of the thematic unit and their own learning. They find themselves reading and writing for real reasons and come to revalue reading and writing as ways of exploring topics of interest to themselves. LD and remedial students may also benefit from the structure of thematic units (Lewis, 1982), although this structure is likely to be student-centered. In addition, the broad curricular focus of thematic units positively influences reading and writing development and academic achievement (Singer, McNeil & Furse, 1984).

A teacher's development of a thematic unit begins, of course, with the selection of a theme or topic. The topic can be selected because it is a required curriculum topic, because the teacher knows that it will inspire students' interests and meet some of their needs, or because the students themselves have suggested the topic or revealed a great interest in it during another instructional experience. Some teachers prefer to develop thematic units around a broad topic, while other prefer a narrower topic. A broad topic frequently has the advantage of permitting more flexibility and creativity, and greater student ownership of the unit. On the other hand, some teachers find narrower topics easier to plan and manage, from the standpoint of both instruction and evaluation.

The concepts to be studied within the thematic unit are developed with the students' interests and needs in mind. Basically, the content the students will be exploring and learning must be identified. "Webbing" is a useful device for involving students in planning what they will study and learn about within a larger topic. The teacher may begin by leading a brainstorming discussion of topics related to a theme and then represent subtopics through the use of a web drawn on the blackboard (see Norton, 1977, 1982 for more information on the use of webbing). Through webbing, the teacher can identify concepts for the thematic unit. For a unit on frogs, for example, a concept might be the life cycle of frogs. Webbing can also be used to encourage students to consider what they know about each subtopic and what they want to know. The subtopics may serve as the basis for dividing into small groups for special interest group study.

In addition to identifying the concepts students will explore, the teacher must also identify what reading and writing instructional goals should be met within the unit. Certainly, plentiful opportunities for reading and writing can be included in the unit as well as lessons in which students extend their comprehension and composition abilities. Teachers' educational objectives for their students should be considered; it is often relatively simply to meet their reading and writing needs within the topic selected for study.

Though teachers need to assume the major responsibility for locating resources for studying the selected topic, students can also be involved in this aspect of planning the thematic unit. Resources available for studying themes are limited only by the imaginations of students and teachers. Information can be obtained from newspapers, magazines, trade books, encyclopedias, people in the community, government agencies, businesses, family members, audio-visual materials, guest lecturers, textbooks, films, tapes, museums, and so on. Annotated bibliographies on selected themes are available in many school libraries (see McGee & Tompkins, 1983). Librarians can also help locate information on various topics, and computer searches of commercial databases (such as *CompuServe* or *The Source*) may be helpful. A number of book publishers are beginning to market databases on selected topics for the school market.

Difficulty is the key issue a teacher needs to confront in gathering reading materials to support a thematic unit. Though students will often deal with more difficult material than we might expect when they are highly interested in a topic, it is important that the majority of the materials gathered are easy enough for students to read if the thematic unit is also to meet students' instructional needs in reading. It is occasionally the case that a topic is not suitable for study because reading materials are scarce. If students are interested in a number of topics, keep this issue in mind in choosing which one they will study. If easy enough reading material can be found for one unit but not another, choose the unit for which reading materials are readily available.

As students study a topic, encourage them to assemble the materials they find on the topic in an organized way, not only for their own continued use but also for the use of other students in the future. Crocker (1983a) recommends that students gather information on topics by building vertical files. Here vast amounts of information on particular topics are brought together, classified, and filed alphabetically in cartons that can then be stored, perhaps in the library. Electronic databases can be constructed in a similar manner. These are worthwhile projects by themselves since they require extensive reading, writing, and organizing. Of course, constructing lessons and activities to support students' learning of concepts and use of reading and writing is a major step in the development of a thematic unit. Continuing the frog unit example, the teacher may decide to have students record their observations of a tadpole's metamorphosis into a frog. Consider both teacher-led or directed lessons as well as activities that may be handled fairly independently by students, such as recording observations.

The lessons and activities that a teacher plans for students should be considered as a point of departure rather than as cast in stone. As the teacher and students live with the ideas, lessons, and materials, they will generate new ideas and lessons, find some not worth pursuing, and adapt many others.

Teachers and students may wish to culminate their study with some sort of project. Again, there is no limit to the number of possibilities here. Possible projects include making a movie, role-playing, writing a TV script, creative dramatics, developing a newsletter, or some formal presentation (Norton, 1977). Burns and Swan (1979) describe a unit on food that included asking students to invent a new cereal and then develop an advertising campaign for the cereal. This campaign included writing slogans, designing billboards, designing and labeling the box, and so on. In another example, a unit on the study and exploration of classical and modern fairy tales by a class of fourth graders culminated in having students write their own fairy tales (Moss, 1982).

Thus far, we have presented the notion of a thematic unit as if it were something a teacher must develop "from scratch." In fact, teachers will find that many school districts have spent considerable time developing thematic units (though they may not be called thematic units) that contain much of what we have already talked about—lists of what students are to learn, resources, lessons, and so on. The missing element in the majority of these units is the infusion of reading and writing as tools for learning about the topic. In these cases, teachers need to think about the reading and writing needs they want to meet as part of the unit study and include reading and writing opportunities and lessons into the unit in order to accomplish their goals.

There are other places to look for prepared thematic units. Mini-thematic units can often be found in well-written science or social studies textbooks. Moss (1984) presents a number of thematic units that are based on the study of literature. Even basal readers that group stories by theme contain the kernel, if not more, of a thematic unit. Finally it should be remembered that thematic units are an approach to curriculum and not a curriculum in themselves. Teachers need to adapt this approach to their own needs and styles while considering the particular students with whom they are working (Lewis, 1982). In other words, the themes, activities, products, and goals of thematic units depend on the needs and interests of particular students and cannot be developed without considering them. Even if teachers develop a thematic unit from the beginning, they'll find that it changes when it is used with a different group of students.

CONCLUSION

The environments within which students learn will affect what they learn, how they learn, and how they feel about learning. We have argued in this chapter that the immersion of students in print, the demonstrations of print they observe, the opportunities they have for reading and writing, especially for different purposes and audiences, and the instructional materials they use can all influence, positively or negatively, their literacy development. This is especially true for children who have experienced school failure.

Teachers must make every effort to ensure that children discover that reading and writing are meaningful, relevant, and purposeful and have frequent opportunities to interact with print as readers and writers. They can do this by carefully looking at what is demonstrated to students about reading and writing in the classroom and the opportunities students actually have to engage in meaningful reading and writing. This chapter has presented a number of ideas for increasing children's engagement with print and for designing environments that are meaningful, relevant, and purposeful. It is only within these sorts of environments that children will develop into lifelong readers and writers. It is only within environments, where there are many diverse reading and writing opportunities that lessons extending students' reading and writing ability and knowledge will be effective.

VI

Developing fluency in reading and writing

David (third grade) reads aloud to his teacher, faltering frequently, pleading with warm brown eyes for help at each difficult word.

Brian (ninth grade) reads aloud even more haltingly than David. Brian claims he cannot read silently and says his attention wanders almost immediately. Five minutes after beginning to silently read a brief paragraph, he is still trying. Brian's writing is equally labored. Though he has a lot he wants to say on paper, his handwriting is so tense and deliberate, he often "loses" his thoughts in the process.

Rita (second grade) has no difficulty with handwriting but her writing is limited to what she can spell. After thirty-two minutes and considerable avoidance behavior, she has committed six words to paper, all of them spelled correctly. The topic, about a cat, has no importance to her; she chose it because she could spell *cat*.

Nonfluent reading and writing are common among learning disabled and remedial students. They read word by word, in a stumbling, choppy manner, doing what has been referred to as "barking at print" (Wardbaugh, 1969). Their writing, if it ever gets started at all, is equally choppy and stumbling. In either case, the students' processing of print is so slow and disjointed that construction of meaning is quite limited.

Fluent reading and writing is characterized by a rapid and smooth processing of text and an apparently effortless construction of meaning. No one is always a fluent reader and writer; each of us can think of situations in which our reading or writing was rendered nonfluent. Thus we cannot set as a goal helping students to become fluent readers and writers in all situations; our goal instead must be to help them become fluent readers and writers in an increasingly wider range of reading and writing situations.

As we have contended, learning disabled and remedial students often know and can do more than we give them credit for. This contention is equally true with regard to fluent reading and writing; that is, your students are almost certainly fluent in some reading and writing situations. It's probably the case, however, that the range of situations in which they are fluent is so limited that you have never observed them to be fluent readers and writers.

This chapter will briefly review reasons why students like David, Brian, and Rita are nonfluent readers and writers and how you, as their teacher, can help them achieve greater fluency. First, we will explore several general strategies that can encourage students to reconsider the nature of written language and the importance of fluency. The rest of the chapter is devoted to specific strategies designed to engage students frequently in fluent reading and fluent writing.

REASONS FOR A LACK OF FLUENCY

A lack of fluency in reading and/or writing can be traced to several interrelated sources—the student's fear of taking risks in the process of reading and writing, and the student's store of knowledge about reading and writing as language. Proficient language users understand that written language exists to communicate meaning; less proficient language users typically believe that reading and writing are done in order to practice written language forms—word recognition skills, spelling, and handwriting (Graves, 1983; Harste & Burke, 1980).

In the authors' experience, when fluent readers and writers are asked what they would like to be able to do better as readers and writers, they usually provide answers focused on meaning: "I need to understand more of what I read" or "I want to write what I mean more clearly." On the other hand, nonfluent students' answers to the same question are usually focused on the conventions or forms of language: "I want to know all the words"; "I want to be able to sound out words better"; "I want to be able to spell better"; or "I need to make my writing neater."

If readers focus too heavily on individual letter/sound relationships or on the recognition of individual words, they cannot concurrently focus on the construction of meaning (F. Smith, 1982a). Nor can a person focus on the construction of meaning in writing if his attention is on spelling, letter formation, and/or neatness (Graves, 1983; Shanklin, 1981; F. Smith, 1982b). Readers and writers who focus on form do not process meaning as they read and write; they process letters, letter sequences, or words. It's no wonder that such students sound as if they are reading word lists or that their writing is so stilted.

Closely aligned with students' notions that reading and writing are done in order to practice the forms of written language is the belief that the goal of this practice is perfection. That is, reading is a matter of correct word recognition and writing, the correct use of conventions. Even adolescent students sometimes think that good readers and writers know how to pronounce and spell almost all words. They have no idea that readers and writers must constantly take risks in their quest to construct meaning, risks that may result in error.

Finally, nonfluent students' store of information about reading and writing as language limits their fluency in reading and writing situations. The instruction provided for nonproficient readers commonly focuses on one aspect of the student's limited store of information about written language: graphophonics. Miscue research indicates, however, that proficient and nonproficient readers do not differ in their use of graphophonics while reading; rather, they differ in their use of syntax and semantics in conjunction with graphophonics (Cambourne & Rousch, 1982; Y. Goodman, Watson & Burke, 1987; Pflaum & Bryan, 1982).

In order to learn to use the three language systems in an interrelated way, the student must read whole text, text in which an author has presented these language systems in an interrelated manner. Essentially, nonfluent readers and writers must learn to treat reading and writing for what they are—language. Once students have become more fluent in reading and writing, attention may be given to their knowledge and use of language forms. This topic will be addressed in more detail in chapters 7 and 8.

CONFRONTING STUDENT BELIEFS

Before we consider instructional strategies designed to engage students more frequently in fluent reading and writing, we will discuss some strategies that help students directly confront their beliefs and/or gain new insight about the nature of reading and writing. A strong belief that reading and writing are the correct practice of language forms often inhibits students' ability to read and write effectively, since their beliefs have an impact on their reading and writing (Harste & Burke, 1980). We have found that reading and writing behavior may become more effective more quickly if beliefs about the reading and writing processes are confronted at the same time that instructional strategies designed to increase fluency are instituted.

Consider the following example. A teacher we know found that it took three months of the school year for her mid- to low-achieving fifth graders to reach an acceptable level of writing fluency. No matter how many times she told her students that she didn't want them to worry about spelling and neatness, that their ideas mattered most in initial drafts, the students wouldn't take risks and continued to do "safe" writing. Only gradually did her students stop writing about things they were sure they could spell; only gradually did they stop balking at frequent writing.

The following year the same teacher was faced with a new class of unconvinced fifth graders reputed to have low self-concepts and a reputation for "dreadful" academic performance and behavior. This time she decided to enlist the previous year's fifth graders to talk with her new class about what they had learned about writing in fifth grade. She constructed a series of open-ended statements for each group to respond to in writing.

For previous students:

1. When my teacher first told us we were all authors, I...
2. At first when I was given a writing assignment, I...
3. When I first found out I was expected to write a book, I...
4. If I were advising other kids about writing, I would tell them...
5. I felt much better about writing once I realized...
6. I first realized that I could really write when...
7. For me, the least enjoyable part of writing was...
8. The most valuable thing I learned from writing was...

For current students:

1. When my teacher tells us that she knows we are all authors, I...
2. When my teacher gives us a writing assignment, I...
3. When I saw the books from last year's fifth graders, I...
4. If I could ask another student one question about learning to write well, I would ask...
5. What scares me about the whole idea of writing is...
6. Writing would be a lot easier if I knew more about...
7. The best part about making a book would be...
8. What makes writing good is... (Clyde, 1981)

Then the teacher arranged to have the two classes meet so that they could exchange their ideas about writing. Hearing their older peers discuss their previous year's experiences—how these experiences had affected their perceptions about themselves as authors and resulted in new insights into the writing process—helped the current students react much more quickly to the teacher's instructional strategies for increasing writing fluency. The fifth graders in the second class wrote fluently by mid-October, in spite of their reputation.

Questions from the reading and writing interview presented in chapter 3 are also suitable as discussion starters about beliefs. "What do you do when you come to something you don't know when you're reading?" often elicits profitable discussions, for example. Comments from acknowledged good readers that they sometimes skip unknown words may result in astonished looks on the faces of poor readers. The astonishment often grows as the teacher nods in agreement and shares an example of how she handled an unknown word she encountered the previous day.

It's not usually useful to hold discussions such as these with only poor readers and writers; less proficient readers and writers also need to hear what proficient students do during the reading and writing processes. By their very nature, "pull-out" programs do not include proficient readers and writers. Yet students who are nonfluent desperately need proficient readers and writers as models. If you decide to arrange for students to share and discuss strategies, the meeting can take place in the pull-out student's regular classroom.

The student's regular teacher may be delighted at the suggestion that you take the whole class for a discussion or a series of discussions. (It's completely unnecessary to identify achievement levels for the sake of these discussions;

the students know already. Your job is simply to help the students share information.) If your pull-out students don't volunteer much during the discussion, review the session when they next come to your classroom, asking them what they learned and what they heard that surprised them.

One model of proficient reading and writing that all students have access to is their teacher. This, of course, demands that you read and write with your students frequently. Telling students what you do when you read and write is only effective if you also show them what you do. As you write and as you read, occasionally mention the difficulties you are encountering and how you solve them or attempt to solve them. For example, as you write, you might say, "Oh, I just remembered something I should have written before. I'll write it in the margin and draw an arrow to show where it goes." Or, if you are reading a story to the students and come across a long and difficult name to pronounce, you might say, "I can't figure out what this name is and it doesn't really matter. I'll use a nickname I make up instead."

As their teacher, you can also help students gain new insights into the reading and writing processes. For example, some students, even adolescents, do not understand what it is that people do when they read silently. In such cases, observation of good silent readers is in order, followed by discussion. You might begin by asking your students to watch you as you silently read a short passage. After you finish, ask them what they saw you do. You'll get answers like, "Your eyes moved quickly from one side to another," "Your lips didn't move," and "You moved around in your chair." Tell the students what the passage was about in some detail and ask them how you know what it was about, i.e., what else you must have been doing as you read that they couldn't see. Sometimes such discussions can encourage major insights such as this one: "Now I understand how people can read to themselves. They have to share it with their brains" (S. L. Smith, 1979, dedication).

After a reading or writing session with students, you might engage them in a discussion about the problems you encountered and brainstorm possible solutions for these problems with an eye to which solutions are more appropriate to the situation. Likewise, encourage students to provide examples of problems from their own reading and writing and to share their solutions.

The ideas presented here are only a few examples of how students can be helped to confront their beliefs directly. As you help students examine long-held beliefs, remember that there is almost no strategy that a student uses (even avoidance!) that isn't appropriate in some settings. It is appropriate to use a dictionary as a spelling aid in editing a piece of writing. On the other hand, it is a strategy that renders a student a nonfluent writer when producing a rough draft of a composition. It may be appropriate to sound out "A-nan-ul-fay-dee-ma" if a student is reading "The Name of the Tree" (Macmillan, 1972) to a friend. Sounding the word out is an unproductive strategy, however, if the student is reading the same story to himself.

The goal in helping students confront their beliefs about reading and writing is not to rid the students of customary strategies. Instead, the goals are to help students put customary strategies into perspective, hurry along their awareness that other strategies exist, and help them begin to understand which strategies are appropriate in which reading and writing situations.

INSTRUCTIONAL STRATEGIES FOR DEVELOPING READING FLUENCY

"Fluent reading depends on the ability to use the eyes as little as possible" (F. Smith, 1982a, 3). In turn, using the eyes as little as possible depends on the ability to predict the language and content of text. Thus, if we want to help a student become more fluent at reading any given text, we must attend to the "match" between text and reader.

The match between reader's and author's thought and language may be addressed either by careful selection of "predictable" material (see chapter 3) or by increasing the reader's knowledge of the text and written language in general. Either increases the likelihood that the student can predict more effectively in the process of reading text and thus read more fluently.

In the pages that follow, we present three techniques that will increase a reader's knowledge of both a particular text and of written language in general, and thus increase reading fluency. The first technique, assisted reading, provides students with a powerful model of fluent reading, and at the same time, increases students' knowledge of the text being read. The second technique, repeated reading, increases students' knowledge of a particular text as they read the text over and over. The third technique, sustained silent reading, operates on the premise that the more we do something, the better we get at it. Thus, the more students read, the more they learn about reading, and the better they are at reading fluently. All three techniques have the potential to increase students' general knowledge of written language; people learn to read by reading. As students gain in their knowledge of written language, what they have learned by fluently reading one text they can transfer to other texts.

Assisted reading, repeated reading, and sustained silent reading can be, and frequently are, used in concert with each other. If the reader with whom these techniques are to be used is extremely nonfluent, it is also important to carefully select highly predictable reading materials. Remember that every reader can be fluent in some situations—the repeated reading of a highly predictable book may yield the first situation in which you observe fluent reading in a particular student. Once a student has experienced reading fluency and understands that reading should sound like language, then the student can be helped to extend that reading fluency to more situations and an increasingly wider variety of materials.

Remember also that oral reading fluency should not be the primary goal for most students; silent reading fluency is far more important. (There are occasional exceptions, such as the learning disabled high school student who desperately wants to participate in the drama club.) Assisted reading must be done orally and repeated reading is often done orally because both the teacher and the student must be able to directly observe fluent reading for a time. Oral fluency instruction is intended, however, only as a way station to what is of real concern—increasing silent reading fluency.

ASSISTED READING

A basic technique for helping students get on the road to fluent reading is assisted reading, sometimes called the "lap method" or "the neurological impress method." Assisted reading can be thought of as the way many parents read with children who beg to read along before school (the lap method). This technique has been around as long as there have been books that are initially too difficult for the children who are interested in reading them. Assisted reading as an instructional technique is usually recommended as appropriate for severely disabled readers (Bos, 1982; Hollingsworth, 1978) as well as emergent readers.

Assisted reading is best done with a text, a whole story, or book that the student has already heard and enjoyed or one that the student is sure to enjoy and find predictable. If the student has not previously heard the text and requires a great deal of support, the instructional session can begin with the teacher reading the book to the student so that the student can not only hear a model of fluent reading but can also begin to build her/his knowledge of the text through hearing it in its entirety. Then the student can be invited to read along with the teacher as the teacher reads the text a second time. Or, if the student needs less support or has heard the story before, the session can begin with the student being invited to read the text along with the teacher.

During the reading of the text, the teacher should read smoothly and evenly (fluently!), lowering her/his voice slightly when it's clear that the student has control of the text, raising it slightly when the student falters. The reading of the text should not be interrupted; the goal is to experience the text through a shared reading of it. Discussion of individual words is usually unnecessary. When it is, the discussion should ordinarily wait until a reading of the entire text has been accomplished.

Several of those who have written about the assisted reading technique recommend that the student "read with his finger" or point as s/he reads (Hollingsworth, 1970, 1978; Schneeberg, 1977). For students who are still learning the voice-print match of beginning reading (Holdaway, 1979), such a recommendation is well worth following. However, students who can track words with their eyes as they read them may find such a recommendation superfluous and, in fact, counter to the development of increased fluency.

Another way to accomplish assisted reading is by having the student read along with a prerecorded tape of a text. Headphones are recommended to reduce distraction (Chomsky, 1976, 1978); multichannel wireless systems have the additional advantage of permitting the student to hear her/himself and the tape recording simultaneously (Hollingsworth, 1970).

Although there are a number of excellent published tape-recordings and corresponding books available to teachers and children, teacher-made tapes are often more valuable because the text selection, reading rate, cues provided, and length of reading can be better adjusted to meet a student's needs and interests (Carbo, 1981). It is possible to save yourself some time by recording your own reading the first time you read a text to a student, thus producing a tape-recording for others to use later or for the same student to listen to again.

Learning disabled students in the United States may qualify for the "Talking Books" program of the Library Service for the Blind and Physically Handicapped, which makes available numerous books and accompanying tape-recordings for home and classroom use by the qualifying student or the teacher of the qualifying student.

In addition to the previous suggestions for conducting assisted reading, the following variations and recommendations are also useful in some instructional situations:

- Ask parents to read with students, their own children or others, in the classroom or at home. Some parents may need to see you model the assisted reading technique; for others, it will feel natural.
- Have children read in pairs. You can read the book to both children, or a child who can read the book fluently can play the previously described role of teacher in assisted reading. (If you use assisted reading with younger students, this pairing and role playing will often occur spontaneously.)
- Arrange to have men record tapes too; the students can benefit from a male reading model.
- Have teacher aides participate in assisted reading. Be sure to model the process for your aide and discuss your goals with her/him.
- Try recording only the first chapter for assisted reading if a book is quite long. This is especially useful for secondary students who sometimes need a gentle assist in getting into a book (Carbo, 1981).
- Try doing assisted reading with a small group (five to six) of learning disabled children. We have seen it work remarkably well with a group of second and third graders unable to read whole text on their own. In such cases, you can handle assisted reading in much the same way as the shared book experience explained by Holdaway (1979).

REPEATED READING

Repeated reading, another technique for increasing reading fluency, is frequently used in concert with assisted reading. Like assisted reading, repeated reading has been around at least since books have been written for children. Parents often tire of repeatedly reading their children's favorite books long before their children do.

Because a single assisted reading of a text is usually not enough to help a student become fluent at reading the text, the teacher, like the parent, may find it necessary to be the lead voice in repeated readings. As the student approximates a fluent assisted reading of a text, the teacher may invite the student to read it alone. If the student falters at some point in the text, the teacher can briefly read along again, beginning with the phrase or sentence in which the student has encountered difficulty. Thus, the teacher uses the situation as an opportunity to provide a model of rereading that preserves the linguistic nature of text.

Several researchers, including Carbo (1978), Chomsky (1976, 1978), Hollingsworth (1970, 1978), and Samuels (1979) have reported significant gains in fluency and in other areas of reading ability in instructional programs that have combined assisted and repeated reading. (See Bos, 1982; and Moyer, 1982 for reviews of research in this area.) Gains were not only noted on texts that were repeatedly read, they were also documented in the reading of new material.

Repeated reading programs in which tape-recordings rather than teachers provide assistance in reading are often instituted. In such programs, students are asked to read along with a taped text of their choice repeatedly until they feel ready to read the text fluently to the teacher independently of the tape-recording. In one such program (Carbo, 1978), the teacher used a large number of texts at varying grade levels, each requiring a ten- to fifteen-minute reading/listening time.

One pull-out teacher we know encouraged those of her intermediate grade students who were reading two or more years behind expectation to read the stories in their on-grade-level basal reader along with her tape-recordings of the texts. The children's pride at being able to read the same material as their classmates was reward enough for the teacher to continue to make tapes for them. When a text was too long, the teacher broke it into natural segments for recording and reading.

Chomsky's (1976, 1978) procedures were somewhat different. She provided tape-recordings of long stories in their entirety and relied on students to self-select portions of the text for rereading until they felt they were ready to read the whole text.

Several researchers have used assisted and repeated reading solely to improve students' word recognition (see Johnson, Johnson & Kerfoot, 1972; and Neill, 1980 for examples), a goal we do not advise. Though the number of miscues ordinarily decreases as fluency increases in very poor readers, a decrease in semantically unacceptable miscues is a better goal than accuracy given what we know about the reading process of proficient readers. Together, an increase in reading speed and a decrease in semantically unacceptable miscues are good indicators that the student is treating reading as language and has become more fluent.

Assisted or unassisted, young children do not often have to be prompted to repeatedly read enjoyable literature. One teacher we know can list at least a dozen library books that her learning disabled second, third, and fourth graders adopted as favorites and read innumerable times during the school year. The teacher tired of the stories; the children never did. Nor do students of any age have to be prompted to repeatedly read text if they sense a gain in fluency (Chomsky, 1978; Moyer, 1982).

Lauritzen (1982) argues, and we agree, that speed and error charting motivators like those recommended by Samuels (1979) and others can be replaced with "motivation by appeal." When students do require external motivation to read texts repeatedly, establishing and/or varying real reading purposes and audiences will provide the necessary appeal. For example, if students were taking part in a play, they would read the play script repeatedly as a matter of course in preparation for the play. Many "natural" activities that call for the repeated reading of text can be used to advantage in school. Descriptions of some of these activities follow. Because some of these descriptions do not provide sufficient information for implementation, references are included that give far more detailed information.

Radio reading

Though developed as an instructional technique for content-area classes, radio reading can provide a reason for the repeated reading of any text, especially at the secondary level (Greene, 1979; also see J. Vacca, 1981). In small groups, each student takes a turn reading a text or a portion of a text (such as a subtitled section of a science chapter) to the other students. The listeners do not have a copy of the text being read; their job is to listen to the reading as if they were listening to the radio. After reading the text, the reader invites discussion of what was read by asking the listeners questions. The role of radio reader rotates until all in the group have had a turn.

Repeated reading may play a role, of course, in the preparation of material to be read during radio reading. The readers quickly understand that they must read their material so that it can be understood by their listening audience. Repeated reading until fluency is achieved is a necessity for listener comprehension.

Readers Theatre

Students of all ages thoroughly enjoy the reading and rereading of scripts in Readers Theatre (Sloyer, 1982). Prepared Readers Theatre scripts are available from Readers Theatre Script Service (P.O. Box 178333, San Diego, CA 92117), and scripts for plays such as those published by Plays, Inc., may be used in Readers Theatre as well. However, we recommend that the students themselves produce scripts from their favorite stories, fables, and folktales. Such an activity is not only an excellent reason for writing—it also prompts repeated reading of the original text as it is adapted to script form. (See Sloyer for detailed instructions on helping students to write scripts.)

In preparation for a performance, students who are assigned script parts read and reread the script. Though props aren't necessary, a little time spent locating or making a few simple props adds to the fun. During the performance itself (other class members are a fine audience), students read the script again. Lines are not memorized as in plays; instead, each player reads from a script held in her/his hand. Students can be expected to read the same scripts many times after a performance for the sheer enjoyment of it. Little do the students know the positive effect of all these repeated readings on their reading fluency.

Choral reading

Choral reading is an interpretive reading of text, often poetry or songs, by a group of voices (Schiller, 1973). Schiller recommends that students themselves work on arranging the text for voices rather than depending on available arrangements, such as those found in choral reading collections by Rasmussen (1962) or Bryan (1971). Once students have a feel for choral reading, such a recommendation is a valuable one since students must read a text repeatedly in order to decide how to prepare it for choral reading. The *Sounds of Language* reading series (Martin & Brogan, 1972) is replete with texts suitable for choral reading as well as choral reading suggestions, especially the reader entitled *Sounds of a Distant Drum*. Shel Silverstein's two collections of poetry, *Where the Sidewalk Ends* (1974) and *A Light in the Attic* (1981) contain possibilities for choral reading selections that will generate enthusiasm in students. A choral reading arrangement of an old song is reprinted below (from Hess, 1968) in order to provide an idea of possible arrangement:

THE POOR OLD WOMAN

SOLO 1: There was an old women (*say it on an ascending scale to discourage singsong*) who swallowed a fly.

ALL: Oh, my! (*Hands on face; act horrified.*) Swallowed a fly? Poor old woman (*tearfully*), I think she'll die. (*Shake heads mournfully.*)

SOLE 2: There was an old woman who swallowed a spider. Right down inside her (*make an agonized face and bring hand down front of body to stomach*) she swallowed a spider.

ALL: She swallowed the spider to kill the fly. Oh, my! (*Same as first verse*) Swallowed a fly? Poor old woman, I think she'll die.

SOLO 3: There was an old woman who swallowed a bird. (*Boy chirps like a bird.*) How absurd to swallow a bird (*disgusted tone*).

ALL: She swallowed the bird to kill the spider. She swallowed the spider to kill the fly. Oh, my! Swallowed a fly? Poor old woman, I think she'll die.

SOLO 4: There was an old woman who swallowed a cat. (*Sound a cat mewing—take time for this.*) F-a-a-a-n-c-y that, she swallowed a cat.

ALL: She swallowed the cat to kill the bird. She swallowed the bird to kill the spider. She swallowed the spider to kill the fly. Oh, my! Swallowed a fly? Poor old woman, I think she'll die.

SOLO 5: There was an old woman who swallowed a dog. (*Sound of dog barking.*) She went the whole hog! (*Incredulous tone—accent on "whole."*) She swallowed a dog.

ALL: She swallowed the dog to kill the cat. She swallowed the cat to kill the bird. She swallowed the bird to kill the spider. She swallowed the spider to kill the fly. Oh, my! Swallowed a fly? Poor old woman, I think she'll die.

SOLO 6: There was an old woman who swallowed a cow. (*Sound of cow bawking*.) I don't know how (*in a helpless voice, shaking head from side to side*) she swallowed a cow.

ALL: She swallowed the cow to kill the dog. (*Speak slowly at first but increase tempo faster and faster*.) She swallowed the dog to kill the cat. She swallowed the cat to kill the bird. She swallowed the bird to kill the spider. She swallowed the spider to kill the fly. Oh, my! (*Stop suddenly*.) Swallowed a fly? (*Shake heads mournfully*.) Poor old woman, I think she'll die.

SOLO 7: There was an old woman who swallowed a horse.

SOLO 8 (*idiotically*): She died?

ALL (*turn toward last speaker, place hands on hips, speak in a disgusted tone*): OF COURSE!

Recording books

Older students can easily be convinced to read very easy material repeatedly if they are asked to make tapes to be used for assisted reading by younger children. Have them listen to one of Bill Martin's (1970c) *Instant Reader* tapes as one possible model for their own recordings. Possible audiences for the tapes include the younger children you serve as a pull-out teacher, the primary teachers in your own or the closest elementary school, the children's wards in hospitals. Less expensive paperbacks of stories are best for recording so that the book may be sent along with the tape to the intended audience.

Reading to young children

Older students can also be easily persuaded to read easy material repeatedly if they are preparing to read to groups of kindergarten or first-grade children. In some cases, reading to youngsters at home is also good motivation for repeated reading.

A different format

Reading several different illustrated versions of the same text or the filmstrip format of a book often stimulates another reading of a text. For example, "I Know an Old Lady Who Swallowed a Fly" appears in two different versions (Adams, 1973; Bonne & Mills, 1961) as well as in a filmstrip published by Weston Woods. Weston Woods is well known for its excellent reproductions of children's books in filmstrip format. Older children can have a wonderful time repeatedly reading a text in preparation for showing the filmstrip of it to a class.

Expecting repeated readings

Good literature often deserves at least two readings, and students deserve to find out what literature offers in the second (or third) reading. This notion is recognized in the Great Books program in which the text is read as least twice prior to story discussion. Instead of reading something new each class period, ask students to choose a text they've enjoyed in the past for a repeated reading.

SUSTAINED SILENT READING

As we said in the introduction to this section, the ultimate goal of the strategies presented here is to increase students' silent reading fluency. While hearing and experiencing fluent oral reading is frequently an important first step for the student who is a slow, halting reader, attention must also be given to the student's silent reading. After all, the vast majority of us spend our time reading silently, not orally.

Sustained silent reading (SSR) is a relatively simple technique that can be used to increase the amount of time students read silently. During regularly scheduled reading periods, students and their teachers independently read material of their own choice. Although a number of studies have been conducted on SSR programs for all ages and proficiency levels, results are often contradictory because of the vast differences in program implementation and the poor tools used for measuring gains. Those who have reviewed these studies (Bergland & Johns, 1983; J. C. Moore, Jones & Miller, 1980; Sadoski, 1980, Schaudt, 1983) suggest that properly implemented SSR programs do enhance reading ability and encourage positive attitudes, and that much has been learned from programs that have failed.

A successful SSR program requires thoughtful planning and implementation. Advance publicity about the program is recommended so that students perceive that teachers see value in the program and are approaching it with enthusiasm. A wide variety of reading materials must be readily available for the students to choose from, and scheduling decisions about when and how often sustained silent reading should occur must be made. We highly recommend daily sustained silent reading for learning disabled and remedial students; they need plenty of time to read. It's generally recommended that SSR periods start out at about five minutes and gradually lengthen to a fifteen-minute minimum as the students begin to complain, "But I just got started!"

A number of those who have evaluated SSR programs (Bergland & Johns, 1983; Gambrell, 1978; McCracken, 1971; McCracken & McCracken, 1978) suggest that the teacher establish particular procedures for sustained silent reading periods and firmly abide by them, at least until the program is well established. In approximate order of importance, here are the recommended procedures:

1. All adults in the room must be engrossed in reading and should not permit interruptions or be visibly distracted by minor disturbances. When SSR programs fail, it is usually because the teacher and/or teacher's aide was "watching" students or using the time to do something other than read. (This procedure can be relaxed once students no longer need to be convinced of the value of reading. At that point, teachers can use this valuable time to read with individual students.)

2. Each student in the room must be reading. Most advocate silent reading, but others recommend that young or very poor readers be allowed to read in pairs and talk with each other about what they are reading (Hong, 1981).
3. Each student should have only one piece of reading material—a book, a magazine, a newspaper, etc. If the material proves unsatisfactory or if it is finished before the period is over, the student may quickly choose another. It may be useful for students to sit near the bookshelves so that traffic in the room is kept to a minimum.
4. Students should make no records or reports. You will know that the periods have become effective when students begin to share spontaneously what they have been reading. If you occasionally share what you have read, students will often follow suit.
5. Teachers should use a timer to determine the end of the period. It keeps both teachers and the students from being clock watchers.

Several problems are commonly encountered when an SSR program is considered or initiated for students, especially poor readers. Teachers frequently dismiss the idea of an SSR program out of hand because they find it difficult to find room in the day for "just" reading. Often this is a matter of reconsidering instructional priorities. Several researchers (J. C. Moore, Jones & Miller, 1980; Norland, 1976) have contended that reading is all too frequently overtaught, leaving few opportunities for students to use reading in fruitful ways. Allington (1980) adds that good readers may become proficient in part because they are assigned greater amounts of silent reading and often read material that is easy for them, both inside and outside the school. If poor readers are to learn to read, they must be extended the same opportunities.

If you decide that providing time for students to read material of their choice is important, you may still face the problem of seeing students for only short periods of the day. In such cases, one of the following suggestions may help:

1. Ask students to come early, to find some reading material, and to engage in SSR until you finish with the students you are currently seeing. As soon as these students leave, find your own reading material and join the next group of students for the remainder of SSR.
2. Arrange to have students' periods overlap; have first period students stay longer and second period students come earlier. Schedule SSR with all the students at once during the overlapping time.
3. Encourage the entire school to schedule an SSR period at the same time. On a rotating basis, take your own reading material and silently read in the classrooms of the students you serve.
4. Ask all your students to join you for SSR at a time during the day other than their regularly scheduled period. The first and last fifteen minutes of the day are frequently possible. Or think about using fifteen minutes of your planning or lunch period. It's a good way to find time for professional journals, a current novel, or the daily newspaper.

Once an SSR program has begun, teachers often encounter another problem—students who have difficulty choosing materials. Remember that all of us gradually learned to choose our own reading materials, usually on the basis of enjoyable experiences in the past or others' recommendations. Because poor readers seldom choose to read, they have had little experience in choosing reading materials and will need your guidance in learning how, at least for a while.

Ross (1978) suggests that teachers elicit from students their criteria for a "good" book so that teachers can become more sensitive to what their students might enjoy. Ross's students suggested the following criteria; the list may give you an idea about what your students might suggest:

- A topic interesting to me.
- Easily readable, print not too small.
- A book I've heard of before.
- Main character my own age and sex.
- A "now" setting, not the olden days.
- Some pictures.
- Paperback.
- Action beginning on page one, not after pages of "dull stuff."

Ross also asked her students to share their methods for choosing a book with each other. Their ideas included the following:

- Ask the librarian for a book in my interest area.
- Look in the subject cards of the card catalogue.
- Wander around, turning head sideways to read title.
- If the book looks attractive, take it off shelf.
- Flip through the pages to see if it looks easy enough.
- Read the "blurb" about the book.

Once you've had discussions about criteria with your students, you can also help them by teaching them strategies they don't know—how to find another book by the same author, for instance. However, the decision about whether material is readable is best left to individual students, even if they make a number of mistakes in that regard. Hunt (1970) states:

When the classroom atmosphere encourages self-selection, usual reading level performances become less meaningful. This author has watched many readers spend many rewarding moments with material which by any standard would be classified as too difficult....If oral reading performances were required...performance would be catastrophic; the material would be classified as well beyond the frustration level. However, when [a student] has chosen the material to read because of personal interest, he can break many of the barriers. (148)

You can also keep your own eyes open for books and other materials that fit students' criteria. Share the good materials you encounter and encourage students to share books with each other as they discover them. Familiarity with a book or its author is a critical factor in its selection for reading (Ross, 1978); aim to help your students be able to say, "Oh, I've heard of that book (author) before" about a large number of books and authors.

When the SSR period begins, students should have already chosen reading material so that they can spend the period reading. Some students require help in thinking ahead about choosing materials. It might help to require students to choose something to read for the next SSR period at the end of each SSR period and to create a special shelf in the room to house their current reading materials. Be sure to put your own reading materials there too.

Another commonly encountered problem is the student who "can't" silently read. Even adolescent students make this claim and/or spend as much as ten minutes silently reading a brief paragraph. Students who spend too long silently reading are usually nonfluent oral readers who also need to be exposed to some of the oral reading fluency techniques discussed earlier in this chapter. In addition, students may benefit from discussions, such as those cited earlier, to develop insights about the nature of silent reading.

"Mumble reading" has been suggested by Cunningham (1978) as an intermediate step that is helpful for many students who have not learned to read silently. In mumble reading, students are encouraged to participate in SSR periods by reading aloud very softly. Bruinsma (1980) states that this sort of quiet reading aloud is visible subvocalization that should be expected of less proficient readers; it differs from the measurable subvocalization that takes place in all of us during both listening and silent reading only in that it is visible in poor readers. Bruinsma also adds that subvocalization sometimes becomes visible even in proficient readers when they experience an increase in textual or environmental demands. Obviously, decreasing textual and environmental demands has the opposite effect; students should do their best silent reading when they have selected material that is highly predictable or familiar from past assisted and repeated reading encounters.

INSTRUCTIONAL STRATEGIES FOR DEVELOPING WRITING FLUENCY

"When we begin working with inexperienced writers our first concern is to get them to produce written language. We can't teach them much about improving their writing until they can produce it with relative ease" (Olson et al. 1982, 11). Several basic principles underlie any attempt to increase the writing fluency of students. First, students must write frequently. Frequent opportunity for writing is the single most common recommendation for improving the compositions of students. "While instruction and evaluation may prove helpful, the more valuable opportunity is the actual writing practice, the expression of ideas" (Lickteig, 1981, 47).

Second, students can be more fluent if they write on topics, usually self-selected, about which they have considerable knowledge. Students' expression of ideas on paper can only be fluent if they have plenty of ideas about the selected topic from which to draw. "The student writer's most important inner resources are words to use in talking about personal experience. Start with what they know and feel—and in their own words" (Kirby & Liner, 1981, 31).

Third, students' audiences, whether themselves or others, must be forgiving of what they initially produce, especially in fluency exercises. As students participate in the fluency strategies suggested in this section, they must put aside their concern for editing—for correct spelling, neat handwriting, and the other conventional niceties produced for the reader. "The habit of compulsive, premature editing doesn't just make writing hard. It also makes writing dead" (Elbow, 1973, 6). Students must shift their attention from conventions to meaning; their initial goal is to learn to express meaning on paper with ease. If a piece that evolves from fluency exercises is good, the student may choose to edit it later for clarity, appropriate use of conventions, and so on.

Not only students, but also teachers (and other readers) must be forgiving and patient if students are to learn to attend to meaning first. Teachers, like the parents of children learning to speak, must initially overlook errors and attend to the meaning students have communicated. It is students' audiences who teach them what to attend to in writing. If the audience, including teachers, is most concerned about students' ideas, students will learn to focus on the expression of ideas when writing. Conversely, if students' audiences are most concerned with form, students will likely focus on form.

In this section we will discuss several strategies useful for increasing writing fluency. Free writing, journal writing, and written conversation are all intended to help students learn to express themselves fluently on paper. As we look at each technique, we will elaborate on several issues common to each—helping students select topics, the value of having the teacher write and share writing with students, and teacher response to what students produce in fluency exercises. In addition, we will give separate attention to helping students overcome spelling and handwriting barriers to writing, two common problems that are serious obstacles to fluency.

FREE WRITING

Free writing is "timed writing in which the writer puts down absolutely anything that occurs to him, without stopping and without making any corrections, for a specified period of time: usually five or ten minutes" (Temple, Nathan & Burris, 1982, 187). Elbow emphasizes the fluent nature of free writing: "Don't stop for anything. Go quickly without rushing. Never stop to look back, to cross something out, to wonder how to spell something, to wonder what word or thought to use, or to think about what you are doing.... The easiest thing to do is just to put down whatever is in your mind. If you get stuck, it's fine to write, 'I can't think what to say, I can't think what to say' as many times as you want; or repeat the last word you wrote over and over again; or anything else." (Elbow, 1973, 3)

Free writing is especially useful for students who compulsively edit as they write and those who are too critical of their own ideas to want to commit them to paper. Students of both types produce little writing, and when they do produce writing, it comes forth slowly and haltingly.

Most students would have plenty to say if they would only leave behind their nearly paralyzing concern about conventions, spelling in particular. Writers cannot concentrate on generating ideas and using conventions correctly at the same time. If their focus shifts to editing to ensure conventional usage, they can lose their ideas. Elbow calls free writing "non-editing." Practiced regularly, [free writing] undoes the ingrained habit of editing at the same time you are trying to produce. It will make writing less blocked because words will come more easily" (Elbow, 1973, 6). Though free writing itself often forces students to shift their focus from spelling (and other conventions), some students need direct and specific help in breaking the spelling barrier to fluency. Strategies for helping students with this particular problem are found in the last part of this chapter.

The other type of writer who benefits a great deal from free writing is the hyper-critical writer. These writers fret and worry so over what ideas to share and whether they are worthwhile that their paper remains blank. Elbow suggests that beginnings are the hardest and that the only way to conquer them is to start writing; "afterwards you can throw away lousy beginnings" (Elbow, 1973, 6). We have told students that they may have to begin with "I can't think of anything to say." When one hyper-critical ninth grader took advantage of our advice and repeatedly wrote only the sentence "I can't think of anything to write" daily for two weeks, we began to worry about whether the strategy was a wise one. Finally, halfway into the third week, the student began to commit his ideas to paper. Later, he told us that he wanted to see what our reaction was to the other students' writing as well as what the other students wrote about before he committed himself to thinking on paper.

Older children in particular sometimes have difficulty in finding a topic to write about during free writing, usually because topics have been chosen for them for years. As Graves (1983) notes, "Children entering school rarely have a problem with topic choice. Older children have already tended to deny their own experiences, what they know, and what they can share with others" (88). With students who "can't think of anything to write about" during free writing (or any other writing session), it's frequently useful to conduct periodic brainstorming sessions. As a group, students make topic suggestions both on the basis of past writing and writing they consider doing in the future. As students make their suggestions, the teacher can write them on the board and ask each student to make a personal list of suggestions that s/he finds of interest. Students should keep their individual lists of possible topics at hand at all times—as something they can refer to when they are stuck and can't think of a topic, and to which they may add more topics as these occur to them.

Topics may also be suggested by the teacher for consideration in free writing as long as they are broad enough so that students can rely on their own experiences and ideas in thinking about them. Kirby and Liner (1981) suggest that students can write about what they hear going on around them, they can write about writing, do memory writing (What were you doing twenty-four hours ago?), or fantasy writing (What would you rather be doing right now?). When you make topic suggestions, make sure that students understand that they are free—in fact, encouraged—to write on a topic of their own choice instead.

Consider varying classroom mood before and during free writing time; it frequently has an impact on which topics students consider and elect to write about. If students have engaged in sustained silent reading or you have read something particularly interesting to them prior to the free writing period, they may choose topics related to the reading. Consider using a variety of background music during free writing time. The music may not only suggest some new topics, it may well soothe the writers so that they can relax and let the words out.

It is as important to write with your students as it is to read with them. Seat yourself where the students can observe you during free writing. It demonstrates the importance of free writing to them and provides them with a good procedural model. Share what you've written during free writing with students. Encourage them to share the bits they like from their own writing. It's also important to share your frustrations on those days when writing is not easy for you, as well as your strategies for coping with the frustrations. Sharing problems and solutions will encourage students to share their problems also. They will learn that even fluent writers sometimes encounter difficulties.

Your responses to the writing produced by students during free writing are critical to the success of free writing. Like the students, you must suspend attention to conventions and focus on what students had to say. One way to avoid attending to conventions is not to read what is produced by students during free writing time. Instead, share orally what you and the students have written as suggested above. Oral sharing certainly requires less time, and it has the added benefit that everyone can gain something from it, including ideas for future topics. During sharing periods, students can either relate something they've written about or they can read aloud something they've written. The latter has the advantage of encouraging students to discriminate what is good from the volume of writing they've produced since the previous sharing session.

Free writing goes by many names: "marathon writing," "composition derby," "uninterrupted writing," and others. The notion of free writing as a sporting event, as the first two names suggest, is appealing to some students and helps them to understand the nonstop nature of the experience. An occasional "composition derby" of the kind described by Holt (1982) may reenergize student efforts during free writing. Holt divides students into teams and gives each member of the team a few minutes to consider a writing topic before beginning. At the signal to "start," students begin writing and must continue to write about the chosen topic until the "finish" signal is given. At this point, they count the number of words they have written and contribute that number to their team's score. Holt found that the class output during the same amount of writing time doubled in a few months and that it tripled for some of the students who were the least fluent in the beginning.

The advantage of free writing is that students can learn to be fluent by engaging in it frequently—to learn to talk rapidly and smoothly on paper about topics of concern to them. "The main usefulness of the exercises is not in their immediate product but in their gradual effect on future writing" (Elbow, 1973, 11). Both Elbow and Olson et al. (1982) note that free writing is often used by experienced writers. Even proficient writers need to loosen up when they sit down to write, "to get words flowing out of their heads, down their arms, through their pens, onto paper" (Olson et al., 1982, 8).

For all writers, free writing encourages the production of language in volume, some of which is worth going back to, even if much of it is eventually discarded. Elbow (1973) notes that if any writer does free writing frequently, "bits and pieces of writing that are genuinely better than usual" will emerge in the volume of writing produced. Free writing helps nonfluent writers produce volume and thus good bits and pieces. It also teaches them that they have innumerable topics to write about and that they should put editing in its proper place as they explore these topics on paper.

JOURNAL WRITING

Like free writing, journal writing is a strategy that provides students with extended practice in committing ideas to paper. In journal writing, students generate a quantity of writing if they write daily, as is recommended. Free writing and journal writing can be one and the same activity. In fact, journal writing may be introduced as free writing at first in order to help students learn to keep their writing moving.

Journal writing is frequently done in a notebook used only for this purpose. Some teachers prefer that students use loose leaf paper, which is filed daily in the student's journal folder. Whatever your preference, ask students to date each of their entries and keep them in chronological order. Such a system enables both you and the student to reread entries and to see progress over time.

Journal writing may proceed more smoothly with some students if you set time and quantity expectations. For example, you might want to require your students to write a minimum of fifteen minutes and a minimum of one page daily. Of course, begin with shorter requirements, especially for highly nonfluent writers. You could use a timer just as suggested for sustained silent reading and free writing.

Kirby and Liner (1981) suggest that there are four different types of journals, each written for different reasons or purposes. The most common type is the *diary journal*, which is used to explore personal ideas, thoughts, and events. Like some adults, some students find diary journals therapeutic—a safe place to think through and explore their thoughts and feelings about events and people in their lives.

If you want honest writing from your students, be careful to respect their decisions about sharing/not sharing particular entries with you or anyone else. As you read and respond to entries students are willing to share, respond with care and thoughtfulness to their concerns and ideas.

Other types of journals include the *writer's notebook*, a place to save ideas for future writing; the *project notebook*, a place to keep track of progress and ideas that are generated during group projects or individual research papers; and a *class journal*, a place where students are expected to summarize, react, and respond to what they are learning, usually in a content-area class (Fulwiler, 1987). See Kirby and Liner (1981) for more details.

Most of the journals written by both children and adolescents that we have seen are difficult to classify according to Kirby and Liner's categories. Though some entries are of the diary type, we find that most students explore a variety of topics and types of writing in addition to personal writing—what is currently being discussed in science class, something they have recently seen on TV or read in the newspaper, and stories of all sorts. We have found that, if the journal is referred to simply as "The Journal" or "The Notebook," and if students know they have the freedom (and responsibility) to choose their own topics, they will discover their own purposes for daily journal writing.

Because journal writing is intended to provide students with frequent opportunities for writing, the content they select for exploration is not important. What is important is that the students have an investment in what they have chosen as a topic. It is not difficult to motivate students to write regularly in their journals if they sense the importance of it, first to you and eventually to themselves.

There are two major ways you can communicate how important the journal is to you. First, you can write along with students when they write in their journals. In most cases, just as in sustained silent reading and free writing, your involvement in the process makes an enormous difference in student involvement. Some teachers use their journals for a wide variety of purposes, just as students do; others use their journals only for professional purposes—to record their observations of students, to work out future plans for the class, and so on. Students also sense that the journal is important if you (and others) respond to what they have written. One way to do this is to read the entries they want you to read and then respond in a manner that makes it clear that you have heard them. "Good entry," for example, does not show that you heard a student's words. On the other hand, a specific, well-placed comment or question in the margin or at the end of a journal entry signals to students that you care about the ideas they have attempted to express. "It sounds as if you were angry when you wrote this. Do you feel better today?" or "Please let me know when your dog has its puppies" are examples of responses that help students know that you've heard them. Remember that if you want the students to concentrate on the expression of meaning in their journals you must limit your feedback to meaning.

Another successful way to respond to student journal entries is to ask students to read entries to the class. One teacher we know assigns students a particular day of the week on which they may share all or part of a single journal entry. Thus, one-fifth of the class shares an entry daily, usually right before the journal writing time. Because the students write on five days but only share one day or less of their writing, what they share is usually worth the attention of the rest of the class. Deciding what to share also has the advantage of making a weekly demand on students to reread their week's entries and to judge which pieces are best and of interest to the class. Since students read what they have written orally to the class, their ideas are attended to rather than their use of conventions. Teachers often schedule this sharing time just before journal writing time because they have found that the entries students share often inspire other students when they consider topics for that day's writing. Teachers also uses sharing time as an opportunity to encourage those who are sharing to continue writing or to return to writing on the topic they have shared, especially when the class asks several questions that alert them to what else they may explore about the topic.

Some students' journals (and free) writing is unreadable because the students have not discovered written language conventions such as spelling and spaces between words. Even if students only produce a series of letters that have no graphophonic relationship to the words they want to use to express their ideas, they can still profitably engage in journal writing if the following procedures are used (adapted from Gaskins, 1982):

1. When students make a journal entry, ask them to write only on every other line.
2. As soon as students finish writing, ask them to read their journal entry to you.
3. As they read, record their ideas in your own writing above or below what they have written, on the unused lines.
4. As in language experience dictations, immediately ask students to read what you have recorded. Point to the words as they read and use assisted reading when necessary.
5. If you do class sharing of journal entries as we have previously suggested, have students stand next to you as they read their selected entry to the class. Again, use assisted reading when necessary.

The results of journal writing are similar to those of free writing. Students become fluent writers by frequently engaging in writing. They learn that they have innumerable topics about which they can write, and they learn to produce a volume of writing. Like free writing, these results are usually more apparent in long-term growth and in the student's other writing efforts. Students may be occasionally asked to select an idea or a piece of writing that is worth reworking from the writing in their journals. If they have been selecting entries to share orally with the class, they will be able to select pieces that are worth revising and editing easily. However, until students are fluent writers, keep in mind that they are gaining more from writing frequently and concentrating on the expression of ideas than from revising and editing.

WRITTEN CONVERSATION

A third strategy that is effective in helping students to write fluently is written conversation (Burke, in Crafton, Hill, House, and Kucer, 1980). In written conversation, two people "talk" to each other about topics of interest to both of them—on paper. The written conversation between fifteen-year-old Brian, a learning disabled adolescent, and his teacher is presented in Figure 6–1. The

---

FIGURE 6–1   A Written Conversation

What was your favorite thing at Epcot? Jirney in to magen ashion land. for futuchfe Whoirld. Canada Whoirld Showcase,

What did you like best about Journey into imagination land? 3D Movie, and exededet

What was the 3·D movie about?

a Kid ass drime that he and his fid flou Kitse.

How long did you stay at Epcot? 15 ours.

What was the weather like in Florida? nis and worrn dan day it ran all day.

---

conversation begins with a question about a recent trip (to the Epcot Center in Disney World). Note the open-ended nature of the teacher's questions to Brian, which encouraged Brian to make relatively lengthy responses.

As they wrote this conversation, Brian and his teacher sat near each other, passing the paper back and forth when they were ready for the other person's response. The nature of the activity encouraged Brian to focus on ideas and to write rapidly so that he could respond quickly to his teacher's conversation with him.

Interestingly, Brian's teacher observed that not only did his writing increase in fluency when he engaged in written conversation, his reading fluency increased as well. Brian typically read his teacher's responses to him far more quickly and with greater comprehension than he read any of his texts.

Some students' writing, as we noted previously in the discussion about journal writing, is unreadable. Nor can some students read what teachers write during a written conversation. For these students, oral language support must be added to what is a silent activity for most students. Brian's teacher, for example, couldn't read part of one of his responses to her and when she couldn't, she asked him to read it to her.

An entire written conversation could be carried on in the same way, with the writer first writing and then reading aloud what he has written before he passes the paper on. Young children and very delayed readers/writers learn a great deal about the relationships between oral and written language in this way, just as they do from language experience dictation. A number of variations on the written conversation technique are possible. Some of the following variations may better suit your students or provide occasional alternatives to written conversation between you and students:

- We have observed a teacher carrying on written conversations with several children at a time, all seated at a round table. Only infrequently did a child have to wait for a response from the teacher.
- Once students understand the nature of written conversation, they may want to carry one on with each other. Students in your class may be paired for written conversation, or older and/or more proficient writers may be paired with your students.
- If students seem to enjoy written conversations with each other, you might consider legitimatizing notes in the classroom or formalize written conversations by setting up a post office in the classroom.
- Written conversation may be carried on using microcomputers. Students can send and respond to "electronic mail."
- You and the student may assume other identities as you carry on a written conversation. For example, a third grade learning disabled student showed up in class one day with two pocket-size rubber gorillas. Instead of taking the gorilla figures away, the teacher made them a part of the instruction by involving the child (as a gorilla named Ligo) and herself (as a gorilla named Mushka) in a written language conversation and adventure (see Figure 6−2).

The written conversation also provides students with rapid feedback on the effectiveness of their written communications. If the writing partner doesn't understand something, a request for clarification can be made just as it is in oral language: "What do you mean..." or "Tell me more about...." The conversational exchange in print, exemplified by that between Brian and his teacher, often encourages fluency both in reading and in writing; the nature of conversation requires that each participant play both receptive and expressive roles. Written conversation also has the advantage of providing the student with an immediate model each time you, as the teacher, read and write with him. As the more proficient participant, you not only model the standard use of conventions in a natural way (see the teacher's spelling model naturally provided for Brian after he misspelled "Journey into Imagination Land") but also the writing process as a whole.

LIFTING THE SPELLING AND HANDWRITING
BARRIERS TO FLUENCY

Some students focus so much attention on handwriting or spelling that it greatly affects their writing fluency. When handwriting is the students' focus, they may define writing as "keeping neat margins, not writing below the line, and having

---

FIGURE 6–2   A Written Conversation: Ligo and Mushka

<u>The Two Gorillas</u>

M: Hi, My name is Mushka.
Let's Go to the Jungle.

L: HiMyname iSLigo
oKLet'shut fora maICe

M: Where shall we look?
Oh No, there's a mountain lion.
What shall we do?

L: LaSrun.

M: Oh No! I tripped.
Help me !

L: oKIwill Helpyou Iwill
Pak youUP

---

good spaces between words" (Graves, 1978, 394). If spelling is the students' focus, they may respond that they were "thinking of a story [they] knew how to spell" (Rhodes, 1981, 773) when asked why it takes so long for them to write.

When spelling or handwriting appears to be a barrier to fluency, direct attention to the problem is sometimes necessary. The major goal is to help students put spelling and handwriting into perspective. In this section we present various strategies that encourage students to focus on the fluent expression of ideas rather than on spelling and handwriting. In most cases, the strategies are designed to lower the mental barriers students have constructed that render their writing nonfluent. In the case of handwriting, however, physical barriers are sometimes the root of the difficulty, and we include strategies for those problems as well.

Some children are convinced that, since they cannot spell correctly, they cannot write. This may be evidenced in minor ways by those students who spend some of their writing time searching for an easy-to-spell synonym for the hard-to-spell word they really want to use. Or the problem may be evidenced in seriously debilitating ways by those students who do not write at all or write extremely little in the allotted time. In the case of those students who have minor fluency problems caused by their synonym-hunting tactics, it's usually helpful to sit with them individually while they write, and as they finish writing each phrase or sentence ask, "What are you going to say next?" Then help them commit to paper the words they used to express their ideas orally, no matter how difficult they are to spell. If the students ask for help with any of the words, reply that they should do the best they can, as quickly as they can. A session or two in which you help a student write down the words as best he can will usually convince even a particularly stubborn student that you mean what you say—spelling is important only in final drafts.

Sometimes it's also helpful to suggest to these students that they underline or otherwise mark words they would like to give more attention to later. If they can mark words quickly as they write, the marking need not interfere with fluency. If, on the other hand, marking appears to cause interruption in the flow of writing, they should wait to do it until after they have finished writing the piece.

One of the major recommendations that Graves (1983) makes for children who are overly concerned with conventions is to heighten the importance of information—or meaning—in writing. One procedure he suggests not only heightens the importance of information but also provides natural spelling support to students. Graves suggests that you have a short two- to three-minute conference with the student about the topic s/he has elected to explore. As the student talks, you play secretary, recording some of the informational words and phrases the student uses in discussing the topic with you. When the conference ends, hand your conference notes to the student, saying "If you'd like to use some of the words you were just speaking, here they are" (Graves, 1983, 208).

When students will not write at all or write very little, more drastic measures may be necessary. One learning disabilities teacher had five second and third graders whose fluency did not increase for several months in the beginning of the school year, even though she involved them in daily writing with a stated and demonstrated focus on ideas rather than on conventions. One day, in despair, she gathered all five of the children around a table with her and gave out paper and pencils to all, including herself. She told the children that she was going to tell them something about herself, a sentence with some very hard-to-spell words, and that they must write down exactly what she said on their papers. She told the children some news about herself, "I am going to go to Hawaii for a vacation," and asked them which words were very hard to spell. Although almost all words were difficult for these children to spell correctly, they immediately picked out Hawaii and vacation. The teacher told everyone to write down what she told them and they did. She praised attempts that included orthographic features of the words as well as the strategies they were using to produce those features. Some of her comments were "I see you are saying the word to yourself to see what sound comes next," and "Great! 'Vacation' does have a 'v' sound at the beginning." Then in turn, each of the five children thought of some news about himself for everyone to write with "hard words" in it.

The session, with each child writing all six sentences, lasted about half an hour. Since the children seemed to leave the session with positive feelings, the teacher repeated it the next day. One of the children asked the teacher on the third day if they could do some more "hardest word" sentences. The teacher told the child that he could write as many sentences and stories as he could think of with all the hardest words in the world! Since that time, the five children have had little trouble quickly "inventing" spellings for what they want to say.

Just as students should be encouraged to focus on ideas in initial drafts rather than on spelling, they should be encouraged to do the same with handwriting. As Graves (1983) notes, "When handwriting flows, the writer has better access to his own thoughts and information" (181). Short term games often help. For example, if the student is one who spends a great deal of time neatly forming letters as s/he writes, conduct races for a week or so in the journal or during free writing: How many words can you write in how many minutes? Or, if the student's problem is that s/he spends a lot of time erasing and re-forming letters, have a "no eraser week" and have the students discuss and show what they did when erasers weren't allowed.

Some students have postural or motor difficulties that render handwriting very labored and difficult and consume a great deal of their energy. In such cases, your intervention may help a great deal. While positional guidelines for fluent handwriting may be consulted (see Graves, 1983, 172–73 as an example), Graves (1983) recommends that a good way to figure out the source of difficulty is to sit next to students and imitate their handwriting. Thus, you should turn the paper at exactly the same angle and place it in the same relationship to your midline, distance yourself from the desk and paper in the same way, hold the pencil in the same way and apply similar pressure to the paper, and position both your elbow and back in the same way. Write for the same period of time that the child writes. You should be able to discover and change those positions that cause the student to labor so hard and to be fatigued. (If the student is left-handed, you might ask a left-handed adult to do this for you and to relate his/her observations. Or consult Howell, 1978; or Enstrom, 1968 for left-handed guidelines.)

If the student appears to have motor problems, several things are worth mentioning. First, many motor problems will virtually disappear or at least improve through writing itself. In other words, sometimes the problem is also the cure. The only cure for a child who is having difficulty learning to ride a bike is to help him ride the bike. The same is frequently true of writing; students' motor difficulties often resolve themselves through the constant, integrated practice that the writing muscles get as the student writes. As Graves (1983) says, "If children have enough writing time, and are in control of their topics, their handwriting improves" (178).

We have observed many students, including children with diagnosed physical difficulties such as cerebral palsy, improve their handwriting abilities through extended daily writing in journals and similar situations. When the children's regular teachers noticed improvement and inquired about the source of it, they were surprised to learn that the children did not go through an isolated handwriting program or visual motor training.

Occasionally, a handwriting disability will exist that doesn't repond to a teacher's help. In such cases, it may be wise to help the student learn another method for fluently recording ideas. Typing, for example, has been successfully taught to even young children (Kaake, 1983; J. L. Rowe, 1959a, b, c) and has been found to make positive contributions to younger and older students who have difficulty with both reading and writing (Fuhr, 1972; J. L. Rowe, 1959a, b, c). Fluency, in particular, can be helped by learning to type. The average handwriting speed for the third and fourth graders in Rowe's study was 11.6 words per minute in comparison to 42 words per minute at the typewriter. Students can also learn to compose at the typewriter or word processor.

CONCLUSION

In this chapter we have discussed strategies for developing fluent oral and silent reading in students whose reading tends to be slow, choppy, and halting. We have also shared several strategies for encouraging reluctant writers. Dysfluent reading and writing are particularly evident in many, perhaps most, learning disabled and remedial students. However, these strategies, while helpful for encouraging fluent reading and writing, can easily be overused. Assisted reading makes little sense for the fluent reader and derby writing is unnecessary for students who already write with relative ease. Some students may tire of journal writing, while other, fluent writers may continue to enjoy putting down their thoughts, feelings, and observations in a journal. But decisions about journals or any other reading and writing strategy must be made on the basis of the development of individual readers and writers. Lots of teachers across North America have their students write in journals every day because they believe students should write in journals. For some students, however, this practice may actually distract them from the writing they want to do. In any case, no particular strategy will necessarily be best for all students. Teachers must make their decisions based on their observations of individual students.

VII

Reading and writing instruction

In the previous two chapters we discussed ways of encouraging students to read and write often. However, though frequent reading and writing is necessary if LD and remedial learners are to become proficient readers and writers, it is not sufficient. As we indicated in chapter 2, reading and writing are fundamentally social processes. Both comprehension and composition are enhanced by lessons in which readers and writers share and extend their efforts at meaning construction. In addition, many students will also benefit from strategy lessons designed to provide them with examples of the sorts of strategies used by proficient readers and writers and to draw their attention to certain aspects of reading and writing that they may be overlooking. In general, reading and writing instruction should encourage students to use and further develop their knowledge of language and of the world to transact meaning with texts for authentic social purposes.

We also wish to reiterate that the lessons or instructional strategies presented here are meant to serve only as models for teachers of LD and remedial students. Effective teachers will modify and adapt these lessons according to their students' needs and invent other instructional strategies. What we present here are lessons we know have been effective with certain teachers and students. The same lessons, applied in the same way, will not work for all students or teachers. We do believe, however, that all teachers can effectively use instructional strategies like those presented here to encourage reading and writing development.

As your students read and write, and as they share their reading and writing with you and others, your observations will indicate where they need to extend their comprehension and composition and what they know and don't know about language and language strategies in reading and writing.

Such observations are the basis for lessons like those presented here. Some lessons may be planned in advance, while others may emerge spontaneously from the immediate situation. In no way should the lessons we present be treated as "prescriptions" to fit all students.

In the remainder of the chapter, we'll return to the "gradual release of responsibility model of instruction" presented in chapter 2 in order to talk about demonstration, discovery, and guided use as general approaches to encouraging literacy development. In addition, we'll treat conferencing and questioning as major topics; sharing and extending lessons and strategy lessons rely heavily on both of them. The information in this chapter will serve as an introduction to the chapters on reading and writing that follow.

DEMONSTRATION AND DISCOVERY

In the "gradual release of responsibility model of instruction" (see Figure 2−2 on page 24), the teacher initiates the development of language information or strategies in one of two ways: through demonstration or through teacher-led discovery. From our observations, demonstration is a seldom-used, but effective, method of teaching students reading or writing strategies. In the following chapters, we'll present recommendations for demonstrating reading and writing strategies such as predicting, self-correcting, revising, and proofreading. When they demonstrate a reading or writing strategy, we encourage teachers to do whatever they want the students to do as readers or writers and to talk aloud about what they are doing. In essence, you say aloud what you normally do rather unconsciously. At first, you may find it odd, and perhaps even difficult, to get in touch with what you usually do intuitively. But you'll find that the students get a lot out of your demonstrations, even when you may not think you've done well. Over time, you'll find demonstrating the strategies you use as a reader or writer more natural, and students will learn even more from your demonstrations.

Demonstration may also be used to teach students knowledge about language. It's a method that is easily incorporated during student dictation of a text and in editing conferences. For example, during a dictation of a Readers Theatre script, one of the authors demonstrated how to translate the dialogue of a story into the dialogue of a play—how to show who is talking in the story and what they are saying by writing the speaker's name followed by a colon and then writing what the speaker says without the quotation marks.

Students can also learn information about language and language strategies through "discovery" of the information or strategy. Although the discovery lessons we present do not involve students in discovery in the true sense of the word, they do help students to learn for themselves how language works. Active student learning about how language works encourages real under-standing and learning on the student's part. Though the lessons themselves may take longer to teach, they are often more effective than simply stating language rules because they encourage children to infer rules and discover them for themselves.

Lessons that help students discover information about language are often taught by comparing texts. The texts may be trade books, students' writing, your writing, or some combination of these materials or other texts. If you want students to discover the characteristic of "threeness" in folktales, for example, comparing a variety of folktales that feature "threes" will encourage that learning. Or if students are using a nonstandard grammatical construction, you might "lift" some of the sentences containing these constructions from their writing and have the students compare them with the way those same sentences would be written in books.

Comparison can also be useful for helping students discover learning strategies. If students are doing poorly on sequencing worksheets in their regular classroom, we might involve them in a lesson in which we ask them to sequence the statements on the worksheet before reading the passage, to read the passage, and then to renumber the sequence where necessary (see M. A. Atwell and Rhodes, 1984 for more detail about this lesson). After the students have experienced success with sequencing in this way, we ask them to compare the procedures they used in the lesson with those they usually follow in completing such worksheets. They might conclude that what was different in the lesson was that they guessed or predicted the sequence and then read to confirm/disconfirm their predictions, and, in the process, read much more actively. Teachers can help students think about other school situations in which predicting on the basis of the final task (e.g., statements to sequence, questions to answer, multiple choices on tests) and then reading to confirm predictions will be useful.

GUIDED USE

Guided use of a language strategy or language knowledge follows demonstration or discovery and should be done within the context of students' natural reading or writing. If you've demonstrated how to translate story dialogue into play dialogue, for example, the next steps are to have students try it themselves with your support, then work with each other under your supervision, and finally work independently. You may find that individual help and review of what was demonstrated or discovered is fine in some cases, but that it's more efficient to provide guided use in a group situation when a number of students have need for it.

One way to provide guided use in a group situation is by "lifting" examples of students' work or language to illustrate the lesson. For example, if you've demonstrated proofreading to students and you conclude that they need guided help in its use, lift a student's composition (or a portion of it) and proofread it as a group. In another example, if you've helped students to discover the difference between "its" and "it's" yet find that they are not consistently using this knowledge, lift sentences containing the words from students' papers and let students consider those sentences as a group.

Lifting students' writing for instruction must be done with care so that students treat each other's work with respect. To help them establish respect for each other's work you need to make some things clear: first, that everyone's work will be considered by the group, including the teacher's; and second, that work does not get lifted because it's poor but because there is potential in it, which the group, working together, can help to achieve. Until students understand this, you might even remind them that if their work is lifted so the group can work on it, at least they won't have to do the work alone!

When we begin lifting student work, we discuss the above issues with students. In addition, we lift the work of several students at a time—a number of sentences from various student compositions that feature the language knowledge or strategy we wish to highlight, the work of those students who are respected by others, and work that is above that done by the poorest students. Using these examples, we set the tone for the remainder of the year. Some teachers make it a point of not identifying the lifted student work, but our preference is to acknowledge whose work it is for several reasons. We find that students make a game of trying to identify whose writing it is anyway, and if the classroom is sharing reading and writing frequently, it's likely that at least some students have seen, heard, and discussed the writing already. We also think it's important to involve the student whose work is being discussed at a different level than the others. For example, if we have lifted sentences to work on substituting more interesting words for overused ones, we usually ask the writer to tell the rest of us which word of those suggested s/he will probably use in revising the composition.

CONFERENCING

A reading conference is a meeting between a reader and someone who is interested in hearing the reader share what s/he has read. Similarly, a writing conference is a meeting between a writer and reader(s) in which the writer shares something about the writing and the reader responds to the writing and/or to what the writer has shared. In either case, conferencing is an important instructional tool throughout the reading and writing processes. A writer may engage in a number of conferences while writing a single text—prior to writing, during writing, and after the writing has been "completed." A reader may also participate in a conference at any point in the reading process as well—before, during, or after reading the text.

Conferencing is a natural part of teaching reading and writing when conferences are viewed as processes by which readers and writers may benefit from sharing what is being read or written. Readers or writers who have difficulty constructing meaning, whether in general or with a specific text, usually benefit from talking about the text with someone. Students experiencing more difficulty require even more frequent conferencing.

Conferencing is also a way for teachers (and others) to learn about students and their reading and writing, and to respond to their current needs as readers or writers. Sharing and extending what students have read or written is the foundation of the conference. However, it's not unusual for a teacher to hold spontaneous strategy lessons to address a particular point or to make a note to plan a strategy lesson to meet a student's needs. Over time, conferencing will contribute to readers' and writers' ability to construct meaning.

The overriding principle that should govern conferences is student ownership of the reading or writing. This principle helps us understand that what the reading or writing is about is not our choice (or at least not our choice only). Decisions about organization or what's to be done with a particular piece of reading or writing must also belong to students. Whenever students begin to read or write for the teacher rather than for themselves as their own first audience, they are less motivated to use reading and writing for their own purposes and less likely to develop into life-long readers and writers.

In general, the kinds of interactions you have with students must be those that help them find their own writing subjects, what they are interested in reading, their own evidence in order to document or detail their subject, their own purposes for reading and writing, a form for the writing that fits the subject, and others with whom to share their reading and writing (Murray, 1982).

How do you, as a teacher, help students retain ownership of reading and writing? The most often repeated advice is by "letting children lead the way" (Cadieux, 1982). That may be an uncomfortable thought for you if you are a teacher who wants to feel in control. But it shouldn't feel so uncomfortable once you realize that letting students lead the way is simply responsive teaching, the kind of teaching done by teachers who individualize instruction. You don't lose by letting students take the lead; you gain by teaching them how to control themselves and their reading and writing. Your control simply takes a different form.

How do you know when a student has provided a "lead" for you to follow in instruction? Most students, especially learning disabled and remedial students, don't march up to a teacher and say, "The next thing I'm ready to do is to proofread my letter before I send it to my pen pal, and I'd like you to help by telling me what I miss when I proofread." But you can learn to spot students' leads and you can encourage them to provide leads.

One way to do this is by opening a conference with questions designed to get students talking about their reading or writing. Broad questions like "How's it going?" or "What are you into here?" allow students to take control of what they want to discuss. Over time, students learn to initiate and take control of conferences from the beginning, providing you with direct leads, e.g., "Tell me whether this makes sense to you."

To spot less direct leads, you must fine tune all your observational skills. When asking questions like "How's the writing going?" you must be prepared to listen closely to what students say. The student's answer will provide you with information about what you should attend to in the conference. When the student's response is brief, like "Fine" or "Awful," you must be prepared to follow up in order to identify the lead—"What is it that's going well/not going well?" Or you may find that a brief answer means "Don't disturb me right now—I'm reading/writing." Whatever the case, follow the students' leads and attend to their focus.

Also, listen to what students say and watch what they do when you are nearby or in the middle of a conference. If you hear a student groan, "I can't spell!," or see a student sit back in her/his chair and say, "Hey, this is a great book!," that's a lead. A child who repeatedly hides a book under the rug is providing a lead, and so is the student who throws down a pencil in disgust. A simple "Why?" is in order and will provide you with useful information. A boy who is obviously struggling over something provides a lead as well—what can you do to help him solve his problem? Even students who aren't doing what we expect them to do provide leads. For example, a girl who engages in an activity other than the writing you have asked her to do is providing you with a lead, either about general feelings toward writing or specific feelings about the day's assignment.

Your comments and questions should keep the student talking once the conference has begun. You can reflect back what you have heard about the content ("So this is a story about your dad's accident over the weekend?") and the difficulty the student is having ("You're having trouble getting through this chapter?"). Your aim is to help students reflect on the topics or issues they've raised and if necessary, to help them figure out how to solve a problem. Thinking aloud helps students extend what they were previously thinking and often helps them move forward in their reading or writing with renewed vigor. Students often find that when they talk out loud about their difficulties, the difficulties suddenly seem solvable. When that's not the case with students who have a negative image about what they are capable of, help them verbalize possible solutions to the problem and choose one to follow through on before ending the conference.

CONFERENCE TIME

For many teachers, a teacher-student conference means sitting down with children individually for some period of time. Since lengthy, individualized conferences are disruptive in many settings, we'll discuss more efficient conferencing strategies.

Recognizing that frequent, brief conferences are usually more effective than long and less frequent conferences is a helpful beginning. Frequent conferences capture students' reading and writing at various points in the process and provide a window into their thinking, their successes, and their difficulties. Short conferences also have the advantage of focusing students' attention on *one* or *two* important and immediate aspects of the reading or writing rather than diffusing attention to other aspects that may not be as important or immediate. Because you are working within the student's "zone of proximal development" (Vygotsky, 1986), conferences are often quite intense. The students (and you) can sustain that intensity for only a short period of time.

Something else that is helpful in managing your conference time with students is to consider the types of conferences available to you in view of your purposes and the time you have. One type of conference that can be very effective is the roving conference (Turbill, 1983). In roving conferences, the teacher moves among students while they are either beginning or ending a period of reading or writing, asking questions and taking mental or actual notes on students' progression in the piece they are reading or writing, who is having difficulties that need attention, and so on. We recommend that you do not sit or kneel down beside students; either movement will suggest that you are willing to stay and talk. It's also unnecessary to read every (or even any) piece of writing or touch the student's book. Instead simply glance at the book or piece of writing and ask the student a few quick questions like, "How's it going?" or "Will you need some help today (or tomorrow)?" A roving conference should be treated as a fact-finding mission done to get a feel for how students in the class are currently operating and to identify those who need more attention than others. Although it's certainly possible to quickly help a few students get on the road to solving a problem they've run into, it's not the main focus of the roving conference. Any individual help provided during this time should be the kind that takes only a quick question or comment.

Group conferences can be convened whenever a number of students are reading the same text and could benefit from a discussion of it, or are encountering the same difficulties in their reading or writing and need a planned strategy lesson. For example, if a student includes character dialogue in her/his story for the first time and shares that story with the class, the attention you give that dialogue is likely to inspire others to try out the technique. Once students begin trying out dialogue, you are likely to observe that they need some help with punctuating it. Pulling together the students who are using dialogue in their stories enables you to present a strategy lesson on dialogue to the group, perhaps saving you from conducting a number of individual lessons on the same topic.

Whole-class conferencing may evolve from the discovery that all the students in your class could benefit from the same sort of discussion or information. Calkins (1986) recommends that teachers begin writing time with "mini-lessons" for the whole class, which take about five minutes and focus on one specific issue or topic. Even students who already know the subject matter of a whole-class conference can consolidate their learning through a group mini-lesson and will provide others with the needed perspective of a more proficient reader/writer.

Peer conferencing is another useful type of conference and not only because it saves the teacher time. In peer conferencing, the teacher may or may not be present as students themselves gather to share their reading or writing and their reading or writing difficulties with each other. The peer conference may involve a pair of students, one of whom is offering help or just a friendly ear to the other, or it may involve a small group or even an entire class. The "author's circle" (Harste, Pierce & Cairney, 1985), a whole-class conference where individual students share work with the other writers in the class, is a fine arena for helping students understand how to offer specific positive comments and specific suggestions to peers. As the teacher, you can demonstrate questions and comments, encouraging students to rephrase and clarify their comments so they are helpful. Whenever you are conferencing with students, remember the power of your demonstrations; what the students hear you say and how the students see you conduct yourself will soon be reflected in the conferences they have with each other.

Of course, you'll still want to conduct individual conferences. Individual conferences are best used for those things that require expertise that no one else in the room has or when others in the room are engaged in their own reading or writing. Above all, remember the maxim that the individual conference should be focused on one or two of the most necessary things the student needs in current reading or writing.

CONFERENCE RECORDS

Many teachers fill out plan books prior to instruction. But conferencing does not lend itself well to prior planning because its underlying principles are to follow students' lead, meet their current needs, and leave ownership in their hands. For a variety of reasons, however, including solid instructional ones, it's important to have a record of the instruction provided to students. Anecdotal records fulfill that purpose for a teacher who uses conferences in teaching.

Anecdotal records are a responsibility that can be shared by teacher and students. The writing folder is often the vehicle recommended for student record-keeping in writing (Bingham, 1982; Graves, 1983). Students can keep track of what they've written and when by recording the titles of their pieces and their completion dates on one side of the writing folder. They can record the topics they know a great deal about and want to write about on another side. On still another side, they can record what they have learned to do in their writing, as well as what they need to work on.

In a like manner, students can also keep reading logs. They can record the titles of the books, articles, etc. they have read and their completion dates. They can record what they want to read about next and specific titles or authors they want to look for. They can make judgments about books by rating books they've read. And they can record the reading strategies (e.g., "Keep reading to see if the author provides more information") they have learned to employ while reading. These student records provide information to teachers about what the student has done, information that teachers can examine for patterns in behavior and in the lessons provided. And not to be overlooked is the usefulness of these records to students, especially in encouraging students to see themselves as increasingly proficient readers and writers.

Graves (1983) offers other ideas for recording conferences as well as ideas for shaping record-keeping to meet both teachers' and students' needs. His final words on the subject emphasize the importance of record-keeping in conferences and apply as much to conferencing in reading as they do to conferencing in writing:

> In most teaching, especially during conference time, teachers don't have time to consult records in order to respond to children. . . . Teachers can't teach with a "cookbook" full of recipes consulted in midflight. Rather, they teach as the situation demands. Records prepare teachers for the teaching moment. Teachers respond effectively during the conference because they have absorbed recorded information. (308)

QUESTIONING

Questioning is so much a part of instruction that we sometimes wonder if teachers at any level would find it possible to get through a day without asking questions. We recommend the use of questions that assist students in sharing and extending their comprehension and composition, and questions that help them discover language strategies and increase language knowledge. Since questions focus students' attention on what is to be learned from text (Reynolds & Anderson, 1982; Wixson, 1983) and have the potential for developing cognitive processing (Guszak, 1967; Ruddell, 1978; Taba & Elzey, 1964), the ways of questioning we propose are not trivial. We consider questioning important enough to accord a significant portion of this chapter to it.

QUESTIONING IN READING

Much of the discussion of questioning in reading has focused on question/comprehension taxonomies such as Bloom's and Barrett's. Barrett (1976), for example, has proposed a taxonomy that assigns reading questions to one of five levels—literal, reorganization, inferential, evaluation, and appreciation—based on the anticipated response of students. Presumably, taxonomies such as these are intended to help teachers examine their questioning strategies and generate questions that encourage a wider range of student responses in order to promote better reading comprehension.

Questioning taxonomies may have limited usefulness, however. We find Barrett's taxonomy and others used for generating questions problematic for a number of reasons. These approaches assume that comprehension levels are sequential and hierarchical in development (Tatham, 1978)—that literal comprehension must be mastered before reorganization, reorganization before inferential, and so on. They also assume that comprehension occurs in discrete categories or divisions, which contradicts what we know about children's cognitive and linguistic development and what we know about the process of comprehension. Two-year-olds can infer what's going on from the "facts" in a situation, if the situation is one within their realm of experience. Why shouldn't this ability to infer be expected in print situations? Also, consider your own experiences with students: Do they have more difficulty telling how the main character in a story feels (appreciation level) or summarizing the events of the story (reorganization level)? Even the most basic understanding of a text requires both inferring and recall of literal information, which contradicts the literal and inferential divisions in the taxonomy.

Beck and McKeown (1981) challenge the notion that these taxonomies actually help teachers understand how to develop questions that promote comprehension. They cite, as an example, two literal level questions for "The Three Little Pigs": "What did the third little pig use to build his house?" and "How many bricks did the third little pig use?" Though both are "equal" questions in that they are both literal, one is trivial while the other is important to an understanding of the story.

Publishers of reading series often suggest that teachers follow a rigid sequence of questioning from "lowest" level to "highest," again under the assumption that students need to demonstrate recall before being led to think at a higher level about a text. Teachers can test this assumption by trying the following experiment. If you use a reading series that includes a suggested sequence of reading comprehension questions, ask the questions listed by the publisher in reverse order from the one suggested by the publisher. If you ask follow-up questions to the higher level questions that require students to provide support or evidence for their responses, you'll find that there's no reason to ask the literal questions because students will have already demonstrated their literal understanding of the text.

Another difficulty with this notion of sequencing questions from lowest to highest levels in instruction is that the sequence may disrupt the flow of the story or the information rather than promote comprehension of the text as a coherent unit. In addition, questions that publishers (and teachers) ask at all levels of the taxonomy are sometimes trivial and may distract students from the essence of the story (Guszak, 1967). In a teacher's guide for "The Little Red Hen," for example, students are asked to recall the steps the hen used in making bread. That sort of question may be fine in the context of reading a bread recipe but in this story, bread-making is only used by the author as an example to support the theme of cooperation in work; another task would have supported the author's theme just as well. As it is, the question distracts students from the theme of the story.

On the other hand, some higher level questions can be answered without any reference to the text (Guszak, 1967) or without demonstrating any understanding of the text. For example, the following questions are listed for postreading discussion of *The Little Red Hen* (Durr et al., 1981):

Which do you think was the hardest work: planting, cutting, pounding, going to the mill, making the bread, or eating the bread? Why? What do you think was the easiest to do? Why?

How do you think the little red hen felt each time the animals wouldn't help her?

How do you think the duck, the cat, and the pig felt when the little red hen wouldn't give them some bread? (53)

In answering these "evaluation" level questions, students who have not read the story can certainly arrive at plausible (and brief) answers on the basis of their own knowledge and the information provided in the questions themselves.

A more recent taxonomy of reading questions (Pearson & Johnson, 1978) is based on theoretical advances in reading; questions are considered within a context that includes both the text and the reader. Earlier taxonomies considered only the text (see Ruddell, 1978 for another exception). That is, instead of simply focusing on questions, Pearson and Johnson's taxonomy considers question-answer relations (QARs). The taxonomy consists of three types of question-answer relations, which are based on the sources readers use to answer questions. The categories include:

- *Textually explicit*: In order to answer the question, the student read or pointed to the appropriate information in a sentence in the text. "Reading the lines."
- *Textually implicit*: In order to answer the question, the student integrated information across sentences in the text. This required the reader to make inferences on the basis of data in the text or generate connections that the author had left unstated. "Reading between the lines."
- *Scriptally implicit*: In order to answer the question, the student used her/his own script or schema in a way that was relevant to the question and the text. Though the question is related to the text, the reader's answer is based on prior knowledge. "Reading beyond the lines."

This taxonomy is much more useful for helping teachers formulate a variety of questions for their students. For one thing, the taxonomy is based on a far more robust view of the reading process and the process of questioning; it suggests that the quality of a question is a function of student response. Thus, a question might fit more than a single category if it invites a response from one reader that is "scriptally implicit" and a response from another reader that is "textually implicit" (see Wixson, 1983 for examples). This taxonomy also indicates that response variation is not only to be expected but to be appreciated.

Once you've become comfortable with the question-answer categories in the taxonomy, you may find it useful to analyze the difficulties students encounter in reading activities that are dependent on questioning. If, for example, you observe that students are sticking closely to the text in a postreading discussion (i.e., giving textually explicit responses), you might consider the following questions:

- Can the questions be reworded so that they more clearly invite the sort of responses/answers you had anticipated? Or at least a larger variety of responses?
- Do students' responses provide clues to their need for greater background knowledge (or to activate what they know)? Is instruction needed in some specific comprehension strategy?
- What about your follow-up responses/questions? Do they help students clarify their responses, expand upon them (Ruddell, 1978), generalize from them about how to respond to these kinds of questions in the future (Riley, 1979), or connect one reader's response with another?
- Are you sure that the text provides the data you think it does for the students to arrive at the response you anticipated? (It's easy to think the information is in the text when it is really in your own background knowledge but not that of the students.)

Although the Pearson and Johnson taxonomy has much to recommend it, it's possible to make instructional applications of this taxonomy that are as inappropriate as the instructional applications of other taxonomies. For example, both trivial and important questions may be constructed (Wixson, 1983), and publishers or teachers may use this taxonomy, just as they have used others, to generate incoherent questions that do not help students understand the text as a whole. Further, it's still possible to generate questions that distract from the essence of the text or to ask questions that can be answered without reference to the text. Although the taxonomy is based on a clear theoretical understanding of the reading process, unless publishers and teachers share that understanding, this taxonomy will not help teachers generate more meaningful questions for their students.

QUESTIONING IN WRITING

Asking good questions is also an important part of writing instruction. In general, questions should be designed to help students discover strategies used by proficient writers in selecting topics, finding details to explain topics, and deciding what needs to be done next in their writing. Graves suggests that questions "may temporarily cause discrepancies between intention and what is on paper. The art of teaching is to ask questions in the midst of the person's competence" (Graves, 1983, 213).

Many writing experts (e.g., Calkins, 1983, 1986; Graves, 1983; Murray, 1982) provide examples of possible questions, which may be helpful for teachers who are just beginning conferences and need to get a better feel for the kinds of questions that are generally successful. Those who give lists of sample questions frequently categorize them; the categories themselves provide information on what sorts of conference topics are possible. However, although it's possible to list questions that are useful in conferences as we do later in the chapter, it's not possible to ask effective questions, questions that will help students learn, without taking into account the students and the context in which they are writing. As Graves says, "Questions cannot be transferred from child to child" (Graves, 1983, 107).

Murray (1982) remarks that he searched for years for the right questions, and although he still finds questions useful in the beginning of his work with students, he also finds that they become unnecessary. Students learn to ask themselves the same sorts of questions and to begin conferences by addressing the questions he might have asked had they allowed him time. That certainly is something to strive for: asking questions that are so predictable and useful, students come to anticipate them and then move to taking control of conferences.

Asking questions that will encourage students to verbalize successes, problems, and solutions to problems in writing is an important part of questioning. However, it's also important to learn to wait for student responses and then to listen to what students are saying. Sometimes the wait can be very long, but the thinking that the student does is well worth it. Your listening skills may be sorely tested for a while. Though we often tell children to listen, we don't realize the intensity of concentration good listening requires until we have conducted conferences. Be patient with yourself as you learn to ask questions, learn to wait, and learn to listen. Be patient with the students as they learn that they must take control of their own writing in order to learn.

PROCESS QUESTIONS

Questions that encourage students to reflect on what they're doing as they read and write can help them consider how they handle various aspects of the reading and writing processes. Process questions in reading and writing may be asked no matter what the content. They help students become aware of what they do before, during, and after writing/reading a text, and why.

For example, questions such as "How did you choose this book to read?" or "How did you choose this topic to write about?" will elicit reflections on aspects of the prereading/writing process—what the student relies on in selecting reading material, what the student considers in selecting writing topics. When questions like these are asked in a group situation, students may discover from each other criteria for text and topic selection they had not previously considered using.

Questions such as "What difficulties are you encountering as you read/write and how are you dealing with them?" will elicit reflections on aspects of in-process reading/writing behavior. Questions such as "Has anything made you think of (title) since you read it? What? Why?" or "Have you learned anything since you wrote this that makes you look at your writing differently?" elicit reflections on postreading/writing behavior. These types of questions can be asked either during individual conferences or in group discussions. Directed to an individual or a group, such questions encourage students to be sensitive to those aspects of reading or writing under consideration. Asked in group situations, such questions encourage individuals to share their experiences and broaden their thinking when they read and write. Even when students can't provide an answer for a question or provide a negative answer, the fact that you've asked it will heighten their sensitivity to the point you've raised. The first time you ask a student about whether s/he has thought again about a piece of reading material since s/he read it may be the first time the student ever even considered that as a possible reading behavior.

In a similar manner, students who have no idea of how they choose reading material or writing topics are likely to pay greater attention to their selection criteria the next time they choose a text or topic because you've asked about it. You can encourage this by asking related process questions: "The next time you choose a book to read (or a topic to write about), pay attention to what kinds of things made you choose that book (topic) over others. How do you suppose you might figure out what makes you decide what book to read (topic to write about)?"

STUDENT-GENERATED QUESTIONS

A lot has been written recently about encouraging students to ask their own questions in reading instruction (Balajthy, 1984; Clark et al., 1984; Cohen,

1983; Kitagawa, 1982; Lindquist, 1982; Singer, 1978; Wong & Jones, 1982). Medway (1981) describes learners as "questioners"—"drawing conclusions, expressing surprise, speculating on implications, formulating hypotheses" (15). F. Smith (1982a), applying the same notion to reading, describes it as a process of getting *the reader's* questions answered.

Encouraging students to ask questions in the process of writing is equally important. In a community of writers, writers are also readers of each other's material who can help each other develop as writers by asking questions of each other as they write. The questions teachers and students ask about each other's writing transfer to individual writing in the form of self-questioning. In conferences with you, students see those aspects of writing that proficient writers need to concern themselves with demonstrated for them. Students learn to ask about those same things in conferences with their peers and ultimately to ask those same questions of themselves in the process of writing. Questions writers ask themselves while they write shape the writing as it is done on a minute by minute basis and encourage writers to reflect on whether or not they are fulfilling their intentions.

It would seem that teaching students to formulate and answer their own questions would stimulate the "questioning" that Medway, Smith, and others describe as important. We will address that topic next, but we can't help but wonder if we are really teaching students to ask questions or whether we are encouraging them to ask questions. After all, children are veteran questioners before they enter school. In school, it becomes clear to many students that teachers ask the questions (for which they often know the answers). But once students are asking the questions, our job is to help them ask the kinds of questions that will facilitate their construction of meaning when they read and write.

Regrettably, in reading, students find themselves responsible for identifying levels of questions by name and for generating questions at a variety of levels in classrooms where teachers have become enamored of question taxonomies and decided that it's just the thing for students, too.

Nothing suggests that learning taxonomic labels (literal, inferential, etc.) is necessary to students' understanding how to ask good questions. On the contrary, we would argue that teaching students question taxonomies in an effort to help them learn how to ask better questions may be detrimental to such an effort. Labels themselves have little or nothing to do with developing a real understanding of what is labeled. Students may focus their attention on trying to remember what the labels are and what they mean rather than on discovering how to use them in any significant way. Further, the traditional categories of comprehension taxonomies are of no more use to students than they are to teachers.

It's important to encourage students to ask questions in reading and writing and then to help them in asking the kinds of questions that will encourage them to construct meaning effectively. To accomplish this, continue to demonstrate questioning strategies by asking questions. But start paying attention to the questions you ask and the answers you get in response (the question-answer relationships); work on changing your questioning if necessary.

Second, invite students to ask questions but do it as if questioning was a natural part of learning rather than the end goal. There's a difference between "What do you want to learn about?" and "It's time to ask each other questions." Involve students in situations such as peer conferencing or group conferencing, in which they are naturally expected to ask each other questions.

Move students from asking each other questions to asking themselves questions as well. Atwell (1984), for example, taught her students to "self-conference." She asked her students to read their pieces to themselves, suggesting that the best writers often spend a great deal of time rereading and thinking about what they have written. Then, the students asked themselves questions from the list of questions in Figure 7—1, which they had constructed together with their teacher after participating in many conferences with each other. They found that engaging in other types of conferences sometimes became unnecessary because they had already asked themselves the questions that others often asked. Even when students still need a conference with the teacher or with each other, previous self-questioning will ensure that the time spent in the conference is much more effective.

The Atwell list is a sophisticated one that may not be entirely appropriate for the students with whom you work. But you and your students will benefit from constructing your own list as Atwell and her students did. Use the emphasis on content in Atwell's list as a guide. Consider the number of questions; help your students think about which important aspects of writing come up most frequently in conferences rather than listing all the questions they suggest. And if you have a small enough group of students, help each student individualize the list at least in part.

Teachers should also consider abandoning "rapid-fire" questioning in reading and writing and providing longer "wait time" for students (Gambrell, 1980; M. P. Rowe, 1974; 1986). Increasing wait time from the usual second or less to about five seconds has positive effects for those asking and answering questions:

- Response length increases.
- The number of unsolicited but appropriate responses increases.
- Student failure to respond decreases.
- Student confidence increases.
- Speculative thinking increases.

You may also wish to demonstrate your own reflections about the sorts of questions you are asking by occasionally talking aloud about the kinds of questions you want to ask the students and why you want to ask them before you ask them. Or if you ask a question that goes nowhere, take a chance and talk aloud about what your intentions were in asking the question, what it was about the students' responses that led you to understand that the question didn't work, and so on. By reflecting aloud about your own questioning process

FIGURE 7–1   Having a Writing Conference with Yourself (from Atwell 1984)

Questions about Enough Information

Have I told where, when, and with whom this is happening?

Have I clearly explained what I mean? Is there any part that might con-
fuse my reader?

Have I described the scene and people so well that my reader can see
and hear my story?

Do people talk? Have I put quotation marks around the words people say
out loud?

Have I used examples to show what I mean, instead of just telling?

What's the most exciting or interesting part of the piece? How can I build
on it?

Questions about Too Much Information

What parts aren't needed — don't add to my point or story? Can I cross
them out?

What is this piece really about? Are there parts that are about something
else? Can I cross them out?

Do I have more than one story here? Which is the one story I really want
to tell?

Is this a "bed-to-bed" piece, going through every event of a day? Can I
keep the important part of the day and cross out the unimportant parts?

Is there too much conversation? too many little details? Have I explained
too much?

Questions about Beginnings

Does my beginning bring my reader right into the action of the story or my
main ideas?

Where does my piece really get going? Can I cross out the first paragraph? the first page?

Questions about Endings

Does my ending leave my reader wondering?

Does my ending go on and on?

How do I want my reader to *feel* at the end? Does this ending do it?

What do I want my reader to *know* at the end? Does this ending do it?

Questions about Titles

Does my title fit what my piece is about?

Is my title a "grabber"? Would it make a reader want to read my piece?

Questions about Style

Have I said something more than once?

Have I used any words too much (such as *and, then,* or *said)*?

Are any sentences too long and tangled up? too short and chopped up?

Have I paragraphed or indented often enough to give my reader's eyes
some breaks? Have I broken up my piece by paragraphing too much?

Is this the way things happened, in this order? Have I grouped together
ideas that belong together?

Does the voice telling the story stay the same — *I* or *he* or *she?*

Does the verb tense stay the same — *present* (I am doing it now) or *past*
(I did it before)?

and the difficulties you encounter, you should help students internalize criteria that will enable them in turn to formulate more effective questions:

- Questions ought to involve students in *thinking* about text, in thinking about constructing meaning effectively.
- Questions ought to involve students in uncovering connections between the text and their experiences, lives, thoughts, feelings, and attitudes.
- Questions ought to involve students in authentic conversation with their community of readers and writers (each other and you) about aspects of the text.
- Questions ought to require the readers or writers themselves to decide what was important about the text and how they can organize a presentation of the text for others.

If you and your students use these criteria to reflect on the relationship between the questions being asked and the sorts of responses they inspire, all of you will soon be asking questions that encourage genuine thinking before, during, and after reading or writing a text.

CONCLUSION

In this chapter we have presented some general ideas about reading and writing instruction that underlie the specific lessons presented in the following chapters. We have discussed demonstration, discovery, and guided use as powerful teaching strategies. We have spent considerable time talking about conferencing as an important tool used by teachers to respond to students' instructional needs and about questioning, which plays such an important role in instruction.

The instructional ideas presented here urge students to take responsibility for their own reading and writing and encourage teachers to reconsider their own roles as they move from being "teachers" to becoming "facilitators" of students' literacy development.

VIII

Prereading instruction

It's been said that reading begins even before a book is opened (Watson, 1978b). That is, even before we open a book we have some expectations about what we'll find between its covers, and these expectations will vary with regard to content, language, and structure from text to text. If we've heard of the author Agatha Christie, for example, our expectations will be even more specific, particularly if we've already read other books by this same author. We expect a mystery with both the characteristics of mysteries in general and of Agatha Christie mysteries in particular.

Prereading expectations or predictions guide our reading when we begin a book. These predictions are extremely important to the process of reading; good readers constantly confirm and disconfirm predictions they've made both before and during reading. The more knowledge readers already have, the more likely their predictions and the easier they will find reading the book. It's clear both from our own experiences as readers and from research that the amount of background information possessed by a reader affects comprehension (Pearson, Hansen & Gordon, 1979). If you want to remind yourself of what it's like to read with inadequate knowledge, try the statistics passage again in chapter 2.

It's not enough simply to have the background knowledge—knowledge must also be activated in order for it to be helpful (Bransford & Johnson, 1972). Many students, however, including LD and remedial students, do not spontaneously activate that knowledge.

Thus, there are two ways that teachers might help students prior to reading a text: they can help students activate the knowledge they already have that is related to the text or they can help students increase their relevant knowledge prior to reading a text. Sometimes both are

143

necessary. The lessons presented in this chapter will either help students activate existing background knowledge, increase knowledge, or both.

ACTIVATING STUDENT KNOWLEDGE ABOUT TEXT

Students' knowledge can be activated in a variety of ways—with and without the concurrent presence of the text that is to be read, with a variety of textual cues when the text is present, and with varying degrees of teacher direction or assistance. Although teacher direction and assistance is important and in some cases absolutely necessary, our focus here will be on presenting lessons in which teacher direction and assistance may be withdrawn gradually as students develop independence in activating knowledge prior to reading. Research indicates that instruction is most effective when students are encouraged to apply strategies independently and to become actively involved in their own learning (Stephens, 1985). Reid and Hresko (1981) note that in most cases, teachers design the strategies that are taught to students, and although LD and remedial students prove amenable to learning the strategies, knowing the strategy does not guarantee that it will be activated (Wong, 1985) or activated in appropriate settings (Deshler et al., 1984). We concur with Reid and Hresko (1981) that, although teacher involvement may be necessary in early instructional stages when a strategy is being learned, teachers must replace their assistance with more and more student involvement, not only in using strategies but also in selecting the strategies that may be of use given the particular demands of the setting.

PREVIEWING THE TOPIC

Teachers have long made it a practice to inform students of the topic of a text prior to reading in order to establish a purpose for reading the text. Basal reader teacher guides are infamous for suggesting exactly how this should be done, sometimes even providing the exact wording. Usually teachers are advised to give students some information from the text or related to it and then have them "read in order to find out." Beck, McCaslin, and McKeown (1981) found that many introductions of topic and purpose are misdirective or too narrow in scope, or divulge excess content. Topic introductions may require that students read for information or ideas that are not contained in the text or that do not reflect the major ideas of the text. Revealing too much about the topic may leave readers with little motivation to read the text.

Topic introductions contribute to another problem, increased student passivity. The teacher provides information and a purpose for reading. The teacher tells the students everything. The teacher does all the talking and the students listen (presumably).

One alternative to this sort of introduction is *already-know time* (Hampton, 1984), which involves students in thinking and talking to activate their *own* knowledge of the topic. Once teachers have presented the topic, they provide no further information but assume the role of discussion leader, drawing information out of the students and encouraging them to organize it. First, the teacher asks students to relate to the group what they already know about the topic. One LD teacher who did this with three sixth graders on the topic of the United States wrote the students' "already-know" statements on large chart paper so everyone could watch as they were written. The following statements were generated by these students during their first brainstorming session:

- The national bird is the bald eagle.
- There are fifty states.
- There are many different kinds of people in the U.S.
- The U.S. is a country.
- There are billions and trillions of people in the U.S.
- The U.S. is a free country.
- There are thirteen white stripes on the flag.
- People come from all over the world to live in the U.S.
- The U.S. is in North America with Canada.
- The U.S. has a President as the head of the country.
- The U.S. has the Empire State Building and the Statue of Liberty.
- The U.S. has lots of beaches on the shores.
- The states have different things they're famous for.

Next students reread their statements and think of questions they have about the topic. When one student isn't sure of the veracity of an already-know statement, another may turn it into a question so that its accuracy can be checked. The students' questions from the first brainstorming session were committed to large chart paper as follows:

- Why can the Russians come here and travel where they want? Why can't we travel where we want in Russia?
- How is life in the U.S. different from life in Russia or China or Africa?
- Is Africa like the U.S.A.—with states?
- Why do they call different parts of Denver by different names? (reference to all the suburbs)
- Why does the President say bad things about the Russians?
- How should they solve the nuclear war problem?
- Who's the President of the world?
- Why do they vote for President every year?
- Does the President have a boss?

On another day, these already-know statements and questions were categorized by the students, a task that generated more statements and more questions. The students developed a whole series of statements and questions about the flag, which revolved around its description, and questions about the origin of its colors and the number of stripes and stars.

As a result of this categorization, students will develop a well-organized body of statements and questions that will, it's hoped, make it easier for them to organize the new knowledge they gain during reading. Most students, even older ones, have greater success with this organization task if the statements and questions are printed on paper and cut apart so that they may be moved about on a desk or tabletop. Encourage students to share various ways of organizing statements and questions. There will be interesting differences that may generate more discussion on the topic.

Langer's Pre-Reading Plan, or PReP (1981, 1982), is a similar prereading strategy. In PReP, the teacher begins, "Tell anything that comes to mind when you hear the word ————." The word (or phrase) is to represent or name the topic the students will be reading about. Or, to get started, you might show the students a picture that represents the topic. As the students respond, the teacher writes their responses on the board.

When the associations with the word, phrase, or picture have been listed, the teacher asks, "What made you think of [*naming each of the responses on the board in turn*]?" This question encourages students to become aware of each other's associations, the genesis of these associations, and their usefulness given the topic about which they will be reading. This step helps students realize that they have information in their heads that they can link to a topic prior to reading. In the final step of PReP, the teacher asks students, "Based on our discussion, have you any new ideas about [the topic word, phrase, or picture]?" This step encourages students to talk about associations that have been elaborated or changed as a result of the discussion.

If a topic is controversial or likely to generate varying opinions or feelings, a debate might be used to help students identify what they already know and believe. Once you've introduced a topic, ask students to write down their views, pro or con, about the topic. Let them share individual views in either a pro or con group, and then hold a debate based on their discussions. After students have read the text, they can compare and contrast their own views with the author's point of view. Of course, students' interpretation of the author's point of view will be affected by their individual opinions.

These lessons are useful not only as prereading activities for a single text but also in beginning a thematic unit that uses a number of texts on one topic. If students are about to begin a unit on insects or on folktales, they can start out by discussing what they already know and what they'd like to know. Or if it is appropriate, they can begin by debating the topic.

Other prereading lessons have been successful in activating students' prior knowledge, but they are not as amenable to eventual student independence. For example, several researchers recommend providing a familiar example of the theme, an event, or whatever is highlighted in the text from students' lives. Gagne and Memory (1978) suggest this approach, which aims to encourage students to discover what the example has in common with the textual passage. Au (1979) also recommends that teachers introduce content from students' experiences into discussions of reading texts, encouraging students to relate their experiences, and then helping students to link their experiences with text content after reading.

Although these researchers have shown that these lessons are successful in increasing comprehension, the lessons themselves are dependent on teachers' rather than students' activation of background knowledge. Even if such lessons may not lead to long-term independence in the use of a particular strategy, some instructional situations could call for their use. Long-term considerations such as independence in using a strategy may be less important when students require immediate comprehension support for a specific text, at least at the time. However, we recommend that you consider ways in which *students* can learn to generate their own ideas prior to reading, especially as you review what we recommend in the section of the chapter on previewing the text.

As students gain some facility in using prereading strategies, remember to encourage them to use these strategies independently, starting perhaps with the support of a small group, then a partner, and then on their own. The strategies used by students may be like those you've presented, or they may be generated by the students independently. From time to time during this move toward the independent use of strategies, review with students how they are activating their knowledge of a topic and why it is important to do so.

PREVIEWING VOCABULARY

Frequently, teachers introduce "new" vocabulary before students begin to read a text. This introduction to new vocabulary is intended to increase students' knowledge of the meanings of words they'll encounter when they read and their ability to recognize these "new" words. Teachers introduce vocabulary in a variety of ways, ranging from putting a word like *pay* on the board, changing the *p* to an *s*, and asking children to pronounce the revised word, to providing students with a paragraph that features the words in context and requiring them to figure out what the words are and what they mean from the context. Probably the most common procedures require students to look words up in a dictionary or glossary prior to reading or to read single sentences featuring the words.

We would argue that such procedures require rethinking. There are a number of assumptions behind such procedures with which many teachers would not agree if they were consciously aware of them or if they had tested them. First, there is the assumption that students do not know the words that are to be introduced—that the words are not in their receptive oral vocabularies. How much time is spent "teaching" students what they already know? And what are we saying to the students who are unsure of their academic abilities when the subtle message they get in such lessons is that they don't know? We need to assume that LD and remedial students possess considerable knowledge, which we can build on in our teaching.

Even when students do not know the vocabulary that is to be introduced, its introduction may not be much help anyway. For most people, learning vocabulary wouldn't help them cope with the statistics passage in chapter 2. It is often the case that definitions of difficult words will not assist a reader in understanding a text in any significant way.

Another assumption underlying these practices is that students must be taught the words they don't know prior to reading. But when vocabulary is "taken care of" in this way, students don't develop independent strategies for word recognition or word meaning. Think of someone you know who has an extensive vocabulary—perhaps yourself. Almost invariably, these people do a lot of reading and they regularly encounter unfamiliar words, which they deal with while they are reading, not before reading. The same strategies proficient readers use to cope with new words can be learned by learning disabled and remedial students.

Yet another assumption is that the words suggested for introduction in teachers' guides are keys to understanding the text. Anyone who has examined the use of these words in the text itself and watched students struggle with other more important words that were not suggested for introduction knows how fallacious this often is. A related assumption is that the particular words that are to be introduced are important enough for each student to learn. Unless the students perceive that a word is relevant, learning is not likely to take place no matter how important teachers or publishers think a word is. Those of us who are inveterate readers bump into words we have not seen before, and we frequently pay little or no attention to them unless we judge them to be of immediate or long-term importance to us.

Given what we know about the reading process and reading development, vocabulary instruction should focus on providing students with the tools they need for dealing with vocabulary as they read rather than on teaching particular words. Specifically, we recommend:

1. Helping students develop independent strategies for recognizing words and their meanings.
2. Helping students judge when individual words they encounter while reading are worth worrying about and when they are not.
3. Helping to develop students' insights about how words are used in text.
4. Encouraging students' interest in words.

If these instructional goals are realized, students will learn to deal effectively with new vocabulary in text and will have the tools to teach themselves the vocabulary they find relevant.

We'd recommend few of the usual strategies for dealing with vocabulary prior to reading a text for the simple reason that they typically don't encourage independent strategies for dealing with new vocabulary. The two prereading strategies discussed below are directly connected with whole texts and involve *student* thinking and *student* talking rather than *teacher* telling. Other strategies for teaching vocabulary will be presented in the chapters dealing with in-process and post-reading instruction.

The first prereading vocabulary lesson, *vocabulary prediction* (M. A. Atwell &

Rhodes, 1984) is easily adapted for use with almost any text, expository or narrative, and at any grade level. The following lesson was used with a group of remedial readers. The teacher chose five words from the fable "The Partridge and the Fox" (Clymer & Martin, 1980), a basal reader story. The teacher wrote each word across the top of the blackboard, leaving plenty of space to write children's definitions. The teacher read a word, provided thirty seconds' "thinking time" for a definition, and then wrote the children's definitions under the appropriate word. The children's responses were as shown in Figure 8–1.

The teacher then asked her students to read the story. As they read, several exclaimed, "I found it! That's what it means!" After reading the story, the children discussed it, and then attention returned to the children's prereading guesses. With each word in turn, the teacher inquired, "What does the word mean as it's used in the story?" and the group looked to see if one of their definitions matched. For "spoke," "wish," and "partridge," the children quickly located the appropriate definitions, already on their prereading lists. "Brush," on the other hand, was used differently in the story than anyone in the group had guessed, as a synonym for "bush." Here is a child's response to that discovery:

CHILD: We forgot to put that one up [on the board]!
TEACHER: Did you know it before?
CHILD: Yeah, I knew it before. It means like a bush.

"Preen" was a word for which students had to guess definitions prior to reading the story. When the teacher asked what "preen" meant in the story, three children took part in the exchange that followed:

CHILD: It means pretty feathers. [*Child reads the sentence with the word in it.*] "The partridge preened her feathers."
SECOND CHILD: It means like she feathered them down, like petted them.
TEACHER: Have you ever seen a peacock preen its feathers?
THIRD CHILD: Yeah, they open them up so they're pretty.

We think you'll agree that this is an impressive lesson, especially for a group of remedial readers from an inner city school, one of whom had language difficulties. It certainly reinforces what we said earlier about several of the assumptions we make in introducing vocabulary to children. These children not only had plenty of experiences to bring to bear on the vocabulary that was being given attention, but they solved *for themselves* the vocabulary they didn't know by reading the text and using the clues contained there.

Note that in this example the teacher didn't discuss grammatical functions with the children. She did note for herself, however, that they had intuitive knowledge of the fact that many words can serve a variety of grammatical functions. Nor did she discuss with these young children the insights that many older students can consciously deal with: that words often have a number of meanings and that various meanings for a single word are sometimes related

---

FIGURE 8–1   Words with Children's Definitions

Brush
brush your teeth
brush your hair
brush the sidewalk
brush the chalkboard
eraser with a brush on the end
brush your clothes off
paintbrush
brush by somebody

The children discussed "sweep" as an alternative to "brush the sidewalk," and "erase"as an alternative to "brush the chalkboard." "Brush by somebody" was dramatized by several children.

Spoke
something on a branch that's
    sharp
talk to somebody
a spoke that's in bike tires
spoke in a needle

A child who had severe language problems was a part of this group and volunteered the first and last guess. The others decided he meant "thorn" by the first guess; the last guess is probably in reference to "spike."

Preen
touch
practice test
preen beef
cut somebody
pinch somebody

This was a new word to the children, and guessing had to be encouraged. The boy with language problems gave an answer that the group discovered meant "prime beef." "Practice test" no doubt came from the "pre" of "pretest."

Wish
wish you had something you
    wanted
make a wish
wish something bad doesn't
    happen
wishbone inside a chicken
wishing well

Note the children's intuitive use of the word in a variety of grammatical functions. The "wishing well" response was followed by a story of how the child used to live by one.

Partridge
the bird in the Christmas song
the Partridge Family on TV
a porch

Some marvelous responses from children who weren't expected to know this word! The last response is a guess from a child who was not familiar with the word.

---

and sometimes not related. Further, this teacher did not insist that children provide definitions in the true sense of the word. She accepted the fact that young children typically use the word in a phrase or sentence or provide a function for the word rather than defining it.

Teaching often grows spontaneously out of students' responses and should be considered the responsibility of everyone in the group. For example, it was the students who figured out that the boy with language difficulties meant "prime beef" when they asked him what he meant and he described the purple markings on the side of meat. On the other hand, in another lesson, the teacher took the responsibility for clarifying a child's response. In response to "tide," the children provided "sea tide," "detergent (Tide)," "tied shoes" and "tied in a race." As the teacher wrote the children's responses, she asked them to compare the spellings of "tied" with "tide" and then led a discussion on the difference between the words.

In general, teachers should prepare this lesson by reading the text that students will read and choosing between six and ten words that students may not know or that have multiple meanings. They can then ask students to give a definition for each word, either orally or in writing, without referring to any source other than their own knowledge, guessing a definition for those they do not know. The group can share and discuss definitions for each word, focusing on the variety of definitions and the semantic similarities of some of the definitions, and if appropriate for the students, perhaps recognizing the various grammatical functions the definitions might play in the text.

After reading the text, ask students to reconsider the words you've selected, discussing how they knew what the word meant in the text, how or if the postreading definition related to any of the prereading definitions, and perhaps, the grammatical function(s) the word played in the text.

Though students may learn new vocabulary items in this lesson, the main goals are to help them gain insight into how words work in our language, how they are used in text, and what clues can help them figure out their meanings. In the process of the lesson, the teacher demonstrates a belief that students already know a great deal about words and that *they* can figure out more. This lesson is a powerful one for vocabulary, but you are likely to find that the direct attention given to words prior to reading the story interferes with text comprehension. For that reason, we recommend that it be used sparingly and that students reread the text after the lesson for greater comprehension.

Another prereading lesson for introducing vocabulary—*conceptually grounded vocabulary*—may be integrated with a number of other lessons presented in this book. As an example, consider the lesson in which students develop and share already-know statements and questions about a topic. As they share the statements and questions, they may use vocabulary not known by everyone in the group. The attention given to this vocabulary doesn't have to be formal— words do not have to be listed, defined, or tested. But if a student uses a word in a statement that may require some explanation or elaboration, encourage the student to explain or define the word: "Would you tell us what you mean by the term ———?" or "Tell us more about ———" is usually all that is needed. The same sorts of questions and discussions are integral to a number of other lessons that are presented in the following sections of this chapter.

If you use a more formal approach to conceptually grounded vocabulary, you might also use the categorizing idea presented earlier in our discussion of already-know statements. Students will have used a great variety of vocabulary in their brainstorming, vocabulary that can be organized into categories or into a semantic web to reveal the relationships among the words. The categorization of vocabulary will generate further thinkng and discussion about the meanings of the words used earlier. In fact, if the categories are referred to during and after reading, students will add new vocabulary as they integrate the words they've learned with the words they already know on their lists.

Once a prereading activity such as the already-know statements has concluded, ask: "Given the topic of the text, what words would you expect the author to use?" Many learning disabled and remedial students need direct questions like this in order to make the connection between the fact that the prereading activity and the knowledge it activated can be used to help them predict and confirm words in the text that may otherwise be difficult.

PREVIEWING TEXT

A wide variety of textual features may be previewed as a prereading activity. Some teachers and researchers focus on engaging students in previewing a single *text feature*, while others encourage the use of several text features in combination. Which text features are appropriate for previewing depends on the nature of the text and what the student might find manageable and useful, given the purpose of the reading. Text features which may be previewed include:

- Illustrations.
- Graphs.
- Charts.
- Titles and subtitles.
- Chapter questions.
- Introductory and summary paragraphs.
- Whole text—scanning.
- Relationship of chapter to other contents of book.

Previewing any of these text features replaces the introduction of the topic by the teacher that we considered earlier. For example, once students have previewed the text in some way in order to discover the topic for themselves, they can generate what they already know about the topic and what they want to know, i.e., a list of questions to be answered during reading. An alternative is to have students generate a list of predictions, on the basis of what they already know, of what they think the author will discuss and what questions they think the author will attempt to answer in the text. With either alternative, keep in mind that conceptually grounded vocabulary development should also be a part of the lesson.

Here are some examples of the text-previewing questions you might ask to encourage students' questions and predictions:

- From looking at the title (or other text features), what do you think this will be about?

- What would you like to know about the title (or other text features)?
- What does this picture (or other text features) make you wonder about?
- From looking at the subtitles (or other text features), what are some questions you expect the author to answer?
- Why do you suppose this graph (or other text feature) was used by the author?

Survey and *Size-up* (Schumaker et al., 1982), two more text-previewing strategies, require students to actively prepare to read. In Survey, students preview the introductory paragraph, the table of contents (to understand the relationship of the chapter to the rest of the book), and the chapter title and subtitles with a focus on chapter organization, illustrations, and summary paragraph. In Size-up, students preview the chapter questions, decide which answers they already know, read the chapter searching for clues to answers to the remaining questions, and recall as many ideas and facts as possible. In Schumaker's study, LD students learned to use these two strategies independently as well as a third strategy, *Sort-out*, a post-reading self-test over the chapter questions.

In a study of the use of text-previewing strategies, Wong and Jones (1982) found that secondary students who learned self-questioning, which included asking themselves why they were reading a passage prior to reading it, also improved their comprehension scores. In contrast, Idol-Maestras (1983) found that, although learning disabled students improved their comprehension scores with a "teacher-guided probing technique" in which they previewed various aspects of the text, comprehension scores deteriorated once the teacher no longer assumed responsibility for implementing each step of the preview. When the teacher, not the students, assumed responsibility for strategy implementation, students did not learn to implement the strategy for themselves. The contrast between the first two studies (Schumaker et al., 1982; Wong & Jones, 1982) and the Idol-Maestras study reinforces the idea that when students play a more active role in initiating and using a strategy, their comprehension improves.

Even when instructional materials discourage text previewing, the procedures suggested for using the materials can be adjusted. For example, if a student is experiencing difficulty with a sequencing worksheet of the kind often found in basal reader programs, an adjustment in how the task is approached will usually pay big dividends. Instead of following the usual directions to read the text and then put the statements that follow into the correct sequence, the student can activate the knowledge he needs to perform well on the task by attempting to put the statements in a logical sequence before reading the text, then reading the text, and finally reordering those statements that do not reflect the textual order. (See M. A. Atwell & Rhodes, 1984 for a more complete description of such a lesson.)

INCREASING STUDENT KNOWLEDGE ABOUT TEXT

We all occasionally find ourselves in reading situations in which we know little about the topic of the text. Sometimes we even feel as if we know nothing. In these situations, we have two choices: to use what knowledge we have to begin to understand the topic or to rely on an outside resource to activate related knowledge in order to help us begin to understand the topic. If we don't do one of these things for ourselves as readers, we risk reading the words on the page without comprehending the author's ideas.

In the same way, we must often increase our students' knowledge about a topic and help them relate new knowledge to prior knowledge. For poor readers, increasing knowledge is important not only from the standpoint of comprehension but also from the standpoint of word recognition. Students whose word recognition abilities are largely dependent on a supportive context will find themselves in a double bind when they have little background knowledge to draw on while they are reading. They are unable to use the information they have constructed during the comprehension process, which might help in word recognition, and unable to recognize enough words to construct meaning.

Teachers frequently assume, especially in the way content-area classes are taught, that students increase their knowledge as a result of reading. Although this is often true, knowledge increases only if students have enough knowledge to attach new information to, and know that they do; if students activate that knowledge (the subject of the previous section); and if the students' reading abilities permit them to deal effectively with the text. We've already shown that poor readers frequently do not have either well-developed strategies for activating knowledge that might be used in understanding text or a well-developed ability to orchestrate cues in text. Adding a lack of information about the topic to these problems puts poor readers in a situation they have no way of handling without outside help, usually from a teacher. This help needs to focus on building knowledge and *then* using it in reading the text.

What this argument implies is that text needs to be used more often, not as a major resource for learning new information but as a summary in a series of experiences designed to build students' knowledge about a topic (Stansell & DeFord, 1981). Many "tried and true" methods for increasing students' knowledge about a topic before they read about it have been suggested, methods that have been used by good content-area teachers for a long time. These lessons are, by necessity, teacher-directed although some involve students in directing some of their own learning once the teacher has provided initial instructional guidance. In the remaining sections of this chapter we will briefly review various lessons for increasing knowledge.

"HANDS-ON" EXPLORATION

If the topic permits, "hands-on" exploration such as that which often occurs in science lab classes, is an ideal way of increasing student knowledge prior to reading a text. Many of the recent studies of "excellence" in American schools have called for more active involvement of students in learning and have noted especially the disappearance of hands-on exploration from schools. Printed explanations cannot take the place of a student's individual discovery or direct observation of a fact, phenomenon, or feeling. In fact, active student observation and exploration makes an author's explanation come alive for the student.

For example, students observe a small pulley in their classroom and operate the pulley a number of times, lifting objects of various sizes, weights, and shapes. As they do so, they learn the appropriate vocabulary, as it is used by the teacher, to discuss what is happening. They find and sketch pulleys in operation outside of school. As a result of these experiences, they are able to draw on a wealth of information when they read about pulleys in their science textbook.

Hands-on exploration is especially important when knowledge is insufficient to support students' reading efforts. Field trips often qualify as hands-on experience—going to a petting zoo or to a museum that encourages students to touch and explore materials—but most hands-on activities can be done right in the classroom. Ideas for hands-on activities can be found in social studies, science, health, and other textbook teachers' guides.

Although the teacher makes the initial decisions about which learning situations will satisfy the students' need for additional information prior to reading, student exploration and observation offers many opportunities for student-directed learning as well. A teacher who is attentive to student leads and notes students' interests and spontaneous comments will be able to capitalize on these leads as students continue to explore the topic.

USING ALTERNATIVE PRESENTATION MODES

Good content-area teachers also know a great deal about presenting new information to students in a variety of alternative modes—films, filmstrips, lectures, videotapes, picture files, records, slides, field trips, graphic organizers or overviews, or any combination of these. Modes of presentation that provide students with more than one source of information are often the most successful; films and videotapes, for example, involve students in both hearing and seeing information simultaneously.

Although some teachers view alternative materials such as film as less academic and thus not appropriate for school except on an occasional and recreational basis, they are being shortsighted. Good students, even as adults, find that they can learn a great deal from materials such as films, which they cannot learn, at least not in the same way, from books. If you took a language-acquisition course in college, for example, you might have had the experience of seeing films of babies at various stages of language development. Such a phenomenon cannot be captured in the fullest sense in a book; observing it in action makes written accounts far more potent and comprehensible.

The key to whether an experience like watching a film is academic in nature or not is what the teacher does with the experience. If teachers consider it important and convey that sense to students it will serve an academic purpose. And remember that if the film or other presentation mode is conceptually dense, you may need to use a prefilm activity to activate student knowledge.

The argument for using alternative presentation modes is even more potent for those students who find learning from text inherently difficult. The alternative modes should not take the place of reading the text itself if one of the educational goals for the student is more effective reading. But it's often helpful to students if you provide alternative presentations prior to reading so that they have more knowledge about the topic to bring to the text. Some students may become interested in reading a book as a result of seeing a film.

Even lectures, which are probably most like texts in their presentation of information (except that the information is conducted through the ears rather than the eyes), have been shown to be helpful to subsequent reading comprehension. Stevens (1982) provided tenth graders with a prereading lecture on the Texan War of 1836 in order to increase their background information and found that students' subsequent comprehension of the related text improved.

The graphic organizer, or structured overview, is an alternative mode of presentation that usually also involves an oral presentation or lecture. A graphic organizer is usually designed by a teacher (though it is sometimes found in students' texts) to provide a framework or structure for the concepts presented in a text. The organizer should graphically depict not only the important concepts but also the relationship of one concept to another.

Examples of graphic organizers for the most common organizational patterns of expository text—cause/effect, comparison/contrast, time order, simple listing, and problem/solution—are provided in many content-area reading textbooks (see, for example, Readence, Bean & Baldwin, 1981). Narrative text can also be graphically displayed using story structure or mapping (McConaughy, 1980). Once the graphic organizer itself has been prepared, it should be orally presented by the teacher prior to students' reading of the text and referred to periodically both during and after reading.

Another sort of advanced organizer for narrative text has been suggested by Graves, Cook, and LaBerge (1983), who provided remedial junior high readers with detailed and lengthy previews of difficult short stories they had been assigned to read. The written previews began with information familiar to the students but also related to the theme or topic of the story. Questions designed to get students to activate and briefly discuss their own experiences were included with the information. A synopsis of the story up to the point of the story climax followed, describing the setting, the characters, the point of view, and the plot. The synopsis was connected to the preceding discussion of students' experiences. The entire preview session, including the reading and discussion, was teacher-led. Although students did not use the previews independently at any point during the study, they read the short stories independently.

Like some of the strategies presented earlier, these teacher-directed strategies are not likely to increase student independence in reading, but they are useful to consider given some of the circumstances in which learning disabled students and poor readers find themselves. A student's comprehension of a particular text does improve with teacher support. In spite of the fact that in these teacher-directed lessons it appears as if the teacher does a great deal of the text processing for the students, students' comprehension of the text, including material omitted from the previews, is significantly higher than when students are not provided with previews (see Graves, Cook & LaBerge, 1983 for a discussion of this point). Such lessons provide the immediate prereading support students need if they find themselves in a situation in which they are assigned difficult independent reading. Keep in mind, however, that support that leads toward long-term independence is far more powerful.

RELATED READING

While it may seem odd to discuss the reading of related texts as a prereading activity, it's probably obvious to you that what you learn from reading one text can be used in understanding another text. What students learn from reading one text generates new background information they can then apply to another text (Crafton, 1983).

Careful structuring of related reading can be of real help to poor readers, especially prior to reading often dry and concept-dense textbooks like those they must deal with in their content-area classes. If, for example, you are aware that students will be studying the Revolutionary War in their social studies class in the near future, it would be helpful to provide them with other less dry, perhaps shorter, and less concept-dense materials in advance of the textbook assignment. For a topic like the Revolutionary War on the secondary-school level, locate other expository and narrative pieces that are easier to read and involve students in exploring the ideas they present before reading their textbook assignments. Easier expository texts might be found in sources such as *Junior Scholastic* and made into a series of "skinny books" (Watson, in press) on the topic. In addition, historical novels about young people of their age who lived during the Revolutionary War period—*My Brother Sam Is Dead* (Collier & Collier, 1977) or *The Secret Soldier* (McGovern, 1975)—may help the period come alive for them.

A good children's librarian in either a school or public library can suggest related texts and help locate them. Or, if your students also need experience in locating materials in the library, involve them in finding their own related texts. Such skills prepare students to cope with textbooks that are simply too difficult for them to handle by finding similar material presented more simply.

CONCLUSION

Readers transact meaning by using their knowledge of language and their knowledge of the world. Even minimal reading comprehension depends on some level of background knowledge. But possessing relevant background knowledge isn't enough; readers must actively draw upon it as they transact meaning with the text. In this chapter we've presented teaching strategies designed to provide relevant background knowledge or help students activate the knowledge they already possess before they begin reading a text.

We also want to say something again about the role of teaching strategies, like those we've suggested, in reading instruction, since teaching strategies have been the source of some debate in the field of learning disabilities. The teaching strategies presented in this chapter are designed to raise student awareness about the importance of their own active involvement in their reading and about the sorts of prereading strategies used by proficient readers. We do not expect that students will totally embrace the strategies we've presented. It's unlikely that they will and we're not sure that this is even desirable. But we do hope that students will be induced to draw upon what they already know as they read. They may adapt the strategies we've used or they may invent strategies of their own. In either case, the key is that they become actively involved in their reading.

IX

In-process reading instruction

Teachers generally spend the majority of their reading instruction time on in-process reading—listening to oral reading or waiting for students to finish silent reading. If that describes your instruction, we hope the chapters preceding and following this one will help you understand the importance of pre- and post-instructional reading activities to reading development and put in-process reading instruction in its place. Because in-process activity will continue to remain an important aspect of your reading instruction, however, this chapter is devoted to instruction during the reading process.

From a socio-psycholinguistic standpoint, there are three goals for in-process reading instruction. Since students learn to read by reading, the primary instructional goal is to encourage as much reading as possible by *every* student. Two things need to be kept in mind in regard to this goal. First, you may be tempted to use many in-process strategies as listening strategies in which you read and students respond as if they had read. Although the strategies are valuable as listening strategies and may be introduced in that way, remember that the way students will learn to use the strategies in the process of reading is by reading, not listening. Related to this point, we will argue in the opening section of this chapter, "Oral and Silent Reading," that the practice of group oral reading detracts from the amount of reading done by each student. We also begin our discussion there because the lessons that follow require you to decide whether to involve students in oral or silent reading in both learning and using the strategy.

The second goal of in-process reading instruction, one that is basic to all reading instruction, is to encourage comprehension. In the second section of this chapter, entitled "Making Sense of Text," we have included various ways of providing support to students as they attempt to make sense of text.

The third goal is to help students develop effective and efficient strategies for dealing with words in text, strategies they can use independently in the process of reading that contribute to the construction of meaning. We will address this topic in the final two sections of the chapter. "Making Sense of Words in Text" suggests instructional strategies for ineffective readers, while "Learning Words and Other Text Features" suggests instructional strategies for emergent readers.

Before we turn to our discussion of in-process reading instruction, however, we need to restate a very important point: Reading instruction, including in-process reading instruction, cannot take the place of having students read texts. Although the instructional strategies in this and other chapters will increase reading effectiveness when used with students who have demonstrated a clear need for instructional assistance, they must not supplant students' opportunities for reading.

ORAL AND SILENT READING

Though professionals in the field of reading have been critical of oral reading practices for years (see, for example, Taubenheim & Christensen, 1978; N. D. Taylor & Connor, 1982; True, 1979), these practices continue almost unabated. By far, group oral ("round robin") reading is the most frequently observed reading activity in schools (Winkeljohann & Gallant, 1979). Our experience is that this is true even in remedial and LD classes. Teachers appear to prefer oral reading over silent reading and sometimes, students do also (Tovey, 1981). The younger the students or the less able they are as readers, the more likely it is that they will read orally rather than silently. Thus, the vast majority of a young child's or a poor reader's time in reading may be spent in listening to others reading text aloud while waiting for a turn to read.

When viewed in light of the in-process reading instruction goals we outlined earlier, oral reading fares less well than silent reading. First, much of the group oral reading that is characteristic of reading instruction does not engender a great deal of reading on the part of the participants (Allington, 1980; Hoffman, 1981). If you have not recently observed a group orally reading, plan to do so soon and keep track of how much actual reading is done by a couple of individual students. The entire group may read a story, but many of the individuals in a group read only a page or two. Watch carefully—some students know how to look as if they're reading without actually doing so. Once you've made your observations, consider seriously whether that page or two of reading (which may be the only reading of text the student does all day) is enough if a child's reading is to develop.

Nor does group oral reading lend itself to the development of effective, efficient, and independent reading strategies. The typical feedback provided by teachers and other students to miscues serves to reinforce the sort of reading observed in poor readers, reading which does not make sense. We will discuss this topic in depth later in this chapter.

In addition, group oral reading interferes with the most basic goal of in-process reading instruction, comprehension, especially for poor readers. When students read orally, their first consideration is usually to read the words correctly. If that is where students' attention is, it cannot be on comprehension at the same time (Hoffman, 1981; Winkeljohann & Gallant, 1979). Some students do so much oral reading with corrections from others that it leads them to believe that correct word recognition is the goal of all reading, including silent reading.

If the amount and kind of oral reading that goes on interferes with students' reading development, why does the practice persist? Apparently, oral reading persists because it has greater payoff for the teacher from the standpoint of management and of gathering information about student's reading, both authentic needs of teachers.

Teachers do need sane management techniques for groups of students, and they do require information on students' reading. The question then becomes: How can the teachers' needs be met so that the reading needs of students can also be met? Ideas about collecting information can be found in our discussion of observing and assessing students' reading in chapter 3. Other ideas about how to manage time during oral reading follow.

- There are many situations in which you can listen to students' oral reading that are much more authentic in purpose than group oral reading. Observations of oral reading can take place, for example, as students read scripts in preparation for Readers Theatre or when they are preparing a story to be read orally to younger children.
- You can listen to one student read while the others in the group are reading the same text silently (Johns, 1982). The student may be asked to read aloud whatever part of the text s/he had just finished reading silently, the next part of the text to be read, or a part of the text s/he found interesting. In individual oral reading conferences such as this, you can help students discover or consolidate problem-solving strategies for word recognition.
- If some or all of the students do not yet read silently, think about ways of allowing independent oral reading and doing it in such a way that the amount of reading can be increased substantially. For example, the students can be paired for oral reading, they can read along with a tape of the story, or they can simply read aloud to themselves.
- As the students read silently, talk with individual students about what they are reading, using questions like those listed in Figure 9−1. In these comprehension-centered reading conferences, encourage students to talk about what they are reading several times during the process of reading— before, during, and after reading a text or part of a text.
- Instead of using instructional time for in-process reading activities, you can use that time for prereading or post-reading activities designed to enhance the meaning students construct during the process of reading. Of course, this means that students will spend some of their independent work time silently reading text.
- Even poor readers *will* read silently on their own. You should firmly establish your expectation that the student will read; you should consider motivation for reading the text. Prereading activities that assist reluctant readers in

---

FIGURE 9–1   Reading Conference Questions

What would you like to tell me about what you've read?

Do you have any confusions about what you've read?

What have you been wondering about as you read this?

How did you decide to read this?

What kinds of things have you been wrestling with as you read this?
How have you solved the problem(s)?

If you had a chance to talk with this author, what would you talk with him/her about?

What do you plan to read next? Why?

Does this make you think of anything else you've read?

Why do you suppose the author gave this (book, article, etc.) this title?

What parts of this have you especially liked? disliked?

Do you like this more or less than the last thing you read? Why?

Is there anybody else in our class who you think would enjoy reading this? Why?

Did you skip any parts of what you have read? What? Why?

What is the main thing the author is saying to you?

Why do you suppose the author began this the way s/he did?

Would you like to be one of the people in this? Who? Why?

What other texts by this author have you read? Are the other texts similar in any way to this one?

Does this text remind you of others you have read?

---

making a connection between prior knowledge and feelings, and the text are important. So are consistent post-reading activities and discussions that firmly establish in students' minds that they must come prepared to post-reading meetings. Be patient but firm in establishing such expectations. If a student arrives at a group meeting without having read the text, ask her/him to silently observe the activities of the rest of the group. Next time you assign independent silent reading, remind that student of your expectations and that you'd like her/him to be able to participate in the group's activities this time. If the activities are ones that students find interesting, it should not be long before they are prepared for them.

- If you are teaching in a situation in which all the students read independently for a period of time, spend some of your time following individual conferences making anecdotal records about individual's abilities, needs, and interests in reading. Such records are invaluable for planning instruction.

MAKING SENSE OF TEXT

The basic responsibility of readers during reading is to make sense of text, to construct meaning in the process of reading. Readers who focus on word recognition rather than on meaning do not make sense of text while they read, nor do those readers who process the words in a text without actively interacting with the ideas presented by the author.

Though prereading activities will certainly help some ineffective readers refocus their attention and more actively process the text, such activities will not be sufficient for others. Even though the prereading activity may be solidly focused on activating students' knowledge about the topic to be presented in the text, some students will not understand that they are to use that knowledge during reading. Others do not sustain their focus on meaning, even though they may begin with that focus.

Nor are post-reading activities, like those we will explore in the next chapter, always sufficient to help students focus on meaning. Meaning must be constructed during reading if meaning is to be extended after reading. If post-reading activities constantly demonstrate to students that constructing meaning during reading is the goal of reading, some students will react by constructing meaning even though they may not have been observed to consistently do so in the past. Other students need additional assistance.

In the following section, we will discuss instructional strategies that help students learn to make sense of text, to monitor whether they are making sense of text as they read, and to learn to use various text features that help make sense of text. All these things will help students make more sense of text during reading and know what to do for themselves when they are unable to do so.

LEARNING TO MAKE SENSE OF TEXT: STRATEGY LESSONS

An effective way to teach students how to make sense of text is to demonstrate it yourself as you read (Davey, 1983; Pitts, 1983). As the teacher, you have frequent opportunities to read aloud to students—stories, excerpts from textbooks, newspaper articles, and so on. As you do so, think aloud about how you are processing text—how you construct meaning, how you decide what's important to know, how you relate information across sentences and paragraphs, how you deal with difficulties in making sense of the text, and so on.

Some of the many strategies you might demonstrate are listed below, along with wording used by teachers we have observed thinking aloud. This list is by no means exhaustive; other strategies that you use as a proficient reader will become apparent to you as you think aloud while reading text to and with students.

- Use your own background knowledge: "Oh, I've ridden a horse before and I know just what the author means when he says the girl was 'saddle-sore.'"

- Create visual images in your mind: "It's as if I closed my eyes and saw what the author is talking about—(describe the scene)."
- Check predictions: "Hmmm—the author isn't having this character do what I thought she would do next. Remember, I thought she was going to. . . ."
- Make an analogy: "This situation is like another one we've read about. . . ."
- Adjust reading rate: "I think I'll skim through this section—I don't think it pertains to what we want to find out."
- Determine what's important to understand from the text: "One way I decide what's important is to keep the subtitle of the section I'm reading in mind and think about how what I'm reading is related to the subtitle."
- Determine what's important to understand about the instructional situation: "The social studies teacher always wants people to be able to answer the questions at the end of the chapter, so I think I'll read them first so I know what information to look for."
- Use easier reading material: "I'm not sure I understand what this means and I know it's explained in this book over here, which is easier to read. I'll use the other book to learn what I want to know instead."
- Use sources other than books: "One way to learn about this is to keep reading this book, but the book is very hard to understand. Let's see if the librarian has a film or filmstrip that might help us."
- Reread: "You know, I don't think I was paying much attention when I read that last section. I'd better read it again."
- Read on: "I don't really understand what the author is talking about here. I hope he explains more in the next page or so."

It is also helpful to have the students discuss what you have done during your demonstration. After you have thought aloud as you read, ask students to help you list the strategies you used. Accept their way of describing the strategies and display the list somewhere in the classroom; keep adding to it and changing it to reflect their understanding more closely until you and your students are satisfied that you have captured a set of strategies useful in making sense of text.

You may also want to conduct some lessons to highlight a particular strategy. For example, some texts lend themselves especially well to having students visualize images of the action or scene described in the text (Clark et al., 1984; Miccinati, 1981; Rose, Cundick & Higbie, 1983). As students reveal what they have visualized during reading, they should discern differences between the images they have constructed, differences based on another strategy they are invoking—using background experience and information.

Encourage students to think aloud (Rose, Cundick & Higbie, 1983), to talk not only about what they have understood from the text but *how* they have understood it. This is often best done in a group situation. For example, one student can read a paragraph and think aloud while others listen and do the same thing silently; other members of the group can comment on the similarities and differences in the strategies they have used while reading silently. Then another student can continue with the next paragraph.

In the beginning, most poor readers need to think aloud at the end of each paragraph or so (sometimes after even smaller chunks of text) if they are to internalize reading strategies and use them consistently. When students are able to read much longer segments or whole texts and relate the strategies they have used during reading, they have internalized the strategies well enough that they no longer need help in monitoring their own comprehension. Your long-term goal is for students to be able to use these strategies independently during silent reading; keep moving them in that direction.

Some students may benefit from incorporating "comprehension rating" when they think aloud about text. Comprehension rating (Davey & Porter, 1982; Fitzgerald, 1983) requires that students rate their own understanding of something they have read by signifying their degree of understanding (e.g., "I didn't understand it very well"). Students may be asked to rate their comprehension of all or parts of a text.

Comprehension rating will also help poor readers to be more effective with yet another "fix up" strategy—learning to frame questions or requests for help (K. Goodman, 1982). Students who rate their comprehension of a text and discuss the meaning they have constructed also find that they have to put into words what it is they do not understand, to specify what parts of the text are causing them difficulty. Requesting help is a social skill that requires knowing how to specify the difficulty clearly enough so that someone is able to supply appropriate assistance.

We recommend the preceding instructional strategies because they are most similar to the processes proficient readers use in making sense of text. There are, however, a number of other worthwhile ways to help students make sense of text during reading that may be useful in a variety of situations and with some students. Some are completely dependent on teacher direction while others may eventually be used independently by students.

Teacher-dependent instructional strategies have one thing in common: the teacher prepares the text to direct students' attention to particular aspects of the text during reading. Of course, in this kind of lesson, students learn the content the teacher has highlighted. Although such strategies are useful in situations in which the sole focus of instruction is on helping students learn the content conveyed by the text, they may not help students learn how to deal more effectively with text.

An example of this sort of teacher-directed instructional strategy is the Selective Reading Guide-O-Rama (Cunningham & Shablak, 1975), which is much like a study guide but has the additional feature of providing written suggestions about how to process the text. The teacher determines what to direct students' attention to in the text and how to direct it. The teacher may ask the students to read a particular section (with identified page numbers) thoroughly and to list three major points made by the author, to skip another section, to read a summary before reading for supporting facts, and so on. Mateja and Wood (1983) showed how the Guide-O-Rama can be used with elementary materials, adding pictures for visual interest. Maier (1980) found that using a similar oral procedure for narratives assisted LD students in providing more organized and thorough retellings of stories.

A similar technique is the use of marginal notations or glossing (Richgels &

Mateja, 1984). The teacher supplies marginal notes keyed to the text, which guide students to focus on particular content and help them discover what reading strategies are best used to learn the content. Richgels and Mateja (1984) illustrate sample lessons, which reveal how glossing can be demonstrated by teachers and eventually used independently by students.

The graphic organizer, which we discussed as a prereading technique, can also be continued during reading. Instead of providing all the necessary information in the organizer prior to reading, the teacher leaves some out. The location of blanks for the missing information clearly shows where it belongs and what its relationship is to the rest of the text (Mateja & Wood, 1983; Pearson & Spiro, 1980; Readence, Bean & Baldwin, 1981). As students read, they fill in the blanks with missing information. This will enable students to discern the structure of a text and the relationships between pieces of information in a text, and to produce their own graphic organizers as they read in order to study and review important concepts. If students are to learn to produce such an organizer independently, however, the teacher needs to help them discuss how they found the missing information and how they knew where it fit into the organizer.

An alternative to the graphic organizer also involves students in filling in missing information but leaves them more in the driver's seat. Remember the already-know statements and questions in chapter 8? While students are reading, they can refer to their categorized statements and questions, confirm or disconfirm what they know, and answer questions their reading has generated.

Other instructional strategies, like notetaking and underlining, are probably more familiar. But teachers often expect students to take notes or underline important information without considering that they may need direct teaching if they are to do either effectively. Again, demonstrating what you do as a proficient note taker and underliner is a very effective way of helping students learn both strategies.

For notetaking, read the selection aloud to students and compose notes on the blackboard or on an overhead projector; think aloud about the process as you do so. Invite students to describe what your demonstration reveals and encourage them to decide what notes you ought to be taking and why. Then have pairs of students take turns reading a selection to each other while the listener takes notes; they can then discuss whether the notes captured the important points of the text and continue on to the next selection (Wood, 1983).

Underlining, another familiar strategy, is also useful in helping poor readers make more sense of text (Dyck & Cox, 1981; Poostay, 1984). To teach underlining (or highlighting), put the pages you will be reading on the overhead and as you read, underline what you consider to be important. Talk about why you are underlining key words and phrases, why you may connect one under-lined portion with another, why you are making notations in the margins, etc. Then, using another selection, have everyone work together on underlining, talking aloud the whole time about what decisions you are making and why. Finally, move to having everyone underline the same selection independently and discuss the results. (Make sure the students understand that there are lots of right "answers" here.)

All these lessons are most effective if you use materials the students are currently reading in their classes; you'll be helping students learn strategies that apply to many texts, but at the same time they'll be learning the content they need in their classes.

Several other strategies for making sense of text depend on a community of readers; that is, two or more students working together to make sense of text. As the teacher, you are part of the process until the students can proceed independently. One of these strategies, ratio reading (Greene, 1979), was explained in chapter 6, which discussed fluency. "Say something" (Harste, 1982) is similar in some ways to radio reading. Working in pairs, students look through a text and decide whether they will read the text orally or silently and how often they will stop reading in order to discuss what they have read. After each has read a paragraph or so, students stop reading and each one "says something" about what has been read. After reading through the entire selection and commenting in this way, the pair writes a summary of the selection and shares and discusses the summary with other students.

An adaptation of ReQuest (Manzo, 1969) is also suitable for helping students work together to make sense of text. In pairs, students read a predetermined piece of text silently, close their books, and then question each other about what they have read. Fitzgerald (1983) recommends an alternate procedure. In pairs, students read part of the text, generate questions for a second pair of students, continue doing this for the length of the text, and then exchange questions with the second pair of students. Each pair then answers the other pair's questions.

So that students learn to ask questions that are focused on important points, participate in the situation in order to demonstrate the sorts of questions that are worth asking. Encourage the students to ask questions that connect ideas across sections of the text, especially if the selections they are reading are short.

INCREASING KNOWLEDGE OF TEXT STRUCTURE

Making sense of text is sometimes difficult for readers because they do not understand how texts are globally structured or organized. To make sense of text, students need to employ intuitively the structures and structural cues authors use to convey meaning in text, both narrative and expository.

Well-formed narrative texts or stories are governed by a story grammar or structure. The "story grammar" includes those elements that researchers (Mandler & Johnson, 1977; Rumelhart, 1975; Stein & Glenn, 1979; Thorndyke, 1977) have found to be typical (stated or unstated) elements of stories:

1. A theme and plot.
2. A plot that contains episodes.
3. Episodes that each contain a setting and a series of events.
4. A setting that includes time, place, and character introduction.
5. A series of events that each contain:
   a. An initiating event that reveals a goal or problem.
   b. Attempts to achieve the goal or solve the problem.

c. Attainment of the goal or resolution of the problem.

d. Reactions of characters to the events.

Children in kindergarten and first grade have been shown to use this basic story structure to comprehend heard or read stories, to remember and recall stories, and to create new stories (Mandler & Johnson, 1977; Stein & Glenn, 1979). Basically, story grammar allows listeners and readers to comprehend or compose a story more easily because the story structure helps them remember the particulars of the story. It should be noted that no one claims that five-year-olds can label or explain story grammar elements; knowledge of story structure, like the majority of our other knowledge about language, is largely intuitive.

It should not be surprising that attempts to teach story structure explicitly to students have had mixed but largely negative results (Dreher & Singer, 1980; Gordon, 1980; Gordon & Braun, 1983; Sebesta, Calder & Cleland, 1982). We agree with the argument that "if [story grammar] is to aid many children, that aid is likely to come from knowledgeable...teachers who act as intermediaries between the story grammar concept and children's use of it as an aid to comprehension" (Sebesta, Calder & Cleland 1982, 184).

Compared to narrative structure, recognizing and using expository structure in texts is relatively sophisticated. Certainly narrative is more often a part of students' lives from the beginning—not only in the stories that are read to them, but also in retellings of family events, in TV cartoons, and so on. Researchers (Meyer, Brandt & Bluth, 1980; B. Taylor, 1980; B. Taylor & Samuels, 1983) have concluded that, compared to proficient adult readers, more students demonstrate an insensitivity to expository text structure and do not use structure to understand and remember information even from well-structured expository or factual texts.

Expository texts employ a wide variety of structures. We have listed the dominant organizational structures below, along with descriptions and cues commonly used by authors (the list is a combination of information from McGee & Richgels, 1985 and R. Vacca, 1981):

- Enumeration.
  Definition: listed bits of information (facts, propositions, events, ideas), sometimes qualified by criteria such as size or importance.
  Cues: first, second, third, next, then, finally, to begin with, most important, also, in fact, for instance, for example, etc.
- Time order.
  Definition: facts, events, or concepts in a chronological or time-ordered sequence.
  Cues: on (date), not long after, now, as, before, after, when, since, during, etc.
- Comparison/Contrast.
  Definition: similarities and differences established among facts, people, events, concepts, etc.
  Cues: however, but, as well as, on the other hand, not only...but also, either...or, while, although, unless, similarly, yet, different from, same as, alike, similar to, resemble, etc.

- Cause/Effect.
  Definition: shows how facts, events, or concepts (effects) happen or come into being because of other facts, events, or concepts (causes).
  Cues: because (of), since, therefore, consequently, as a result (of), this led to, so that, nevertheless, accordingly, if...then, thus, since, and so, etc.
- Problem/Solution.
  Definition: describes a problem and a solution and/or considered solutions.
  Cues: problem, difficulty, solution, etc.

Teachers should use narrative and expository text structure research in constructing activities for students that will help them use or further develop their intuitive knowledge of text structure. Reading professionals (see Beck & McKeown, 1981; Bruce, 1978; Fowler, 1982; Golden, 1984; K. Marshall, 1983; McConaughy, 1980; M. M. McGee & Richgels, 1985; Meyer & Freedle, 1979; Moldofsky, 1983; Moss & Oden, 1983; Rand, 1984; Sadow, 1980; Whaley, 1981) have written extensively about how teachers might take advantage of this research, and their instructional recommendations can be summarized as follows:

1. Read to students. Students develop an intuitive knowledge of narrative and expository structure by hearing and reading well-formed stories and expository texts. Some reading material designed for instructional purposes, e.g., primers, does not qualify as well-formed. If your students have little background in literature, begin with well-formed stories, such as the classic folk and fairy tales in which story structure is most salient, and expand to a wide range of narratives. Be sure to read expository text to students often, including younger children.
2. Encourage students to compare story elements across narratives and text structures across expository texts. With narrative material, compare new stories with past stories. Questions such as, "Does this story remind you of others we've read?" or "How does the boy's problem in this story differ from the boy's problem in the last story we read?," will encourage intertextual comparisons and, of course, discussion of story elements. A thematic unit based on a variety of narratives that feature a particular theme is helpful in encouraging students to make intertextual ties and discover story elements.

   In expository text, students can compare different structures within the same context and the same structure in different contexts. Meyer and Freedle (1979) provide examples of the first; they prepared three differently structured passages (compare/contrast, cause/effect, and enumeration) containing basically the same content. Students read all three passages and then discussed how the author organized or structured the information differently from one passage to another. Teachers can help students discover the differences, listing what students have observed for each of the passages on the board as they talk and encouraging them to generate a label to describe the overall organization.

   Using the same teaching procedures, you can also provide students with several passages that all feature the same structure but are concerned with different topics. You may wish to end this kind of lesson by referring to the label and the cues provided by researchers who have studied expository structures. However, do not insist that students use the labels researchers have invented; inventing their own labels leads to greater understanding.

3. Ask questions that lead students to notice and use various story elements or expository text structures. For example, here are some questions (from Marshall, 1983) you might ask during and after reading to help students focus on particular story elements:

- Initiating event:
  What is _____'s problem?
  What does _____ have to try to do?
- Attempts:
  What did _____ do about _____?
  What will _____ do now?
- Resolution:
  How did _____ solve the problem?
  How did _____ achieve the goal?
  What would you do to solve _____'s problem?

Here are some questions that will encourage students to attend to expository text structure:

- As (after) you read, write down the similarities and differences the author reveals with regard to...
- As (after) you read, jot down the problem the author discusses and list the solutions suggested.

Prereading discussions that establish a broad purpose for the students' reading will also help them key into important story elements or text structure: "Read to find out who the main characters are, what problems they are having, and how they solve those problems" or "Read to find out what steps are necessary in rotating tires on a car." Your goal is to help students learn to set purposes for themselves.

4. Involve students in story retellings, summaries, storytelling, drama, role-playing, or anything else that stimulates them to generate a story they have heard or read as a whole. In doing so, the students must work at generating a structure for the content. If students need guidance in such activities, ask questions that will help them include and structure the story elements.

5. Involve students in writing that encourages active thought about text structure, whether narrative or expository. Students can write narratives, both self-generated and based on literary patterns they have discovered in other stories. McGee and Richgels (1985) recommend a writing lesson in which students generate an expository text on the basis of a graphic organizer of a published expository text. After the students have written their text, they compare it to the original, focusing especially on the expository

structure and the cues they have used to create it. Many teachers assume that students can respond to writing tasks like "compare and contrast" without teaching students how to structure such a response, what cues might be beneficial to the reader, etc. Lessons like these should not only increase students' ability to use particular structures in essay exams or in assignments in content areas, they also increase their comprehension of expository structure during reading.

6. Provide students with open-ended frames to fill in as the text is read a second time or after reading. Narrative frames can be designed to focus on setting, character analysis, plot, or other single or multiple story elements. Fowler (1982) offers several story frames as examples, including the following one, which focuses on story plot:

In this story, the problem starts when _____
_____. After that,
_____.
Next, _____
_____. Then, _____
_____. The problem is finally
solved when _____.
The story ends when _____.

Expository frames can be designed to focus on the particular expository structure that has been used in the text being read. Here is an example of a frame used in reading a problem/solution expository structure:

In this passage, the problem is defined as _____
_____.
The various solutions that have been suggested include _____,
_____,
_____, and _____.
The author believes that _____
is the best solution because _____.

Though a frame can be helpful in focusing students' attention on story elements or expository structures, it can also be constraining and thus frustrating to students. The frame can become less constraining if you have the students copy the frame onto a sheet of paper as they fill it in, allowing the students to determine the amount of space they need for their answers. Also, encourage students to delete or add to the frame if they find it necessary to do so to capture the essence of the text.

Besides the global structures authors employ for narrative and expository text, they also use many other textual cues to structure meaning across sentences and paragraphs. Some of these cues are found in almost every text, while others are specific to a particular kind of text. We take many of the cues for granted—using "a" instead of "the" when a new topic or character is introduced, using subtitles to capture the main idea of the succeeding paragraphs, that one topic must logically precede another, referring back to an already explored topic, and so on.

An interesting way to call students' attention to these structural cues is the puzzle strategy lesson (Kucer & Rhodes, 1986). Basically, a text that is cut into pieces (usually paragraphs and subtitles, although a paragraph may also be cut into sentences in order to explore cues across sentences) is put together by the students, who discuss their reasons for the decisions they make during the task. These reasons, of course, are the cues the author used to structure the text as it was written. As students repeat this lesson with a number of texts, they'll discover a variety of cues that writers use to help their readers understand text (which they can use in their own writing to help readers understand text).

MAKING SENSE OF WORDS IN TEXT

Probably the most obvious characteristic of poor readers is that they don't make sense in the process of reading. Because these students frequently produce semantically unacceptable miscues, they provide listeners with little sense of what the text is all about. If a semantically unacceptable reading of the text mirrors the meaning that students construct as they read, it is unlikely that much learning occurs during reading.

For most students, oral reading behavior correlates highly with comprehension (Beebe, 1980); the student who produces many semantically unacceptable miscues usually constructs little meaning while reading. But there are always exceptions. It is not always the case that students who "butcher" text orally do not understand what they have read. Students who consistently produce poor quality miscues while reading text but show that they have constructed appropriate meaning may have made sense of print for themselves but may not feel the need to correct miscues for the benefit of those listening (D'Angelo, 1982). Unless there are extenuating circumstances (e.g., embarrassment over oral reading), such students do not need the instruction outlined in this section. These students are making sense to themselves, either by silently self-correcting (Recht, 1976) or by constructing appropriate meaning on the basis of redundant information.

However, most students who produce text orally that doesn't make sense to the listener are not making sense to themselves either. Frequently, if such students can be helped to make sense, comprehension will improve. It is these students that the strategies in the next section and elsewhere (Y. Goodman & Burke, 1980; Johns, 1975; Maring, 1978) will benefit most.

LEARNING TO MAKE SENSE OF WORDS IN TEXT:
STRATEGY LESSONS

What readers who don't make sense when they read need to learn is simply not to tolerate such a situation in reading any more than they would in speaking or listening. We usually begin by asking students to identify which of a number of sentences don't make sense and why. The "why" helps the student focus on the word(s) creating the absurdity in the sentence. For example, we used the following paragraph with a boy named Adam:

> I like to kick my soccer donut. Every day, after school, I go outside and kick it around. Sometimes I go over to my bear's house and ask him to play soccer with me. Sometimes I go over to the soccer field and kick it by myself.

It's important in the lesson or two that is usually necessary to have students *read* the sentences or paragraphs; when they listen, they can already distinguish what makes sense from what doesn't and only need to apply the same active "sense-making" strategies in written language.

Once students have learned to apply what they know about sense-making in oral language to written language, they must learn what information they can use to help themselves make sense of words in the text and what strategies they can use when they find word identification difficult. Poor readers' information sources and strategies are typically quite narrow; they usually rely on others (often the teacher) or "sounding out" for word identification. They need to broaden their sources of information and their strategies.

Through a series of lessons, Adam, for whom we wrote the preceding soccer donut passage, discovered a number of new sources of information he then began to use. In his own words, here is his list of new sources of information:

- Look at pictures. (illustrations)
- See how long word is. (word length)
- Think of what rhymes. (rhyme scheme)
- It says the same thing over and over. (repeated structures)
- Think about what I know. (background knowledge)

We don't have space to describe all the lessons that led to Adam's list of new information sources, but we'll describe one to help you think about the lessons your own students need.

To help Adam discover that he should rely on his background knowledge while reading, we presented him with some words from a Mother Goose rhyme that we thought would be difficult, isolated from the context and in a list— "nimble," "quick," and "candlestick"—and asked him to read them. He could not. We then asked him to recall and say the "Jack Be Nimble" rhyme and then to read the rhyme. After pointing out to him that he had just successfully read the three words he could not read a few minutes earlier, we asked him why he could read them this time. After we talked about his discovery, Adam added "Think about what I know" to his list.

In a follow-up lesson, we asked Adam to tell us the story of "The Three Little Pigs" and as he did so, we jotted down some of the words he used to tell the story:

- The first little pig.
- The big bad wolf.
- "I'll huff and I'll puff and I'll blow the house down."
- House of straw.

We showed Adam the list of words he had said, asked him if he would find those same words in a book containing "The Three Little Pigs" story, and then asked him to read the book, keeping in mind the words he knew would be there as he read.

We also helped Adam discover new reading strategies. In his words, they included the following:

- It needs to make sense.
- Read it over again. (reread)
- Read the rest of the sentence.
- Read the rest of the paragraph.

We'll describe the lessons we did with Adam that helped him learn to read the rest of the sentence. We presented Adam with sentences containing cloze blanks at a spot in each sentence where many possibilities could make sense. The information *beyond* the blank in the sentence was what Adam needed in order to decide which of many possibilities made sense within the context of the whole sentence. So that Adam couldn't possibly use the information beyond the blank at first, we covered up the remainder of the sentence and asked him to make at least three guesses that made sense. Thus, for the following sentence, we covered "in the pool" and he made a number of guesses, each of which was written below the blank.

> Let's go_____in the pool.
> now
> fishing
> shopping
> to the movies

After Adam had made his guesses, we uncovered the rest of the sentence and asked him to read the whole sentence and tell us if any of the guesses made sense. When Adam could read the whole sentence, he revealed what he knew must make sense ("swimming"). (Take care to help students understand that it is highly unlikely that they could come up with something that would make sense in a whole sentence like this when part of it is covered; there isn't enough available information.)

As we worked with Adam during this lesson, we asked questions like "How did you figure out that 'swimming' made sense for the blank?" "Is the information before or after the blank?" "What if you had come across a word here [*pointing to the blank*] and you didn't know what it was—where would you have found more information about the word?" "Then what might you do if you come across a word or an idea you don't understand when you are reading?" Adam quickly became aware that the information he needed to figure out words could sometimes be found beyond the word itself. To his list of strategies, Adam added "Read the rest of the sentence."

Once poor readers have learned about various sources of information as well as strategies like rereading and reading beyond the word, cloze may be an appropriate next step. Cloze passages require students to make decisions about which information sources and strategies are most appropriate in various situations (see Jongsma, 1980 for a review of research on cloze instruction). As students read and encounter the blanks in the passage, they use their knowledge of syntax and semantics to decide what makes sense in the blank.

When we have observed cloze lessons in classrooms, students are usually given a cloze passage and asked to write what makes sense in the blanks, or they are provided with "maze" exercises in which they are to select the word for the blank that best makes sense from among several choices. It is our opinion that neither exercise is in the best interests of students *if* the goal is to improve their ability to make sense *while reading*. Reading requires automatic processing and reliance on the reader's own information sources. Writing the answers permits considered responses rather than the quick responses required in reading. Maze exercises not only permit a considered response, they also provide information instead of encouraging readers to use what they already know.

If the goal is to help students learn to make sense consistently as they read, we recommend instructional cloze procedures, which require that readers respond as they do when they read naturally in whole text without blanks. Readers should be provided with a cloze passage (a short but "whole" text at a level considered easy for them) and asked to read the passage silently and then aloud at a normal pace, filling in as many blanks as possible without slowing their rate. We often do this in group situations in which students read in unison, helping each other maintain a normal reading pace. Of course, when students encounter blanks, they often give a variety of responses. As the students recall their choices after unison reading, write their responses in the blanks on an overhead transparency of the cloze exercise so that everyone can refer to them.

The follow-up discussion should center on which sources of information they used to decide which word or phrase made sense in the blank, on the placement of clues in relation to the blank, and on strategies necessary to make the passage make sense. In other words, responses should be considered *after* the exercise rather than during the exercise itself. Gradually, post-reading discussions will have an impact on in-process reading behavior.

Sometimes students learn to respond effectively in cloze exercises but do not transfer the strategies and information they used to make sense in the cloze exercises to everyday reading situations. That is, the students know that they should make sense while reading and do make sense as long as there are blanks; but when they encounter difficulties in a typical text, they don't consistently choose to make sense, reverting instead to overuse of the graphophonic system. For example, if American students encounter the page from Langstaff's *Oh, A-Hunting We Will Go* that reads, "We'll catch a lamb and put him in a pram," they may try to sound out the word "pram" rather than use the information from the illustration to substitute a word from their own background that makes more sense, like "stroller."

Teachers can provide two kinds of assistance for those students who need to learn that sense-making should take precedence over conflicting graphophonic cues. The first kind of assistance can be given in any oral reading situation. If the student is trying to sound out "pram," for example, cover the print so the student is forced to use the illustration instead of graphophonic cues and ask "What would make sense there?" When the student responds with a word or phrase that does make sense, ask her/him to read the sentence again, this time substituting the word or phrase that makes sense for the word in the text. After the student has finished reading the text, discuss the strategy, helping the student to understand that substituting a word that makes sense and continuing to read is preferable to getting stuck on sounding out or reading a word that doesn't make sense.

Substitution lessons may also help these students. Substitution passages are constructed in the same way as cloze exercises and procedurally may be used in the same way. The only difference is that instead of replacing words with blanks, the words are left in the text and simply underlined, as follows:

The brown bears, lean-flanked and rough-coated from their long winter's sleep, would <u>amble</u> down off the high snow fields and <u>congregate</u> along the spawning streams. There would be <u>colossal</u> battles for choice fishing sites; but once those were decided, the animals would all settle down to eating their fill every day as the returning salmon fought their way upstream to spawn. Herds of seals and sea lions would <u>mass</u> on jutting points of land and along rocky shores of islands to dip into the run for their annual feast. They would charge into the nets of <u>seiners</u>, ripping them to shreds, and spend hours searching for the opening to a fish trap, trying to get at the thousands of salmon inside. Eagles, hawks, crows, and foxes would <u>vie</u> with the brown bears, seals, and sea lions at every stream and sandbar. Over all would circle <u>hordes</u> of screaming gulls scouring land, sea, and beaches, cleaning up, to the last <u>morsel</u>, every crumb left by previous feeders. (Morey, 1965, 18−19)

In substitution lessons, students read at a normal pace, and when they encounter an underlined word, they substitute another word that makes sense.

(Your demonstration of substitution is probably the best procedural explanation.) Don't tell the students to substitute a synonym; that requires them to read the original word and substitute a synonym for it, a situation that involves processing the word in the text and then processing a synonym for it, which is quite different from the processing that occurs when readers don't know a word. You simply want the students to learn that one way they can respond to a word they don't know in the text is by substituting another than makes sense even if it doesn't look like the one in the text. This sort of lesson is not designed to teach a student a cavalier attitude toward the author's words. The goal is to help students understand that, when they must choose between substituting a word that looks like one in the text but which does not make sense and substituting a word that makes sense but does not look like the one in the text, the latter response is usually more effective while the former usually interferes with comprehension.

TEACHER FEEDBACK TO MISCUES

One particularly important line of reading research into helping students make sense of words during reading has to do with the feedback teachers provide to students' miscues during oral reading. Miscue feedback research reveals a characteristic profile in teacher feedback to the miscues of poor readers. It also sets forth recommendations about the feedback that ought to be given to students during oral reading. Interestingly, the feedback recommended for poor readers is characteristic of that which teachers frequently provide to good readers.

CHARACTERISTIC FEEDBACK

The teacher provides the student with the word that has caused the student difficulty and/or calls attention to graphophonic cues (Allington, 1980; Hoffman & Clements, 1984; Lass, 1984; McNaughton, 1981; Pflaum et al., 1980; Spiegel & Rogers, 1980).

The teacher provides feedback immediately at the point of difficulty or miscue (Allington, 1978; Hoffman & Clements, 1984). Wait time between miscue and feedback is less than three seconds (Hoffman & Clements, 1984).

RECOMMENDED FEEDBACK

The teacher accepts those miscues that do not greatly change the author's meaning (Hoffman, 1979; Hoffman & Clements, 1984; Recht, 1976). The teacher may comment positively about a miscue that reveals attention to meaning (Lass, 1984).

When a miscue disrupts meaning, the teacher waits to intervene until the end of the paragraph or sentence (Hoffman, 1979; Hoffman & Clements, 1984; McNaughton, 1981) or until the student has finished reading.

When we read with students, we favor assisted reading if the student is having a fair amount of difficulty constructing meaning and silence if the student is having little difficulty constructing meaning. Semantic prompts like the following may be needed or prove useful in developing a student's reading strategies:

SEMANTIC PROMPT	READING SITUATION
"Keep reading and see what makes sense there."	Useful if you see semantic cues ahead that will help the student.
"Did that sentence make sense? Read it again so it makes sense this time."	Useful when students continue to read with no sign that they have not understood.
"Is there a clue in what you've read so far (or in the picture) that tells you what would make sense there?"	Useful when textual cues (or picture clues) prior to the difficulty will help the student understand the meaning of the word.

These sorts of prompts are helpful because each of them alerts students to precisely what strategy they should use. Once students understand that they can read on, reread, and use picture cues to make sense of words in text, you should help students move toward greater independence in their selection of strategies. Replace the semantic prompts above with "What can you do when it doesn't make sense?," alerting students to the fact that something needs to be done yet putting them on the road to deciding independently which strategy is appropriate in the reading situation.

A comparison of the feedback to one child's miscues provided by two different teachers will serve to illustrate the positive and negative impact of variations in teacher response on meaning construction during oral reading. The child was a third-grade girl named Florine who was attending a learning disabilities resource room on a daily basis. She spoke a Southern black dialect, which was evident in some of the miscues she produced during reading. In the following excerpts miscues are coded in the usual way except for the circled *T* throughout the passage, which represents the *teacher's* interventions.

During the first half of the school year, Florine had attended an LD resource room that operated within a socio-psycholinguistic framework. In this classroom, Florine read numerous children's books with her teacher. The pattern of feedback when she read *Neat and Scruffy* (Gale, 1975) is consistent with other observed instances of her reading (see Figure 9–2).

As Florine read *Neat and Scruffy*, the teacher listened to the story and enjoyed it with the child. (Think about the difference between listening to a story and listening to a student read words.) There is only one *T* in the miscue markings because the teacher remained silent so that Florine could assume responsibility for the reading. The teacher's silence provided Florine with the opportunity to process and utilize ensuing textual cues and self-correct when they didn't "fit" with her miscue.

The teacher's single intervention occured on line 13 when Florine paused for about ten seconds and then proceeded to try to sound out "short." After giving

1. *Neat and Scruffy*

One time Ⓒ *w– had*
2. Once there ⌐was a man with neat hair ✓   ✓ Florine laughs.

Ⓒ *w– had*
3. and he had a ⌐wife with neat hair. ✓

4. One day they had a baby boy.

Ⓒ *Then love*
5. ⌐They loved him very much but

Ⓒ *
6. ⌐he had scruffy hair.   *he wa–
he went up uh stair.

And
7. ∧ The baby grew

8. and GREW

Ⓒ *u– una–*
9. ⌐until he was big enough to go to school.

Ⓒ *He Mother* Ⓒ *Dad* Ⓒ *look + ed*
                                    liked
10. ⌐His Mummy and ⌐Daddy ⌐looked at him.

Ⓒ *Then comb*
11. ⌐They combed his scruffy hair

■ *wouldn't* Ⓡ
12. but it would ⌐not be neat.   ■ F: They cut his hair!

Ⓒ *Then   skru–*
13. ⌐They cut⌐ it short ▼   ▼ T: They cut it what?
F: Small.
T: They cut it real . . .
Like I got mine.
F: Short!
T: Yeah! Good!

14. but it grew

15. and GREW.

16. So he went to school with scruffy hair

17. and he GREW ▼   ▼ F (pointing to
picture):
This first, this
second,
this third.

Ⓒ   Ⓒ *Dad*   T: (Chuckles)
18. until he was ⌐(as) big as his ⌐Daddy.

Florine time, the teacher provided a semantic cue rather than the word or a graphophonic cue like "sh." Note that the semantic cue the teacher provided was one outside the text—a reference to her own short hair. A semantic cue that would have been more helpful to Florine's long-term reading development would have been a semantic prompt referring to something within the text: "Florine, is there something in the picture that tells you what would make sense there?"

Although the teacher listened with only a single intervention as Florine read this story, she had taken a more active role in providing miscue feedback when she started working with Florine. At the beginning of the year, the girl's miscues were frequently semantically unacceptable and were not self-corrected. The teacher used the sorts of lessons we presented earlier in these pages as well as semantic prompts during oral reading in order to help the girl learn how to make sense of words.

When a dialect speaker is effectively processing text, as Florine is in reading *Neat and Scruffy*, dialect miscues are often predominant, a sign that meaning construction is occurring. The construction, "One time was a man had neat hair" is perfectly acceptable within Florine's oral language patterns, and unlike many teachers who correct dialect miscues (Tovey, 1979), the LD teacher treated them as acceptable.

Let's contrast Florine's reading in the first half of the school year with the reading she did after her move into the second teacher's class. During the second semester, Florine read out of a basal text, *A Risky Trip* (Richardson, 1976), in "round robin" fashion. The pattern of feedback revealed in Figure 9–3 was consistently observed across reading situations and students.

Note how the teacher fits the characteristic teacher feedback to miscues profile. She responded to miscues by providing Florine with the correct word or an occasional graphophonic prompt. The teacher assumed responsibility for both identifying the miscue and correcting it. In other words, the teacher did a great deal of the reading Florine should have been doing.

Correct word recognition was highly important to this teacher, even when Florine's miscues made sense. Note, for example, the feedback provided for the miscue "cat" in line 5001; the teacher corrected the child by supplying "kitten." A distraction caused the teacher to miss the miscue of "the" for "a" in line 4006, but she corrected the same meaningful substitution in the following line.

The teacher also fits the characteristic miscue feedback profile from the standpoint of timing—where and how quickly she provided miscue feedback. This teacher provided less than a second wait time when Florine produced a miscue. Because the teacher provided feedback immediately at the point of the miscue, Florine could not use the context following the miscue to make a determination about whether what she was reading made sense.

What is instructive about comparing the readings of the first and second passages is the impact of the teachers' differing miscue feedback on Florine's processing of text. When she read the *Neat and Scruffy* passage earlier in the school year, Florine had consistently produced semantically acceptable miscues or self-corrected those that were not. In other words, she used the strategies that

FIGURE 9–3   Interaction During Oral Reading: *A Risky Trip* (Richardson 1970, pp. 40–41)

4001   If the kitty wiggles, the can will

4002   tip.

4003   If the can tips, it will fill up and

4004   drop to the bottom of the pond.* ▶

↑ Interruption by other student;
T provides directions.
*T repeats entire sentence.
▶ T: Please continue, Florine.

4005   That will be too bad!*

4006   To be at the bottom of a pond in

4007   a can is not funny.

4008   It's not a bit funny.

5001   Mr. Hopper has seen the kitten in

5002   the big can.

5003   The kitten has not seen him.

5004   We can see him, but she can't.**

T repeats entire sentence with emphasis on **we and **she**. T: When the words are written dark, we say them louder.

proficient readers use in constructing personal meaning. She exhibited the sorts of reading behaviors, especially self-correction, that allow readers to teach themselves about reading in the process of reading.

Later in the school year, on the other hand, Florine's miscues typically did not make sense, and she did not self-correct. The second semester videotapes of Florine reveal a child who has become dependent on someone else to determine whether text makes sense; she glances at her teacher for help at the slightest difficulty. With a teacher who provided the sort of feedback typically given to poor readers and with a text chosen for its readability rather than its predictability, Florine no longer uses the proficient reading strategies she had developed.

Teachers can also provide assistance to students regarding miscues made during silent reading using an instructional strategy called "reader selected miscues" (Hoge, 1983; Watson, 1978a). Students identify the miscues they have made during silent reading and the teacher helps them resolve the miscues by focusing on strategies for identifying words and their meanings.

Prior to reading, students are provided with slips of paper about the size of a bookmark, which they can use to mark the difficulties they encounter while they read. At the end of the reading period, students select three to five miscues for attention. They copy the sentences containing miscues onto the markers and underline the difficult words or phrases. On the other side of the marker, students write their names, the page number from which the sentence was copied, and, if students are reading various texts, the title of the text.

Occasionally, when students are unable to identify their difficulties during reading, they need to be taught how to do so. We recommend that these students tape-record their oral reading and then listen to it with you, locating sentences that do not make sense and words in each sentence that do not make sense.

Once you have collected the markers from the students, you can categorize them to determine common difficulties or patterns of difficulties. Instruction focuses on helping students identify options available to them when they have difficulties like those they've marked. Strategy lessons such as the "naming" lesson (Y. Goodman & Burke, 1980) may also be used to help students understand how to deal with specific difficulties. The goal is to help students with the *types* of miscues they have identified, though learning specific new words and word meanings will certainly occur in the process.

It is also occasionally useful to discuss miscues that students have either resolved for themselves or judged as less important to discuss than others. Such discussions heighten student awareness of the positive strategies they do use and help them understand that all readers encounter difficulties that make little or no difference to their construction of meaning.

Reader selected miscues is an instructional strategy with a number of features we believe are important in a lesson highlighting making sense of words in text. First, seeing patterns in their own miscues helps students understand that there are widely applicable strategies for making sense of words in text. Second, the lesson puts the student in the driver's seat; the students identify for themselves whether or not a miscue has caused a loss of meaning and whether they need assistance. Third, there is great potential for vocabulary development, vocabulary that the students themselves have identified as important to understanding the text. Finally, if the teacher facilitates this lesson so that students help each other solve problems, the sense of a community of readers will continue to develop.

LEARNING WORDS AND OTHER TEXT FEATURES

Readers have language strengths they can rely on as they learn about the graphophonic system if whole text is available to them. Whole text embodies graphophonic, syntactic, and semantic cues that permit emergent readers to use their already developed knowledge of language as they encounter text features that are new to them.

Unfortunately, many teachers make the assumption that students cannot read whole text until they have achieved a certain level of mastery over phonics and word recognition. For students who have a great deal of difficulty learning about the graphophonic system in isolation, such an assumption is deadly. They may never read a whole text. When whole text is not available to students, they do not have the opportunity to learn how to orchestrate the graphophonic, syntactic, and semantic systems effectively during reading. And readers who have serious difficulty learning the graphophonic system cannot learn to compensate for that difficulty because the syntactic and semantic cues that might support them are not available.

Let us provide an example. When fourteen-year-old Rich was referred for remedial help, we discovered that he could read only three words in the very simple story he was asked to read. When we read sentences to him from the text and asked him to reread the sentences, pointing to the words as he did so, we found that he had not even stabilized a voice-print match in reading. Rich was clearly still an emergent reader at the age of fourteen.

In investigating Rich's instructional history, we found that teachers had worked intensively with him for years, first struggling to teach him the alphabet and then teaching him sight words. When these strategies didn't work, a number of carefully structured phonics programs were used, one of which was still being used on a daily basis in his special ed classroom. In our first meeting with him, Rich pleaded, "I want to learn to read. But please don't teach me the alphabet and the sounds again." When we asked if he had ever read a book, Rich looked at us in amazement and said, "How can I? I don't know any words."

Though Rich's case is certainly extreme because of his age, many younger students have experienced difficulty in learning the graphophonic system in isolation. As a result, they haven't had the opportunity to read whole text, which has deprived them of other language information.

Language information can be made available to students like these during assisted and repeated readings of predictable texts. However, teachers who use predictable texts (including language experience dictations) with emergent readers often report, "But the kids have just memorized the story!" Students may be aware of the same phenomenon; although Rich experienced great joy in reading a book on his own, he also reflected, "I'm just remembering it."

In these observations, teachers and students are identifying a real dilemma. On the one hand, the students have experienced a lack of success in learning the graphophonic system through isolated sound/letter and word instruction. On the other hand, some poor readers pay little or no attention to the graphophonic system when reading whole predictable text. Though the students feel a sense of satisfaction in being able to read a book independently, their learning of the graphophonic system cannot proceed satisfactorily if they do not attend to the graphophonic cues in the text.*

The solution to this dilemma, helping students attend to the features of print or the graphophonic system within the context of whole text, is the subject of this section. Our discussion will begin with two instructional strategies, pointing and graphophonic prediction check, which can be used to draw students' attention to print features whether or not they have prior familiarity with text. Then we will explore several instructional strategies that are dependent on student familiarity with text.

POINTING

Pointing is useful in establishing a voice-print match for an emerging reader. Children need to learn what words are and how they are represented in print. Although it is impossible to explain such a thing, it is an easy matter to demonstrate it so that the child intuitively learns about the nature of words and word boundaries, and the directionality of print. As you read books to children, you simply point to the words as you read. In a group situation, this necessitates the use of big books or large print charts so that all the children in the group can experience how the eyes (indicated through pointing) and voice work together. Though pointing usually necessitates a bit of slowing down in oral reading, avoid choppy, word-by-word reading. At various points in their emergent reading, children learn different aspects of text features from observing the voice-print match. Some may be learning that the English language is represented from left to right and top to bottom. Some may learn that a syllable does not necessarily make a word, a common hypothesis. Others may learn something they did not know about particular words. For example, a child who is observing the voice-print match of a sentence like "I've got to hurry home after school today" may realize for the first time that the oral "gotta" is represented by two words in print.

Once students have established a basic voice-print match on a familiar text, they should take over much of the pointing during reading. The student's behavior in pointing provides evaluative information for both the teacher and the child. For example, we recently observed a child in a classroom reading "Mary Had a Little Lamb," pointing to the text as she read. When she arrived at the line "And everywhere that Mary went," she pointed and read as follows:

---

*Children who learn to read prior to school entrance often teach themselves by attending to graphophonic cues within stories they have memorized during parents' repeated readings. Undoubtedly, some poor readers will teach themselves in the same way once they have the opportunity to experience whole text. However, because of the passivity of many poor readers, teachers must frequently play a role in calling students' attention to the graphophonic system in print.

> [*pointing*] And everywhere that Mary went
> [*reading*] And every   where that Mary...

Because the girl still had one word left to say and no words left to point to in the line, she knew something was wrong. The teacher, alert to the instructional moment, briefly introduced compound words, showing the girl how "every" and "where" were combined into a single word.

Pointing is often thought of as a bad habit and in some cases it is. However, for children who need to learn how language is represented in print, it is the only way teachers have of demonstrating that basic notion. It is also helpful for those children who find pointing the only way of keeping track of where they are in text.

For students who have a well-established sense of voice-print match and can track print with their eyes, pointing has a well-deserved reputation as a bad habit. Revealing to students that grown-up readers do not point and reminding them not to point may solve the problem. However, pointing may be a symptom of an underlying problem—the student's belief that reading is a word-by-word process. In that case, you also need to address this underlying belief if pointing is to stop.

GRAPHOPHONIC PREDICTION CHECK

Another technique useful in helping students attend to graphophonic information is encouraging them to check their predictions against ensuing graphophonic cues in the text. In a first reading of a text, it is often easy to encourage such prediction checks.

For example, if children are reading *Did You Ever See?* (Einsel, 1962), every pair of pages in the book offers opportunities for prediction checks. For instance, one page says, "Did you ever see a crow?" and the students in the class predicted that the paired page might say "blow," "row," "grow," "hoe," or "mow." When the page was turned so that they could check their predictions, the students could tell from the picture that the author had chosen "row." In order to call attention to the print cues, the teacher pointed to the word on the page and asked, "How else do you know this says 'row'?" The children, of course, told the teacher that the word began with an *r*.

Some texts and situations lend themselves nicely to calling attention to print after a first reading of the text. In fact, the remaining instructional strategies in this chapter are most successful if students have experienced the text so many times that it is "memorized," or almost so.

SEQUENCING TEXT PARTS

One technique that directs attention to the features of print is like a game to many students. They are provided with parts of a familiar text (sentences of a text or lines of a rhyme), one part to a "strip," and asked to put them in order or to sequence them in the way the author did.

With a group of students, the best materials to use for sequencing are tagboard sentence strips. The strips may be sequenced in a wooden or cardboard pocket chart, or magnets may be fastened on the back for use on the blackboard. The size of the print on the sentence strips should permit everyone in the group to view the print easily.

If students need a great deal of teacher support in attending to print features, the teacher may begin by asking the students, "What is the first sentence/line we need to look for?," and once the children have located a strip (correctly or incorrectly), "How do you know that says, '(whatever the sentence is)'?" The session can continue in the same way with the teacher asking what sentence ought to come next and inquiring about what features helped the children choose the strip.

As the students suggest the features they are attending to, the teacher may reinforce their choices and call attention to others. If the students' choice of a strip is incorrect, it is usually possible to reinforce the feature that the child was attending to and then call attention to another feature that makes the difference between the correct and incorrect choice. For example, if the children are sequencing lines from "One Two, Buckle My Shoe," and the child chooses "Seven, eight" instead of "Shut the door" and tells you that he found the strip with the letter *s* at the beginning, you can put the two strips next to each other and say something like, "Yes, you are right. This strip does have *s* at the beginning, but so does this one. How do you know which one says "Shut the door"? Or if the child's choice was correct in the first place, you might put the "Seven, eight" strip next to the correct one and ask, "Why did you choose this one instead of this one?"

Cut and paste worksheets are another way of engaging children independently in the same activity. The worksheet reproduced in Figure 9–4 was used with children who were highly familiar with *The Great Big Enormous Turnip* (Tolstoy, 1968). Rather than using the lengthy whole text, note that only the portion representing the important repeated sequence was used.

Here are several other related ideas:

- If the tagboard sentence strips are laminated, they last a very long time and may be left for children's independent use in a learning center. One teacher we know has about a dozen sequencing sets, each for a different predictable book or piece of poetry. The center is a frequent choice of her learning disabled students.
- Small desk sets of sentence strips can also be made and laminated for repeated use. They can be stored in envelopes labeled with the name of the book from which the sentences were taken.
- Not all texts are useful for this sequencing activity, even when they are predictable. Bill Martin's sequence for *Brown Bear, Brown Bear* (Martin, 1970a), for example, could be almost entirely rearranged without affecting the sense of the story. (On the other hand, we've observed students mix the sequence up for their friends to read—a great way to encourage attention to

---

FIGURE 9–4   Cut and Paste Worksheet

CUT and PASTE worksheet

cut on the dotted lines

The old woman pulled the old man.

The mouse pulled the cat.

The granddaughter pulled the old woman.

The old man pulled the turnip.

The cat pulled the dog.

The dog pulled the granddaughter.

paste or glue here in order   NAME:

---

print.) Generally, try to locate books that have a logical sequence, one that wouldn't make sense or would sound odd if it were rearranged.

REGENERATING A TEXT

Engaging children in making a copy of a text is another activity that is helpful in calling children's attention to the way print is used in a familiar book. The activity can be very engrossing and will result in a text students can call their own, especially important in situations where students have few or no books in their homes.

The page reproduced as Figure 9–5 (DiMartini, 1987) is one of the pages of a Mother Goose collection that was regenerated with great delight by second- and third-grade learning disabled children. In regenerating the rhyme, the

---

FIGURE 9–5   Page from a Mother Goose Collection (DiMartini 1987)

BAA, BAA BLACK SHEEP   NAME_____

Fill in the blanks with a word that makes sense.

Baa, baa _____ sheep,

have you any _____?

Yes, sir, yes, sir, three bags full;

one for _____,

and one for _____,

and one for the little boy

who lives down the _____.

---

students filled in the blanks with the missing words; some retrieved a book of Mother Goose rhymes from the classroom library shelves, others copied from a chart showing the rhyme, and still others relied on their own knowledge of the spellings. The day after these books were completed and taken home, there were many stories about how they were read to brothers and sisters and cousins during the previous evening.

INNOVATING ON AN AUTHOR'S STRUCTURE

Instead of, or in addition to regenerating a text using an author's original words, call students' attention to print by having them use an author's original

---

FIGURE 9–6   Extension for *Q Is for Duck* (Rhodes 1985; Elting & Folsom 1980)

Name _____

____ is for Monster.   Why?

Because _____
_____

____ is for Dinosaur.   Why?

Because _____
_____

____ is for Gorilla.   Why?

Because _____
_____

____ is for Teacher.   Why?

Because _____
_____

____ is for _____. Why?

Because _____
_____

---

structure to create new texts. Many predictable books, songs (Mateja, 1982), poetry, and the like are suitable for creating a new version of an original text.

For example, a group of learning disabled children innovated on the structure of *Brown Bear* and dictated pages to their teacher for an illustrated Christmas version. The first page said, "Santa Claus, Santa Claus, what do you see?" and the last page, "We see presents under the tree!" As each page was dictated, the teacher involved the children in learning about the graphophonic system by asking them to spell some of the words borrowed from the book and by asking for the beginning letters in some of the words that were different from those in the book.

As another example, the worksheet reproduced as Figure 9–6 is one of a series of extensions (Rhodes, 1985) for *Q is for Duck* (Elting & Folsom, 1980), a marvelous book for children who need to attend to aspects of the graphophonic system. This worksheet borrows the author's original structure and substitutes words that most students enjoy: monsters, dinosaurs, and the like. The end of the worksheet calls for the child's choice of words entirely.

Using the author's structure to produce a new text is not only valuable for children who are learning about the graphophonic system but also for children who are learning about other features of print. For instance, two fourth-grade girls who were writing another version of *Fire! Fire! Said Mrs. McGuire* (Martin, 1970b) referred to the original text to figure out how to use quotation marks in the version they worked out:

"Snow! Snow!" said Ms. Low.
"Where? Where?" said Mr. Glare.
"Up there!" said Mrs. Pear.
"In the sky!" said Mr. Li.
"Get the Shovel!" said Mrs. Lovel.
"Scoop it up!" said Mr. Lup.

MATCHING

There are various matching activities that also help children attend to the print of a familiar text. Begin the lesson by reading or perhaps sequencing a familiar text. Then pass out individual word cards to the children with important words from the selected text. For "Jack Be Nimble," you might pass out "Jack," "jump," "candlestick," "nimble," and "quick." Each child in turn brings a card to the pocket chart and puts it in the pocket, covering up the matching word. If the child knows the word, s/he can then tell what it is; if not, s/he can read (while pointing) the verse from the beginning up to the word in order to discover what it is.

GAMES

A number of the techniques for calling attention to print can be incorporated into games. For example, matching is the basis of games such as Bingo and Concentration. Both games, however, are difficult for children unless they already have a fairly good knowledge of the print features of the text. Here are some examples of how the games may be prepared and played:

- Cloze sentences can be the basis for either a Bingo or a Concentration game. In a Bingo game for *The Great Big Enormous Turnip*, a square containing the sentence "The old _____ pulled the old woman" could be marked if the caller called "man." In a Concentration game, the cloze sentence and the cloze response would be the matches.
- Bingo cards may be prepared with phrases or sentences from text children have read. For example, bingo cards could contain sentences and phrases from "The Three Little Pigs," such as "Little pig, little pig, let me come in" and "The first little pig." Cards for the person who is the "caller" could include matching sentences and phrases, such as "What the wolf said when he knocked on the pigs' door" and "The pig who made a house of straw." The same ideas can be used to construct a game of Concentration.

Other board games or games based on TV show games can also be constructed, both to call students' attention to print and to extend their comprehension of literature. For more information, including how to engage students in constructing games based on their favorite books, see Morris (1987).

READING VERSIONS OF A TEXT

Often, various versions of children's text exist in literature, especially when the text is a folktale, fairy tale, rhyme, song, tall tale, fable or some other literary genre that has been passed on for years. Sometimes there are major differences between versions and sometimes only minor ones. For emergent readers, those versions that feature minor differences in wording are most suitable. When students read the second text, they should find that they can handle it as well as the first version because both are so similar. Finding the differences between the versions and wondering about them is intriguing. Some book pairs with minor variations, which students may enjoy exploring, include:

- P. Adams. *There Was an Old Lady Who Swallowed a Fly*. New York: Grosset & Dunlap, 1973.
  R. Boone and A. Mills. *I Know an Old Lady*. New York: Rand McNally, 1961.
  S. Kellogg. *There Was an Old Woman*. New York: Parents' Magazine Press, 1974.
  N. B. Westcott. *I Know an Old Lady Who Swallowed a Fly*. Boston: Little, Brown, 1980.
- B. S. de Regniers. *Catch a Little Fox*. New York: Seabury Press, 1970.
  J. Langstaff. *Oh, A-Hunting We will Go*. New York: Atheneum, 1974.
- R. Quakenbush. *Go Tell Aunt Rhody*. Philadelphia: J. B. Lippincott, 1973.
  Aliki. *Go Tell Aunt Rhody*. New York: Macmillan, 1974.

Older emergent readers also enjoy exploring different versions of texts and speculating about the reasons for the variations. They may even want to predict which version might be more popular with younger children and find out whether they are right by reading various versions to young children, leading them in a discussion of the versions, and taking a vote on their favorites.

CONCLUSION

As we've noted throughout this book, reading isn't a matter of simply decoding the author's intending meaning. Readers actively construct meaning by drawing on their knowledge of the world, their knowledge of language, and their knowledge of print conventions as they interact with a text. Good readers use a variety of active strategies to make sense of print as they read. In this chapter we've presented some strategies to encourage poor readers to become actively involved in making sense of text and of words in text. Although these strategies can help students, they are no substitute for lots of reading.

Post-reading instruction

Post-reading instruction follows the reading of some text—
a story, a poem, or some other kind of reading material.
Typically, post-reading activities have focused on a discussion of what's been read, a discussion that can be
characterized as a test of students' comprehension (Crafton,
1982). The teacher asks a question ("Mary, what did he do
then?"), a student replies ("He went back to his house."),
and then the teacher evaluates the students' response ("Are
you sure? Tom...?") (Buttery & Powell, 1978; Kitagawa,
1982; Lehr, 1984). Worksheets also figure prominently in
post-reading instruction. However, these activities encourage a narrow view of the purposes and processes of
reading. In particular, they encourage students to read for
someone else's purposes and not their own.

In this chapter, we'll discuss post-reading instructional
strategies that encourage the sharing and extending of
comprehension as an alternative to the traditional activities
that dominate most post-reading instruction. We'll suggest
a variety of ways to help students engage in thinking about
the text after reading. Many of the activities will be familiar;
they're frequently referred to as "enrichment" activities,
the sorts of activities that are done "if there's time." It's our
position, however, that sharing and extending comprehension with a community of readers is basic to improving
reading comprehension, including what are considered
lower "levels" of comprehension. Ryan and Torrance (1967),
for example, improved the abilities of the poor readers
in a seventh-grade class 7.5 months for every month of
instruction by engaging them in activities such as writing
new endings for stories, writing plays, and making dioramas.
It's clear that sharing and extending activities deserve to be
thought of as central to reading instruction rather than
enrichment.

Much of what we'll recommend depends on the development of a community of readers who share their understanding of texts with each other. The readers with whom you work may not have any sense of community at first, but sharing and extending activities—and time—will help to develop a community of readers. Once that sense of a community develops, the sharing and extending of texts begin to grow more from the students' own purposes and less from teachers' assignments.

There are a number of general instructional goals for post-reading instruction. First, encourage students to reflect on what it is that they've learned or experienced (and what they haven't learned or experienced) in reading a text. Second, extend each student's comprehension of the text through a rethinking of the text. Finally, make every effort to help students relate texts not only to their lives but also to other "texts" they have read, seen, or heard. This will help students integrate what they've read with what they already know, which from our perspective is what reading comprehension is all about.

We will address these three goals in the instructional recommendations we make in this chapter. The first and major section of the chapter suggests instructional strategies designed to help students share and extend their comprehension of a single text and, in the process, to establish a community of readers. In the second section, we discuss how these same instructional strategies can be used productively with multiple texts or text sets. Finally, we'll discuss situations in which students must comprehend text for someone else's purposes, in particular, when they must prepare for some school assignment, such as a test.

SHARING AND EXTENDING A TEXT

If your circumstances don't permit students to work together (if, for example, you work only with individual students), you must revise your role so that you and the student can become a community of two readers who can share their comprehension of text. Unless students can talk with someone else about their understanding of a text, it's unlikely that they will extend the meaning they constructed originally. And if students talk to you about what they've read and do not receive your insights about the text in return, they will probably view the situation as a comprehension test. Thus, in the following lessons, respond as a reader does to the text, preferably in the same manner in which you have asked the student to respond. In other words, if you have asked the student to sketch a response to the text, you should sketch a response as well. Even when you are working with a group of students, try consistently to assume the role of another reader in the community; you'll be surprised how your participation contributes to both the development of a community of readers and the development of students' knowledge about the nature of proficient reading.

ORAL SHARING AND EXTENDING

Certainly the most common way of sharing and extending comprehension is through oral discussion of a text. However, the usual pattern of teacher question, student answer, teacher evaluation must be broken in order to more fully involve students in post-reading activity.

One way to encourage authentic oral sharing and extending is by returning to the already-know statements, questions, and predictions generated during prereading instruction. Guide students' attention back to the prereading lesson and encourage them to reflect on what was discussed then in light of what they have since actually found in the text. When their questions are not answered by the text, encourage students to consider why. When predictions aren't borne out, encourage students to think about why. Ask students to compare their prereading discussion with what they learned from the text while you talk as little as possible. Help them learn to listen well to each other and to relate one idea to another by demonstrating these skills yourself and by asking questions such as, "Tony, how did what you just said relate to what Ann said earlier?"

Another way to involve students in post-reading discussions is to ask them to formulate questions based on their reading (Kitagawa, 1982; Singer, 1978), questions to which they would like to hear everyone else respond. At first, the questions may be the sort that only require single, short, text-based answers. Formulating your own questions along with students will give you an opportunity to demonstrate the questioning process (see the reading conference questions in chapter 7) and encourage more open-ended discussion. Before actually discussing students' questions, write them down and then have the group decide the order in which they would like to address them. The questions might be listed in sequence or grouped according to their subject matter, helping you to facilitate a more coherent discussion. If you want to help students consider the nature of their questions directly in order to improve them, hold a debriefing session on questions at the conclusion of the discussion. Ask "Which questions did we spend the most time responding to? Why?" "Which questions could we answer without thinking much? Could some of the questions be changed to make us think about the relationship of what we read to our own experiences? How?"

Oral retelling of a text also provides students with an opportunity to extend their understanding of its meaning (Y. Goodman, 1982) because they must compose their retelling in their own words. Although in situations in which all the students have read the same text, retellings can be characterized more as testing than as sharing and extending, a retelling may be used to initiate the sharing and extending of a single text. After one student has completed a retelling to which everyone else has listened (including the teacher for purposes of assessment), the rest of the group (including the teacher) might write questions for the student. Some questions should encourage the student to expand on something that was only mentioned in the retelling, others should encourage the student to reflect on feelings or attitudes toward some part of what was retold, and still other questions can encourage relating the text to other texts the group has read. In turn, the student being questioned is free to turn the question back to the questioner, e.g., "I've told you what *I* think about what Jefferson did. What do *you* think?"

Students who enjoy narrative retellings might be encouraged to become involved in telling stories to their peers or to younger audiences (Farnsworth,

1981; Kingore, 1982; Livo & Rietz, 1985) as a related way of sharing and extending their comprehension of narrative text. Livo and Rietz (1985) suggest the following steps for *storytelling*:

1. Choose a favorite story that is familiar and easily remembered. Stories with a strong story grammar or pattern, such as cumulative stories and stories with repeated events, are good ones for beginners.
2. Practice the story to become comfortable with telling it—outlining the features of the story, telling it into a tape recorder, telling it to a young child, a family member, etc.
3. Consider the effect of storytelling conventions on the potential audience and suggest options for ways to use language, noises, movement, body language, and facial expression.
4. Arrange for an accepting audience, probably classmates or a younger group of children. Again, after the event help the student reflect on the storytelling.

Several techniques can help students identify, share, and extend major points in their reading, especially of expository material. You might ask students to choose what they consider to be an interesting, important, or confusing part of text (a sentence or two, not more than a paragraph), to read that part to the rest of the group, and to invite the group to comment on it or to *say something* (Harste, 1982). Or you might ask them to jot down questions or points of agreement and disagreement with the author, to share one or more of these with the rest of the group, and to invite reaction from the group (Burke, 1982). If the reading selection stimulates a *debate*, the points of agreement and disagreement might be used to establish pro and con debate panels (Brenneman, 1985).

Text dramatization is another way of orally sharing and extending students' comprehension of the text (L. C. Hendersen & Shanker, 1978; Micinatti & Phelps, 1980; Miller & Mason, 1983; Vawter & Vancil, 1980). For the purposes of sharing and extending comprehension, dramatization need not become a theatrical production. Informal, quickly devised dramatization is equally effective and less time-consuming.

Dramatization can take a variety of forms—putting on a play, acting out mime, or creating a flannel board story, for example—using whole texts or parts of a text. Different students might decide to dramatize different parts of the same text. Instead of sticking close to the original text, they can try recasting it in the form of a monologue or dialogue in which other students take roles (Bixby et al., 1983). Students might, for example, dramatize the wolf talking to himself about how he might capture the pigs.

Again, encourage students to think about what they've experienced by dramatizing the text, why they chose to dramatize particular portions of text over other portions, problems they encountered in carrying out the dramatization, and what they might do differently next time.

WRITTEN SHARING AND EXTENDING

Writing, which by its very nature is reflective, can play a role in increasing the comprehension of text (Hennings, 1982; Squire, 1983; Stotsky, 1983). For example, students may be asked to write summaries of a text (K. Taylor, 1984), to do "precis writing" (D'Angelo, 1983), or to complete story frames (Fowler, 1982) in order to encourage them to retell the salient points of texts in their own words. If the purpose of writing *summaries* is to assess the student's understanding, and the audience for the writing is only the teacher, the writing only serves to test comprehension. On the other hand, if students write summaries as part of a collection intended to help each other locate good reading material, then the summaries are being shared and have the potential to extend someone else's comprehension. Summaries may also be shared orally as a means of encouraging the sorts of class discussions we described earlier in the section on sharing retellings. When students write summaries to share with others, encourage them to go beyond the "facts" and to respond personally to the texts they've read. (See L. Smith, 1982 for examples of the sorts of responses students are capable of when they have an interested audience.)

Some students may have difficulty summarizing what they've read. For these students, teachers can model summarizing by sharing their own summaries of text. Students may also be encouraged to discuss other students' summaries or to examine summaries like those on book jackets or at the end of content-area textbook chapters (see Alvermann, 1984; D'Angelo, 1983; K. Taylor, 1984; and B. Taylor & Beach, 1984 for other suggestions on how to help students learn to summarize).

Another way of helping students to reflect on what they've read is to follow a reading session with *journal writing* (Hallenbeck, 1983). Kirby and Liner (1981) note that discussions are far better if students first read, then write about their reading, and then, finally, discuss what they have read (and written). Students' journal entries about their reading will usually be much more open-ended than their summary writing. The major audience is more likely to be the students themselves too, rather than the teacher. However, the same principle that holds true in summaries also holds true in journal responses to text; the journal entries need to be shared, discussed, and responded to if students' motivation to write in their journals is to remain high. When students are reading the same text, sharing journal entries has real potential for extending comprehension, especially if the students have identified with particular characters or situations and reflect that in their writing. It's also useful here, as elsewhere, to encourage students to reflect on their journal writing compared to that of other students and to think about adopting a different writing direction or focus from time to time. Some of the conferencing questions in this and other chapters may help students rethink what sorts of responses they might make in a journal after reading a text. For example, if you want students to put themselves into the author's shoes, you might pose questions like these after students have read Robert Frost's poem, "Stopping by Woods on a Snowy Evening":

- Where do you like to go when you have decisions to make? Is your place like the author's place in any way?
- If you were the author of this poem, what promises might you have been thinking about?

Another idea that extends comprehension is writing in *a different format* from the original text. If, for example, students have just read a historical novel, they might write a newspaper piece depicting the events and setting portrayed in the book.

An example from a Readers Theatre lesson with a group of young children in a Chapter I reading program illustrates the potential of writing in a different format for sharing and extending reading comprehension. These second and third graders had just read a story called *The Missing Necklace* (P. Moore, 1971) and were dictating the story as a script when they encountered these sentences: "Mrs. Pig wanted her friends to come to a picnic lunch. She called and asked them" (2). Because a script naturally demands more conversation between characters than a story does, the children decided to represent the two original sentences in their script as follows:

NARRATOR: Mrs. Pig wanted to have her friends come over to have a picnic.
MRS. PIG: Will you come to my picnic, chipmunk?
CHIPMUNK: Yes, I will be there.
MRS. PIG: Do you want to come to my picnic lunch, sheep?
SHEEP: Yes, Mrs. Pig, I'll be right over!
MRS. PIG: Hello, turtles, will you come to my picnic lunch?
TURTLES: Yes, we'll be right over, Mrs. Pig.
MRS. PIG: Cat, will you come to my picnic lunch?
CAT: I'll be right over, Mrs. Pig.

In order to dictate this portion of the script to the teacher, these children had to recall all the characters that attended the picnic and thus had to be phoned, and then create the conversations Mrs. Pig might have had with each of them. It was quite a feat for these children to engage in a task they had set for themselves, and it certainly extended their comprehension of this scene in the story.

Engaging students in writing an addition to or replacement for a text, either before or after they have read the entire text, is another way to share and extend comprehension of texts. Creating new text demands that students consider what the author has written so that the new text "fits" with the old. While most LD and remedial students will find writing texts in which their changes are consistent with the author's context challenging enough, some will also benefit from the additional challenge of trying to emulate the author's style. Invite these students to write new text so that readers will not be able to differentiate between their work and that of the original another.

One of our favorite lessons is to engage students in writing a new ending for a story before they have read the author's ending. This lesson works best as part of a week-long learning center activity. First, select a short story that has a point near the end where a variety of predictions about the story's ending might be made (one we like to use with secondary students is Thurber's "Unicorn in the Garden"; our prediction point is just as the police and psychiatrist arrive). Make a copy of the story with the ending cut off at the prediction point you've selected and place it in the learning center.

You might leave the story at the center on Monday and give students until Thursday to read it and write an ending. Students can put their endings in a folder with a warning sign on the cover: "Do not read until you have written your own ending!" On Friday, students share their endings orally and discuss the similarities and differences across endings, what sorts of things led them to end the story in the way they did, and so on. When students read the author's ending, it usually inspires them to further discussion. Sometimes students prefer one of their endings to the author's.

Students might also be asked to write a new section to fit into a text they've already read—an episode in a story, a stanza in a poem, more facts in an expository piece, and so on.

When students discuss their writing and reflections, the discussion often takes them far afield of the original text. When that happens, it's helpful to end the discussion with a question that brings students back to the original text, e.g., "What do you understand better in this text (or about what this author did to create the text) as a result of our discussion?"

SHARING AND EXTENDING THROUGH GRAPHIC REPRESENTATION AND ART

Art has long been used in classrooms to represent what students have learned in study units or from reading a text. Some teachers specialize in creative ways of engaging students in representing what they have learned from reading through art—in models, dioramas, mobiles, paintings, dressing up as book characters, and so on. Students usually enjoy such projects and benefit from them personally. But if these projects are going to promote other students' learning as well, they must be orally shared with others, not just displayed. For example, a scene depicted in a shoe box diorama means little to students who have not read the story from which the scene was chosen. Even when students have read the same book, the scene may mean something different to them than to the student who created it. Thus, the artist should be encouraged to talk with other students about what the art represents and why the student chose to represent that particular part of the text. In turn, the artist may invite the other students to share the textual meanings that have occurred to them as a result of viewing the art work.

We have worked with many pull-out teachers who have understood the value of having students represent what they read through art and other creative approaches but who haven't felt that they worked with students for sufficient periods of time to permit such lessons. One way to deal with time constraints is to make time for students to work on such a representation elsewhere—at home, in the regular classroom, or at another time and place. If this is possible, meet with the students to talk about what they want to accomplish, what materials they need to gather and what they need to do in order to complete the project, and about how the students will keep you informed of their progress. When students finish their projects, they should share them with the group.

A lesson using art that takes very little time is one called *sketch to stretch* (Siegel, 1984). After students have finished reading a text, they're asked to make a rough sketch of what the text meant to them or what they learned from it. After students have completed their sketches, they share them orally, comparing what they chose to sketch and why, and relating what they sketched to the text. Teachers should word their instructions carefully so that students don't all end up with similar sketches, a situation that isn't conducive to extending comprehension. We've involved students of all ages in sketching after reading both narrative and expository materials (even texts about how to study effectively) with marvelous results. In this lesson, students spend far more time in discussing and extending their comprehension of the text through the sketches than in producing them.

Another instructional strategy, *mapping* (Davidson, 1982) or *webbing* (Freedman & Reynolds, 1980; Gold, 1984), combines writing and graphic representation. Students are asked to recall the major points of an expository text or some of the elements of a narrative text and to organize the points or elements graphically to represent their relationship. Essentially, this is a post-reading, student-produced graphic organizer much like the graphic organizer that teachers present to students prior to reading. Lesser points or elements are usually added as well and are mapped so that their relationships to each other and to the major points in the text are also apparent. Swaby (1984) recommends that students' ideas about the text and how those ideas relate to their lives be highlighted by adding questions that graphically emerge from the core of original information in the map or web. (See Swaby, 1984, for examples.) As they do this lesson, students not only discuss what they have learned and how it relates to their lives but also how what they have learned might be organized, graphically illustrated, and thus more easily remembered.

SHARING AND EXTENDING THROUGH GAMES

Games are another way to motivate students to read or to help them reexperience reading materials in new ways. For example, you may wish to consider developing board games based on a work of children's or adolescent's literature (Harste, Burke & DeFord, 1976; J. Morris, 1987). Game cards and game boards can be designed to invite students to share and extend their comprehension of a book and to use a variety of reading strategies for making sense of words in text. Game boards and cards can also be developed to reinforce students' learning of content-area concepts from their textbooks or from nonfiction works (Strom, 1980).

Once your students have read a number of books, you might consider different sorts of games, similar to some TV game shows. Kettel (1981) suggests a quiz show in which students on opposing teams field questions or clues developed from each book or piece of reading material. Whichever team first signals that it can provide the appropriate title for the clue or answer the question, and does so correctly, earns points. Once students have experienced this game format, they may come up with other formats—Concentration or Jeopardy, for example.

Although participation in games like these may help students share and extend their comprehension of text, they will benefit even more if they participate in preparing the games (J. Morris, 1987; Nichols, 1978). If you see a number of different groups of students during the day, you might consider having one group make up a game for another.

SHARING AND EXTENDING TEXT SETS

In most classrooms post-reading activities typically involve a single text, but Henry (1974) notes that this represents "a preoccupation with the skills that are entailed in reading the work (text) singly without relating it to other works" (1).

Although the ability to comprehend a single text is certainly important, relating information across texts may be more important for developing students' knowledge. In this section, we'll present lessons that go beyond single texts and lessons that encourage students to relate one text to another, to share and extend comprehension through comparison, contrast, and synthesis across texts. Single text lessons don't have to precede lessons involving text sets. Lessons involving text sets and single text lessons are both important. Even in a single text lesson, you can encourage children to relate the text to other texts they have read in the past through questions like, "Does this story remind you of others we have read?"

Text sets involve multiple texts—some combination of books, poetry, newspaper articles, and so on—related in a way that permits students to compare and contrast the texts or to synthesize information from all of them. More broadly conceived, text sets can also include material other than written texts—movies, filmstrips, records, and the like. The texts may be alternative versions of the same story, examples of the same genre (e.g., fairy tales or "how and why" stories), or texts that feature a similar structure, or the same character, theme (sibling rivalry, honor), plot, or topic. Text sets are almost always a natural feature of thematic units. We describe various types of texts sets in the following pages.

Crafton (1983) recommends that students who are studying in a content area read a variety of texts related to a topic, what she refers to as *conceptually related* texts. In the study of vaccines in a science class, for example, students may read different texts to answer the same question: "What are the successes and problems with vaccines?" In reading to answer these questions, students may read a variety of expository texts—encyclopedias, nonfiction trade books, biographies of scientists involved in vaccine research, recent magazine articles, transcripts of TV documentaries, newspaper articles, and so on. Many topics even lend themselves to a combination of expository and narrative texts in the same text set (see McClure, 1985 and Moss, 1978 for examples).

Sharing *genre related texts* extends the meaning of individual texts and understanding of the genre itself. For example, Moss (1982; 1984) recommends that students read, compare, and contrast fairy tales or folktales in order to discover common characteristics. Kimmelman (1981) recommends that folktales be grouped into text sets according to the specific sort of plot that underlies the folktale. One of our favorite genre text sets is "how and why" stories, which abound in children's literature. Some of the books that might be included in a "how and why" text set include:

- V. Aardema. *Why Mosquitoes Buzz in People's Ears*. New York: Dial Press, 1975.
- B. Elkin. *Why the Sun Was Late*. New York: Parents' Magazine Press, 1966.
- M. Hirsh. *How the World Got Its Color*. New York: Crown, 1972.
- R. Kipling. *How the Camel Got His Hump*. New York: Spoken Arts, 1976.
- R. Kipling. *How the Leopard Got His Spots*. New York: Walker, 1973.
- R. Kipling. *How the Rhinoceros Got His Skin*. New York: Walker, 1973.
- D. McKee. *The Day the Tide Went Out*. New York: Abelard-Schuman, 1976.

Informational pieces can be grouped into text sets in much the same way. For example, we cut out the "Far-out Facts" columns from several years of *World* magazine and used them as a text set. Individual students read a single column and shared what they had learned with the group, relating the content of one column to another where appropriate. After all of the columns had been read over a number of days, the students categorized the columns (Far-out Facts about Insects, Far-out Facts about Plants, etc.), a task that involved them in another discussion of content, and pasted them by category into a book that became part of the classroom library.

Another type of text set features texts with a similar *structure*. The structure may be quite apparent, such as the highly cumulative or repetitive structure found in predictable books, or it may be less obvious, such as the compare/contrast or problem/solution structures found in expository materials.

Yet another type of text features the same characters or people. Even as adults, we seek out reading material that features *characters* we have met and liked in other books. How many of us, having read *Clan of the Cave Bear* (Auel, 1980), couldn't wait to meet the heroine again in *Valley of the Horses* (Auel, 1982)? Authors write series stories featuring the same characters for all age groups.

Many students will also enjoy discussing *different versions* of the same story. Students frequently find it interesting to compare the movie and book version of a story, such as *Where the Red Fern Grows* (Rawls, 1974) or *The Outsiders* (Hinton,

1980). It's especially easy to find different versions of traditional folktales. The versions can be surprisingly different, and the differences often lead to interesting discussion and writing. For example, in the text sets listed below, there are two versions of *The Miller, His Son, and the Donkey*, one told in standard English and the other in dialect. In the *Jack and the Beanstalk* text set, one of the texts is a modern-day version of the tale.

- M. Calhoun. *Old Man Whickutt's Donkey*. New York: Parents' Magazine Press, 1975.
- R. Duvoisin, illus. *The Miller, His Son, and the Donkey*. New York: McGraw-Hill, 1962.
- R. Briggs. *Jim and the Beanstalk*. New York: Coward, McCann, & Geoghegan, 1970.
- W. DeLaMare. *Jack and the Beanstalk*. New York: Alfred A. Knopf, 1959.
- J. Jacobs. *Jack and the Beanstalk*. New York: Henry Z. Walck, 1975.

Expository text sets may feature different accounts of famous (or infamous) people. Comparing biographies of the same person is always interesting and presents the readers with some critical reading opportunities, especially if an autobiography is also available. For readers who require shorter texts, you might try comparing pieces on the same person from *Time, People, National Enquirer,* and the newspaper for the same effect.

Cassidy (1984) describes a way to organize text sets for student use and gives an example of a theme-based text set. In his example, a fifth-grade teacher placed three stories illustrating courage in a manila folder and wrote "Courage" on the outside of the folder. The first story, "Nobody's Better Off Dead" by Quentin Reynolds, is the true story of a basketball star who, because of an accident, must fight to live and then regain the use of his limbs. Another story, "High Above Niagara's Waters," taken from an old basal reader and made into a "skinny book," is about a man who walked a tightrope above Niagara Falls. The third story, "The Old Demon" by Pearl Buck, concerns a woman who sacrifices her life by releasing the "old demon river" from its dam to stop a Japanese military advance.

The teacher printed questions on the inside of the manila folder to encourage students to synthesize what they had read:

- What is your definition of the term "courage" that encompasses all of the individuals in these stories? Tell how each fits the definition.
- Of the three individuals, who was the most courageous? List at least three reasons for your decision.

Cassidy notes that, although the teacher used this folder with all her students, she adapted the activity for her poor readers by reading the two more difficult selections to them and having them read the third. Because you are working exclusively with poor readers, try to find materials that are within the students' reading capabilities.

You can help students interact with text sets in a number of different ways. Individual students can read/see/hear two or more texts in a set and compare/contrast or synthesize information from the texts. Or individual students in a group can each take responsibility for one of the texts in a set and share what was read/seen/heard with other students in the group, comparing/contrasting and synthesizing information as a group.

You can formalize sharing sessions by using a strategy called "jigsaw" (Aronson, 1978). If you have nine students in the group and three related texts, divide the students into groups A, B, and C. Each group receives a different but related text from the text set; each individual in a group receives the same text to read and become an expert on. After the students have each read a text, they meet together in the A, B, and C groups to clarify and confirm the information with others who have read the same text. Then the groups reorganize so that there is an A, B, and C person in each group; each individual teaches the others about what s/he read and discussed. The new group is also responsible for tying the information together into a whole.

Students who need support in identifying important information in expository material or in synthesizing that information across texts may find data charts useful (Crocker, 1983b; McKenzie, 1979). (See chapter 11 for specific information.) Data charts are applicable not only to reading expository material but also to reading narrative material when you want students to focus their attention on comparing story elements.

Many of the lessons we have already reviewed for single texts are also suitable for use with text sets. Some oral discussion and dramatization ideas, writing follow-ups, art and mapping activities, as well as game ideas can be used with multiple texts. Though you'll be able to generate other ideas by reviewing earlier sections of this chapter with text sets in mind, here are a few to get you started:

- Consider a chapter in a book to be a text and the whole book to be a text set. Smith (1978) suggests that if each student reads a single chapter, and the students then retell the chapters in order, the students can "read a book in an hour," an idea that should be especially appealing for reluctant readers. A related idea may encourage students to finish a book: Several students read and retell the first several chapters; interested students can finish the book on their own.
- Using the structural characteristics or the genre characteristics of a text set, students can write another text. For instance, once students have experienced the *Jack and the Beanstalk* text set, which includes a modern-day version of the tale, they may be interested in constructing modern-day versions of other folktales or fairy tales. Each student's new text may be rightfully considered to be a part of the original text set.
- Using the idea of dialogue dramatization, students can carry on a dialogue based on a similarity they have discovered across stories. For example: Using Snow White and Sleeping Beauty, compare how they met their princes.
- An interesting Readers' Theatre script can be created if students use parts of

a series of books featuring the same character. For example, one Ramona Quimby adventure might be selected from each of Beverly Cleary's *Ramona* books and rewritten into a script.

- The literature quiz show (discussed previously) could be tailored to a particular text set. For example, a quiz show could be prepared for Lloyd Alexander's *Prydain Chronicles*.

The references we recommended in our discussion of thematic units are also useful in identifying text sets for your students. In addition, rely on a good children's librarian for help, especially if you have identified a couple of texts and want to add others to round out the text set. Another way to locate text sets is to look for ready-made sets, with texts already grouped by the publisher. Basal readers, for example, frequently group stories into a unit by theme or feature stories that you can group simply by rearranging the order in which they are read. What you will have to add are the activities and questions that help students relate one text in the set to another.

LEARNING TO ANSWER QUESTIONS

Teachers often assume that students who have problems in answering questions at the end of a text or completing worksheets have had difficulty reading the text or have read it carelessly. But it may be that these students don't know how to go about the task of answering questions. Students who don't understand question asking and answering may experience difficulty in school because questions are a prominent feature in teachers' instruction and assessment.

The Pearson and Johnson question taxonomy presented in chapter 7 has been used by Raphael and others (Hahn, 1985; Raphael, 1982, 1986; Raphael & McKinney, 1983; Raphael & Pearson, 1982, Raphael & Wonnacott, 1981) to help students understand how to answer instructional questions more effectively. The technique is based on the relationship that exists between questions and the texts to which questions refer and the prior knowledge of the reader.

Raphael (1986) outlines question-answer relationships (QARs) that may help students understand the potential sources of information useful in generating answers to questions. The QARs are "Right There," "Think and Search" (or "Putting It Together"), "The Author and You," and "On My Own" and are defined as shown in Figure 10–1 (from Raphael, 1986).

Raphael (1986) recommends the following steps:

1. Introduce the QAR concept. Students may first be introduced only to the top level of the QARs, "In the Book" and "In My Head." Once students understand the two basic categories, introduce the subdivisions of each category, perhaps using the preceding explanations on an overhead. On short passages, demonstrate how you answer questions by showing the students where you found the answers; each QAR is labeled as it is demonstrated.
2. Provide students with short passages to read and discuss as a group.

FIGURE 10–1   Question – Answer Relationships (QARs) (From Raphael 1986)

In the Book QARs

Right There
The answer is in the text, usually easy to find. The words used to make up the question and words used to answer the question are **Right There** in the same sentence.

**Think and Search
(Putting it Together)**
The answer is in the story, but you need to put together different story parts to find it. Words for the question and words for the answer are not found in the same sentence. They come from different parts of the text.

In My Head QARs

Author and You
The answer is *not* in the story. You need to think about what you already know, what the author tells you in the text, and how it fits together.

On My Own
The answer is not in the story. You can even answer the question without reading the story. You need to use your own experience.

Following the reading of the passage, solicit answers to questions. Rather than focusing on the correctness of the answers, help students focus on the information source for the answers by asking questions, such as "How do you know the answer was _____? Can you prove it in any way? Does the text tell you the answer? If not, how do you know it?" and so on.

3. Provide students with increasingly longer passages and an increasing number of questions. As they gain experience, they should progress from group to individual responses and from total teacher guidance and feedback to independent use. The end goal is to help students use QAR information independently to deal more effectively with everyday instructional materials.

With remedial and LD students, we recommend that you include other related information in these lessons. It comes as a shock to many poor students that those who succeed in school often read the questions they are expected to answer before they read the text, including those on standardized tests. It's an easy task to incorporate that feature into any QAR lesson, along with your demonstrations of how to go about answering questions.

Students can be more successful in their classes if they spend some time using QAR information to analyze each teacher's questions and expected responses, and the textbook's questions and expected responses. Some teachers and some textbooks avoid "Right There" questions, while others are very dependent on those sorts of questions in both daily work and tests. Students who are aware of what QARs are likely in each class are better able to meet the expectations of that class. Students who perform poorly on an exam or assignment can often be helped to understand how to perform better in the future by learning to recognize the predominant types of questions and answers.

STUDY READING

Studying as a general topic is outside the scope of this book. We would, however, like to address briefly what's been referred to as "study reading": "careful and deliberate reading in order to understand and remember both details and major ideas presented in a text" (Friedman & Rowls, 1980, 241). Study reading is usually done by students to prepare themselves to take a test. Study reading strategies must help students identify the major ideas and important supporting details in the text and then organize that information so that they can more easily commit it to memory. Additionally, students must learn that effective study reading is different from "cramming."

One strategy that helps students identify and organize important written information is the *post organizer* (H. Robinson, 1983; R. Vacca, 1981). It's essentially the same as the graphic organizer and uses mapping or webbing. Sometimes teachers supply students with a list of the concepts and vocabulary to be learned (especially for tests) and, in such cases, the students may begin by organizing the information.

If identification of the major ideas and supporting details has been entirely left up to the students, a group brainstorming effort at this stage is probably essential along with feedback from you. If at all possible, have the students check the brainstormed list of ideas and details with the content-area teacher. Remember to help students keep in mind what types of information the teacher typically requires to be remembered (see the QAR discussion) as they identify important information.

Group effort is also useful for organizing ideas and details once they've been identified. Students will have an easier time organizing ideas if they write each piece of information on a card or a scrap of paper. In small groups or individually, engage students in organizing their information by having them move the slips of paper around on a tabletop. Encourage them to use the text when they need an explanation of an idea or detail or need to review the relationship of one idea to another. As they finish, ask them to compare how they've organized information with other students. It's perfectly natural that one student's way of organizing will differ from another's; the key is whether the students can defend their arrangement of ideas and whether they will find them useful, given their study goals. If you have also organized the important ideas, share your arrangement of information with the students as well so they can see one way an experienced reader thinks about the information.

Once students have arranged the text in a way that is useful for study, they should copy the information as they have arranged it onto a sheet of paper so that it is handy for studying. The information can be used as students refer back to the text and reread portions of it and as they question themselves and each other about the information in the organizer, or as you conduct "fake pop quizzes" (Readence, Bean & Baldwin, 1981). As we noted in our earlier discussion of games, students will benefit more from such quizzes if they have a hand in making up the questions or quiz items.

Be prepared to assist students through the post-organizer process of study reading well in advance of when they will need to have learned the information, especially if this is the first time students have used the process. As students are assigned chapters or portions of chapters in a content-area class for which they need your support as a resource teacher, begin to work on post organizers for each chapter. Once an organizer has been completed (a lengthy process at first), it is better to spend a small amount of time on review activities stemming from the organizer every day than to cram them into a day or two.

Before we end our discussion of study reading, we'd like to say a few words about a well-known and widely discussed instructional strategy for study reading, *SQ3R* and all its variations. SQ3R is solidly based on what is known about how proficient readers study and learn from text when they must commit the meaning of the text to memory. The steps in the instructional strategy are:

- **S**urvey: The student previews the reading material in order to determine the overall content and organization.
- **Q**uestion: The student establishes a purpose for reading by reviewing the questions posed by the teacher or publisher, or by changing the headings and subheadings to questions.
- **R**ead: The reader reads in order to answer the questions s/he raised in the previous step.
- **R**ecite: The student closes the book and attempts to answer the questions that were raised.
- **R**eview: At a later time, the student again attempts to answer the questions that were raised.

SQ3R originated years ago as a study reading strategy for college students (F. Robinson, 1961). Since then, it's been recommended in virtually every secondary content-area reading textbook published. Certainly many of the recommendations we have made in this and other chapters are consistent with the theoretical basis of SQ3R and engage students in similar steps, albeit not in a single instructional strategy.

R. Vacca (1981) has stated that, unless they are mature readers, secondary students have a difficult time using SQ3R independently. It certainly can be expected that LD and remedial students will experience difficulty using SQ3R independently. This does not mean that it isn't a worthwhile instructional strategy for poor readers, but it does mean that they can't be expected to use it without teacher guidance in some or all of the steps. Like some of the other instructional strategies we have discussed, including the post organizer, SQ3R requires guidance through the process, guidance which is well worth the time when an important instructional goal is learning the content of a text.

CONCLUSION

In this chapter we've discussed a number of teaching strategies to help students comprehend what they've read. In particular, we've discussed a number of teaching strategies to help students share and extend their comprehension of texts and strategies for dealing with very specific purposes for reading, like preparing for tests. We hope these strategies will help you assist students in integrating what they've read with what they know. We also expect that post-reading strategies will, over time, affect how students prepare to read texts in the future. In this way, post-reading strategies affect prereading strategies.

In the last three chapters, we've discussed teaching strategies that take place before students read, while they read, and after they've read a text. These divisions refer to what teachers do and not what we expect of students; that is, we don't expect students to use one set of strategies before they read, another while they're reading, and so on. Overall, we expect these teaching strategies to draw students' attention to the sorts of reading strategies good readers use. We want them to understand that reading is an active, purposeful, and meaningful process through which they construct meaning from text. In the process, they make sense by using a variety of strategies to integrate what they are reading with what they already know. The instructional strategies we have presented can help students develop into mature readers. But again, effective teachers will use our suggestions only as models for their own instructional strategies, which will be affected by their beliefs, their working environment, and mostly by their students. There are no cookbooks for teaching reading—effective teachers make their own decisions about how to help students based on their observations of the students' reading and what they understand about proficient reading behavior.

XI

Composition: Choices and instruction

When people write they not only compose—that is, make choices about content and language—they also transcribe. They encode their meaning in print using the conventions of spelling, punctuation, handwriting, and grammatical usage. Transcription is what a secretary does when s/he "does not have the bother of actually thinking of the words" (F. Smith, 1982b, 21).

Composition, the topic of this chapter, and transcription, the topic of the next chapter, compete for the writer's attention during writing (F. Smith, 1982b). Where writers focus their attention, on transcription or composition, determines what they accomplish during writing. If composition receives the most attention, the writer concentrates on ideas and language choices but may neglect transcription, resulting in mispellings, fragmented sentences, and illegible handwriting. Conversely, if transcription receives the most attention, the writer will concentrate on written conventions and pay less attention to communicative intentions or the needs of an audience.

This isn't a serious conflict for proficient writers, who know that their first concern as writers must be to address problems regarding what to say and how to say it, to consider their purposes, their topic, and the needs of their potential audience. Learning disabled and remedial students, on the other hand, often focus on transcription rather than composition when they write. Instruction for these students must help them not only attend to composition problems as their first concern but also orchestrate content and language choices during composition.

In this chapter, we'll discuss how to help students as they compose by considering such issues as topic selection, audience, voice, language choices, and revision.

TOPIC SELECTION

Writing begins with a purpose that usually includes some topic, e.g., "I promised my grandmother I'd write a letter this week and let her know what I want for my birthday." School writing should also begin with a purpose and a topic. But topic selection and definition are often difficult for students who have written infrequently. Students need to learn how to go about selecting topics and how to define the scope of their topic. Many students write about such broad topics that they neglect the specifics that give writing life.

In general, students should select their own topics for writing. Students who select their own topics not only learn how to choose writing topics independently, but when they select topics well they also achieve significant growth in the information they present about topics, in the organization of information, and in the use of conventions (Graves, 1983). Further, students who choose their own writing topics feel a sense of ownership—of their topics and their writing. From this sense of ownership comes the motivation to express ideas effectively, a very different motivation from that often driving students—to finish the writing assignment as quickly as possible.

Students' best writing arises out of their own experience (Graves, 1983), and even students from "disadvantaged" homes have a wealth of firsthand experience to draw on. Students can also draw on knowledge acquired indirectly from school, TV and movies, the oral and written stories of their peers, and so on. These experiences form the basis of our students' writing.

Unfortunately, many students are convinced that they have nothing worthwhile to write about, nothing that others would care to read about. As one girl put it during a conference, "There's nothin' interesting about me or my family." In such cases, our job is to convince students (and sometimes ourselves) that they do have experiences that are unique and worth relating. Such students need to believe that they have something worthwhile to say and to *feel* the interest of others in their experiences and their lives.

Perhaps the easiest way to help students identify and develop topics from their own experience is to listen to students as they talk with each other and with you. While we were visiting a school, a sixth-grade LD student told us all about heavy construction machinery—what the various machines were used for, how to drive and repair them, and so on. When we asked if he'd ever written about this topic in his classroom, he told us, "The teacher don't let us write about stuff like that. Besides, she don't know I know that stuff."

Teaching writing demands that we know a lot about our students. Unless teachers show genuine interest in students and their experiences, students will not write about, and may not even come to value, what happens in their lives. Graves (1983) recommends a technique to help us find out what we know about our students. He suggests that teachers first write down the names of all their students from memory and then try to write down one or two of the student's interests next to each name. This type of exercise can draw our attention to the students we need to get to know better—by talking with them while walking the class to the lunchroom or while waiting for the remainder of the class to arrive for the period. Teachers who don't know their students well may have a difficult time helping them learn to identify and select writing topics.

Helping students create topic lists can ease topic selection as well as alert teachers to students' interests. Ask students to brainstorm a list of what they do after school and on weekends. As they suggest things, have them expand upon them a bit. For example, if the students all watch TV, ask them which programs they watch or who their favorite characters are. List their comments on the board as potential writing topics. Teachers should also participate in the discussion and share what they do after school and on weekends. When the brainstorming session is over, everyone, including the teacher, should read the list and copy those topics they know a lot about. This could be done on successive days with other general questions or topics, such as family, trips, things I worry about, special events, intriguing characters in my life, or school. This activity works best in a group where students can hear each other's potential topics and borrow appropriate ones for their own use.

Lists of topics can be stapled to the inside of students' writing folders for them to refer to whenever they have difficulty selecting a topic. Remind students to add new experiences or other ideas they've thought of to their lists. As students talk with you and with each other about their lives—like the boy who was interested in heavy machinery—call their attention to possible topics and remind them to add these topics to their lists.

Teachers can also help students learn to limit or expand their topics and at the same time, help them see that the same topic can be the basis of more than one piece of writing. One young man wrote about a topic on his list, basketball, and then crossed the topic off. The teacher had a conference with him and several others who had listed sports as potential topics, in order to brainstorm various subtopics. The boys came up with related and more specific topics, such as "My favorite professional team," "How to play the guard position," "The most difficult thing to do well in basketball," "My best game this year," and "Losing games." The conference not only alerted students to the fact that they had plenty to say (if they wanted to) about their chosen sport but also that a number of other topics on their list could be treated in the same way. This sort of lesson is especially valuable for students who tend to select broad topics and write about them in a very general manner. Narrowing the topic naturally leads students to use more detailed information.

Demonstrating topic choice is another way to help students. In front of the class, you might jot down three or four possible topic choices, relating some details about each topic as you write it down. Choose one of the topics, sharing with students why you chose that topic over the others (your reasons may have to do with how you currently feel about the topic, the amount of information you have, that it's what you want to think about most, and so on). Demonstrate how you can add your other topics to your list of future topics. Then write with the students and share your efforts at some point; the students will also learn from seeing how you developed your piece from the topic you selected, which details you included and excluded, what else you added that you hadn't talked about previously, and so on.

Teachers are sometimes frustrated by students who seem to be stuck on a particular topic. Perhaps the students are playing it safe; that is, they are writing about topics for which they can spell the words. If thus is true of your students, consult our recommendations about spelling barriers in chapter 6. If students appear to be simply enamored of a topic, you might consider our earlier suggestions for helping students narrow their topic or explore different aspects of it. You might also consider the following recommendations from Graves (1983):

- Read over the student's writings and examine them to see if the student is showing growth in some areas. Sometimes students choose the same topic repeatedly so that they can focus on learning to control particular aspects of their writing without having to think much about a topic. An old topic allows them to do that.
- Ask yourself if enough time is being provided for writing. Students who write frequently will more quickly satisfy their need to write about the same topic repeatedly.
- Ask the student about why s/he keeps writing on the same topic repeatedly and see if the student can provide some insight for you.

When students must deal with assigned topics, help them cope with the situation by bringing their own experience to the topic. For example, if students are assigned to write a report about an insect at the end of a unit on insects, help them select an insect they already know something about. Or if a particular insect is assigned, help them understand how they can use what they know from previous experiences with insects to write about this particular one. If students are given a choice of topics, help them to identify which topic they know the most about. If students are given a broad topic like "What I did this summer," help them learn to focus on a specific event so that they are more likely to use specific information rather than banal generalities.

AUDIENCE

As we said earlier, writing begins with a purpose, which includes a topic and a potential audience. Too often when students write in school, they write only for their teachers. If teachers typically *evaluate* rather than *read* students' writing, students will write lifeless pieces, concerned more with getting a good evaluation than with communicating. In addition, if students come to believe that a positive evaluation is beyond their reach, they may write very little, if at all.

Writers need to learn to write for themselves first, since they will typically be the first readers of what they've written. As we write this book, for example, we read our own writing over and over again, concerned first with whether it makes sense to us. While we're writing, we frequently doff our writers' caps and put on our readers' caps, standing back and reading almost as if we had never seen the text before. Some poor writers don't read and reread their own writing, either as they produce it or afterwards. If this is true of your students, demonstrate how you read and react to your own writing and encourage them to do the same with their writing. Also encourage students to reread selected pieces of their writing to help them develop a sense of what they like (and perhaps don't like) about it. We find, and your students probably will too, that our reactions to our writing often change after a day or two has passed. Let students experience that as well.

Writers rarely write only for themselves; they also need to consider the needs of other audiences. For example, as we wrote this book, we were not only writing for ourselves, we were also writing for you. To do that, we found it helpful to recall the many conversations we've had with teachers, as well as our own experiences as classroom teachers and what we would have wanted to know about reading and writing. Murray (1968) suggests that a writer "must know what his reader knows, what his reader doesn't know, what his reader needs to know, and what his reader wants to know" (3). The ultimate success of our efforts depends, in part, on how well we've listened to and observed other teachers and on how well we remember what we knew, didn't know, needed to know, and wanted to know as classroom teachers.

This connection or identification between writer and reader, which was so helpful to us, has interesting instructional implications for helping writers find readers who can understand them. An especially poor writer needs to find a reading audience who will be "a good listener who can go more than half the way to see what the writer has to say" (Murray, 1968, 42). In other words, as we begin helping our students write for various audiences, we need to begin with those audiences that are willing not only to try to understand the student's writing but who also share enough of the writer's world that they can do such things as "filling in" information and figuring out intended words that are not well represented by the student's spelling. As writers get to the point where their writing doesn't demand so much from readers, the range of potential audiences increases.

The following list of potential audiences (adapted from Kirby & Liner, 1981, 134–35) ranges from audiences who are well known to the student and share the student's world to those who are unknown and do not share that world completely:

- Peers
  - in class
  - in other schools
  - generalized peers (children of the world)
  - in other classes
  - pen pals
  - in the school newspaper
  - famous peers
- Teachers
  - classroom teacher
  - resource teacher
  - other teachers
- Wider known audiences
  - parents
  - neighbors
  - parents' friends
  - principal
  - relatives

- Unknown audiences
  - newspaper editor
  - athletes
  - unknown offenders
    (the person who
    threw all the trash
    on the highway)
  - information sources
  - heroes
  - TV and movie
    personalities
  - citizen groups
  - authors
  - corporations
  - governmental
    bodies and
    officials

You'll note that teachers are only one potential audience for students' writing. However, it's likely that students will expect their teachers to evaluate their papers rather than read them to understand their ideas. It may take some time (and other audiences) before students understand that you wish to be a reader rather than an evaluator. Still, you must balance the need to be a sympathetic audience with the need to help students write more effectively so that they can write for larger and wider audiences.

Group peer conferencing is another effective way to provide feedback to writers on the effectiveness of their writing. When students hear, read, and discuss each other's writing, they may begin to see that revisions are necessary; that is, their writing didn't have its intended effect on their audience. At the end of the conference, teachers may wish to summarize what's been said and ask writers if they plan any changes as a result of the discussion. If students wish to make revisions, be sure they know that they needn't rewrite the entire piece in order to add something in the middle, for example. This, of course, is one advantage of allowing students to compose using a word processor.

Feedback can take other important forms as well. Students who write invitations to a book fair and observe that people arrive as planned have received feedback that their communication was understood. Students who get their letters to the editor printed in the school newspaper have also received feedback that their writing was understood and appreciated. So have students whose books are published and read by others. In most of these cases, however, the feedback, while important, cannot be acted upon. This sort of generalized feedback cannot take the place of teacher and peer conferencing.

It's also helpful to engage students in lessons designed to help them consider the influence of audience on the choices writers make about content, form, tone, style, and conventions. One way to do this is to ask students to consider the effects of audience on speech. Teachers might engage students in discussions about the differences in their language when they are talking with their friends on the playground or the gym and when they are talking to an adult authority. Teachers could use a chart like this to help structure such a discussion:

	CONTENT	TONE	VOCABULARY	FORM
Friends				
Policeman				

It's also possible to have the same sort of discussion by providing students with paired sentences like the following (from Williams, Hopper, & Natalicio, 1977), and inviting them to discuss the likely audiences for each sentence in the pair and how and why the speaker changed the form of what s/he was saying:

- May I have your attention, please?
  Shut up and listen.
- Don't bug me.
  Can we discuss it later?
- I beg your pardon?
  Huh?
- Shall we go?
  Let's get out of here!
- What do you want?
  May I help you?

Speakers vary their use of language unconsciously, but a student may need help to "understand that he should do with calculation in his writing what he does naturally in his speech" (Murray, 1968, 42).

Students can also discuss the intended audiences for tapes of radio and TV commercials, and ads from newspapers and magazines. Then, using the comparison technique, ask them to consider how each ad might be different if it were written for a different audience, selling warm-up suits to senior citizens, for example.

Other lessons can help students not only become aware of audiences and their influence on writing but actually begin to consider what they know and use it in writing. One idea is to have students select a real, approachable audience and address that audience directly. Before they write, students could profile the audience, especially if the audience is less well known and/or understood by students. Profiling the audience demands that students consciously ask themselves questions that writers intuitively ask whenever they write:

- What do members of the audience know about the topic? Feel? Believe?
- What are their backgrounds? (age, education, living environment, jobs, leisure activities, hobbies, etc.)

Writers need to identify information about the reader that may be in conflict with what they are about to say if they hope to be at all convincing or believable. They must also consider potential areas of agreement, common background, and so on in order to establish common bonds with the reader.

A special audience students might profile is a teacher in another class who evaluates students poorly on writing assignments. Pull-out teachers can help students profile the teacher for whom they are writing by asking questions such as: What are the teacher's expectations regarding content? What are the teacher's expectations about length? What are the teacher's expectations about the use of conventions? Students who understand the needs and concerns of teachers as audiences will more effectively address those needs and, as a result, will receive more positive evaluations.

Another way to encourage student writers to consider the needs of audiences is to ask them to read their writing to their peers, who will respond from the intended audience's point of view, posing questions, concerns, and arguments like those the audience is likely to pose. Over time, writers will learn to anticipate and answer their readers' needs. The discussion on self-conferencing in chapter 7 includes a number of questions students can raise about their own writing in anticipation of the needs and concerns of their audience.

Students might also write about the same topic for different audiences and then compare the resulting pieces of writing in order to identify audience-related differences. In a lesson (adapted from Eisele, 1978) students read the following telegram (from "Letters Home" in *Harper's*, June 1974).

Mr. and Mrs. Frederick E. Kingsley:

The Secretary of the Army has asked me to express his deep regret that your son, Private First Class Thomas E. Kingsley, died in Vietnam on 20 March 1971. He was on a military mission when an automatic explosive device placed by a friendly force detonated. Please accept my deepest sympathy. This confirms personal notification made by a representative of the Secretary of the Army.

> Kenneth G. Wickham
> Major General USA
> The Adjutant General
> Department of the Army
> Washington, D.C.

After reading the telegram, students are assigned to write one of the following, using information from the telegram and inventing other material as necessary:

- A short story for the soldier's local small hometown newspaper.
- A report of the incident from the officer in charge to his superior officer.
- A short story for a big city newspaper reporting the death of a soldier from a nearby small town.
- An argument in a speech to gain support for the war.
- An argument in a speech asking for an end to the war.
- A letter from Private Kingsley's parents to the soldier's grandparents.

Before and after writing, students discuss the potential audience in each situation in terms of how that audience would affect their decisions as writers. In such a lesson, students discuss such issues as what information is needed; what format might be required; and how conventions might vary from one piece to another as a function of audience. In this assignment, for example, an official form and formal language are best for the report, which probably would be typed, while another piece, like the grandparents' letter, would use a "friendly letter" format and tone and would probably be handwritten.

Although lessons like this will help students understand the effect audience has on writing, writing for real reasons and for real audiences is far more profitable for developing a sense of audience, since real audiences provide authentic feedback. In earlier chapters we presented a number of ideas for encouraging students to write for a variety of authentic audiences. Here are some additional suggestions:

- Have students read what they've written to each other frequently at various points in the writing process. Students are more likely to revise in response to listener questions while they're in the process of writing something than if they consider themselves "finished."
- Publish writing in a variety of ways—in bound books, in class or school newspapers, on bulletin boards, etc.
- When notices for school functions need to be sent to parents, involve students in composing them.
- When students have complaints or compliments, encourage them to write to the proper authorities—the principal, the PTA, the newspaper editor, etc.
- If students from other classes are to be invited to participate in or watch an event, involve the students in composing the invitation.

VOICE

A fifth grader sits down at a new word processor in his Chapter I class on the day of the Challenger space shuttle accident and writes. Chan talks to the machine about his pride in being able to use it and works through the events of the day. He comes back to his writing the next day and adds to it, almost as if he has to let the word processor know what he has found out (see Figure 11−1). Through Chan's writing comes his "voice"—his own personal expression of his response to the events he wants to understand.

Voice is not something that is unique to writing. How often do we hear something a friend has said and think, "That sounds just like her!" Yet if we heard another friend say the same thing, we'd think it odd. Nor is voice something that happens only with language; artists also have "voice," the distinctive style through which they express themselves. Even the style of an orchestra conductor is recognizable to the knowledgeable listener. Assisting students in releasing their voices so that their writing sounds like them or reveals something about them is an important instructional goal.

Self-selected topics and audiences will certainly encourage students to use their voices. A student who feels ownership in a piece of writing, who is speaking from the authority of his own concerns, interests, and experiences, will be more likely to write with the honesty, the authority, the style, and the voice that makes for good writing. Compare the notes that students write to each

---

FIGURE 11–1   Chan's Writing on the Word Processor

```
I AM THE ONLY ONE WHO NOS HOW TO WORK

YOU.I AM VERY SARY FOR THE AXODNT  THIS

MORNING SEVEN PEPOL WER KILLD THIS

MORNING SOME OF THE TECHERS WOR KRING.I

MY SELF DONT THINK ANY ONE SERVIVD,BUT

THAY DONT NO IF ANY ONE SERVIVD. I DONT

RELY NO IF ANY ONE SERVIVD.BUT THE WHAY

IT LOOK NO ONE SERVIVD BUT LOOK CAN BE

DSEVING. BUT WEN I FIND OUT I WILL BE

BACK,THAT IS  ALL I NO RIGHT NOW. I AM

BAKE THIS IS WEDNEDAY ,29 1986, ALL OF

THE PEOPLE   DIDE THAY SID IT ON NOSE

LASS NIGHT THAY HAVENT EVEN FOWND A PEES

OF THE SPASHATL. THE LAST WORD THAT THAY

SAID WAS CHALLENGER GO AT THROTTLE UP.

SMITH. ROGER. GO AT THROTTLE UP.

FIREBAL
```

---

other with the other writing that they do. Do the other pieces of writing reveal the "voices" that the students use in their notes?

Writing in the first person is more likely to release students' voices. Talking about what they've decided to write about, remembering why they had originally selected the topic, and reading pieces aloud will all help students use their voices in writing. Marking the parts of their writing where their voices are clearest and sharing those with other students will also help young writers get a feel for the elusive thing called "voice."

Some more direct lessons may also encourage students to discover other important aspects of voice in writing—that their voices change in relation to their feelings about a topic and that they can adopt a variety of voices in their writing. So that students discover the changing nature of the writing voice, Kirby and Liner (1981) suggest asking students to do what they call "mad talking," "soft talking," and "fast talking." In "mad talking," students spend a few minutes brainstorming about various things, people (unnamed), or situations that make them angry. In "soft talking," students brainstorm about a person or thing (live or inanimate) that could use some comforting. In "fast talking," students brainstorm about situations in which they need to convince or persuade someone to do or believe something. After brainstorming has produced a number of ideas, provide time for individual students to choose something from the list, or to think of something else, and then to "talk" on paper using their angry, comforting, or persuading voices.

When they have finished writing, students can share what they have written by reading it aloud and considering whether each paper sounds as if the person is "talking" with an appropriate voice (e.g., does the person sound angry? Which paper sounds the angriest? the least angry? why?). If your students are capable of more in-depth thinking about the issue of voice, engage them in comparing some angry, comforting, and persuading papers and considering what characterizes each voice. Encourage students to think of other voices and try them out, to identify them in the compositions they've written, and to choose an old composition and rewrite it with a different voice.

Another idea requires that students write from several different points of view using a new voice each time. Kirby and Liner (1981) suggest that students first write about a favorite possession, one they have strong feelings about, using their own voices in the first person. Or begin by having students write in the first person about an event that involved others. Once they have completed this piece of writing, invite students to write about the same event from another point of view. For example, once a teenager has written about his portable stereo from his own point of view, have him write about it as if he were his mother, his best friend, etc. (It's much easier for students to "feel" the difference in voice if they write from the point of view of someone who reacts much differently to the object or situation.) No matter which voice writers adopt, have them write in the first-person "I" form. When these pieces of writing are shared with others in the group, have listeners try to identify who is speaking. Has the writer captured the "voice" in such a way that readers/listeners can identify the likely writer/speaker?

You may also wish to draw students' attention to the voices of published authors. Discuss how particular authors share their opinions or feelings with their readers. You might suggest that students rewrite stories or parts of stories from a different point of view (Crafton, 1984). Can you imagine, for example, how the voice in "The Three Billy Goats Gruff" would change if it was written from the troll's viewpoint?

Although it's easier to help students use their voices if they're writing about their own experiences in the first person, don't neglect to encourage them to do the same in their stories and their expository writing. Once students understand the nature of "voice," begin calling attention to its use in a wide variety of contexts.

DEVELOPING CONTENT THROUGH SPECIFICS

I like football. It is the best game. Football is my favorite sport. (written by a sixth-grade student)

This composition contains only general statements with no supporting details or specifics. It's the sort of composition students write when they don't possess specific supporting information or don't use what they have.

In order to use specifics in a piece of writing, students need to be aware of what they see, hear, taste, smell, and feel. Those of us who are amateur photographers know the feeling of looking at the visual world in a different way after peering through the camera lens and learning to frame pictures. Even without the camera, we still look at the world as if we were taking photographs to capture scenes in various ways. Writing is somewhat similar; that is, once you've written and tried to capture an event or scene in words, you begin to look at other events and scenes through a writer's eyes, attending to specifics of what you hear, see, or feel. Although the lessons that follow will help students learn to identify specifics and use them in their writing, writing itself enables students to sharpen their perceptions just as picture-taking enables photographers to sharpen their perceptions of the visual world.

The following lessons can help students attend to a number of things related to the notion of specifics, including what specifics contribute to writing, how to gather specifics, and how to use specifics in writing. In order to understand what specifics contribute to writing, students need to compare materials that do and do not contain specifics about the same topic. This is an easy lesson to construct if you first find some materials that contain specifics and then rewrite them in more general terms. For example, in Figure 11−2 we used a portion of *But Not Stanleigh* (Steiner, 1980), which is full of specifics (left column) and rewrote it to express only the general meaning (right column).

We asked students to read and compare each version, focusing on details Steiner used that were not included in the more general version and how they helped readers. We also involved the students in thinking about which senses Steiner used to generate specifics. A good follow-up to a discussion like this would be to have students locate places in recent compositions of their own where they could incorporate specifics.

Another useful lesson is to discuss writing that both "shows" and "tells." Writing that "tells" is general; it relies on words that describe what's been seen (pretty), heard (loud), felt (sad), tasted (tangy), smelled (sweet), or touched (hot), revealing the writer's conclusions about some experience. Writing that "shows" contains specific information about what the writer has sensed or experienced, leaving the reader to infer the writer's conclusion.

Writing frequently contains both "telling" and "showing," but the "telling" reveals the writer's conclusion, while the "showing" supports the writer's conclusion through specifics. Discussing such a piece of writing is useful in helping students understand the difference between showing and telling before

---

FIGURE 11–2 Specifics and General Meaning: *But Not Stanleigh* (Steiner 1980)

Specifics	**General Meaning**
Bumpty, bounce. Bumpty, bounce. Stanleigh ran into a field, a field of flowers. Swish, swish. Swish, swish.	Stanleigh ran into a field.
He found a tall flower. He pulled the blossom down so he could see it better. He put his nose into its yellow center. Ummmm. It smelled sweet.	He found a flower and smelled it.
For a long time Stanleigh lay on his back in the grasses and flowers. Then he heard a noise. Bubbly, gurgle. Bubbly, gurgle. Rolling over, he ran, looking for the sound. Soon he smelled water. The bubbly gurgle sound was water.	He found water.
Stanleigh put his paws in the water. The water was cool, and it moved. The water in his dish just sat there.	He touched the water.

---

they use specifics to "show" in their own writing. An example we've found especially useful is a short poem entitled "Afraid of the Dark" (Silverstein, 1974, 159). Before students read the poem, we share a memory of being afraid of the dark and encourage students to do the same.

As students share their brief stories, we keep using the words "show" and "tell" so that they really understand the connection of those words to their examples. We might say, "Checking inside your closet for monsters every night is a good detail to *show* us that you were afraid of the dark. If your mother saw you do that, she probably knew you were afraid of the dark even though you didn't *tell* her so." Finally, the students read and discuss the poem together, looking for lines that "show" and lines that "tell."

After discussions like these, ask students to find sentences in recent compositions that "tell" instead of "show." For instance, the boy who wrote the piece on football quoted earlier chose "Football is my favorite sport." As a class, students can consider several such sentences and list specifics that would lead a reader to the writer's conclusion. For example, to "show" that football is a favorite sport, the students suggested the following supporting details:

- I watch football every Sunday and Monday.
- I play football with my friends every chance I get.
- For my birthday, I asked for a new football and a football helmet.
- When my mother really wants to punish me, she won't let me play football.
- I read all the articles in the newspaper on football.
- When I grow up, I want to play pro football.

Have students work on another example or two in small groups until everyone has developed a list of specifics for a general statement from a recent piece of writing. The following day, ask the students to use their lists to write a paragraph that "shows" readers instead of "tells" them. The students can choose details from their lists and add other details that have since occurred to them. With the help of his classmates, the boy who wrote "My favorite sport is football" revised it as follows:

> My favorite sport is football. I watch the football games on TV every Sunday and Monday with my dad and read all the articles in the paper about the games on Monday and Tuesday. I practice football over at the park with the D&W team and we play a league game every week. When my mother punishes me, she grounds me. Then I get really upset because I can't play with the team that week.

In sharing these revisions with each other, students may wish to read everything but the "telling" sentence, the first sentence in the football paragraph. If students have done a good job of "showing," their classmates are likely to be able to guess the "telling" sentence.

Besides encouraging readers to come to their own conclusions, specifics are also useful in clarifying an author's intended meaning. Writing instructions for a common task is probably the best way to help students understand the importance of specifics. One popular lesson requires students to write clear and complete directions for making a peanut butter sandwich (Murray, 1968; Yoakley, 1974), assuming that the reader has never made a peanut butter sandwich before. Once students have finished writing their directions, the fun begins as directions are read aloud and followed to the letter. When students watch the teacher trying to put peanut butter on an invisible piece of bread because the bread wasn't mentioned in the directions, they quickly see where they need to revise their writing. Of course, this activity can easily be adapted to a number of other situations. It is also interesting to have students share examples of incomplete or inexplicit instructions they come across outside of school (instructions for assembling a model car, for example).

Writers sometimes choose topics for which they lack sufficient specific information, or they may overestimate what they do know. In such cases, they must spend some time gathering specifics by observing the subject and finding out information about the subject. To help them understand how to do that, students can be assigned to select a place and the people (or animals) in it for close observation. Murray (1968) suggests that students spend some time recording visual specifics, some recording what they heard (including chunks of dialogue that "capture" the place), and some recording smells, tastes, physical feelings, and so on. The more details students collect, the easier it will be to write a piece that "shows" the place being described. Extraneous details can always be excluded.

Vergason (1974) recommends a similar assignment using specifics to describe a single person. He suggests that once students have selected a person to observe, they surreptitiously observe that person over a five-day period, capturing a variety of moods and situations by using all their senses, noting mannerisms, and recording quotes that are typical or provide insights into the person's attitudes, opinions, and speech patterns. When students discuss or write about the person they've observed, they should protect the person's identity. Murray's and Vargason's assignments may also be combined.

Of course, not all compositions permit direct observation. In such cases, specifics must be gathered from secondary sources, such as trade books, reference books, interviews, and brochures. Gathering specifics for reports demands generating questions (or subtopics) to be addressed in the report. Ideally these questions should come from students themselves but the reality is that teachers often require students to address certain subtopics. For example, after studying insects a teacher may ask students to write about an insect of their choice and to include in their report information about the insect's habitat, what preys upon the insect, and what the selected insect eats.

Learning disabled and remedial students frequently have had little experience in writing reports. They need to be taught the process—from how to generate questions to be answered in the report and how to gather specific information to answer the questions to how to organize that information into their final report. One of the most useful techniques we have encountered in teaching students to write reports is the data chart (Crocker, 1983b; McKenzie, 1979). A data chart for the insect report assignment could look something like the one shown in Figure 11–3.

We recommend that teachers construct data charts *with* students rather than *for* them. Construction of the chart itself ought to be part of the report-writing process. If, for example, students are given the insect assignment in another class, we begin by having them tell us what they understand the assignment to be, giving special attention to those things the teacher has specified should be discussed. Each aspect should be turned into a question and entered by the student in a column of the chart (see the first three columns on the chart as examples). Any other questions students want to answer in their report (see the last two columns on the chart as examples) should be entered as well. Then show the students the function of the horizontal columns. Note that students will often have background information that can be recorded in the "me" column. Or they may be able to make direct observations and record those observations in the "me" column. The "sources" columns should be filled in

FIGURE 11–3   Data Chart for Insect Report Assignment

	What is the habitat of _____?	What eats _____?	What does _____ eat?	What does _____ look like?	How does _____ harm/help man?
Me					
Source #1					
Source #2					
Summary					

with the names of the books, magazine articles, encyclopedias, and similar sources they have used to locate information. Encourage students to check the information from one source by comparing it with other sources. Sometimes they'll locate conflicting information; at other times, they'll simply find more information. The summary column encourages students to synthesize the information from all their sources and forms the basis for the report itself.

Again, encourage students to seek details during the information-gathering process; it's the details that will make their report worthwhile for others to read. The search for details may well raise more questions in students' minds; these questions may be added to the chart if there is sufficient time and energy to do more investigation. Although this shouldn't be imposed on them as a rule, students often find that each column lends itself to a paragraph in the report if enough details have been gathered. Because their data charts provide them with the information they need, they can then turn their attention to which paragraph ought to be first, second, and so on. Writing the paragraphs on separate index cards and moving them around allows students to organize the report in a variety of ways before they select one. A useful strategy lesson for more sophisticated writers at this point would be to help the students create transitions between the paragraphs that need them. For example, in the insect report, a transition could be very useful between the two paragraphs resulting from columns two and three.

As in all strategy lessons, remember that your main instructional goal is to help students do independently what you have demonstrated. Expect that a series of lessons in teaching students how to write reports will take a great deal of time as you guide them through the required steps and spend time on each (including things we haven't discussed, such as learning to locate books using the card catalogue, and so on). Teaching students to observe with all their senses and put their observations into words or to gather specific information from secondary sources and use that information in a report provides important writing lessons. Your main goal, here as elsewhere, is to help students discover strategies that will be useful to them in any number of learning situations.

LANGUAGE CHOICES

Writers constantly make choices about language as well as content. They make complex decisions about structuring sentences, paragraphs, and entire texts and about selecting vocabulary that best conveys their meaning. These choices are, of course, interdependent and also relate to topic, audience, purpose, and the like. This section will explore a number of instructional issues and lessons that will help students consider the available choices in their sentences, paragraphs, and texts.

The choice of a specific *text structure* grows out of the writer's purpose. If the student's purpose is to tell a story, a narrative structure is the appropriate choice. If the student needs to write an essay exam, an expository structure is probably more appropriate.

Students can usually choose an appropriate text structure intuitively if they have determined purpose, topic, and audience for themselves. However, they may be at a loss if the teacher defines the writing purpose, topic, and audience. For example, if students are asked to write an essay on the causes of the Revolutionary War, they need to understand the teacher's purpose before they can choose an appropriate text structure. Students who don't understand that text structure grows from writing purpose may think, because of the word "causes" in the assignment, that they need to use a "cause/effect" text structure, especially if they've been introduced to text structure terminology without understanding it. If students understand that their purpose is to list various causes of the war and elaborate on them, they understand that the structure they need is one of "enumeration," whether or not they know the terminology for the structure. In other words, text structure choice is a natural outgrowth of understanding the purpose for the writing, whether it is initiated by the student or the teacher.

Avoid assignments that ask students to use particular text structures and generate purposes for which the text structure would be appropriate, e.g., "write a compare/contrast essay on a topic of your choice"; and assignments that treat text structure as a numerical formula, e.g., "wrtie a five-paragraph theme on honesty." If applied formulaically by teachers or students, text structures, whether narrative or expository, lead only to poor writing. A well-selected topic, a meaningful purpose, and a teacher who works effectively with students to help them create meaning are the keys to learning to make effective language choices about text structure.

The text structure lessons we referred to in our discussion of reading in chapter 9 will also help students with their writing, since choosing text structure in writing relies on intuitive knowledge gained largely by reading. If students have done little reading of expository texts, they can't be expected to have much knowledge of how those texts are structured when they write. Specifically, an adaption of the graphic organizer lessons presented in chapter 9 can help students prepare for writing papers and exams. Students could generate the information for a graphic organizer on the exam question we posed earlier about the causes of the Revolutionary War, based on the information they've learned in their social studies class. Then, with your guidance, they could compose an essay together, as McGee and Richgels (1985) suggest, focusing on the text structure and how the ideas relate to one another within that structure.

Paragraphs alert readers to topic changes, but they do not stand alone. As parts of a larger text, paragraphs must relate to the text as a whole and to other paragraphs in the text in ways that maintain a coherent structure. But, since paragraphs function *within* a text it makes little sense to teach students how to write "good" paragraphs before allowing them to write text. Paragraphing is a part of writing texts, a way that writers consider the needs of their audience.

Students need to learn about the nature of paragraphs and how paragraphs function within texts. However, most of us would throw up our hands just thinking about trying to explain the precise functioning of paragraphs within texts, even to secondary students. What we need to do is to provide experiences that increase students' intuitive knowledge about the function and structure of paragraphs. Of course, the primary source of information about paragraphs is students' reading. However, some lessons directly draw students' attention to paragraphs.

The puzzle strategy described in chapter 9 can be helpful. As students order the paragraphs of a text in some logical way, they deal with the kinds of choices authors make about paragraphs—which paragraphs are gathered under which subtitle, how paragraph topics are related to each other, how authors use transitions between paragraphs, and so on. If students cut their own writing into paragraphs, they can try various arrangements of paragraphs, sometimes generating new ways of thinking about texts in the process.

The same strategy can be used to help students achieve an intuitive feel for the choices authors make in arranging sentences into paragraphs. Several paragraphs that make sense out of context can be selected from a text. Sentences in each paragraph may be written separately on strips of paper and given to students in random order. As students order the sentences to construct paragraphs, they'll discover that they can usually determine which sentences go together and why—that they are related by topic. Additionally, by ordering sentences within each paragraph they will also develop an intuitive sense of how sentences are related to each other within paragraphs.

The puzzle strategy can also be used with paragraphs from students' compositions. Students might rewrite each of their sentences on separate strips of paper and then move them around, creating a variety of "new" paragraphs. In addition, students might rearrange sentences from each others' compositions, allowing the original author to see it in a fresh way. When moving sentences, students may discover that one sentence really doesn't fit with the rest of the sentences in the paragraph. In such cases, they can elect to delete the sentence, to add other sentences to it so that the sentence has a paragraph of its own, or to consider whether the sentence would fit better in a different paragraph.

It might also be useful to heighten students' awareness about when to indent or paragraph in their compositions. One way to do so is to provide a text (a published author's or a student's) without paragraph indentations and involve students in locating those places where they think paragraphs might be marked. In a follow-up discussion, ask students to explain their decisions. They are likely to talk about such issues as paragraphing cues (e.g., repetition of content words, shift in topic, wording such as "in conclusion") and length (Bond & Hayes, 1984). Remember that paragraph indentations can occur at a variety of reasonable places; don't let students conclude that the author's original way is the only way to do it.

Like text structures, paragraph structures shouldn't be taught in terms of formulas that ignore the larger context within which they occur. Too often, students are taught that paragraphs always begin with a topic sentence, which is followed by other sentences (usually specified as four) that supply supporting details. Even a brief examination of published texts provides evidence that paragraphs are not consistently constructed in such a manner. Consider the following paragraphs:

Korean young people feel that they must always obey their parents. The father is especially respected, and his advice is always sought. In 1981 Korean young people were asked this question: "Do you want to choose your own husband or wife, or do you want your parents and a match-maker to choose for you?" More than seventy percent of both males and females answered that they wanted their families to choose for them.

Some countries are called melting pots because so many races of people live together peacefully. Korea has only one race of people, but it is a melting pot of ideas. Because powerful countries have invaded their land many times, the people have been forced to listen to new ideas. If they liked the ideas, they fit them into their own lives. They made them Korean. (Farley, 1983, 23–24)

The first paragraph does begin with a topic sentence. In the second paragraph, however, the topic sentence is the second sentence. Topic sentences can occur in a variety of places in paragraphs, and sometimes they aren't used at all, leaving the reader to determine the main idea.

Any time writers compose sentences, they make decisions about vocabulary and sentence structure. Since these choices are made within the context of whole texts, instruction in sentence structure and vocabulary use should also occur within the context of whole texts. The act of composing and getting feedback through vehicles like conferences will naturally enlarge a student's language repertoire. If teachers determine that directed lessons are necessary to help students understand the choices that are available to them in sentences, *sentence expansion*, *word substitution*, and *sentence combining* may be useful.

In order to help students understand the choices available in sentence expansion, we find sentences in their writing that have the potential for expansion. Recently, in a Chapter I class, we lifted a sentence from each student's composition and wrote them on the board. Where words or phrases could be added to the sentences in order to expand them, we inserted a caret and asked for ideas from students about what might be added. The students supplied a number of ideas for expansion, which we wrote on the board above the caret. Then the student who wrote the sentence was asked to decide which word or phrase s/he preferred from among those suggested, keeping in mind not only what words and phrases were interesting but also which best fit the original context.

Another day we again asked students to look at sentences lifted from their writing, but this time they themselves were to identify places in their sentences where ideas could be expanded. Finally, we asked students to locate sentences that could be expanded in their own compositions, to expand those sentences, and then to share the results with their classmates. Eventually, students were observed attending to sentence expansion when they were revising their own writing.

Similar procedures may be used in the case of "overused" words—"pretty," "nice," "happy"—or slang terms such as "awesome." The only difference is that the word or phrase to be considered is underlined so that substitutions can be made. It's often revealing if sentences that feature the same overused word are lifted from various compositions; students discover that they can replace the overused word with any number of more precise words. One teacher we know even goes so far as to "trash" overused words in her class. Students write the words they are going to try not to use in the future on small cards and throw them into a garbage can for overused words. A bit of humor in lessons like these can go a long way in helping students think about making more effective word choices in sentences.

Some students overuse phrases in their writing, phrases that are "empty" in the sense that they're simply placeholders. A typical example, "I like... because...," comes from a writing sample written by a boy named Jeremy after a trip to a museum:

> I liked that Cheetah because it pulled up that deer. I liked the zbra because uve his shrips. [I liked the zebra because of his stripes.]
> I liked the Tyrranasaurus Rex because of his sharp teeth and he's a meat eater and that's why I like him.
> I liked the gold at the musem because it is shiny.
> I liked the saber tooth tiger when he was going to jump on the dinosaur.

To help Jeremy, the teacher gave him stick-um paper and asked him to cover up all his "I like" and "because" wordings with it, leaving the important facts he had written/dictated about his trip. Next, the teacher demonstrated how to rewrite two sentences chosen by Jeremy so that they did not feature "I like... because...." The two sentences were rewritten as:

> The saber tooth tiger was going to jump on the dinosaur. [*which the boy decided he wanted to be rewritten again*: The saber tooth tiger looked like it was going to jump on the dinosaur.]
> The zebra had stripes.

Jeremy himself rewrote the other sentences without "I like...because..." and then discussed with the teacher how his new piece compared to his old piece. Since Jeremy has abandoned his overuse of "I like...because...," he has made good strides in the kinds of sentences he constructs in his compositions.

Finally, students can learn a great deal about the language choices available to them through sentence combining (Nutter & Safran, 1983, 1984; see S. L. Stotsky, 1974, for a review of research). Moffett (1968) suggests that "the learner must hear and read many sentence constructions that would not initially come to his mind. But he needs to try out the forms he takes in" (168). Students can use sentence combining to try out various sentence forms. We don't recommend commercially developed exercises, however. First, students need to understand that sentence combining is a language *choice*, not a requirement. Through playing around with various sentence combinations, students learn that it's their choice whether the sentences should be combined, and if they are to be combined, how to combine them. It's only through comparing various combinations of the same sentences that students can sense the subtle changes in meaning caused by the various sentence combinations and the effect of those changes in meaning on the composition itself. Moffett says, "Only a comparison of sentence alternatives—in the context of what the author is trying to accomplish—will teach judgment" (1968, 177).

Teacher demonstration, lifting, and comparison are all techniques that can be used to help students, either in group lessons or individual conferences, consider sentence combinations. A teacher might choose, for example, the following three sentences from a student's composition for consideration:

My dog's name is Blacky.
He likes to play with me.
He likes to catch the Frisbee.

Some of the combinations the group might consider include:

My dog Blacky likes to play with me and catch the Frisbee.
Blacky, my dog, likes to catch the Frisbee and play with me.
Blacky, my dog, likes to play with me, especially when I
throw the Frisbee.
When I want to play Frisbee, I can count on my dog Blacky to
play with me.

In the beginning, teacher demonstration is important in showing students what sentence combining is. As students begin to understand the notion of sentence combining, teacher demonstration is important in presenting new combinations to students that they haven't consider themselves. Occasionally, challenge students to generate as many different combinations as possible for the two or three sentences you've lifted from a student's composition. Of course, you can also participate and demonstrate more combinations to add to their lists.

In individual conferences, you might ask students to think about how a couple of sentences from their composition might be combined, either for greater effect or to reduce redundancy. Whether the sentence combining work is done in a group or individually, however, the last step ought to be to ask the students whose writing is being considered what their decision is regarding the ideas that have been generated. As in the case of sentence expansion or substitution ideas, the students should make choices based not only on what sounds interesting to them but also on the context from which the sentences were lifted. Remember too that students have the right to decide not to revise but to stick with their original sentences.

REVISING

For many purposes, composition includes not only planning to write and getting ideas on paper but also the process of revision. Revising requires that authors "revisit" their thoughts to consider whether they've fulfilled their purposes. Revision "is what the writer does after a draft is completed to understand and communicate what has begun to appear on the page. The writer reads to see what has been suggested, then confirms, alters, or develops it, usually through many drafts. Eventually a meaning is developed which can be communicated to a reader" (Murray, 1982, 73).

Writers attend to various aspects of writing when they revise their work—the content or the specific information they've selected to develop the topic, the voice they've adopted for the audience, and the decisions they've made about text structure, sentence structure, and word choice. Writers also consider a number of levels when they revise. At a global level they might consider whether to delete a whole section of text, while at a focal level they might consider whether to add a descriptive word. "Revisiting" a composition can thus result in deletion, addition, reorganization, no change, or a combination of these.

Proficient writers often revise with little or no feedback from an audience. They're able to stand back from their writing and adopt a reader's stance, judging the text for its value to their readers. As they revise, they use a variety of strategies. They move back and forth between various aspects of their writing that need revising and between global and focal levels. To do all this, they read to monitor their writing, to decide what needs revision; once the writing has been revised, they read again to monitor their writing. When proficient writers do seek feedback from others, they often specify what they want feedback about and then decide whether to pay attention to it or not. Inexperienced writers need to learn to do the same things. They learn by seeing revision demonstrated by their teachers and fellow students, by being encouraged to revise by their community of readers, and by experiencing for themselves the potential of revision.

Revision is not unknown to young writers, no matter how inexperienced as writers they are. Revision takes place every time students rearrange their folders or desks or decide to take a different way home from school. More akin to writing, it takes place when they draw something, look the drawing over, and make changes. Capitalizing on this everyday experience with revision, Catroppa (1982) describes a lesson to help students understand revision in writing. During the lesson, students work and revise in the medium of clay and then work and revise in the medium of writing, and, finally, compare the two experiences.

Although revision is not unknown to inexperienced writers, they approach revision differently than proficient writers do because of differences in their development and experience. For example, Calkins (1986) describes third graders' writing revisions in this way:

Even when the youngsters make substantive content revisions, their revisions tend to be corrections. Their purpose is to make the text match the subject that was in their mind when they began writing. Often children will find that a draft doesn't match "what really happened." This leads them to insert information or to write a new draft, which is meant to be a more accurate or more complete version of the first. In the child's mind one draft is replaced by a second. This means that the two drafts do not exist simultaneously in the writer's mind, nor are they used as a lens for discovering new meanings, new subjects. (87)

In addition to differences in development, inexperience with the writing process at any age can lead students to approach revision in different ways. For example, students may resist revision because they have chosen a topic in which they do not have substantial personal investment, or because they feel that producing new writing is more important than revising old writing. They may not be motivated to revise because they don't have a vision of what their audience wants or needs, or simply because they consider getting the message down on paper enough. Further, students may have observed over their years in school that "revisiting" writing has often meant what we refer to in the next chapter as editing, a chore they find distasteful because they haven't experienced the end result of having their work published.

Conferences can help students learn to value revision and to make specific revisions. When authors hear feedback from readers over time, they begin to incorporate that feedback into the writing process. They learn to anticipate the questions that listeners/readers might ask and to answer them in their revisions. They learn to look at their current writing with the sense of distance characteristic of readers and to incorporate the information and structure that readers want and need.

Some conference questions help students learn to judge the value of the information they've included: "Why did you choose this topic?" "What part did you like best?" "What will interest your readers most?" and "Read the part that tells most what this piece is about." Questions like these help authors decide not only what is worth keeping and perhaps expanding but eventually what is worth discarding from a piece of writing. Students often revise only by adding information "until [they] can value one part of the story over another, and know how to heighten meaning through the exclusion and reorganization of information" (Graves, 1978, 156).

Conference questions also help students move from focal revision to more global revision and away from the notion of revision as "correction." For example, if students are encouraged to find sections of their writing that seem essential to their intent and to talk about why those sections are significant, they may discover new meaning in their writing. If they are asked to consider and experiment with another approach (e.g., another point of view) or to fix in their minds exactly who their audience is and to read and revise with that audience in mind, they're likely to move toward larger or more global revisions (Calkins, 1986).

As we noted earlier, an author's revision is helped along by direct feedback from listeners/readers who hear/read a draft of a composition. But if readers are to provide feedback that is helpful to the author, they must learn to do so. Of course, in learning to provide feedback to other authors, students also learn how to provide feedback to themselves as author. That is, they learn to ask themselves questions that generate ideas about revision, thus internalizing the revision process.

Students need to learn strategies for making revisions. Some students resist revision because they think it means rewriting the entire piece or because it "messes up" their writing. Others use revision strategies that are not always effective; erasing, for example, may be an effective way to substitute one word for another but not to change large blocks of information.

In all these situations, students benefit from lessons in which teachers demonstrate revision strategies. Depending on what you see as students' revision needs, consider demonstrating the following revision strategies with your own writing:

- Cutting and taping or stapling.
- Drawing arrows to places where additions could be made (e.g., margins).
- Using codes to denote where additions coded the same way fit into text.
- Crossing-out words, lines, whole blocks of text.
- Using carets to insert information.
- Numbering to reorder paragraphs.
- Writing on one side of the paper.
- Writing on every other line.
- Leaving large margins for additions.
- Any other revision strategy you use as an author.

Of course, the mechanical process of making revisions is much easier for students who use word processors.

One way to regularly organize feedback from readers to authors and to encourage revision is the "Authors' Circle" (Burke, 1985). The Authors' Circle involves the following steps:

1. A group of students, usually three or four, gathers, each with a piece of writing "in process." The teacher should join the group regularly, at least in the beginning, and as a member of the group, should share writing from time to time as well.
2. One person begins by reading her/his writing aloud to the other group members. It's the job of the others to listen as well as possible.
3. Each listener in the group "receives" the writing by telling what s/he liked best about the piece. Students need to be helped to make specific comments as they receive writing. As one of the group, the teacher also receives the writing and in so doing, demonstrates receiving.
4. A group member asks the author, "What (part) did you like best about your piece of writing?" and the author replies to the question.

5. A group member asks the author, "What (part) has given you trouble in this piece of writing?" and the author replies to the question.
6. Each listener may then make suggestions to the author regarding the concerns the author has raised. The author is encouraged to take notes about the suggestions but should not comment on them or defend what s/he did.
7. The authors' circle proceeds with each author in the circle having a turn to read, to have his/her work received, and to seek suggestions for potential revision from the listeners.
8. When the authors' circle has finished its work, each author privately considers the suggestions the group has made and makes decisions about revision of the writing. If it supports the students' thinking, before leaving the group each might be asked to reply to this question: "What do you think you might do about the suggestions/comments you heard in the Authors' Circle?"

Revision makes sense for any piece of writing in which the student remains interested and/or which the student wants to publish, but it makes sense only at the level of revision the student can handle. The point is not to have the student produce the piece of writing as you would have produced it, but to extend what the student is doing as a writer in the revision process. Extending what the student can do is the goal of conferences: "Revisions that children make as the result of the conference can be at a much higher level than those made when the child is working and reading alone" (Graves, 1983, 153).

Once students understand the point of revision and its potential, it may become as important for them in the writing process as it is for proficient writers. Students who are regularly invited to "revisit" an old piece rather than to start a new one may find new joy in writing—discovering new meaning in the old. Murray (1982) captures well the potential of revision for learning disabled and remedial students:

> In my teaching of "remedial" students, the exploration of a subject through many drafts is the single most significant motivating factor. Teachers constantly make the judgment that their least motivated students will not write many drafts, when in fact they are often the students who most quickly write many drafts once they experience the excitement of exploring a subject with language. (84)

CONCLUSION

In this chapter we have discussed writing composition—the choices authors make about the content and language of their writing in light of their topics, purposes, and the needs of their audiences. In most cases, students learn to write by having frequent opportunities to write for authentic audiences who provide feedback about the communicative effectiveness of the writing, i.e., did the writing do what the writer hoped it would? Other data about writing will come from students' reading.

In some cases, especially with learning disabled and remedial students, feedback from audiences may not be enough. These students may also require more explicit instruction in the "art of writing," which the lessons presented in this chapter are meant to provide. Remember, too, that these lessons should complement students' authentic writing and should never replace having students write for their own purposes on topics of their own choosing. In fact, most of the lessons presented here use students' actual writing as the basis for instruction. The purpose of students' writing must be to fulfill personal intentions, not to master the content of instructional lessons, and these lessons are important only insofar as they help writers to do so.

XII

Transcription: Choices and instruction

Written language conventions are primarily for the benefit of readers. Predicting and sampling print during reading require that readers have a clear idea of what letter forms (handwriting) and what letter sequences (spelling) will appear and how language units will be marked (punctuation). The conventions shared by the community of readers and writers (Fish, 1980) are the basis for the contractual agreement that exists between readers and writers (F. Smith, 1982b; Tierney & LaZansky, 1980), without which both writing and reading would not be possible.

However, written language conventions are arbitrary and are never absolute. The use of conventions changes over time (witness the increased use of dashes in writing), and in any case the appropriateness of conventions depends on context. For example, a letter to a friend often requires different uses of capitalization, punctuation, and even spelling (e.g., thru vs. through) than a formal paper. Additionally, conventions are sometimes purposefully misused by writers who want to be distinctive (E. B. White's poetry does not use capital letters) or wish to capture a mood or a particular dialect (Alice Walker's *The Color Purple* is full of unconventional usage and spelling). Conventions are important only insofar as they help writers fulfill their communicative intentions. Conventions should be the focus of writers' attention during editing, while composition should be the focus during drafting and revising.

This isn't to say that writers have no interest in conventions during drafting and revision. At every point in the act of writing, there are a myriad of opportunities for students to work at transcription or the use of conventions. In addition, teachers can provide some assistance and instruction in conventions in the midst of writing, but there is not much point in editing for conventions unless there is an

239

audience for the writing. When they edit, students need to understand that they are refining conventions as a courtesy to their readers. Students who write for personally important audiences usually need no other motivation to want to edit.

This chapter will address the teaching of writing conventions as part of the writing process, specifically during editing. The writing conventions we will consider are spelling, punctuation (including capitalization), handwriting, and grammatical usage. The final section of the chapter will deal with helping students learn to orchestrate all aspects of editing.

SPELLING

Spelling is a developmental cognitive process (E. Henderson & Beers, 1980) that requires not only a basic knowledge of orthographic rules but also strategic application of those rules (Gerber & Hall, 1981). It's clear from the literature examining children's spelling errors that unconventional spelling is an attempt to use orthographic information in a strategic and logical fashion (see Read, 1975; E. Henderson & Beers, 1980). This is as true of learning disabled (see Gerber, 1984) and remedial students as it is of normally achieving students. The poor spelling of almost all LD and remedial students does not look different from the spelling of younger, normally achieving students (Bookman, 1983; Gerber & Hall, 1981; Gerber, 1984; Holmes & Peper, 1977; Nelson, 1980). Thus, spelling development as described earlier in this text applies to learning disabled and remedial learners as well as to normally achieving students.

Learning to spell is not a matter of memorizing the spelling of words (Beers & Beers, 1977). If spelling were merely a matter of memorizing words, we wouldn't be able to spell words we'd never seen (and sometimes never heard) before. The word lists of commercial spelling programs seem to suggest that spelling is memorization, but if memorizing the words from commercial spelling programs accounted for how many words each of us could spell, we wouldn't know how to spell many (figure out how many words you'd know at the rate of twenty per week times the number of weeks in a school year times the number of school years you used a speller).

Our discussion of spelling instruction will be based on several important assumptions. First, if spelling is a cognitive process, "learning to spell requires the active, hypothesis-testing involvement of the learner" (Zutell, 1978, 849). Therefore, students, not teachers, should take responsibility for spelling during writing. If students request help, a consistent reply of "Spell it the best you can" and the acceptance of students' efforts will usually assure students' active involvement. On the other hand, providing students with word spellings or with strategies like "Write the first letter and draw a blank for the rest of the word" relieves them of responsibility and discourages hypothesis testing. (See chapter 6 for a discussion of removing spelling barriers.)

Second, we will operate under the assumption that "spelling is for writing" (Graves, 1977, 90) and that important learning about spelling takes place *as* students interact with print (Gentry & Henderson, 1978; Lancaster, Nelson &

Morris, 1982; Zutell, 1978). Therefore, none of our instructional recommendations for spelling will be very useful unless they are embedded within authentic reading and writing.

We'll talk about spelling instruction in terms of the developmental continuum we presented in chapter 3. We'll provide recommendations, for example, that will help a phonemic speller toward using the knowledge and strategies of letter name spellers, but we will not expect the phenemic speller to become a correct speller without moving through the other points on the developmental continuum first (although this could happen). We begin with instructional recommendations for the prephonemic speller.

INSTRUCTION FOR PREPHONEMIC SPELLERS

The prephonemic speller needs to discover that there is a regular and systematic correspondence between oral and written language. Repeated reading of a book aloud to students, especially when they can observe the print as it is read, will help develop that insight; students will begin to notice that every time you read the same book/page/line, you read it the same way.

Involving students in language experience can also encourage them to see that correspondence. A teacher assigned to provide extra help to a first grader named Tommy discovered that Tommy's regular teacher had only very recently placed him in the first pre-primer because she didn't believe that children were ready to read until they knew the alphabet, and Tommy had had a great deal of trouble learning it. The next time the special teacher met with Tommy, she brought along a series of Snoopy pictures cut from newspaper comic strips. Each picture featured Snoopy doing something different. The teacher gave Tommy time to look over the pictures and then asked him which one he wanted to paste in his booklet first. Tommy chose one and pasted it on top of the page, leaving the rest of the page for a dictated description of what Snoopy was doing. Tommy then dictated a simple sentence for each page: "He's digging," "He's reading," "He's sitting on his dog house," and so on. After a few pages, Tommy stopped the teacher and said, "There's something suspicious about this!" and pointed out that the "He's" looked the same on all the pages.

Some spellers have the knowledge needed for spelling but don't use it when they spell (Gerber, 1984; Gerber & Hall, 1981). If you ask some prephonemic spellers what letter *box* begins with, they can tell you *b*, but if they write about their lunch boxes, you won't see a corresponding *b* in their writing. One way to approach this problem is to sit beside students as they begin to write, ask what they intend to write about, and then help them record what they want to say. After listening, ask them what the first thing is that they want to say. Many will give you a whole sentence; if so, ask what the first word is. Demonstrate how you listen to the word and ask what the student hears. Ask the student to write down the letter that represents the sound s/he hears and then listen for the next one. The student will be able to isolate few sounds, sometimes only the first letter of each word. Expect the student to write down only those that s/he can isolate, not all the ones you hear. Do this for just a couple of minutes, perhaps for the span of a single sentence. Stop by the student's desk again the next day and spend a couple minutes doing the same thing. When you see the student representing sounds with letters on her/his own, you know the lesson has taken and that the student can now teach her/himself a great deal about representing sound/letter relationships.

Another way to help prephonemic spellers learn to use their graphophonic knowledge during writing is to engage them in a written conversation. We used this technique to help Joseph, the second grader who read his random string of letters as "Jack and Jill" (see Figure 3–2). Because Joseph had revealed a knowledge of graphophonics during instruction, we knew that we only had to help him discover that writing was systematically representational.

One of us began a written conversation with Joseph by writing, "Hi! What is your name?" The teacher read the message aloud to Joseph, pointing to each word as she did so. Joseph looked up and said, "I don't know how to write 'My name is Joseph.'" The teacher helped him write "My name" in the way suggested above, asking him what word he wanted to write first, what sounds he heard as they said the word together, etc. Joseph knew how to spell "is" and his own name and finished off the sentence on his own.

Next the teacher asked Joseph if he wanted to ask her a question. Joseph grabbed the pen but then sat in dismay, finally saying that he didn't know how to write "What's your name?" The teacher read and pointed to the first line of the conversation again, saying that there was probably something there that might help him. The light went on in Joseph's eyes and he immediately set to work, copying what the teacher had written from the first line, even adding the "Hi!" He learned his lesson so well that he had no trouble locating "have" and "brothers" from the line above or in copying "Do you have any . . ." in the following part of the conversation. The teacher helped Joseph listen to the sound of "daughters" in order to help him write it. By now, Joseph was feeling so successful that even after the teacher left, he asked his regular teacher, who had been observing, more questions. Note that Joseph corrected to the conventional spelling of "daughter" by finding it in an earlier part of the conversation. (See Figure 12–1.)

Joseph isn't unusual. Children often don't use what they know, sometimes because they lack the strategies. The teacher revealed to Joseph that he could use his knowledge about print by relying on two strategies—using the print in his environment (in this case, in the conversation) and listening to and representing the sounds in words. With one lesson, Joseph's writing moved from being prephonemic to being phonemic. Joseph had already the knowledge to be a phonemic speller; what he needed to learn were strategies to enable him to use his knowledge.

INSTRUCTION FOR PHONEMIC SPELLERS

Helping phonemic spellers become letter name spellers involves similar instructional strategies, except that here, you need to help students examine the words they are trying to represent more carefully. If the student is representing

---

FIGURE 12–1   Joseph's Written Conversation

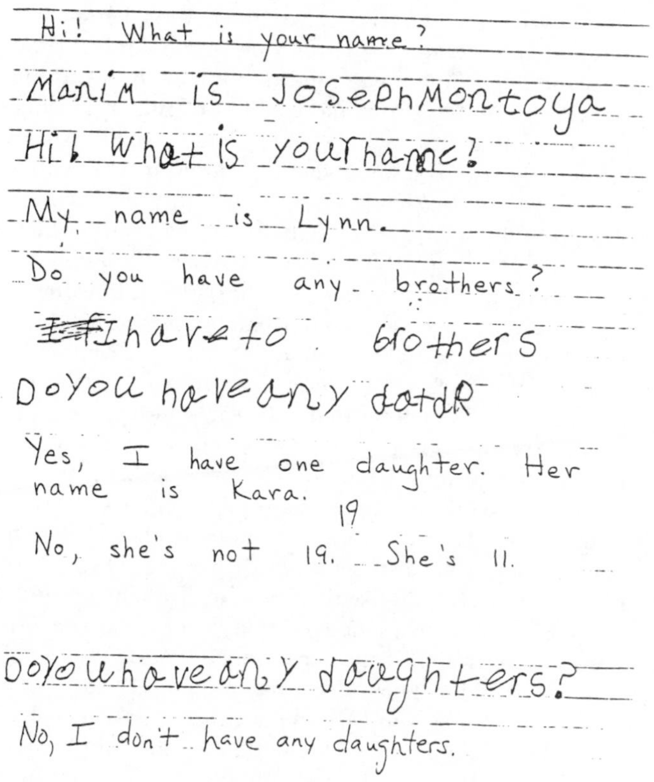

Hi! What is your name?

Marim is JosephMontoya

Hi! What is yourname?

My name is Lynn.

Do you have any brothers?

~~If~~ I have to brothers

Do you have any dotdR

Yes, I have one daughter. Her name is Kara.

No, she's not 19. She's 11.

Do you have any daughters?

No, I don't have any daughters.

---

only a few sounds, the teacher can help the student listen for the other sounds as well. The teacher can demonstrate how s/he listens to one syllable in a word at a time, and then to the sounds in each syllable, inviting the student to listen along and represent all the sounds s/he hears. In the case of the child who wrote *rainbow* as "RAbPED," for instance, the teacher might say something like, "Let's listen to the word again in parts, like what you were doing. You have the first two sounds that you hear in *rain*. Let's listen to the end of *rain—rain* [*drawing the word out like a rubber band and slightly emphasizing the end*]. Write down the sound that you hear—where will it go? That's right, after *r* and *a*. Now, let's listen to the second part of *rainbow—rain-bow*...*bow*...*bow*. You have the first sound of *bow*, don't you? Now, let's listen to the second sound—*bow* (again drawing the word out and slightly emphasizing the *o* sound on the end). Good— you hear an *o* too—where will you put it?"

Again, frequent but brief lessons are more helpful than long and infrequent ones. The above lesson on *rainbow* is probably enough for most students, though some may benefit from one more word or so in the same time period. Observe to see if students begin to syllabicate where necessary and draw out the sounds of the words as they write independently. As students get better and better at analyzing words with less and less help from you, you might just simply stop by their desks and suggest, "See if you can think about how this word sounds again and add to your spelling of it." Also reinforce the student's increasing representation of sounds by saying such things as, "When you listened to that word, look at all the sounds you heard. You know just how to do it" (Giacobbe, 1986).

At this point (and for that matter, at any point in a child's spelling development) be careful not to give students more information than they can handle. For example, you should be very satisfied with "ranbo" at this point and not say such things as "I know you can't hear them, but there's also an *i* after *a* and a *w* after *o*." This sort of information *may* be helpful to a more developed speller but not to a student you are trying to guide into becoming a letter name speller. Too much information may destroy a student's growing confidence that spelling is something that s/he can control.

One way to incorporate this process into group instruction is to involve students in a bit of the spelling while you record their language experience dictations. As you write what the students are dictating, ask them to help you with the spelling of sounds that you know might push the students a little further. For example, if you have students who are regularly capturing the first and last letters of words and you'd like them to start listening for middle letters, you can encourage them to think about a few middle letters as you write. As you write down "One day we watched the gerbil make a nest," you might ask the students to listen to the middle part of "gerbil." When they suggest letters that they've heard (for example, *r*), simply write out the word as usual and as you are doing so, say, "Yes, there is an *r* in the middle of the word *gerbil*," pointing to the *r* as you do so. It's easy to individualize instruction by involving particular students in spelling appropriate to their needs. If the group contains students who are only representing the first sound of a word, they may benefit from being asked to think about how words end rather than about midword letter/sound relationships.

Even when you try to avoid it, you will occasionally find that you have asked students to help you spell something you cannot acknowledge as conventional during a dictation. For example, if you made the mistake of asking the students to help you spell "One" in the sentence above, you may well get a reply that the word begins with *y*. In each cases, we find it best simply to say, "That *is* how you could spell it in your writing but it's actually written this way." Then write the word quickly and move on.

Students who don't know some of the sound/letter relationships will learn them from those who do as they help you construct dictations on paper. However, be careful not to overdo your attention to sound/letter relationships during dictations; keep everyone's attention focused on meaning construction.

INSTRUCTION FOR LETTER NAME SPELLERS

Once students become (predominantly) letter name spellers, they *can* analyze and sound out words independently. But what they still need to learn is that spelling is also visual. That is, knowledge about how words *look* must now be developed through reading and instruction. Once letter name spellers begin reading, they're likely to be confused at some point by the differences between their own spellings and the conventionally spelled words they encounter in books. You may find, for example, that students have difficulty reading their own writing. And it's also likely that students will suddenly be very dissatisfied with their invented spellings and want to spell words "right" (Bissex, 1980).

Their discomfort is a sign of growth. When students get to this point, they're beginning to incorporate visual information into their knowledge of spelling and need reassurance in order to continue writing fluently. You can reassure them that their spelling will become more conventional with time and continued writing; reviewing the progress they've already made as spellers by looking over old papers sometimes helps. Reinforce the notion that getting ideas on paper is of utmost importance before worrying about spelling; it may help to promise that you'll provide the conventional spellings of a few words when students have finished writing.

Help students understand also that reading is important and that they may teach themselves to spell a number of words as they read. Rejoice publicly when a student informs you that s/he's just figured out that "uv" is really spelled "of" in books. That's a marvelous self-teaching strategy that is also used by adults.

The instruction you provide at this point also needs to draw students' attention to the visual information contained in conventional spellings. When a student requests help with spelling or when you decide to provide help, tell the student to "think about what the word looks like." If you provide the student with a conventional spelling in place of an unconventional spelling, any "That's the way _____ sounds but it's not the way it looks" (Bissex, 1980). You can respond in the same way as you continue to involve the students in the recording of language experience dictations. At this point, if some students have not discovered some conventions—that the first sound of "chewing gum" is represented by "ch" rather than the "h" that letter name spellers often use, for example—involve them in spelling words featuring that letter sequence as it is naturally used during language experience.

In addition, refer students to print in their environment—suggest that they look for the words they're having difficulty with in books, on signs, labels, charts, etc. If students don't realize that they can use the spellings you've previously used in written conversations, show them the potential for doing that. In all these cases, try to encourage independent strategies in students. Let *them* think of a book they've read in which they might find a particular word rather than directing them to a specific book. Eventually, encourage students to think of which strategy is appropriate to use. Discuss the usefulness of various strategies from time to time. Don't recommend a dictionary to students at this stage of their development. How could a letter name speller who thinks that "elephant" begins with "l" ever find "elephant" in a dictionary, no matter how easy the dictionary is?

As students progress toward transitional spelling, they'll learn more and more conventional spellings for frequently used words if they are both reading and writing. And when students begin to spell frequently used words conventionally, recognize their learning so that they know what they've done and how to do it again. Say things like, "You used to spell 'my' as 'mi' and I've noticed that you spell it 'my' now like it's spelled in books. How did you learn that?" If students can't verbalize how they learned to spell the word, say something like, "When you read, you see "my" a lot. I'll bet you noticed how it looked and started to make your words look like the words in books." In other words, encourage students to recognize that they can learn a great deal about spelling from reading and attending to what words look like in print. (We don't mean here to focus the student's attention on spelling instead of meaning while reading; be careful that you don't overdo such comments.)

INSTRUCTION FOR TRANSITIONAL SPELLERS

Once students begin using transitional spellings, it's useful to encourage them to edit for spelling. Students may be asked to mark those words in their writing that "don't look right" (notice how visual attention is invoked) *after* they've finished writing something that requires editing for an audience. Students who have visual information can be very successful in finding words that don't "look right." The more visual information they have, the more successful they'll be at locating and self-correcting their unconventional spellings.

One self-correction strategy that students can be taught is one that many of us use as proficient spellers. When students decide that a word doesn't look right, ask them to rewrite the word a number of different ways and then decide which spelling looks the best. (Note again how attention is directed to visual information.)

Once students can locate their spelling errors, decide what they can handle in editing with relative ease yet still be challenged to learn. You might, for example, ask some students (those with less visual information) to find three of the words they've underlined in books or somewhere else and then correct them. Other students (who have more visual information) can use the "write it several ways and see what looks best" strategy. Don't ask students to fully edit for spelling unless there's a reason to—an audience who will be reading their writing. Even then, if the amount of spelling that needs to be corrected is potentially overwhelming, have them do part and you, another person, or a computer program can assist with or simply correct the rest.

We recommend that commercial spelling programs be avoided unless they include specific lessons that address students' needs. It's easy enough to develop an individualized spelling list for transitional spellers by helping them learn to spell words they use in their own writing; the words they study are those they use frequently and misspell. One technique is to have each student learning five or six of these words at a time. If the student has an assigned desk, we like to tape a small index card containing the words at the upper right hand corner of the desk. If the student has no desk, the card may be kept paper-clipped to the writing folder and pulled out each time the student writes. The words are selected from the students' writing on the basis of potential frequency of use and student interest. Consult students to decide which new word(s) to put on the index card, but emphasize the criteria of frequency by asking, "Are you likely to use this word a lot in your writing?"

Writing the word(s) on a card is an appropriate time for a quick lesson in which the student's spelling of each word is compared with the conventional spelling *by the student*. Thus, "often" is placed next to the student's spelling "ofen" and the student might say something like, "There's a *t* in it. You can't hear the *t*. I could remember the *t* if I pronounce it ' off+ten' when I write it."

We work with index cards rather informally; that is, students know which words are on their card, and each time they use one of them in writing, they use the card to copy the word or to check their spelling. We tell students that once they no longer have to look at the card to write or check a word it's time to replace the word with another one (and to have another quick comparison lesson). Thus, the student is always learning five or six words. Emphasize the students' responsibility in knowing when to tell the teacher that they're ready for a new word. A list of all of the words the students has learned during the year provides a record of learning for both teachers and students.

Another instructional strategy (Ganschow, 1981; Marino, 1981) is to collect unconventional spellings from students' work over a period of time and to categorize the errors, listing the conventional spelling next to each unconventional spelling. Invite students to consider words that belong to the same category and hypothesize the "rule." In this way, students can revise their current rules in a situation in which the need to do so is personally evident. For example, a teacher decided to help students understand the differences between *their*, *there*, and *they're*, words that she observed her students misspelling and misusing in their writing. She collected sentences from her students' writing in which these words were used correctly and incorrectly and grouped them together according to how the particular word *ought* to be spelled. To keep students from being distracted, she corrected all other misspellings in the students' sentences.

The teacher then gave each student a copy of the sentences and told them that the sentences underneath the word *there* all had the word *there* in it, sometimes spelled correctly and sometimes spelled another way. She said the same about the sentences listed under *their* and *they're*. The students' were asked to read each sentence and to correct the spelling if necessary to match the word under which the sentence was grouped. Then each student was asked to talk with another student about how the word was used in each category of sentences. In other words, students themselves were asked to infer the rule for why the word was spelled the way it was in each of the three sets of sentences. The students then shared their findings and became involved in thinking of ways to remember which spelling was connected to which function or meaning. Some of what the students discussed follows:

- *there*
  1. Defined as "a place," "a direction."
  2. Noted that "here" was in "there."
  3. Since "here" was also "a place or direction," and was in "there," that was a way to remember the spelling of "there."
- *their*
  1. Defined as "a group that had something or owned something."
  2. Noted that "their" was followed by a noun while "there" wasn't.
  3. Tried to figure out how to remember that the spelling was "ei" and not "ie" and noted that all three words began with "the," including "their."
- *they're*
  1. Stands for "they are."
  2. Noted that if they substituted "they are" for "they're" and it made sense, then the word must be the short (contracted) form of "they are."

Encourage students to generate their own wording for these and for any other rules you feel it necessary to teach by examining categorized words that demonstrate the rule. If students themselves are actively involved in figuring out the rule, they will understand it better than if they try to memorize a rule.

Some students find the development of a personal word dictionary or word bank a useful resource for spelling. Teachers can help students add to their dictionaries or word banks when they are editing their writing by asking, "Which of the words we've worked on would you like to add to your word bank?" Encourage students to choose words they're likely to use in future writing. Word banks are a useful resource as well if you find that students benefit from "word sorts," categorizing words according to a specified feature.

Don't overdo the use of a personal or published dictionary or word bank. Don't suggest or allow its use during writing, since it disrupts the construction of meaning. Even when it is used after writing in order to edit, limit its use to only a few words, words the student cannot figure out otherwise. While a published dictionary provides correct spellings, it doesn't encourage students to hypothesize about words.

It may be useful for some students to take regular, informal spelling "tests." For example, students could pair off and quickly test one another over words on their personal index cards. Or students might be regularly tested over high frequency words displayed on a room chart for everyone's reference. (Make sure that the students understand that the words on the chart are those they use regularly and naturally in their writing.) Such tests are not meant to be graded, and in fact, it's recommended that the words to be tested remain in view during the test to assure success (Marino, 1981). Thus, the "test" is a means of engaging students once again to think about words and how they work. These "tests" should take no more than five minutes.

There are a number of word games that students enjoy and that will encourage a greater awareness of possible letter sequences, the relationships between words, and so on. Though these games are not related to students' writing, they do rely on students' vocabularies and encourage greater awareness of how spelling works. Keep the games in perspective; they cannot take the place of frequent reading and writing for developing spelling.

"Hangman" is an old childhood favorite, a game that demands that a student think about such things as what could come before and after certain letters, what letter sequences are likely and so on. "Boggle," "Spill and Spell," "Scrabble," and "Word Mastermind" (see Marino, 1981) are others that will help students think about words and consider various possibilities and relationships. We recommend that you sit alongside students and encourage them to verbalize their thinking as they play. If you find that the students are not using strategic thinking about letter sequences to play a game (see Marino, 1981 for examples), you may want to play the game also so that you can think aloud and demonstrate the strategies you use. Do this with a light touch—you don't want them to avoid playing games because they seem like academic exercises.

Students who have learned the visual patterns of spelling and who spell frequently used words correctly, still may not have discovered that words with similar meanings tend to have similar spellings (e.g., sign, signal). Temple and Gillet (1984) call these students *derivational* spellers. Reading widely, writing more, and studying word derivations are helpful to these students, who may also be helped simply by your calling attention to base words and affixes as needed when they edit their writing.

Some students may continue to be transitional spellers despite our efforts. Though we certainly don't advocate halting instruction, we do find that some students need to learn other strategies for coping with what can be a serious matter. One common coping strategy is to ask someone to proofread their writing for them. Don't assume that students know, without discussion, when it is appropriate to ask for help and from whom to seek it. Help them to understand that to determine when to request proofreading assistance involves thinking about who the audience will be for their writing and what the audience requires in terms of correct spelling (and other conventions). Also talk with them about finding good spellers around them who are willing to take the time to do what they ask. Remind students that even people in prominent positions can be poor spellers, and that they hire secretaries with precisely this skill in mind.

There are other coping strategies that might also be useful for some students under some circumstances. One is the *Bad Speller's Dictionary* (Krevisky & Linfield, 1963), a small pocket dictionary in which students may find common misspellings of words followed by their correct spelling. Another is a dictionary used by secretaries only for the purpose of looking up commonly misspelled words. These dictionaries don't feature definitions except when necessary; they exist only to help people with spelling. Another possibility for students with access to computers are word processing programs and electronic typewriters that check and sometimes correct spellings.

UNUSUAL SPELLING DIFFICULTIES

Occasionally you'll encounter a student who has an unusual spelling problem. One we met was John, a seventh grader whose spelling rendered his writing unreadable. His mother had enrolled him in our university Reading and Writing Center for help. One of John's first pieces of writing, about *Where the Red Fern Grows* (Rawls, 1974), was written in the following way:

dele is a huert. he wons	(Billy is a hunter. He wants
a dog. he like to huot	a dog. He likes to hunt
in the uoads. I thing he	in the woods. I think he
is nete. I lthe to hoint.	is neat. I like to hunt.
I like dogs to he will	I like dogs too. He will
a dog	get a dog.)

John had been in a learning disabilities classroom since first grade and none of our usual approaches to spelling seemed to help. When the teacher who had been assigned to John at the university helped him sound out words, he'd spell "hunter" as "hunert." Asking him to study the conventional spelling of the word and then to reproduce it from visual memory didn't work either, nor did the strategy of writing it down several different ways. But John could read his own writing immediately after writing it and could underline most of the words he had spelled unconventionally. The second fact was especially surprising, since John's teachers described him as a "nonreader."

Every week, John's university teacher involved him in writing down his assignments, something the boy's mother was quite happy to follow through on at home. John wrote the following list of assignments one week, providing a sample that gives an idea of how poor his spelling was, especially when his heart was not in the writing.

rede p 135	(read to p. 135
thing a blte the soide	think about the story
blkah polhe book	bring poetry book)

The teacher regularly recopied the assignments so that John's mother could read them. One week she invited John to help by telling him, "I'm going to write down your assignments now. You help me with the spelling as I write. What does *assignments* start with?" The boy answered *a* and then, as the teacher wrote the *a*, he spelled out the remainder of the word—*-ssignments*. He proceeded to spell the majority of the other words he had just spelled incorrectly in his list of assignments, and the ones that were still incorrect were far closer to the conventional spelling than his original spellings had been. The teacher was completely amazed.

In ensuing lessons, the teacher found out that John's pattern was always the same—he could spell many words orally, but the moment he put a pencil in his hand his spelling ability disappeared.

It occurred to us that there might be a way to help John cope with his difficulty. Relying on the knowledge that John could read what he'd written, we began to involve him in self-correcting spelling after he had completed his original drafts. He followed this routine: 1) He read the first word in the sentence, 2) he spelled it aloud, and 3) as he spelled each letter aloud, he wrote the letter. He continued the same routine with the next word and so on.

This was slow but it worked rather well, though some days were better than others. Eventually, John spontaneously began doing some oral spelling while writing his first draft. For example, here's the original draft he wrote when he had completed his reading of *Where the Red Fern Grows*:

> The red Fern lencht is that a Inend boy and flre wer walking and frzze to died. and in the summer thay find the ren Fern grow by dobies. The ren Fern mene that the dobies. of Billy dogs well allways de ther. Billy fledl dete win he know he's dogs spernt wood de ther for afer.

After he had finished his first draft, John edited the writing, using the routine he had been taught and produced the following:

> The red fern legend is that an Indian boy and girl were walking and froze to death. In the summer they found the red fern growing by their bodies. The red fern means that the bodies of Billy's dogs will alway's be there. Billy felt better when he knew his dog's spirit would be there forever.

In editing his draft, John was given help changing "find" to "found" (a grammatical problem), changing "dobies" to "bodies" in both places where he used it (a reversal problem), and changing "allways" to "always," his only remaining spelling problem. It was his own idea to look up the spelling of "legend" in the book.

John had essentially learned to translate what he had written through an aural mode that was working, making his pen follow what he spelled aloud. His feelings about what he had experienced and learned during the semester of individual help were summed up when he wrote and rewrote the following:

> 1. redeing the red fren help me de cusdes I did think I codk.

> 1. reading the red fern helped me becaise I didn't know I could read it.

(Remember that we had been told that John was a "nonreader." The teacher had begun reading *Where the Red Fern Grows* to John because she knew he could relate to the story due to some recent past experiences. Because he wanted to hear the story faster than the teacher could read it in her sessions with him, he asked to take it home and have his mother read it. When his mother didn't have time, John decided to try it out. We realized that John had been reading the book on his own one day when his mother came in and told us, "I have always been told he couldn't read. If he can't, I don't know why he reads this book all the time and tells me about what he's read." Until the time John left us, he still sounded as if he couldn't read whenever he was asked to read orally. However, it was clear he could read silently.)

2. I that I wodt have to ride off lafsh card dut in stude I ride a dook.

2. I thought I would have to read flash cards instead I read a dook.

(John was certainly aware of the differences between his past and current instructional experiences.)

3. spelling help me. I ride didnd now

3. spelling helped me because of writing on paper I read better now because of writing.

(The teacher asked John to add some information about "why" when he rewrote. Note John's intuitive sense of the connection between reading and writing development.)

4. spelling out and wting out the wake and pot in senoch

4. spelling out loud helped me and wting out the words and putting in sentences

(Here John is referring to the breakthrough we made in how to help him cope with his spelling.)

We share this story about John because we want our readers to know we are aware that not all poor spellers' needs are easily met. We think John's story reveals how important instructional observations are as well as being able to formulate creative ways to help such students.

PUNCTUATION

Periods, quotation marks, apostrophes, capital letters, commas, and so on (even parentheses and dashes)—all are aspects of punctuation, conventions governed by arbitrary rules that assist readers in making sense of text because they mark off units of language. Students can be expected to hypothesize or invent rules for punctuation just as they do for spelling and other conventions (Cordeiro, Giacobbe & Cazden, 1983; Edelsky, 1983). For example, Cordeiro, Giacobbe, and Cazden documented first graders' hypotheses about periods, finding that some students thought that periods should be placed after each syllable, some after each word, some at the end of each line, some at the end of the page or writing, and some at the end of phrases. All of these hypotheses make linguistic sense if you consider that punctuation is intended to mark language units.

However, the development of at least some aspects of punctuation, unlike spelling, may be very gradual. Consider the developmental data on sentence fragments, for example. Whether a sentence is or is not a fragment, of course, is dependent on whether a period has been placed at the end of a sentence or at the end of a portion of a sentence. "Sentence sense" seems to be fairly well understood by about fourth grade since even low-proficiency nine-year-olds write an average of .6 sentence fragments per hundred words. However, high proficiency seventeen-year-olds write an average of .5 sentence fragments per hundred words, a decrease of only .1 over a period of eight years (Mellon, 1975). From this data, it might be concluded that virtually no learning takes place with regard to punctuating sentences during those years but, in fact, the

> data mask some significant changes that are occurring. Though the proportion of sentence fragments may remain fairly stable beyond a given age or grade, the types of fragments apparently change over the years as students attempt to express new kinds of semantic relationships and to employ new kinds of syntactic constructions. (Weaver, 1982, 443)

Thus, as the students learn to punctuate a syntactic construction that they've been using in their writing for a while, they also begin trying out new constructions that they do not know how to punctuate, and those errors replace the old ones. Weaver puts it so well: "growth and error go hand in hand."

Students discover the conventions governing punctuation from observing how others use it in their writing, from hypothesizing about its use in their own writing, and from teacher instruction. Once students discover a particular aspect of punctuation, they can be expected to use it in an unconventional manner before moving to conventional use. Many of us have seen writing like the first grader's story in Figure 12–2, in which the child's discovery of

---

FIGURE 12–2 Discovery of Apostrophes

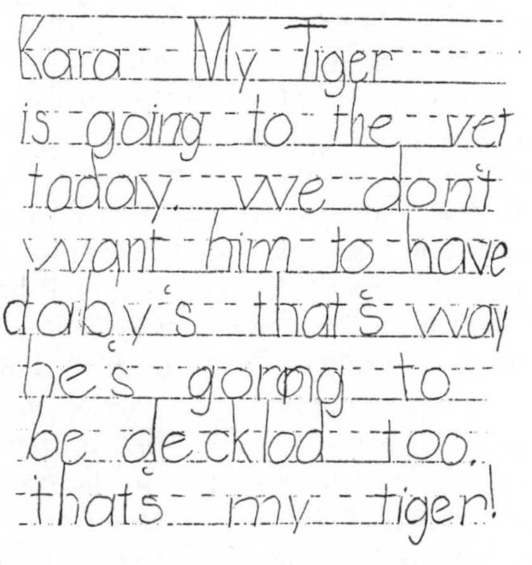

Kara – My Tiger
is going to the vet
today we don't
want him to have
daby's that's way
he's going to
be deckload too.
thats my tiger!

apostrophes is being explored and is overgeneralized. This phenomenon should be expected of all students, including learning disabled and remedial students.

Punctuation should be taught as students' writing indicates the need for it. For example, if students begin using dialogue in their story writing, teach them quotation marks. Punctuation is often taught during editing conferences when students are finalizing a piece of writing for an audience. The teacher demonstrates the use of an aspect of punctuation and often provides an explanation. Some aspects of punctuation may require a functional explanation. For example, Cordeiro, Giacobbe, and Cazden (1983) demonstrated the use of a possessive apostrophe while saying,

> When something *belongs* to someone else, we put one of these little marks (showing as she speaks). We call that an "apostrophe" and we add the "s." That lets the reader know that "my friend's house" (pointing to the child's text) means that the house belongs to your friend; it doesn't mean "lots of friends." (326)

Cordeiro, Giacobbe, and Cazden (1983) also explained quotation marks during editing conferences:

> Someone is talking on this page. If we could hear her talking, what would she say? (Student reads.) Well, we have some marks that we put around the words people say, before the first word and after the last. (327)

Not all aspects of punctuation can be explained in this way, however. One of the most common problem areas for students is punctuating the end of a declarative sentence, which requires a decision that is based on syntactic rather than semantic or functional knowledge. Though teachers might use a functional explanation such as, "Put a period where you hear your voice drop or where you stop," such rules are inevitably found to be wanting. "The notion...that periods represent relatively long pauses in speech...just does not hold up. Speakers often pause longer within sentences than between them" (F. Smith, 1982b, 154). A syntactic explanation such as, "A sentence contains a noun subject and a verb" will only make sense to students who have an understanding of grammatical terminology, and even then it doesn't explain why "Stop!" is a sentence while "Coming from the background that I do" is not a sentence.

Cordeiro, Giacobbe, and Cazden (1983) recommend that students' intuitive knowledge of what is and isn't a sentence can best be developed by demonstrating to students where periods ought to be placed without explanation. Thus, teachers might say something like, "Yes, periods belong here, here, and here (pointing to each spot where the student used a period conventionally). But they don't belong here and here (pointing to the spots where the student placed periods unconventionally). And you need one here" (pointing to a spot where the student needs to add a period). Once a student's writing has been edited, ask the student to read her/his piece aloud in order to get a feel for the conventional placement of each period. This sort of instruction encourages the development of an intuitive knowledge of punctuation.

As students increase their intuitive knowledge of punctuation, they can assume greater responsibility for editing their own writing. If a student continues to need a great deal of guidance in editing, the teacher may say, "Read this sentence and see where a period (comma, etc.) might help your readers." A student who needs less guidance might be asked to read the same sentence and see what punctuation might be added. Students who need less guidance may be asked to reread their pieces and check the punctuation independently. As we stressed in our discussion of editing for spelling, students should be given more and more responsibility for editing for punctuation but not overwhelmed. Balance your expectations against a student's ability to meet them.

Punctuation can also be addressed as teachers "lift" pieces of writing and use them to work on punctuation and compare conventional and unconventional punctuation. For example, a secondary LD teacher whose students had written letters to obtain information for a social studies project observed that a number of the students had not capitalized words of personal address, such as "Mr.," "Dr.," "Ms." The teacher constructed two columns, one in which the students' writing was featured (dr. Smith) and one in which conventional writing was featured (Dr. Smith). The students were asked to compare the two columns, to verbalize what they had learned, and then to use that information to edit their letters for this convention.

Some very difficult punctuation concepts seem best addressed by comparison. Students usually have difficulty understanding that direct speech is marked with quotation marks while indirect speech is not. In such cases, a comparison of direct and indirect speech sometimes eliminates the confusion. Examples like the following may be taken from familiar books or students' writing:

- Mom said that she was going to the store.
- Mom said, "I'm going to the store."

If students don't use the punctuation they know during editing, it may be that they don't know how to proofread for punctuation. In such cases, a group of students may benefit from proofreading a "lifted" piece of writing. Any student's writing may be used; placing it on an overhead is best because you can more easily help students to focus on the particulars under discussion. Demonstrate how you go about proofreading for punctuation and then involve the students. Help them understand that you ignore other problems like spelling when you are proofreading for punctuation, that you read one sentence at a time and check for "sentence sense" before checking for punctuation within and between sentences. If you also find yourself teaching students about aspects of punctuation that haven't come up before, such as capitalizing and underlining book titles, teach these lessons quickly so that the focus remains on proofreading.

You might also involve students in "lifting" examples of punctuation from their environment. For example, if you do a comparison lesson between "its" and it's" (where a semantic difference is signaled by punctuation), an interesting follow-up is to suggest that students find examples of the use of these words and "lift" them for sharing with the class. Students will find the convention misused everywhere—grocery store signs, garage sale signs, movie billboards, and perhaps even the school newspaper. This sort of follow-up will cement students' learning.

Learning to punctuate, like learning to spell, never ends as long as we read and write. How many of us, for example, are certain about how to use semicolons? Also, like spelling, punctuation rules are continually evolving and may vary depending on which set of style rules are consulted.

HANDWRITING

As Donald Graves put it so well, "Handwriting is for writing" (1978, 393). In other words, the only reason to learn handwriting is to communicate with others or with ourselves. If a student's handwriting doesn't require unusual effort from readers or from the student him/herself in producing it, there is little reason for the student to be receiving handwriting instruction. Students who write with an audience in mind learn that legible handwriting is important if they're going to communicate with readers successfully.

Learning to print or to write in cursive does not require that students do handwriting exercises in isolation. Students can learn handwriting as they write meaningful text simply by being invited to write messages of their own and by being helped with those letter formations or letter sequences the teacher observes as being difficult. Students who need handwriting instruction ought to receive it while copying their own compositions for publication or, at the minimum, while copying something—a poem, for example—they have selected because they want their own copy of it.

Children who need help with their handwriting can be effectively and efficiently grouped for instruction, just as students with similar needs are grouped for instruction that addresses conventions. If you observe that several students are writing letters from the bottom up rather than from the top down, for example, work with them and have them copy or recopy whatever they've chosen. If students have difficulty writing a letter or connecting letters in cursive, demonstrate how to write the letter or letter series, let them try it out, and then have them focus on that letter or letter series in the next thing they copy. Before students make a final copy of their writing, have them underline in their rough copy the problem letter(s) they want to focus on; it will help them remember to make an extra effort when they encounter those letters.

Some students (like John, the boy whose spelling we have discussed at length in this chapter) may reverse letters in their writing, even in cursive writing. Reversals, which are common in young children's writing, are the result of a lack of experience with print. The same is true of the reversals that older students make in both LD and remedial programs; these students are often no more experienced with print than a much younger, normally achieving child. (For more on this topic, see Nelson, 1980; F. Smith, 1982a; and Vernon, 1957).

Even students who are excellent readers and writers reverse letters, but this doesn't usually interfere with literacy development.

Problems with reversals are often exacerbated by the excessive attention they receive. Some students become so concerned about possible reversals they ask, "Is this the right way?" as soon as they've finished writing a letter they know causes them problems. In such cases, it's best to give students the sort of support they can use on their own so that some of the anxiety and pressure they have built up over the problem is relieved. For example, if a student regularly reverses *b* and *d*, consider putting some guide words featuring the letters, like *dog* and *cab*, nearby so that the student can refer to them. The best place to put the words might be on the upper corners of the student's desk, in this case, *dog* on the left and *cab* on the right so that the circular part of the words face outward from the desk. After a few months of increased success, ask the student if her/his image of the words on the desk is so good the cards can be removed. Whatever your solution to the problem, it must reduce student anxiety.

Other ideas for dealing with handwriting difficulties are presented in the section on "Lifting the Spelling and Handwriting Barriers to Fluency" in chapter 6.

USAGE

Traditional grammar instruction (e.g., teaching parts of speech or diagramming sentences) has no effect on grammatical usage in students' writing. In fact, "the teaching of formal grammar has a negligible or, because it usually displaces some instruction and practice in actual composition, even a harmful effect on the improvement of writing" (Braddock, Lloyd-Jones & Schoer, 1963, 38; for a lengthy discussion of this topic, see Moffett, 1968, 155–87).

Teachers are legitimately concerned about students' grammatical usage, however, especially in their writing. "The differences between nonstandard and standard English are primarily differences in usage, not grammar" (Jaggar, 1980, 26). Many consider "He don't have dessert" and "He don't have no dessert" to be poor grammar. Actually, they are examples of nonstandard English usage and reflect complex grammatical rules learned from a speech community in which they are acceptable. Although the rules are different from those that govern the standard "He doesn't have any dessert," the knowledge of grammar that produced all three sentences is equal. Rather than being a linguistic problem, usage often represents social or cultural differences. Regrettably, those who use nonstandard English are frequently branded as unintelligent.

Usage problems are also common among students (and adults) who speak and write standard English. Some of the more common problems include:

- Use of pronouns: How many of us would say "The teacher is I" (correct usage) rather than "The teacher is me" (incorrect usage)?
- Subject-verb agreement: "Each of the girls has money" not "Each of the girls have money."

- Inconsistent verb tenses within a piece of writing.
- "Dangling" modifiers: "Exhausted and feeling ill, I went to bed" not "Exhausted and feeling ill, the bed felt good when I climbed in."

Usage develops through oral and written language use and direct study. In general, the instructional strategies that address usage are similar whether the usage difficulty stems from specific dialect differences or is common across dialects.

Since the speech communities in which students live are the most influential forces in the development of usage, the school community as one of these speech communities has the potential to be a powerful force in usage development. The more speakers and writers in the school community employ standard usage, the more likely it is that students will also use it. As Moffett argues, "If standard English grammar, as a behavior, is considered desirable, then let 'disadvantaged' students speak with those who use the standard dialect. They will learn it the same way they learned their local dialect, and for the same reason— that they are members of a speech community where it is native" (1968, 158).

However, several powerful forces can operate in the opposite way—peer pressure, strong identification with the home speech community, and no identification with those who speak the standard dialect in the school speech community. Students may choose not to use the standard dialect because they feel that it compromises their own identity or that they'll never have a need for it, since they don't envision themselves becoming functional members of a standard English-speaking environment (K. Johnson, 1970). If students who speak nonstandard English are to learn and employ standard usage, their aspirations must change, and positive relationships with standard English speakers are important.

Another powerful and natural force in usage development is literature (Cullinan, Jaggar & Strickland, 1974). The usage found in books is probably the single best model for students because it is produced by professional writers, who consider usage well before publication. Those who hear literature read and read literature independently know more language than those who don't (Chomsky, 1972). Repeated read-alongs of books that feature certain standard usages, read primarily for pleasure, also have the secondary advantage of repeatedly engaging students in producing standard usage (Tompkins & McGee, 1983). In addition, retelling, storytelling, dramatization, and writing a new story using the book as a model all encourage students in the repeated use of standard English as a natural part of instruction (Strickland, 1972).

In addition to immersing students in positive standard English environments and encouraging frequent interactions with books, instruction in usage can also be helpful if students are mature enough to reflect on language itself and can detect differences between their written dialect and standard written dialect. Usage instruction can take the form of teacher demonstration, comparison, and/or lifting. But before we provide instructional examples, we need to consider how a teacher decides which usage problems or differences to focus on in instruction.

Since usage problems or differences vary from region to region, school to school, class to class, and student to student, the teacher needs to begin by surveying the usage differences and problems that exist among students (Pooley, 1974), through observation of writing and speech. The list does not have to be exhaustive. Instead, it should feature those usage problems or differences that appear most often and that are most likely to stigmatize students or brand them as "uneducated." Obscure or pedantic usage "problems" should not be targeted for instruction; our rule is that if we hear or see well-educated adults frequently using the same grammatical forms, the usage problem is probably not worth instructional time. Temple and Gillet (1984) recommend that the list contain no more than ten to fifteen prioritized problems to be addressed over the course of a school year. For some students, even that is too much; adjust your instruction accordingly.

How you refer to students' usage during instruction is important. Avoid "wrong," "nonstandard," "incorrect" or any other term that could be construed as a negative reflection on students. Instead, use writing as the major force it is in usage. We prefer to talk with students about "book language" and "home language" when we discuss usage in writing. Or if the situation calls for a speech model, have students think about "TV language"—talking like Dan Rather ("CBS News"), Bryant Gumbel or Jane Pauley (NBC's "Today Show"), Knowlton Nash (CBC's "The National"), or some other newsperson. However, don't demand that students replace their home language with book or TV language or even encourage it. Instead, your goal is to add standard usage to the students' language repertoire so that they may choose the usage appropriate to the situation. Since there is general agreement that formal writing features standard usage (but how much of students' writing is formal?), we prefer to help students with usage in writing and assume that they can make the same usage choices in speech situations that call for it. But do remember that "there really is no right or wrong usage. Usage choices are either appropriate for the situation or not appropriate" (Fisher, 1980, 63). Thus, while "book language" is most appropriate for formal writing, "home language" is most appropriate on the neighborhood baseball diamond or in informal writing of notes to friends.

Teacher demonstration may be useful when particular aspects of usage are being attended to for the first time, when instructional time is short, or when the usage issue is too complex for the student to deal with any other way. For example, while editing Delores's paper, the teacher decided to call attention to usage in one of her sentences: "I like to go to school for I could be real smart." The teacher substituted "so" and "can" for "for" and "could" and said: "This is the way the sentence would be written in a book. Read it aloud so you can get a feel for how it sounds." In doing this, the teacher was developing Delores's intuitive knowledge of how words and tenses are used in standard English. Although Delores was a ninth grader, the teacher didn't talk with her about the differences between "for" and "so," nor did she give Delores the rule about keeping tenses consistent within a sentence. When Delores read her piece of writing to a small group of students, she again produced the standard usage and heard how the sentence sounded. Note that the teacher kept this lesson quite brief, attending to usage in only one sentence.

Comparing usage is another useful technique, especially when the same usage problems or differences arise frequently in students' writing. This usually requires collecting a number of sentences in which usage problems occur before the lesson can be taught. For example, a teacher working with two girls, both dialect speakers, observed that they weren't using plural "-s" and past tense "-ed" endings consistently in their writing. Because the students occasionally used the endings, the teacher assumed that the girls knew of their existence and function but not at a conscious enough level for them to make a choice about using the endings appropriately. The teacher looked through a number of the girls' recent compositions and located sentences that contained words without "-s" and "-ed" endings. She wrote the girls' sentences on a piece of paper and then, below each one, rewrote the sentences "as an author would in a book" (see Figure 12–3).

The teacher asked the girls to examine the pairs of sentences and explain the differences. They not only spotted each of the differences, they spontaneously arrived at the rules: that "-s" was used at the end of a word when talking about more than one and that "-ed" was used when talking about things that had already happened. If the girls had not spontaneously generated the rules, the teacher would have asked them to look at the sentences and figure out how they would know in the future when to add "-s" or "-ed" to words in their writing.

Many points of usage may be taught in the same way, ranging from replacing "Me and Bobbie" with "Bobbie and I" and avoiding split infinitives ("She helped the children to fill the glasses correctly" rather than "She helped the children to correctly fill the glasses") to sophisticated discussions about appropriate usage when writing character descriptions or trying to capture the essence of a character in the character's dialogue. In the latter case, of course, the students may need to work in the opposite direction—to study and replicate dialectical or nonstandard usage. It is also quite interesting to compare usage in songs and poems that creates certain effects, such as a rhyme scheme. For example, students might compare the lines, "We three Kings from Orient are. Bearing gifts we travel afar" with the sentence, "We are three Kings from the Orient" and discuss what the lyric writer might have had in mind when deciding how to write the first line of the song.

The final technique, lifting text, is also useful, especially when you've already demonstrated or compared certain aspects of usage. Provide part of a composition or an entire one written by a student for students to edit for usage as a group. As students change usage on their own, record their choices in writing. You might also issue specific challenges to them: "Let's take a look at the pronouns John used in his piece of writing. Which are used the way they would be in a book? Which are not? How would those be written in a book?"

We want to close this discussion of usage with a caveat. Teachers must be cautious when teaching standard English to nonstandard speakers. Language is very personal. It not only allows us to communicate, it also enables us to proclaim our membership in social and cultural groups. Questions about the

---

FIGURE 12–3   Comparing Usage

First I had to wait in the waiting room until he call me.

First I had to wait in the waiting room until he called me.

I really don't like snow because when you are really dress up . . .

I really don't like snow because when you are really dressed up . . .

At home for the last three day . . .

At home for the last three days . . .

I'm going to take my camera and take pictures of my teachers and children and some friend too.

I'm going to take my camera and take pictures of my teachers and children and some friends too.

---

use of standard or nonstandard dialects are questions of appropriateness, not correctness. Successful writers (and speakers) must learn that standard English is appropriate in certain contexts and that dialects may be appropriate in other contexts. When we encourage students to write for a range of purposes and audiences, we give them opportunities to use both standard and nonstandard language in their writing. In this way they learn appropriate usage, rather than correct usage.

EDITING AND PUBLISHING

Writers engage in transcription not only when they get their original thoughts on paper, but also when they edit and publish their work. Editing requires that the writer use standard conventions, while publication requires that the writer put the piece of writing into its final form before it is released to an audience of readers.

In earlier sections of this chapter, we shared some ideas for helping students learn and use each of the major conventions of transcription—spelling, punctuation, handwriting, and grammatical usage. These recommendations may be employed in group lessons or in conferences with students after they have drafted and revised their writing. For the sake of convenience, we presented ideas in a linear way, but we do not want to leave the impression that editing is linear. Instead, when students need to learn to do what proficient writers do, they must orchestrate what they know about writing conventions in independently editing their own work. Most of us edit by reading our work and changing what needs changing in the order in which it occurs to use while we read. This requires not only skill in proofreading and knowledge about conventions but also experience in editing.

Let's repeat that editing only makes sense if writers have readers. That's why we are also including a brief discussion about publishing students' work. Publication is an important way to provide a natural impetus for editing. Editing is extra work for the author, who does it only to facilitate the reader's efforts to understand and appreciate the author's work. Thus editing is being treated here as the final step prior to publication.

In this section we'll recommend instructional strategies to help students learn how to edit writing. Although editing may seem very easy to those of us who are proficient writers, students can't just be told, "Edit your paper." They need to learn how to edit.

If we think back to "the gradual release of responsibility model of instruction" (Pearson & Gallagher, 1983) presented in chapter 2, editing instruction may begin with a teacher *demonstration* of editing. This can be done by making an overhead of a student's piece of writing (one which has been selected and then revised for publication) and editing it in front of the students, all the while commenting aloud on how you are going about the editing process. Ask students to observe carefully what it is that you do to edit a piece of work and perhaps even take notes on what they observe. Make sure they observe such things as how you read, how much you read, and that you read repeatedly when necessary, as well as how you mark changes—crossing out unconventional spelling and writing conventional spelling above, using a special editor's mark to show a new paragraph, and so on (the conventions of editing will be different for students using word processors).

When you have finished, discuss the process that students observed and begin to make a chart of their editing observations that includes procedures and marks. You may find that you need to demonstrate the process to students several times before they are able to observe all the aspects of editing that are important. If any piece of writing you use for demonstration takes more than ten or fifteen minutes to edit, finish the piece another day.

Once students have a feeling for the editing process, involve them as a group in the process, still using an overhead and a piece of student writing (Cramer, 1978). Encourage them to edit the paper aloud, while you guide the process as much as seems necessary. A major goal for students during these group editing sessions is to proofread for conventions rather than to read for meaning. *Proofreading* is a delicate balance between a heavy focus on conventions and a concern for meaning. After all, meaning determines such things as the placement of punctuation and the spelling of words when there are competing homophones (*their* and *there*, for example). As students learn and refine their understanding of editing, encourage them to revise the group's editing chart. You may even want to have students write the editors of the local newspaper and ask for their editorial marks and tips. If you're working with small groups of students, attempt to use every student's writing for at least one editing session. In the process, help each student to understand her/his strengths and weaknesses in the use of conventions so that each one begins to know where to concentrate more and less effort during editing.

When you think that students have developed some editing skill in this guided way, we recommend establishing an *Editors' Table* (Burke, 1985) where students rotate the responsibility for editing their own and others' writing prior to publication. At the Editors' Table, the editorial board works on writing turned in by fellow students. The work turned in to the editors should have already been shared in Authors' Circle (see the previous chapter) and revised. The editors' first job is to read to see if any further revisions need to be made for the sake of clarity. If they find a need for revision, they must confer with the student who wrote the piece about what they feel needs revision and ask the student to revise. As Burke emphasizes, editors need to understand that no one except the author has the right to change the meaning or structure of the text. Authors also have the right to reject revision recommendations.

The editors read the piece again when they edit. They correct spelling, punctuation, and usage to the best of their knowledge and prepare the writing so that it is ready for final copying (rewriting by the student, typing by someone else, or printing from the word processor). The editors can consult you, as the teacher and "Managing Editor," for help with editing problems; and as Managing Editor, you may also make the final decision about whether a piece will be released for publication.

Depending on whether a piece needs to be edited to "perfection" and on the editing skill of the current editors, a piece of writing may not be edited to the point where it is suitable for publication. In this case, as Managing Editor you may finalize the editing. Or if students' manuscripts are being typed, you may turn the final editing over to whoever types them.

Be sure to rotate those who serve as editors so that every student may participate in this learning experience. It's helpful to have a range of abilities on any given editorial board, and you may want to consider that when deciding on a rotation schedule. Once students have participated in editing in this way, they'll become increasingly able to self-edit or to edit with the help of another student.

Publication is the final step for some writing. Like editing, publication is not necessary for all pieces of writing; you may want to establish a rule of a maximum of two publications per month for each student (Harste, Pierce, & Cairney, 1985). Learning to choose pieces for publication helps students develop better judgment about what is worthy of publication and what is not.

Publication can take many forms—a bound book featuring one student's piece of writing or the collected works of several students, often about the same theme or topic; publication in the class or school newspaper; a wall display at eye level in the classroom or school; submission to a newspaper or magazine; reproducing with a ditto master for handing out to everyone. Some methods of publication motivate students to write more than others do. Observe individual students and see what they get most excited about. For example, many consider themselves to be real authors only when they've published a bound book. Directions for binding books can be found in numerous places; your school media center should be able to provide some. In addition, consider requesting that the school invest in a binding machine to make publication easier. Also consider setting up a *Publication Table* in you classroom containing materials often used for publication—a typewriter, good paper, markers, bookbinding materials and directions, and so on.

Published writing needs to be recognized and celebrated. One way to do so is to establish an *Author's Chair* in the classroom (Graves & Hansen, 1983), a special chair from which students and teacher read trade books and the students' own published writing. Whether students read a trade book or their own writing, the same routine is followed, a routine quite like that for Authors' Circle described in the previous chapter. First, authors read their published writing and students "receive" it by telling the author what they liked specifically about the piece and revealing what they thought the piece was about. Next, listeners ask the author questions that range from how the author decided on the topic to those that clarify parts of the story.

When the teacher or a student reads from a trade book, the group follows the same routine—students receive the writing and then ask questions about it— but since the author is not present, they speculate on what the answers to their questions might be. When this routine is used frequently with both student work and trade books, students begin to internalize the questions and use them to guide their own revisions prior to publication. "The [student] rewrites with a sense of what the class will ask when he or she reads the piece from the author's chair" (Graves & Hansen, 1983, 182).

Writing can also be celebrated by selecting an *Author of the Week*. In the classroom that Graves and Hansen (1983) studied, the author's photo and a list of her/his published works were posted on a bulletin board. The student's books were placed in pockets for other students to read and comment on in writing. The student chose her/his favorite published book for the teacher to make five copies of for other students to read during reading time. Try out some of these ideas and establish your own Author of the Week traditions.

Finally, consider an *Authors' Party* at some point in the year. Invite families and friends to see the students' publications and to hear them read.

CONCLUSION

In this chapter we have discussed the use of conventions in writing and instructional strategies for helping students learn to use conventions effectively. But students should not learn conventions like spelling, punctuation, and grammatical usage as a separate body of knowledge or as a measure of literacy. These conventions are useful only insofar as they help writers to fulfill their intentions. A piece of writing may be judged perfect in its use of conventions but still fail to achieve its purpose. Students should learn about conventions as they write and as they consider the needs of particular audiences. And, as we've said already, students should wait until they're ready to edit their writing to focus on conventions, since close attention to conventions during composition will detract from their ability to construct meaning for their readers.

XIII

Collaborating with students, teachers,
parents, and administrators

Throughout this book we've presented instructional and assessment strategies to help LD and remedial teachers promote the reading and writing development of their students. However, LD and remedial teachers aren't alone in their concern about their students' reading and writing development, nor do they have the sole responsibility for their students' literacy development. Many individuals share an interest in students' literacy development, including regular classroom teachers, school administrators, and parents. And, of course, the students themselves have an important role in their own literacy development. Reading and writing instruction should not be limited to the efforts of LD and remedial teachers. The prospects that learning disabled and remedial students have for developing into life-long readers and writers increase when parents, teachers, administrators, and students work together toward their common goal—literacy.

But as we all know, teachers, parents, and administrators don't always work together. In fact, there is often little collaboration or even cooperation among the various people who can affect students' reading and writing development. It's not that everyone working with the child isn't concerned—they usually are—it's just that their efforts are rarely co-ordinated. There are exceptions, of course, but too often the contacts that LD and remedial teachers have with regular classroom teachers, parents, and administrators are limited to occasional progress reports. This is partly due to teacher education programs and school environments that rarely stress how teachers can and should work with each other or with parents. But differences in attitudes and beliefs about reading and writing—how reading and writing should be taught, assessed, and so on—can be another barrier to collaboration. Parents, teachers, and administrators may find it difficult to work together when they perceive serious differences in their ideas about how reading and writing should be taught. This is a real problem for holistic teachers who find their beliefs about reading and writing in conflict with the beliefs of those with whom they must work closely.

The purpose of this chapter is to present ideas for developing collaborative relationships between teachers, parents, administrators, and students so that more effective literacy programs are available to LD and remedial students. We'll give special attention to working in situations where the beliefs of others about instruction differ substantially from those of the LD or remedial teacher.

ESTABLISHING EXPECTATIONS ABOUT YOUR READING AND WRITING CURRICULUM

Before collaborative relationships can be developed, it is necessary to help students, parents, other teachers, and administrators become aware of your approach to reading and writing instruction. It isn't necessary to change beliefs, although it would certainly be helpful to students' literacy development if it happened. Your goal is to establish expectations about students' reading and writing curriculum and some understanding about your rationale for the curriculum.

We recently observed a group of three-year-olds playing school. It was apparent that these children had some expectations about what goes on in school, even though they themselves had never been in a school. Once children have been in school for a short time their expectations become clearer. These expectations about schooling are shaped by their own school experiences and the expectations of their parents. Parents also have expectations (conscious or unconscious) about the type of instruction their children will receive in school, expectations that are shaped by their own school experiences. Parents' expectations may also be affected by the school experiences of their children and the mass media. No doubt, the media attention given to the "back-to-basics" movement has affected the beliefs of many parents.

The expectations of students, teachers, parents, and administrators merit consideration by all teachers but especially by LD and remedial teachers whose educational philosophy may not be shared by those with whom they work. Actually it's unlikely that LD or remedial teachers will find themselves in a situation in which there is universal agreement on instructional philosophy. But LD and remedial teachers who take a holistic approach to reading and writing instruction may be especially likely to find their educational philosophy in conflict with that of others. The question is, does it matter? Is it really necessary that parents, teachers, students, and administrators share a common educational philosophy? Of course not. It isn't necessary or, perhaps, even desirable that everyone share a common philosophy. In any case, such a state of affairs is highly unlikely.

But serious consequences can result when people's expectations about instruction differ. When expectations aren't met, people may become confused, and suspicion and distrust may develop. Many people not only believe that reading and writing instruction must focus on teaching isolated "basic skills" (e.g., sight word recognition, letter-sound correspondences, spelling), they also believe that students who have not learned to read and write well have faltered because of a failure to master these so-called basic skills. When LD and remedial programs do not feature the mastery of isolated skills, parents, teachers, and administrators may lose confidence in the LD or remedial teacher, which lessens the potential for collaboration. (A helpful definition of what we consider the basic skill in reading to be may be found in J. Taylor's 1977 article, "Making sense: The basic skill in reading.")

One of the top priorities for LD and remedial teachers is to change expectations where necessary. If we know that our teaching will be different from what is expected, we need to let it be known what can be expected from us. We need to inform teachers, parents, and administrators about the nature of our reading and writing curriculum and the rationale behind it. Otherwise we risk being judged according to expectations we may not share.

THE EXPECTATIONS OF STUDENTS

Although we stated earlier that it is not necessary that everyone come to share our beliefs about reading and writing in order to develop collaborative relationships, students are an exception. Unless students come to revalue reading and writing as meaning construction processes, they will not become the readers and writers they are capable of becoming. In fact, K. Goodman suggests that changing students' expectations about the value of reading and writing in their lives is the single most important thing we can do for them as teachers.

> Revaluing is essential. If those pupils are to become literate, they must lose the loser mentality. They must find the strength and confidence to take the necessary risks, to make the literacy choices, and to enter into functional literacy events. Whole language teaching helps pupils value what they can do and not be defeated by what they can't do; it helps them trust themselves and their linguistic intuitions, to become self-reliant in their sense of what they are reading. Whole, relevant, meaningful language...can help them build productive meaning-seeking strategies. Eventually they will come to realize that making sense is all that reading and writing are about. (K. Goodman, 1986b, 56)

Everything we have written in this book is intended to help students revalue reading and writing as meaningful, purposeful processes. Every decision you make as a teacher to implement what we have presented or to invent your own curriculum with students must remain within that overall intention if students are to revalue literacy in their lives.

THE EXPECTATIONS OF PARENTS

Misunderstandings that arise between teachers and parents can frequently be traced to differing expectations. Teachers who accept invented spellings in their students' writing, for example, often find themselves in conflict with parents. Some parents view invented spellings as "mistakes" and may view teachers who fail to correct these spelling mistakes as lazy or incompetent. Some parents may even take "uncorrected" spellings as evidence that the teacher doesn't know how to spell and wonder how their child will learn to spell if the teacher doesn't correct mistakes and give correct spellings. Parents often believe that they learned to spell as a direct result of their teachers' corrections and are suspicious of teachers who don't teach this way. Parents who are poor spellers will often argue that they didn't learn to spell because they didn't get enough phonics instruction.

This kind of situation is avoidable, however. LD and remedial teachers needn't become helpless victims of parental expectations. We can affect the expectations of parents. For example, LD and remedial teachers can inform parents when students enter their programs that in certain situations, students' invented spellings will be accepted. Teachers can tell parents that it makes little sense to worry about correct spelling with students who produce very little writing, often because of excessive concern with spelling conventions. Remind parents of their willingness to accept misarticulations and ungrammatical utterances when their children were learning to use oral language. Show parents writing samples from students in previous years. Let them see how the acceptance of invented spellings can affect children's writing fluency. Share evidence with parents that invented spellings do evolve into standard spelling over time, and let them know what form your spelling instruction will take.

Teachers need to consider what opportunities they might have to share what they'll be doing in their literacy programs with parents, e.g., how they'll handle spelling and why. Communicating with parents is an important factor in developing a collaborative relationship. Periodic newsletters, individual parent conferences, IEP staffings, open houses, meetings with groups of parents, and telephone calls are some of the possibilities for communicating with parents that we will describe in more detail.

The "good news" phone call

Regular telephone calls are a personal and effective way to communicate with parents. However, many parents dread phone calls from teachers since they usually focus on some problem. Parents of LD and remedial students have usually had many such phone calls. The following account is illustrative.

TEACHER: Mrs. Jones, this is Mr. Dudley-Marling, Stanley's teacher.
PARENT: What has he done now?
TEACHER: No, everything is fine, Mrs. Jones...
PARENT: I'm sorry but I can't do anything with Stanley either.
TEACHER: No, you don't understand. I'm calling to tell you that Stanley had a great day. He selected and read a book on his own. He wrote in his...

PARENT: Well, what do you want me to do about it? Maybe his father can talk to him.

TEACHER: No, Mrs. Jones...

It took several minutes for this parent to realize that the teacher was calling to share good news because she'd never had this kind of call before. In the past teachers had only called when there was a problem.

Teachers can routinely use phone calls to share student progress, develop collaborative efforts, and let parents know what teachers expect and why. Even though some LD and remedial teachers have relatively large numbers of students, it should be possible to phone each parent once every four to six weeks by making only one phone call a day. It's important to remember that phone calls will be most effective if they focus on the positive and largely ignore student problems, at least until a strong, trusting relationship has been developed between teacher and parents. Don't start out with the "good news" and then add "but...."

Parent conferences and open houses

Parent conferences and open houses are excellent occasions for sharing information about your reading and writing program. Open houses at the beginning of the year may feature slide presentations of the previous year's program with specific examples of reading and writing activities. They might also include an informal discussion to deal with parents' concerns and curiosity about your program. Parent meetings are times when teachers can let parents know what they do and why, e.g., why they accept invented spellings or why they depend on children's literature instead of workbooks and basal readers. Parent meetings can also be used to share ideas about reading to children, suggestions on books to read, writing with children, and so on.

Individual parent conferences are also effective for keeping parents informed about your literacy program and their child's progress. However, it's important that the information shared with parents be precise and accurate. Very general comments about a student's progress usually leave parents less than satisfied.

While there will be little disagreement about the potential effectiveness of face-to-face parent contacts, many teachers are skeptical about the likelihood of parents' attendance. Most of us have experienced parent conferences or parents' night when only a few parents showed up. However, there is evidence that high rates of parent attendance are possible if there is a concerted effort to get parents to attend, if there is the promise of valuable information, or if the students "show off" what they've learned/done for their parents. For example, Granowsky, Middleton & Mumford (1979) reported very high rates of attendance at parent conferences in an inner-city school in Dallas, Texas, when mass media was used to advertise parent meetings, conferences were scheduled at times convenient to parents, student work was presented, and information was shared with parents that helped them get involved in their children's learning. Parents were given concrete reasons for attending school conferences.

Classroom visits

Classroom visits are an invaluable way for parents to learn about what goes on in their child's class. Visiting parents have the opportunity to observe your teaching and to see samples of students' work. Additionally, parents will get some ideas they can use to encourage reading and writing at home. Classroom visits will be most effective if parents are able to make several visits. Parents who rarely visit the classroom will see only an isolated bit of what's going on. Parents will be more likely to return for additional visits if an effort is made to make them comfortable, even to the point of providing comfortable furniture for them (Lamme, 1981). Parents will also be more comfortable, and will learn more, if they are encouraged to participate actively in your reading and writing program. Parents can read to children, conduct writing conferences, help in the preparation of materials, and so on.

The IEP conference

Many LD teachers, and some remedial reading teachers, participate in team meetings in which general instructional plans and strategies are developed. These conferences provide teachers with excellent opportunities for sharing information about their programs and developing collaborative relationships with parents. Involving parents in goal setting and program planning will increase the prospects of collaboration. Goal setting can include specific parental responsibilities in a child's literacy program, e.g., reading daily to the child, family reading times, and so on.

Newsletters and written information

Newsletters and other written information can also be used to inform parents about what their children are doing in the classroom and what they might do for their children at home. Some teachers send a newsletter telling parents that they will be accepting invented spellings and why, which can then be followed up in phone calls and parent conferences.

Periodic newsletters can be prepared by teachers but they can be more effective if they are developed and prepared by the students themselves. In a remedial reading class in Denver, for example, students jot notes on a calendar each day about what they have done in class before they return to their regular classrooms. Every two weeks they use these notes to write letters to their parents explaining what they have done and what they have learned during the previous two weeks. In another class for emergent readers, students dictate a group letter to their parents, which is copied and sent home. This serves as both a source of information for parents and as reading material for students.

Now, more than ever before, information written for parents about literacy development is available. We recommend that you select information to share with parents that encourages them to involve their children in reading and writing in natural, everyday activities, with everyday materials, and for a variety of purposes. Pamphlets, booklets, and books that are written specifically for parents are listed in Rhodes and Hill (1985). Many are brief and so inexpensive that they might serve as "take homes" on back-to-school night or after parent-teacher conferences.

Home visits

Although home visits are time-consuming, parents are often much more comfortable in their own homes than they are at school. During home visits teachers can share information about their classroom programs, discuss a student's progress, and share ideas with parents for working with their children at home.

It's unlikely that you will affect parents' expectations with a single newsletter, phone call, or face-to-face meeting. Frequent communication about your goals and your teaching methods will be necessary. Open communication with parents will diminish the prospects of conflict while improving the prospects of collaboration. Again, these contacts will be more effective if you are explicit about the goals and the direction of your literacy program and if you share concrete examples of students' work. Parents who understand what we are doing and why are far more likely to work with us, and of course, working with us will lead to a better understanding of what we are trying to accomplish.

THE EXPECTATIONS OF TEACHERS AND ADMINISTRATORS

Efforts should also be undertaken to affect the expectations of administrators, regular classroom teachers, and others with whom you work. Misunderstandings between LD and remedial teachers and other professional educators may permanently damage working relationships, leading to ineffective instructional situations for students and, occasionally, negative teaching evaluations. Therefore, it's imperative that you consider the expectations of the significant people with whom you work. This doesn't mean that they need to understand everything you do, but that you should anticipate areas of potential conflict and address these before problems arise.

Probably the best method for establishing expectations is frequent personal contact. Talk with teachers and administrators as often as you can and let them know, generally, what you will be doing and why. You can do this naturally. It's quite natural, for example, to discuss with regular classroom teachers the reading and writing programs of students for whom you share responsibility. Most principals are pleased to have the opportunity to hear what's going on in classrooms in their schools.

Share samples of students' work with teachers and administrators. Draw their attention to developmental changes, and briefly share what you will be doing to foster continued development. Provide detail only if it's requested. Display students' work in the halls outside your classroom and encourage students to share their reading and writing with students in their regular classroom. Invite teachers and administrators to visit your classroom—you may be able to encourage visits by providing coffee and donuts before school once every two or three months. You might also offer to teach lessons in the regular classroom. Use opportunities like these to define your curriculum and to invite collaboration.

Share useful articles on teaching reading and writing with teachers and with the principal. Some schools have procedures for circulating interesting books and articles. You might also leave copies of interesting articles about reading and writing in the teachers' lounge or in other areas likely to be used by teachers. If teachers express an interest you might consider holding mini-workshops or sponsoring study groups. You might also make staff aware of interesting speakers or conferences in your area. You may even be able to influence the selection of workshop speakers in your school. The teachers' lounge is a good place to share some of your successes. Teachers might be impressed to hear that, after years of resistance to writing, little Mary Smith is churning out books. You may also find them really interested in your curriculum when you share writing from your LD or remedial students that is as good as or better than the writing done by normally achieving students in their classes. Participating on key committees, especially curriculum development and text-book selection committees, is another way to define expectations and, of course, influence school policy.

In all of this, you need to be patient. Remember that your goal is to make clear what can be expected of your curriculum and develop collaborative relationships, not to "convert" everyone to your point of view. Even this relatively modest goal may take several years. If you affect beliefs about reading and writing, it will only happen after good relationships have developed and because the teachers and administrators have had their interest piqued and have begun to ask questions.

Avoid using jargon in your discussions with teachers and administrators, including terms like "holism" or "whole language." Also avoid excessive enthusiasm. Most of us are put off by jargon and by bandwagons. Just let teachers and administrators know that what you are doing is providing what you believe encourages literacy development in the students with whom you are working. In some cases it may also be important to let teachers know that you are not ignoring aspects of reading and writing that they feel are important either. It's just that you approach these aspects of written language instruction differently.

Many LD and remedial teachers lament the difficulty of finding mutually convenient times to meet with regular classroom teachers. Certainly regular classroom teachers do have busy schedules. While it may be difficult to find large blocks of time to meet with teachers, there are usually lots of smaller time periods when teachers are available. Frequent two or three minute meetings are sometimes more effective anyway. You can share a sample of a student's work or briefly review a student's reading or writing progress just before school, between classes, during preparation periods, during recess, and so on. If you're unable to find convenient meeting times, ask teachers to list several times during the day when they are available for five minutes. It's unlikely many teachers won't find five minutes during the day to meet with you. Most will be especially willing to meet regularly with you if they come to expect that something useful to them will emerge. But be brief! If you habitually take lots of teachers' time, you may encounter an increasing reluctance to meet.

DEVELOPING COLLABORATIVE RELATIONSHIPS

While it's important to make clear what can be expected of your curriculum for students, parents, teachers, and administrators, this is only a first step in developing collaborative relationships. In the sections that follow we present some ideas for developing collaborative relationships with students, parents, teachers, and administrators.

COLLABORATING WITH STUDENTS

Recently, James Ysseldyke of the University of Minnesota taught a learning disability course at York University in Toronto. At one point Professor Ysseldyke paired the students in the class, all of whom were teachers, and presented them with a memory task to teach each other. When they were done he asked students to report on their "teaching" experiences. Interestingly, a significant number of the students in the class reported that, when they assumed the "teacher" role, they began by asking the "student" how they would like to be taught. Though this is a logical, efficient way to proceed, how many of us ask our students how or what they want to learn?

Our students are our most important collaborators. We can teach but we can't force learning; learning is a student's prerogative. We not only need to let our students know what we will be doing and why, but we should also involve them in goal-setting, materials selection, scheduling, evaluation, and program planning. The importance of student input is most apparent with high school age students, but even our youngest students should have some input into the educational decisions that will affect their lives.

Why not ask students what books they'd like to read and what they'd like to learn about? Some students may be able to tell us that they would rather not come to a special program for reading and writing but would prefer to have something worked out in the regular classroom. All but the most immature students can effectively participate in the decision-making that occurs in an IEP conference. After students have been in our programs for a while we can ask for their evaluation of our teaching strategies. Which strategies do they feel are most helpful to them? Which do they find less effective? They can also be involved in the evaluation of their own reading and writing development (see N. Atwell, 1982). If we're faced with a decision such as whether or not to introduce word processors into our classrooms, we might request student input. If we think students have too little information to provide input, we can least let them evaluate the effectiveness of such innovations as the word processor after they've been introduced as part of the curriculum.

Involving students in educational decisions will increase the prospects of their continued cooperation in their own education and their sense of owner-ship, since they share the responsibility for decisions. In general, we should treat our students as partners in developing and implementing reading and writing curricula. As we've noted throughout this book, students must actively participate in their reading and writing development. We can't succeed without their commitment.

COLLABORATING WITH PARENTS

Parents are an important influence on children's literacy development, and evidence suggests that parental involvement in students' reading programs will positively affect students' reading performance (Schuck, Ulsh & Platt, 1983). A number of effective programs have been established in various countries for increasing parents' participation in their children's reading (see Criscuolo, 1978; Quisenberry, Blakemore & Warren, 1977). Parents can also be a valuable resource in the classroom. In this section we'll discuss ideas for involving parents in their child's reading and writing development at home and then involving parent volunteers in the classroom curriculum.

There are a number of ways of involving parents in their children's reading and writing development at home. All of them simply recognize the ways that parents have used for generations to support literacy development in the home. Some parents will already be doing all or most of the things we will mention, while others will need a great deal of support and encouragement to implement these ideas.

1. All parents should be encouraged to read aloud to their children, regardless of age. Reading to children can affect reading achievement (Teale, 1978) and is the easiest, most natural, and effective way to involve parents in their child's reading and reading development (Jones, 1981). Most parents will find the *Read-Aloud Handbook* (Trelease, 1985) a useful resource for good read-aloud materials as well as for hints on establishing a routine of reading aloud as an enjoyable experience.
2. Parents can learn how to respond effectively to children's oral reading. Suggest that they sometimes read texts to their child first, before the child reads it to them. Demonstrate the technique of assisted reading to parents so that they can use it to support their children's reading (Hoskisson, Sherman & Smith, 1974). Encourage parents not to limit the amount of discussion of a text or the accompanying pictures. Suggest that they avoid criticism and allow the child plenty of "wait time" or "thinking time" before providing assistance with words. You may also wish to instruct parents in the use of strategies like "Read on a little" (Bartlett, Hall & Neale, 1984). Parents who learn how to respond to their children's oral reading find that reading becomes an enjoyable activity for them both rather than one that everyone dreads (Bartlett, Hall & Neale, 1984).
3. Parents can be encouraged to take advantage of environmental print in natural situations, e.g., reading road signs while driving, reading advertise-ments and labels while shopping, reading recipes while cooking, etc.

4. Parents can be encouraged to provide a variety of reading materials for their children, including books and magazines. Advise parents on good children's and adolescent literature, perhaps sending home lists of books and magazines that parents might want to buy for their children just before Christmas (Vukelich, 1984) or the student's birthday. At group meetings share the titles of books you have seen students enjoy at school, and encourage parents to share titles of books they have seen their children enjoy at home. Most parents will find Michele Landsberg's (1986) *Guide to Children's Books* an excellent guide to children's and adolescent literature.

   Encourage parents to visit local libraries with their children regularly. Keep them informed about school book fairs and special reading programs at libraries and suggest that parents consult librarians for titles of books their children might enjoy. Local libraries frequently have regular story times. Also recommend bookstores that stock good selections of children's and adolescent literature. Some children's bookstores also feature story times and visits by authors of children's and adolescent literature. You might even consider establishing a book lending library for parents at school (Brieling, 1976) if parents don't have easy access to other sources of books. Some parents might also be interested in courses on children's and adolescent literature.

5. Encourage parents to read with their children. Seeing their parents regularly reading will have a positive effect on children's reading development (O'Rourke, 1979). Suggest that parents take advantage of every opportunity to let their children observe them reading, to see them as readers. Taking advantage of environmental print as suggested above is helpful. Some parents may be comfortable setting aside a family reading time every night when everyone in the family looks at books, newspapers, or magazines. As little as fifteen minutes will be helpful. Remind parents of the power of imitation; if parents read and write, it is much more likely that their children will also read and write.

6. Encourage parents to write with their children. Parents can, for example, write letters with their children. A letter to grandma could be a family activity. Children also can help their parents develop grocery lists. Some families keep regular journals that provide a record of family events as well as a model for writing. Parents show their children what writing is about and how it is used when their children see them as writers. Parents can also write to their children, perhaps sticking a note in their lunch boxes. Many families have blackboards or bulletin boards in the kitchen where family members write messages to each other. Information about children's development in writing as well as other ideas for encouraging writing in the home may be found in two books written especially for parents, *Write from the Start* (Graves & Stuart, 1985) and *Writing Begins at Home* (Clay, 1987).

This is only a sampling of ideas for encouraging parental involvement in students' reading and writing. Most teachers will be able to think of many more. Many of the ideas in this book for encouraging students to share what they've read and written may also be used by parents. There are a number of additional resources available for involving parents in the literacy program. Quisenberry, Blakemore, and Warren (1977) have produced an annotated bibliography of three dozen articles with ideas and plans for developing parent involvement programs in reading.

One caution is in order here. Reading (and writing) is often a source of considerable stress between parents and their LD or remedial children. Therefore, it's important that parents be encouraged to focus on reading and writing experiences with their children that are especially likely to be natural and enjoyable. Parents should not be encouraged to teach reading or writing skills but rather to help their children find as many opportunities as possible for purposeful and enjoyable reading and writing. The sorts of ideas we have shared here involve parents in time-honored ways in their children's literacy development and minimize stress for both parents and children. In some cases, however, parents may find any involvement in their child's reading and writing program stressful. Teachers should be alert to this possibility and consciously avoid making parents feel guilty if they aren't able, or willing, to participate in their child's reading and writing program.

Parents can also be a valuable resource for teachers. Parents possess useful information about their child's literacy development; they can inform teachers about children's reading and writing experiences at home, their favorite books, their interests, and so on.

Parents can also be very helpful within the classroom. Some parents may be able to volunteer regularly in the LD or remedial classroom. They may also be able to volunteer in the regular classroom, thereby allowing the regular classroom teacher to provide special attention to children having reading and writing problems. Parents can aid in materials preparation and repair, bookbinding, fund raising, and so on. But they can also help students to read and write in school in the same way they do at home. Parents may, for example, read to or with individual children or groups of children. If provided with instruction, some may also be able to help teachers implement many of the instructional strategies we've discussed in other chapters.

Parents can contribute to the curriculum by sharing their hobbies or careers (Lamme, 1981). Lots of reading, writing, and oral language can accompany these sorts of presentations. Some parents may be skilled storytellers. Others may be willing to share some of their own writing with your class (Lamme, 1981). Many parents can also contribute to classroom projects, perhaps serving as a resource for some thematic unit or helping students locate information for a class project (Rhodes & Hill, 1983).

Using parents as aides or volunteers is initially a time-consuming project that demands organization, but it's worthwhile since it provides more one-to-one help for your students, more variety in their exposure to literature and other written material, and more flexibility in your use of resources (Lamme, 1981). Significant and active parent participation in literacy programs will affect parental expectations and their ability and willingness to contribute to the literacy development of their own children at home while increasing your effectiveness in the classroom.

COLLABORATING WITH TEACHERS

Many learning disabled and remedial students are typically served in resource rooms or pull-out programs, yet spend the majority of their time within the regular classroom. Others are served by the special teacher within the regular classroom setting. Whatever the situation, we can't overlook the influence of regular classroom teachers on the reading and writing development of LD and remedial students. As LD and remedial teachers, we are far more likely to influence the reading and writing development of our students if we're able to collaborate with regular classroom teachers.

Strong collaborative relationships with regular classroom teachers are more likely if we can involve them in initial assessment, goal setting, and other decision-making. It's unrealistic to expect teachers to feel ownership in a student's reading and writing curriculum if they're not included in the decision-making and planning process (Alvarez, 1981).

We would expect regular classroom teachers to know a great deal about the reading and writing development of the students with whom they work. Yet, except for making the referral, many teachers have little to do with placement or instructional decisions regarding LD and remedial learners, despite the fact that they will continue to share the educational responsibility for these students.

Even classroom teachers who do not share your reading and writing philosophy can be effectively involved in the assessment of LD and remedial students if you structure the information you request. Encourage teachers to talk about students' oral reading in useful ways by asking them if the students' oral reading "mistakes" make sense. Don't ask if the student can read or not; ask *what* the student can read. Encourage the teacher to talk about students' writing samples by asking questions such as, "Does the student talk about important aspects of her/his world in writing?" and "From the student's spelling, what can you tell that s/he knows about sound/letter relationships?" Encouraging teachers to share information in this way will ensure that you get usable instructional information and not just a catalog of students' deficits. These sorts of questions may also encourage classroom teachers to view reading and writing in new ways.

You may also wish to observe students in their regular classes and then discuss with teachers what you observed about the students' literacy development. Make sure that the focus of your observation and your conversation afterwards remains on the student and the student's work, not on the teacher.

Once student strengths and needs have been identified, work with regular classroom teachers to establish cooperative plans for a reading and writing program. When will the student come to the resource room and for how long? How will the student's needs be addressed in the resource room *and* the regular classroom? One need that will, no doubt, be identified is the need to do lots of reading and writing. If you sense a willingness to address this need in the regular classroom, you'll be able to suggest lots of strategies that will increase the fluency of LD and remedial students as well as the other students in the class.

Often classroom teachers will be sympathetic to goals like increasing the amount of reading and writing in classes but worry about whether this goal and its increased demands on their time will detract from other things they feel they should be doing. Be sympathetic to this concern. A great deal is expected of regular classroom teachers, and demands for accountability have increased. You might consult with these teachers to help them include reading and writing "across the curriculum," perhaps by collaborating on a thematic unit that is carried out in both the regular classroom and your classroom. Many teachers resist new ideas for teaching reading and writing because they feel they barely have time to do what they are already doing. Often this is because they see reading and writing as skills that are taught in a particular block of time. Show them that reading and writing are a logical part of a history or geography lesson. Better yet, demonstrate this to them by offering to teach lessons in their classes. If you are both doing a thematic unit, this can be a natural extension of your work together.

You can also help overcome teachers' concerns about time by helping the students on your caseload within the regular classroom rather than in a "pull-out" situation. This is especially effective when a number of students on your caseload are from the same classroom. In some situations, you might also offer to include other students from the class who the teacher thinks could benefit from your attention. Offer to provide greater opportunities for reading and writing during independent work times by setting up a listening center. You might also help the classroom teacher develop a volunteer program to provide more individualized attention for reading and writing in the classroom. Many teachers would be much more willing to conduct reading and writing conferences, for example, if they had the assistance of another adult in the room.

Working collaboratively with regular classroom teachers is the most effective way to influence teachers' beliefs about reading and writing. Your efforts will not only affect the reading and writing curriculum of your students, it will also affect the curriculum of all of the teachers' students. If you're successful in developing these kinds of relationships with regular classroom teachers, you may find your role within your school shifting. You may work with students more within the regular classroom and consult more with those teachers who request it.

COLLABORATING WITH ADMINISTRATORS

School administrators can, of course, be important allies. They can provide physical resources and emotional support that may significantly affect school literacy programs (Barnard & Hetzel, 1976). Too often administrators are viewed only as obstacles, and many of us are only too happy when administrators ignore us and our programs. This attitude is unfortunate. We shouldn't be satisfied with a principal or supervisor who would rather focus attention on regular classroom programs or administrative concerns. School administrators have a lot to offer us.

As we said earlier, begin by addressing the expectations of the administrators with whom you work. Inform them about what you are doing in your literacy program and why. Many administrators are grateful to receive the latest information on reading and writing instruction. Additionally, solicit their active involvement in your program, including reading and writing occasionally with your students.

You can also work with principals to establish schoolwide literacy programs, such as sustained silent reading, paperback book programs, or writing programs. Schoolwide literacy programs can broaden the literacy experience of LD, remedial, and normally achieving students throughout the school. Efforts by the principal in support of schoolwide literacy programs may prevent, or at least minimize, future reading and writing failures.

Administrators can also help you establish volunteer programs, arrange for time to consult with teachers and other school staff, locate community resources, and establish schoolwide information-sharing networks. They can also help you develop parent programs, arrange in-service sessions, encourage collaboration by school staff, and seek donations of reading and writing materials, if necessary.

Remember that many administrators too feel accountability pressure. When that pressure is great, time, patience, curricular changes that work within the system and continued communication from you regarding student growth will eventually lead to greater support from your administrator in making greater curricular changes.

COLLABORATING WITH OTHERS

A number of people within the school and community can also contribute to your literacy program. For example, school librarians can be very helpful in the selection and acquisition of reading materials. Many librarians are also well acquainted with microcomputer technology and can assist you with your decisions in this area. Some may also be accomplished storytellers or oral readers and therefore able to affect your students' reading selections and habits.

Because of their expertise in oral language development, speech and language therapists can be a useful resource in helping you and classroom teachers incorporate effective oral language situations into your curriculum. There are, no doubt, a number of other school staff—school psychologists and guidance personnel, clerical and custodial staff—who may be willing to share skills or interests that can contribute to your language program. We have encountered janitors who were great storytellers, and other staff members may be able to share a musical interest with your class. In short, there are a number of ways to involve school staff in your oral language and literacy program in order to affect the education of your students.

People from the community can contribute to your literacy program in much the same way. You can probably discover children's authors, poets, storytellers, and musicians who are willing to share their skills with your class or, perhaps, the entire school. Senior citizens, many of whom are retired teachers, provide an especially valuable pool of volunteers (Cassidy, 1981). Additionally, peer tutors can be used effectively in LD and remedial programs. And don't forget the potential value of having your students read and write with younger students. Consider contacting Schools of Education at local colleges or universities to recruit students as volunteers. If you use volunteers in your classroom, it's important that you require regular, long-term commitments and as with parents, have well-established activities so they can spend their time with your students in effective ways.

STRATEGIES FOR DEALING WITH IMPOSED CURRICULA

Learning disability and remedial teachers usually have considerable freedom in their selection of materials and teaching strategies. However, there may be instances in which LD and remedial teachers must deal with curricula imposed by administrators with very strong expectations about skills instruction. Perhaps all the teachers in the school, including resource staff, are expected to use the same "skill building" reading series, children are tested according to their mastery of skills addressed in these programs, and teacher evaluations are linked to student success. Some LD teachers may labor under skills-oriented IEPs developed by someone else. And all LD and remedial teachers who function as resource teachers must give some consideration to the regular classroom curriculum, which often includes a skills-oriented approach to reading and/or writing.

These curricular constraints cannot be ignored. The success of LD and remedial students in the regular classroom, teaching evaluations, and, in extreme cases, continued employment may depend on teachers' ability to deal with curricula over which they have little control. It is much more common, however, for regular classroom teachers to have to deal with mandated curricula. If we wish to influence these teachers, we must know how to help them implement holistic reading and writing programs within the framework of an imposed curriculum. In this section we will discuss some strategies for dealing with imposed curricula.

HELPING TEACHERS DEAL WITH IMPOSED CURRICULA

Teachers who feel constrained by an imposed curriculum should first check their perceptions. Are they, in fact, required to adhere slavishly to a curriculum to the exclusion of any other approach to reading and writing? In most cases they are not. We've known many teachers who have satisfied their principals with an explanation of how and why they would like to either supplant or supplement the adopted reading program. The principals' usual concern was that the proposed program made sense for the students.

If a principal is reluctant to permit a departure from the adopted curriculum, teachers should not give up. They should continue to lobby for the freedom to implement meaningful reading and writing activities in their classroom. Ohanion (1981) described her efforts to obtain the principal's permission to read books with her students during the lunch hour. The principal agreed to this proposition on the condition that the assigned reading time continue to focus on the teaching of reading skills. Ohanion's students ate their brown bag lunches while Ohanion read to them and they looked at books on their own. We don't suggest that teachers give up their lunch period, but extraordinary efforts are occasionally required to introduce actual reading and writing into the classroom.

Most teachers do have freedom, perhaps more than they realize. Even where imposed curricula exist, these curricula only indicate that teachers should do certain things, use certain materials, and so on. Teachers are rarely required to do nothing else, although Ohanion's experience reminds us that this can happen. In all but the rarest cases, teachers do have the opportunity to encourage meaningful reading and writing, even within the context of a skills-oriented curriculum.

For example, if teachers are required to use skills-based reading and writing programs, they don't usually have to use these programs exclusively. They can devote a segment of the reading or language arts period to more meaningful activities, such as journal writing and sustained silent reading, which involve students in the reading and writing of actual texts. As we noted earlier, regular classroom teachers can also be encouraged to teach reading and writing "across the curriculum," incorporating meaningful reading and writing opportunities in content areas.

If teachers examine what they do with their skills-based programs, they find that they already make choices about what to use and not to use in the curriculum. No teacher we know uses materials exactly as they are written. Most teachers, for example, skip the "enrichment" or "language extension" portions of the basal reader teacher's guide and choose to spend their time on skills exercises and worksheets. Teachers could continue to use the basal reader and move toward more meaningful reading and writing if they made a different choice. Teachers could choose to skip the skills exercises and worksheets and spend their time instead on the enrichment and extension activities. Those activities often feature meaningful reading and writing or at least offer the potential for incorporating reading and writing.

Even when teachers use mandated skills exercises and worksheets, they can certainly spend less time at it. In our experience, students spend lots of time doing worksheets that could be completed in relatively short periods of time. When children are given a reward for satisfactorily completing worksheets, they finish worksheets that formerly took up to thirty minutes to complete in as little as five minutes with no apparent effect on performance. Many students may find the opportunity to read their favorite stories sufficient reward for completing tedious worksheets (Deardorff, 1982). We're not advocating worksheets or behavioral rewards. It's just that if teachers find they must use skills worksheets in their classes, these can done more quickly than they usually are so that "extra" time is available for real reading and writing.

Many teachers are afraid to abandon skill-oriented writing and reading instruction because of the effect this might have on their students' performance on the achievement tests that are often used to gauge the performance of students and teachers. This is a reasonable concern. Standardized reading and writing tests, which may focus on isolated skills, are widely administered throughout North America. Teachers concerned about the effects of introducing a more meaningful approach to written language instruction on children's test performance need to be reassured. They need to be reminded that holistic approaches to reading and writing do attend to what are referred to as "skills" like punctuation, spelling, and word recognition (Hansen, 1987). Writing skills or conventions are addressed during editing, when it becomes necessary to standardize writing for the sake of readers. As we have noted, readers must consider graphophonic rules, but children learn and use them as they read, not before they read. Teachers who encourage meaningful reading and writing will positively affect students' performance on reading achievement tests (see, for example, K. Goodman, 1986b; Singer, McNeil, & Furse, 1984; Teale, 1978). On the other hand, there will be some students who develop into effective readers although they never do well on skills tests (Jackson, 1981).

HELPING STUDENTS DEAL WITH IMPOSED CURRICULA

Throughout this book we've stated our position that the mastery of isolated, fragmented skills is not a prerequisite to successful reading and writing. Students will learn the skills necessary for reading and writing *as* they read and write. But in some cases, isolated skill instruction may be necessary, not as a strategy for teaching students to read and write but as a strategy for helping LD and remedial students survive in regular classrooms where "doing skills" is required.

Obviously we want to do everything we can to promote the reading and writing development of our students. However, it's also important that our students reach a point where they no longer need us. They must learn to function within the context of ordinary reading and writing curricula. Sadly, in some classrooms it isn't enough to be able to read and write real text for real reasons. In some classrooms, reading and writing competence requires the demonstration of the mastery of various skills, e.g., sound-blending, syllabication, capitalization, and so on.

In some instances, the LD or remedial student may understand the skill but have problems with worksheets or tests. Sometimes, the format is problematic; at other times, students do not perceive that an exercise calls for the very knowledge they apply in their reading and writing. We once encountered a student who struggled endlessly over worksheets requiring her to circle the words that rhymed from a list of words. We knew this student could produce rhymes. We had heard her make up rhymes in her LD classes. It turned out that the student was confused by the visual aspects of the task—some of the words that rhymed were spelled quite differently (e.g., make-steak).

LD and remedial teachers should attempt to identify the specific kinds of problems their students have with reading and writing in the regular classroom through observing and talking with the students involved. If it appears that the task itself might be the problem, they can address this in the resource room. It may be a case of teaching the student how to go about completing a particular worksheet rather than teaching the skill.

In rare cases, it may be necessary to teach skills like sound-blending directly. When this happens, LD and remedial teachers should remember that what they are doing is teaching "school survival skills" and not reading. Be honest with students when this happens. Don't deceive them into believing that what you are doing is teaching reading, but do tell them that they may have to learn some things that make little sense if they're going to succeed in a particular situation. If such skills instruction is attempted, it should not be done until the student has discovered that reading and writing are meaningful and purposeful and has achieved a reasonable level of fluency. At that point, it may be possible to help students make a connection between the skill as it is being taught and something they already know and do in reading and writing.

CONCLUSION

Children learn to speak in environments in which they are surrounded by meaningful talk. Parents and their children talk to each other almost constantly. Reading and writing are difficult for many children simply because they have relatively few opportunities to use written language in purposeful ways or see written language used by others in purposeful ways. We have discussed the importance of developing effective literacy learning environments in an earlier chapter.

At the same time, we recognize the limited influence of some LD and remedial teachers on their students' literacy learning. LD and remedial teachers may see some of their students for as little as thirty minutes a day, and in many cases, this isn't enough time to provide children with adequate opportunities for reading and writing. We don't mean to minimize the effect of LD and remedial teachers on their students' reading and writing development but to emphasize that they will be much more effective in promoting literacy among students if they establish collaborative relationships with regular classroom teachers, administrators, parents, and the students themselves. Effective collaborative relationships depend on mutual trust and respect, but once they have won respect and trust, LD and remedial teachers have a good chance to promote meaningful reading and writing for students throughout the day. Only through collaboration with others can we hope to involve our students in meaningful print, both in and out of school.

Predictable trade books for young children
Compiled by Lynn K. Rhodes
and Darlene Crow

Aardema, Verna. *Bringing the Rain to Kapiti Plain*. New York: Dial Press, 1981.

———. *Why Mosquitoes Buzz in People's Ears*. New York: Dial Press, 1975.

Abisch, Roz. *Around the House that Jack Built*. New York: Parents' Magazine Press, 1972.

Adams, Pam. *Old MacDonald Had a Farm*. Restrop Manor, Purton Wilts., England: Child's Play International, 1975.

———. *There Was An Old Lady Who Swallowed a Fly*. Restrop Manor, Purton Wilts., England: Child's Play International, 1973.

———. *This Old Man*. New York: Grosset & Dunlap, 1974.

Ahlberg, Janet and Allan. *Each Peach Pear Plum*. New York: Scholastic Book Services, 1978.

Alain. *One, Two, Three, Going to Sea*. New York: Scholastic Book Services, 1964.

Albright, Nancy. *I Know an Old Lady Who Swallowed a Fly*. Orlando, Fla.: Moonlight Press, 1984.

Aliki. *At Mary Bloom's*. New York: Greenwillow Books, 1976.

———. *Go Tell Aunt Rhody*. New York: Macmillan, 1974.

———. *Hush Little Baby*. Englewood Cliffs, N.J.: Prentice-Hall, 1968.

———. *My Five Senses*. New York: Thomas Y. Crowell, 1962.

Allen, Pamela. *Bertie and the Bear*. New York: Coward-McCann, 1984.

———. *Who Sank the Boat?* New York: Coward-McCann, 1982.

Appleby, Ellen. *The Three Billy-Goats Gruff*. New York: Scholastic, 1984.

Asbjornsen, P. C., and J. E. Moe. *The Three Billy Goats Gruff*. New York: Brace & World, 1957.

Asch, Frank. *Happy Birthday, Moon*. Englewood Cliffs, N.J.: Prentice-Hall, 1982.

———. *Just Like Daddy*. Englewood Cliffs, N.J.: Prentice-Hall, 1981.

———. *MacGooses' Grocery*. New York: Dial Press, 1978.

———. *Monkey Face*. New York: Parents' Magazine Press, 1977.

Ayer, Jacqueline. *Nu Dang and His Kite*. New York: Harcourt, Brace & World, 1959.

Aylesworth, Jim. *Tonight's the Night*. Chicago: Albert Whitman, 1981.

Balian, Lorna. *The Aminal*. New York: Abingdon Press, 1972.

———. *Where in the World Is Henry?* Scarsdale, N.Y.: Bradbury Press, 1972.

Barchas, Sarah E. *I Was Walking Down the Road*. New York: Scholastic Book Services, 1975.

Barrett, Judi. *Animals Should Definitely Not Act Like People*. New York: Atheneum, 1980.

Revised 1986 by Darlene Crow, graduate student, University of Colorado, Denver. Originally published in article by Lynn K. Rhodes, "I can read! Predictable books as resources for reading and writing instruction," *The Reading Teacher* 34 (1981). 511–18.

————. *Animals Should Definitely Not Wear Clothing*. New York: Atheneum, 1977.

————. *I'm Too Small. You're Too Big*. New York: Atheneum, 1981.

Barton, Byron. *Buzz Buzz Buzz*. New York: Scholastic Book Services, 1973.

Battaglia, Aurelius. *Old Mother Hubbard*. New York: Western (A Little Golden Book), 1970.

Bauer, Caroline Feller. *My Mom Travels A Lot*. New York: Frederick Warne, 1981.

Baum, Arline and Joseph. *One Bright Monday Morning*. New York: Random House, 1962.

Baylor, Byrd. *Guess Who My Favorite Person Is*. New York: Charles Scribner's Sons, 1977.

Becker, John. *Seven Little Rabbits*. New York: Scholastic Book Services, 1973.

Beckman, Kaj. *Lisa Cannot Sleep*. New York: Franklin Watts, 1969.

Bellah, Melanie. *A First Book of Sounds*. Racine, Wis.: Golden Press, 1963.

Berenstain, Stan. *The Berenstains' B Book*. New York: Random House, 1971.

Berenstain, Stan and Jan. *Bears in the Night*. New York: Random House, 1971.

————. *The Berenstain Bears and the Spooky Old Tree*. New York: A Bright and Early Book (Random House), 1978.

Bishop, Claire H. *The Man Who Lost His Head*. New York: Viking Press, 1942.

————. *Twenty-Two Bears*. New York: Viking Press, 1964.

Bishop, Claire, and Kurt Wiese. *The Five Chinese Brothers*. New York: Coward, McCann & Geoghegan, 1938.

Blair, Susan. *The Three Billy-Goats Gruff*. New York: Scholastic Book Services, 1963.

Blocksma, Mary. *The Best Dressed Bear*. Chicago: Children's Press, 1984.

Bloome, Enid. *Dogs Don't Belong on Beds*. Garden City, N.Y.: Doubleday, 1971.

Boone, Rose, and Alan Mills. *I Know an Old Lady*. New York: Rand McNally, 1961.

Brand, Oscar. *When I First Came to this Land*. New York: G. P. Putnam's Sons, 1970.

Brandenberg, Franz. *A Robber, A Robber*. New York: Greenwillow Books, 1976.

————. *I Once Knew a Man*. New York: Macmillan, 1970.

————. *I Wish I Was Sick, Too!* New York: Penguin Books (A Puffin Book), 1978.

————. *Nice New Neighbors*. New York: Greenwillow Books, 1977.

Brenner, Barbara. *Mr. Tall and Mr. Small*. Reading, Mass.: Addison-Wesley, 1966.

Brown, Marcia. *The Three Billy Goats Gruff*. New York: Harcourt, Brace & World, 1957.

Brown, Margaret Wise. *Four Fur Feet*. New York: William R. Scott, 1961.

————. *Goodnight Moon*. New York: Harper & Row, 1947.

————. *Home for a Bunny*. Racine, Wis.: Golden Press, 1956.

————. *Little Chicken*. New York: Harper & Row, 1943.

————. *The Friendly Book*. New York: Western (A Little Golden Book), 1954.

————. *The Important Book*. New York: Harper & Row, 1949.

————. *The Runaway Bunny*. New York: Harper & Row, 1942.

————. *Wheel on the Chimney*. New York: J. B. Lippincott, 1954.

————. *Where Have You Been?* New York: Scholastic Book Services, 1952.

Brown, Ruth. *A Dark, Dark Tale*. New York: Dial Press, 1981.

Buchanan, Joan. *It's a Good Thing*. Toronto: Annick Press, 1984.

Buckley, Helen E. *Grandfather and I*. New York: Lothrop, Lee & Shepard, 1959.

————. *Grandmother and I*. New York: Lothrop, Lee & Shepard, 1961.

Burke, Carolyn L., and Jerome C. Harste. *All Kinds of Cats*. Worthington, Ohio: School Book Fairs, 1983.

Burningham, John. *Mr Gumpy's Motor Car*. New York: Thomas Y. Crowell, 1973.

————. *Mr. Gumpy's Outing*. New York: Holt, Rinehart & Winston, 1970.

————. *The Shopping Basket*. New York: Thomas Y. Crowell, 1980.

Burningham, John. *Would You Rather...* New York: Thomas Y. Crowell, 1978.

Byars, Betsy. *Go and Hush the Baby*. New York: Viking Press, 1971.

The Bus Ride, illustrated by Justin Wager. New York: Scott, Foresman, 1971.

Cameron, Polly. *"I Can't" Said the Ant.* New York: Coward-McCann, 1961.

Campbell, Rod. *Dear Zoo.* New York: Four Winds Press, 1982.

Carle, Eric. *Have You Seen My Cat?* New York: Franklin Watts, n.d.

———. *The Grouchy Ladybug.* New York: Thomas Y. Crowell, 1977.

———. *The Mixed Up Chameleon.* New York: Thomas Y. Crowell, 1975.

———. *The Very Busy Spider.* New York: Philomel Books, 1985.

———. *The Very Hungry Caterpillar.* Cleveland: Collins World, 1969.

Carrick, Malcolm. *I Can Squash Elephants!* New York: Viking Press, 1978.

Carrier, Lark. *There Was a Hill...* Book Studio USA (distributed by Alphabet Press, Natick, Mass.), 1985.

Cauley, Lorinda B. *The Three Little Kittens.* New York: G. P. Putnam's Sons, 1982.

Charlip, Remy. *Fortunately.* New York: Parents' Magazine Press, 1964.

———. *What Good Luck! What Bad Luck!* New York: Scholastic Book Services, 1969.

Chase, Richard. *Billy Boy.* San Carlos, Calif.: Golden Gate Junior Books, 1966.

Chess, Victoria. *Poor Esme.* New York: Holiday House, 1982.

Child, Lydia M. *Over the River and Through the Wood.* New York: Coward, McCann & Geoghegan, 1974.

Christian, Mary B. *Nothing Much Happened Today.* Reading, Mass.: Addison-Wesley, 1973.

Chwast, Seymour. *The House That Jack Built.* New York: Random House, 1973.

Cleveland, David. *The April Rabbits.* New York: Scholastic, 1978.

Cole, Brock. *The King at the Door.* Garden City, N.Y.: Doubleday, 1979.

Cole, Joanna. *Bony-Legs.* New York: Scholastic, 1983.

Conover, Chris. *Six Little Ducks.* New York: Thomas Y. Crowell, 1976.

Cook, Bernadine. *The Little Fish That Got Away.* Reading, Mass.: Addison-Wesley, 1976.

d'Aulaire, Ingri and Edgar. *Animals Everywhere.* Garden City, N.Y.: Doubleday, 1940.

DeLage, Ida. *Am I a Bunny?* Champaign, Ill.: Garrard, 1978.

Delton, Judy. *I'm Telling You Now.* New York: E. P. Dutton, 1983.

Demers, Jan. *What Do You Do With a...?* Worthington, Ohio: Willowisp Press, 1985.

de Paola, Tomie. *The Comic Adventures of Old Mother Hubbard and Her Dog.* New York: Harcourt Brace Jovanovich, 1981.

———. *The Friendly Beasts.* New York: G. P. Putnam's Sons, 1981.

———. *Mary Had a Little Lamb.* New York: Holiday House, 1984.

———. *Now One Foot, Now the Other.* New York: G. P. Putnam's Sons, 1981.

de Regniers, Beatrice Schenk. *Catch a Little Fox.* New York: Seabury Press, 1970.

———. *The Day Everybody Cried.* New York: Viking Press, 1967.

———. *How Joe the Bear and Sam the Mouse Got Together.* New York: Parents' Magazine Press, 1965.

———. *Jack and the Beanstalk.* New York: Atheneum, 1985.

———. *The Little Book.* New York: Henry Z. Walck, 1961.

———. *May I Bring a Friend?* New York: Atheneum, 1972.

———. *Red Riding Hood.* New York: Atheneum, 1972.

———. *So Many Cats!* New York: Clarion Books, 1985.

———. *Something Special.* New York: Harcourt, Brace & World, 1958.

———. *Waiting for Mama.* New York: Ticknor & Fields (Houghton Mifflin), 1984.

———. *What Can You Do With a Shoe?* New York: Harper & Row, 1955.

———. *Willy O'Dwyer Jumped in the Fire.* New York: Atheneum, 1968.

Dodd, Lynley. *Hairy Maclary.* Milwaukee, Wis.: Gareth Stevens, 1985.

Domanska, Janina. *Busy Monday Morning.* New York: Greenwillow Books, 1985.

———. *Din, Dan, Don, It's Christmas.* New York: Greenwillow Books, 1975.

———. *If All the Seas Were One Sea.* New York: Macmillan, 1971.

———. *Little Red Hen.* New York: Macmillan, 1973.

————. *What Do You See?* New York: Collier Macmillan, 1974.

Dragonwagon, Crescent. *I Hate My Brother Harry*. New York: Harper & Row, 1983.

Duff, Maggie. *Jonny and His Drum*. New York: Henry Z. Walck, 1972.

————. *Rum Pum Pum*. New York: Macmillan, 1978.

Durrell, Julie. *Mouse Tails*. New York: Crown, 1985.

Eastman, Patricia. *Sometimes Things Change*. Chicago: Children's Press, 1983.

Eberts, Marjorie, and Margaret Gisler. *Pancakes, Crackers, and Pizza*. Chicago: Children's Press, 1984.

Edwards, Dorothy, and Jenny Williams. *A Wet Monday*. New York: William Morrow, 1976.

Einsel, Walter. *Did You Ever See?* New York: Scholastic Book Services, 1962.

Elkin, Benjamin. *Six Foolish Fishermen*. Chicago: Children's Press, 1957.

Elting, Mary, and Michael Folsom. *Q is for Duck*. New York: Clarion Books, 1980.

Emberly, Barbara. *One Wide River to Cross*. Englewood Cliffs, N.J.: Prentice-Hall, 1966.

————. *Simon's Song*. Englewood Cliffs, N.J.: Prentice-Hall, 1969.

Emberly, Barbara, and Ed. *Drummer Hoff*. Englewood Cliffs, N.J.: Prentice-Hall, 1967.

Emberly, Ed. *Klippity Klop*. Boston: Little, Brown, 1974.

————. *London Bridge Is Falling Down*. Boston, Mass.: Little, Brown, 1967.

————. *The Wing on the Flea*. Boston: Little, Brown, 1961.

Ets, Marie Hall. *Elephant in a Well*. New York: Viking Press, 1972.

————. *In the Forest*. New York: Viking Press, 1944.

————. *Just Me*. New York: Viking Press, 1965.

————. *Play with Me*. New York: Viking Press, 1955.

————. *Talking Without Words*. New York: Viking Press, 1968.

Farber, Norma. *As I Was Crossing Boston Common*. New York: E. P. Dutton, 1973.

Flack, Marjorie. *Ask Mr. Bear*. New York: Macmillan, 1932.

Foster, Joanna. *Pete's Puddle*. New York: Harcourt, Brace & World, 1950.

Gackenbach, Dick. *A Bag Full of Pups*. New York: Ticknor & Fields (Houghton Mifflin), 1981.

————. *Claude the Dog—A Christmas Story*. New York: Clarion Books (Houghton Mifflin), 1974.

Gág, Wanda. *Millions of Cats*. New York: Coward-McCann, 1928.

Gage, Wilson. *Squash Pie*. New York: Greenwillow Books (William Morrow), 1976.

Galdone, Paul. *Cat Goes Fiddle-i-fee*. New York: Clarion Books (Ticknor & Fields Houghton Mifflin), 1985.

————. *The Gingerbread Boy*. New York: Seabury Press, 1975.

————. *Henny Penny*. New York: Scholastic Book Services, 1968.

————. *The Little Red Hen*. New York: Scholastic Book Services, 1973.

————. *The Old Woman and Her Pig*. New York: McGraw-Hill, 1960.

————. *The Teeny, Tiny Woman*. New York: Clarion Books (Ticknor & Fields Houghton Mifflin), 1984.

————. *The Three Bears*. New York: Scholastic Book Services, 1972.

————. *The Three Billy Goats Gruff*. New York: Seabury Press, 1973.

————. *The Three Little Pigs*. New York: Seabury Press, 1970.

Gale, Leah. *The Animals of Farmer Jones*. New York: Western (A Golden Book), 1952.

Galloway, Priscilla. *When You Were Little and I Was Big*. Toronto: Annick Press, 1984.

Gelman, Rita Golden. *More Spaghetti I Say*. New York: Scholastic, 1977.

————. *Mortimer K. Saves the Day*. New York: Scholastic Book Services, 1982.

Gerstein, Mordicai. *Roll Over!* New York: Crown, 1984.

————. *William, Where Are You?* New York: Crown, 1985.

Gibbons, Gail. *The Seasons of Arnold's Apple Tree*. San Diego: Harcourt Brace Jovanovich, 1984.

Ginsburg, Mirra. *The Chick and the Duckling*. New York: Macmillan, 1972.

————. *Good Morning, Chick*. New York: Greenwillow Books, 1980.

————. *The Strongest One of All*. New York: Greenwillow Books, 1977.

Gomi, Taro. *Coco Can't Wait!* New York: William Morrow, 1984.

Gordon, Sharon. *Drip Drop*. Mahwah, N.J.: Troll Associates, 1981.

Gorsline, Douglas. *The Night Before Christmas*. New York: Random House, 1975.

Goss, Janet L., and Jerome C. Harste. *It Didn't Frighten Me!* Worthington, Ohio: School Book Fairs, 1981.

Graham, John. *A Crowd of Cows*. New York: Harcourt, Brace & World, 1968.

Graham, John. *I Love You Mouse*. New York: Harcourt Brace Jovanovich, 1976.

Greenberg, David. *Slugs*. Boston: Little, Brown, 1983.

Greenberg, Polly. *Oh Lord, I Wish I Was a Buzzard*. New York: Macmillan, 1968.

Greene, Carol. *The Insignificant Elephant*. New York: Harcourt Brace Jovanovich, 1985.

Griffith, Helen V. *Mine Will, Said John*. New York: Greenwillow Books, 1980.

Guilfoile, Elizabeth. *Nobody Listens to Andrew*. Chicago: Follett, 1957.

Hall, Donald. *Ox-Cart Man*. New York: Viking Press, 1979.

Hamsa, Bobbie. *Animal Babies*. Chicago: Children's Press, 1985.

———. *Dirty Larry*. Chicago: Children's Press, 1983.

———. *Polly Wants a Cracker*. Chicago: Children's Press, 1986.

Harper, Anita. *How We Live*. New York: Harper & Row, 1977.

———. *How We Work*. New York: Harper & Row, 1977.

Harste, Jerome C. *A Dog to Love*. Worthington, Ohio: School Book Fairs, 1983.

———. *A Horse of Course!* Worthington, Ohio: School Book Fairs, 1983.

Harste, Jerome C., and Carolyn L. Burke. *Animal Babies*. Worthington, Ohio: School Book Fairs, 1983.

Hawkins, Colin and Jacqui. *Old Mother Hubbard*. New York: G. P. Putnam's Sons, 1985.

Hazel, Beth, and Jerome C. Harste. *My Icky Picky Sister*. Worthington, Ohio: School Book Fairs, 1982.

Hazen, Barbara S. *Tight Times*. New York: Viking Press, 1979.

Hearn, Emily. *TV Kangaroo*. Champaign, Ill.: Garrard, 1975.

Heide, Florence P. and Roxanne. *A Monster Is Coming! A Monster Is Coming!* New York: Franklin Watts, 1980.

Heide, Florence P., and Sylvia Worth Van Clief. *That's What Friends Are For*. New York: Four Winds Press, 1970.

Heilbroner, Joan. *This Is the House Where Jack Lives*. New York: Harper & Row, 1962.

Heller, Ruth. *Animals Born Alive and Well*. New York: Grosset & Dunlap, 1982.

———. *Chickens Aren't the Only Ones*. New York: Grosset & Dunlap, 1981.

Higgins, Don. *Papa's Going to Buy Me a Mockingbird*. New York: Seabury Press, 1968.

Hill, Eric. *Where's Spot?* New York: G. P. Putnam's Sons, 1980.

Hillman, Priscilla. *A Merry-Mouse Christmas ABC*. Garden City, N.Y.: Doubleday, 1980.

Hines, Anna. *Come to the Meadow*. New York: Clarion Books (Ticknor & Fields/ Houghton Mifflin), 1984.

———. *Taste the Raindrops*. New York: Greenwillow Books, 1983.

Hirsh, Marilyn. *Could Anything Be Worse?* New York: Holiday House, 1974.

Hoberman, Mary Ann. *A House Is a House For Me*. New York: Viking Press, 1978.

Hoff, Syd. *Who Will Be My Friends?* New York: Harper & Row, 1960.

Hoffman, Hilde. *The Green Grass Grows All Around*. New York: Macmillan, 1968.

Hogrogian, Nonny. *One Fine Day*. New York: Macmillan, 1971.

Hoguet, Susan R. *I Unpacked My Grandmother's Trunk*. New York: E. P. Dutton, 1983.

Holland, Margaret. *African Animals*. Worthington, Ohio: School Book Fairs, n.d.

Hooper, Meredith. *Seven Eggs*. New York: Harper & Row, 1985.

Houston, John. *A Mouse in My House*. Reading, Mass.: Addison-Wesley, 1972.

Hutchins, Pat. *Don't Forget the Bacon*. New York: Greenwillow Books, 1976.

———. *Good-Night Owl*. New York: Macmillan, 1972.

———. *Happy Birthday, Sam*. New York: Greenwillow Books, 1978.

———. *One Hunter*. New York: Greenwillow Books, 1982.

———. *Rosie's Walk*. New York: Macmillan, 1968.

———. *The Surprise Party*. New York: Macmillan, 1969.

———. *Titch*. New York: Collier Books, 1971.

———. *Tom and Sam*. New York: Macmillan, 1968.

———. *You'll Soon Grow into Them, Titch*. New York: Greenwillow Books, 1983.

———. *The Very Worst Monster*. New York: Greenwillow Books, 1985.

Isaacsen-Bright, and Margaret Holland. *No, No, Joan*. Worthington, Ohio: School Book Fairs, n.d.

Isadora, Rachel. *I Hear*. New York: Greenwillow Books, 1985.

Ivimey, John W. *Complete Version of Ye Three Blind Mice*. New York: Frederick Warne, 1979.

Jacobs, Joseph. *Master of All Masters*. New York: Grosset & Dunlop, 1972.

Jeffers, Susan. *All the Pretty Horses*. New York: Macmillan, 1974.

———. *Three Jovial Huntsmen*. Scarsdale, N.Y.: Bradbury Press, 1973.

Johnston, Tony. *The Quilt Story*. New York: G. P. Putnam's Sons, 1985.

Joslin, Sesyle. *What Do You Do, Dear?* New York: Young Scott Books, 1961.

———. *What Do You Say, Dear?* Reading, Mass.: Addison-Wesley, 1958.

Joyce, Irma. *Never Talk to Strangers*. New York: Western (A Little Golden Book), 1967.

Kafka, Sherry. *I Need a Friend*. New York: G. P. Putnam's Sons, 1971.

Kahn, Joan. *You Can't Catch Me*. New York: Harper & Row, 1976.

Kalan, Robert. *Jump, Frog, Jump!* New York: Greenwillow Books, 1981.

Kane, Sharon. *The Farmer in the Dell*. Chicago: Rand McNally, 1967.

Keats, Ezra Jack. *The Little Drummer Boy*. New York: Macmillan, 1968.

———. *Over in the Meadow*. New York: Scholastic Book Services, 1971.

Keller, Holly. *Too Big*. New York: Greenwillow Books, 1983.

———. *Will It Rain?* New York: Greenwillow Books, 1984.

Kellog, Steven. *Can I Keep Him?* New York: Dial Press, 1971.

Kent, Jack. *The Fat Cat*. New York: Scholastic Book Services, 1971.

———. *Silly Goose*. Englewood Cliffs, N.J.: Prentice-Hall, 1983.

———. *Twelve Days of Christmas*. New York: Parents' Magazine Press, 1973.

Kessler, Ethel and Leonard. *Do Baby Bears Sit in Chairs?* Garden City, N.Y.: Doubleday, 1961.

Kessler, Leonard. *Do You Have Any Carrots?* Champaign, Ill.: Garrard, 1979.

Kherdian, David. *Right Now*. New York: Alfred A. Knopf, 1983.

Kipling, Rudyard. *The Elephant's Child*. New York: Harcourt Brace Jovanovich, 1983.

Klein, Leonore. *Brave Daniel*. New York: Scholastic Book Services, 1958.

Klein, Leonore. *Only One Ant*. New York: Hastings House, 1971.

Kline, Suzy. *Don't Touch!* Niles, Ill.: Albert Whitman, 1985.

Knight, Hilary. *Hilary Knight's The Twelve Days of Christmas*. New York: Macmillan, 1981.

Kohn, Bernice. *How High Is Up?* New York: G. P. Putnam's Sons, 1971.

Kowalezyk, Carolyn. *Purple Is Part of a Rainbow*. Chicago: Children's Press, 1985.

Krasilovsky, Phyllis. *The Man Who Didn't Wash His Dishes*. Garden City, N.Y.: Doubleday, 1950.

Kraus, Robert. *Leo the Late Bloomer*. New York: Windmill Books, 1971.

———. *Whose Mouse Are You?* New York: Collier Books, 1970.

Krauss, Ruth. *Bears*. New York: Scholastic and Harper & Row, 1948.

———. *The Carrot Seed*. New York: Harper & Row, 1945.

———. *Everything Under a Mushroom*. New York: Four Winds Press, 1973.

———. *The Happy Day*. New York: Harper & Row, 1949.

———. *A Hole Is to Dig*. New York: Harper & Row, 1952.

———. *What a Fine Day for . . .* New York: Parents' Magazine Press, 1967.

Kwitz, Mary DeBall. *Little Chick's Story*. New York: Harper & Row, 1978.

Langstaff, John. *Frog Went A-Courtin'*. New York: Harcourt Brace Jovanovich, 1955.

———. *Gather My Gold Together*: *Four Songs*

for Four Seasons. Garden City, N.Y.: Doubleday, 1971.

——. *The Golden Vanity.* New York: Harcourt Brace Jovanovich, 1972.

——. *Oh, A-Hunting We Will Go.* New York: Atheneum, 1974.

——. *Ol' Dan Tucker.* New York: Harcourt Brace & World, 1963.

——. *Over in the Meadow.* New York: Harcourt Brace Jovanovich, 1957.

——. *Soldier, Soldier, Won't You Marry Me?* Garden City, N.Y.: Doubleday, 1972.

Laurence, Ester. *We're Off to Catch a Dragon.* Nashville, Tenn.: Abingdon Press, 1969.

LeSeig, Theo. *In a People House.* New York: Random House, 1972.

Lester, Helen. *It Wasn't My Fault.* Boston: Houghton Mifflin, 1985.

Lexau, Joan. *Crocodile and Hen.* New York: Harper & Row, 1969.

Leydenfrost, Robert. *The Snake that Sneezed!* New York: G. P. Putnam's Sons, 1970.

——. *Ten Little Elephants.* Garden City, N.Y.: Doubleday, 1975.

Lionni, Leo. *A Color of His Own.* New York: Pantheon Books, 1975.

——. *Little Blue and Little Yellow.* New York: Ivan Obolensky, 1959.

Littledale, Freya. *The Magic Fish.* New York: Scholastic Book Services, 1967.

Livermore, Elaine. *One to Ten, Count Again.* Boston: Houghton Mifflin, 1973.

——. *Three Little Kittens Lost Their Mittens.* Boston: Houghton Mifflin, 1979.

Lobel, Arnold. *How the Rooster Saved the Day.* New York: Greenwillow Books, 1977.

——. *King Rooster, Queen Hen.* New York: Greenwillow Books, 1975.

——. *On Market Street.* New York: Greenwillow Books, 1981.

——. *The Rose in My Garden.* New York: Greenwillow Books, 1984.

——. *A Treeful of Pigs.* New York: Greenwillow Books, 1979.

Low, Joseph. *My Dog, Your Dog.* New York: Macmillan, 1978.

Lubin, Leonard B. *This Little Pig.* New York: Lothrop, Lee & Shepard, 1985.

Mack, Stan. *10 Bears in My Bed.* New York: Pantheon, 1974.

——. *Where's My Cheese?* New York: Pantheon, 1977.

Maestro, Betsy. *Through the Year with Harriet.* New York: Crown, 1985.

Maestro, Betsy and Giulio. *Traffic, A Book of Opposites.* New York: Crown, 1981.

Maris, Ron. *Are You There, Bear?* New York: Greenwillow Books, 1984.

Martin, Bill. *Brown Bear, Brown Bear.* New York: Holt, Rinehart & Winston, 1970.

——. *Fire! Fire! Said Mrs. McGuire.* New York: Holt, Rinehart & Winston, 1970.

——. *I Reach Out to the Morning.* Glendale, Calif.: Bowmar (A Bill Martin Freedom Book), 1970.

——. *Spoiled Tomatoes.* Glendale, Calif.: Bowmar (A Bill Martin Freedom Book), 1970.

Matthias, Catherine. *I Love Cats.* Chicago: Children's Press, 1983.

——. *Out the Door.* Chicago: Children's Press, 1982.

——. *Over-Under.* Chicago: Children's Press, 1984.

——. *Too Many Balloons.* Chicago: Children's Press, 1982.

Mayer, Mercer. *All By Myself.* New York: Western (A Little Golden Book), 1983.

Mayer, Mercer. *I Am a Hunter.* New York: Dial Press, 1969.

——. *I Was So Mad.* New York: Golden Press, 1983.

——. *If I Had . . .* New York: Dial Press, 1968.

——. *Just For You.* New York: Golden Press, 1975.

——. *Just Go to Bed.* Racine, Wis.: Western (A Golden Book), 1983.

——. *Me Too!* New York: Golden Press, 1983.

——. *What Do You Do with a Kangaroo?* New York: Scholastic, 1973.

——. *When I Get Bigger.* Racine, Wis.: Western (A Golden Book), 1983.

Mayers, Patrick. *Just One More Block.* Chicago: Albert Whitman, 1970.

McClintock, Mike. *A Fly Went By.* New York: Random House, 1958.

McDaniel, Becky B. *Katie Couldn't.* Chicago: Children's Press, 1985.

——. *Katie Did It.* Chicago? Children's Press, 1983.

McGovern, Ann. *Stone Soup*. New York: Scholastic, 1968.

———. *Too Much Noise*. New York: Scholastic, 1967.

McKee, Craig B., and Margaret Holland. *A Peacock Ate My Lunch*. Worthington, Ohio: Willowisp Press, 1985.

———. *The Teacher Who Could Not Count*. Worthington, Ohio: School Book Fairs, n.d.

———. *Time to Swim*. Worthington, Ohio: School Book Fairs, 1983.

———. *The Turned-Around Taxi*. Worthington, Ohio: Willowisp Press, 1985.

McKee, David. *I Hate My Teddy Bear*. New York: Clarion Books, 1982.

McKissack, Patricia C. *Who Is Who?* Chicago: Children's Press, 1983.

McLeish, Kenneth. *Chicken Licken*. Scarsdale, N.Y.: Bradbury Press, 1973.

McLeod, Emily W. *One Snail and Me*. Boston: Little, Brown, 1961.

McMillan, Bruce. *Kitten Can...* New York: Lothrop, Lee & Shepard, 1984.

McMillan, Sally H. *I Used to Be Afraid*. Worthington, Ohio: Willowisp Press, 1985.

Memling, Carl. *Hi, All You Rabbits*. New York: Parents' Magazine Press, 1970.

———. *Ten Little Animals*. Racine, Wis.: Golden Press, 1961.

Merriam, Eve. *Do You Want to See Something?* New York: Scholastic Book Services, 1965.

Minarik, Else Holmelund. *Little Bear*. New York: Harper & Row, 1957.

Mizumura, Kazue. *If I Built a Village...* New York: Thomas Y. Crowell, 1971.

———. *If I Were a Cricket...* New York: Thomas Y. Crowell, 1973.

———. *If I Were a Mother...* New York: Thomas Y. Crowell, 1968.

Moffett, Martha. *A Flower Pot Is Not a Hat*. New York: E. P. Dutton, 1972.

Moncure, Jane B. *Animal, Animal, Where Do You Live?* Chicago: Children's Press, 1975.

———. *Love*. Elgin, Ill.: Child's World, 1980.

———. *Pets Are Smart*. Chicago: Children's Press, 1976.

———. *What Will It Rain?* Chicago: Children's Press, 1977.

Mosel, Arlene. *Tikki Tikki Tembo*. New York: Holt, Rinehart & Winston, 1968.

Most, Bernard. *If the Dinosaurs Came Back*. New York: Harcourt Brace Jovanovich, 1978.

Neasi, Barbara J. *Just Like Me*. Chicago: Children's Press, 1984.

Newsom, Carol. *An Edward Lear Alphabet*. New York: Lothrop, Lee & Shepard, 1983.

Nic Leodhas, Sorche. *All in the Morning Early*. New York: Holt, Rinehart & Winston, 1963.

Nixon, Joan L. *If You Say So, Claude*. New York: Frederick Warne, 1980.

Noble, Trinka H. *The Day Jimmy's Boa Ate the Wash*. New York: E. P. Dutton (Dial Books for Young Readers), 1980.

———. *Jimmy's Boa Bounces Back*. New York: E. P. Dutton (Dial Books for Young Readers), 1984.

Nodset, Joan L. *Who Took the Farmer's Hat?* New York: Harper & Row, 1963.

Numeroff, Laura Joffe. *If You Give a Mouse a Cookie*. New York: Harper & Row, 1985.

O'Neill, Mary. *Hailstones and Halibut Bones*. Garden City, N.Y.: Doubleday, 1961.

Oppenheim, Joanne. *Have You Seen Trees?* New York: Young Scott Books, 1967.

Palazzo, Tony. *Animals 'Round the Mulberry Bush*. Garden City, N.Y.: Doubleday, 1958.

Palmer, Helen. *Why I Built the Boogle House*. New York: Random House, 1964.

Parker, Ed. *Three Billy Goats Gruff*. Mahwah, N.J.: Troll Associates, 1979.

Paterson, A. B. *Waltzing Matilda*. New York: Holt, Rinehart & Winston, 1970.

Paterson, Diane. *If I Were a Toad*. New York: Dial Press, 1977.

Patrick, Gloria. *A Bug in a Jug and Other Funny Rhymes*. New York: Scholastic, 1970.

Pearson, Tracey C. *Old McDonald Had a Farm*. New York: E. P. Dutton, 1984.

Peppe, Rodney. *The House That Jack Built*. New York: Delacorte Press, 1970

Petrie, Catherine. *Joshua James Likes Trucks*. Chicago: Children's Press, 1982.

———. *Sandbox Betty*. Chicago: Children's Press, 1982.

Pienkowski, Jan. *Dinner Time*. Los Angeles: Price, Stern, Sloan, 1980.

———. *Gossip*. Los Angeles: Price, Stern, Sloan, 1981.

Pinkwater, Daniel M. *The Big Orange Splot*. New York: Hastings House, 1977.

Piper, Watty. *The Little Engine That Could*. New York: Platt & Munk, 1961.

Plume, Ilse. *The Bremen Town Musicians*. Garden City, N.Y.: Doubleday, 1980.

Polushkin, Maria. *Mother, Mother, I Want Another*. New York: Crown, 1978.

Pomerantz, Charlotte. *Where's the Bear?* New York: Greenwillow Books, 1984.

Preston, Edna M. *One Dark Night*. New York: Viking Press, 1969.

———. *Squawk to the Moon, Little Goose*. New York: Viking Press, 1974.

———. *Where Did My Mother Go?* New York: Four Winds Press, 1978

Provensen, Alice and Martin. *Old Mother Hubbard*. New York: Random House, 1977.

Quackenbush, Robert. *Clementine*. Philadelphia and New York: J. B. Lippincott, 1974.

———. *Go Tell Aunt Rhody*. Philadelphia and New York: J. B. Lippincott, 1973.

———. *No Mouse for Me*. New York: Franklin Watts, 1981.

———. *Pop! Goes the Weasel and Yankee Doodle*. Philadelphia and New York: J. B. Lippincott, 1976.

———. *She'll Be Comin' Round the Mountain*. New York: J. B. Lippincott, 1973.

———. *Skip to My Lou*. Philadelphia: J. B. Lippincott, 1975.

———. *There'll Be a Hot Time in the Old Town Tonight*. Philadelphia and New York: J. B. Lippincott, 1974.

———. *Too Many Lollipops*. New York: Parents' Magazine Press, 1975.

Raskin, Ellen. *Who, Said Sue, Said Whoo?* New York: Atheneum, 1973.

Reinl, Edda. *The Three Little Pigs*. Natick, Mass.: Neugebauer Press (Picture Book Studio USA), 1983.

Rey, Margret. *Pretzel*. New York: Harper & Row, 1944.

Rice, Eve. *Goodnight, Goodnight*. New York: Greenwillow Books, 1980.

Rokof, Sandra. *Here Is a Cat*. Singapore: Hallmark Children's Editions, n.d.

Satchwell, John. *Odd One Out*. New York: Random House, 1984.

Sawyer, Ruth. *Journey Cake, Ho!* New York: Viking Press, 1953.

Schackburg, Richard. *Yankee Doodle*. Englewood Cliffs, N.J.: Prentice-Hall, 1965.

Scheer, Jullian, and Marvin Bileck. *Rain Makes Applesauce*. New York: Holiday House, 1964.

———. *Upside Down Day*. New York: Holiday House, 1968.

Sendak, Maurice. *Chicken Soup with Rice*. New York: Harper & Row, 1962.

———. *One Was Johnny*. New York: Harper & Row, 1962.

———. *Pierre*. New York: Harper & Row, 1962.

———. *Seven Little Monsters*. New York: Harper & Row, 1977.

———. *Where the Wild Things Are*. New York: Scholastic Book Services, 1963.

Seuss, Dr. *Green Eggs and Ham*. New York: Random House, 1960.

Seymour, Dorothy Z. *The Sandwich*. New York: Wonder Books, 1965.

Shapiro, Arnold. *Squiggly Wiggly's Surprise*. Los Angeles: Price, Stern, Sloan, 1978.

Sharp, Paul. *Paul the Pitcher*. Chicago: Children's Press, 1984.

Shaw, Charles B. *It Looked Like Spilt Milk*. New York: Harper & Row, 1947.

Sherman, Ivan. *I Do Not Like It When My Friend Comes to Visit*. New York: Harcourt Brace Jovanovich, 1973.

Shulevitz, Uri. *One Monday Morning*. New York: Charles Scribner's Sons, 1967.

Siewert, Margaret, and Kathleen Savage. *Bear Hunt*. Englewood Cliffs, N.J.: Prentice-Hall, 1976.

Silverstein, Shel. *A Giraffe and a Half*. New York: Harper & Row, 1964.

———. *The Giving Tree*. New York: Harper & Row, 1964.

Simon, Mina and Howard. *If You Were an Eel, How Would You Feel?* Chicago and New York: Follett, 1963.

Simon, Norma. *How Do I Feel?* Chicago: Albert Whitman, 1970.

———. *What Do I Do?* Chicago: Albert Whitman, 1969.

———. *What Do I Say?* Chicago: Albert Whitman, 1967.

Singer, Marilyn. *Will You Take Me to Town*

on Strawberry Day? New York: Harper & Row, 1981.

Skaar, Grace. *What Do the Animals Say?* New York: Scholastic, 1972.

Slobodkin, Louis. *Thank You—You're Welcome.* New York: Vanguard Press, 1957.

Slobodkina, Esphyr. *Caps for Sale.* Reading, Mass.: Addison-Wesley, 1940.

Smith, Susan M. *No One Should Have Six Cats!* Chicago: Follett, 1982.

Smoak, Dona V. *Ride, Richie, Ride.* Worthington, Ohio: School Book Fairs, 1983.

Smoak, Dona V., and Isaacsen-Bright. *Crazy Town.* Worthington, Ohio: Willowisp Press, 1985.

Sonneborn, Ruth A. *Someone Is Eating the Sun.* New York: Random House, 1974.

Soule, Jean C. *Never Tease a Weasel.* New York: Parents' Magazine Press, 1964.

Spier, Peter. *The Erie Canal.* Garden City, N.Y.: Doubleday, 1970.

———. *The Fox Went Out on a Chilly Night.* Garden City, N.Y.: Doubleday, 1961.

———. *London Bridge Is Falling Down!* Garden City, N.Y.: Doubleday, 1967.

Stanley, Diane. *Fiddle-I-Fee.* Boston: Little, Brown, 1979.

Stanovich, Betty Jo. *Big Boy, Little Boy.* New York: Lothrop, Lee & Shepard, 1984.

Stevens, Janet. *The House That Jack Built.* New York: Holiday House, 1985.

Stevenson, James. *Could Be Worse!* New York: Penguin Books (Puffin Books), 1977.

Stobbs, William. *One, Two, Buckle My Shoe.* London: Bodley Head, 1984.

———. *The Little Red Hen.* Oxford: Oxford University Press, 1985.

Stone, Elberta H. *I'm Glad I'm Me.* New York: G. P. Putnam's Sons, 1971.

Stover, JoAnn. *If Everybody Did.* New York: David McKay, 1960.

Sutton, Eve. *My Cat Likes to Hide in Boxes.* New York: Parents' Magazine Press, 1973.

Tafuri, Nancy. *All Year Long.* New York: Greenwillow Books, 1983.

———. *Have You Seen My Duckling?* New York: Greenwillow Books, 1984.

Tanz, Christine. *An Egg Is to Sit On.* New York: Lothrop, Lee & Shepard, 1978.

Thomas, Patricia. *"Stand Back," Said the Elephant, "I'm Going to Sneeze!"* New York: Lothrop, Lee & Shepard, 1971.

Thomas, Sharon, and Marjorie Siegal. *No Baths for Tabitha.* Worthington, Ohio: School Book Fairs, 1982.

Tolstoy, Alexei. *The Great Big Enormous Turnip.* New York: Franklin Watts, 1968.

Tresselt, Alvin. *How Far Is Far?* New York: Parents' Magazine Press, 1964.

———. *It's Time Now!* New York: Lothrop, Lee & Shepard, 1969.

———. *What Did You Leave Behind?* New York: Lothrop, Lee & Shepard, 1978.

Udry, Janice M. *A Tree Is Nice.* New York: Harper & Row, 1956.

Viorst, Judith. *Alexander and the Terrible, Horrible, No Good, Very Bad Day.* New York: Atheneum, 1972.

———. *Alexander, Who Used to Be Rich Last Sunday.* New York: Atheneum, 1979.

———. *I'll Fix Anthony.* New York: Harper & Row, 1969.

———. *My Mama Says...* New York: Atheneum, 1981.

Vipont, Elfrida. *The Elephant and the Bad Baby.* New York: Coward-McCann, 1969.

Vogel, Ilse-Margaret. *The Don't Be Scared Book.* New York: Atheneum, 1964.

Waber, Bernard. *Ira Sleeps Over.* Boston: Houghton Mifflin, 1972.

Wadsworth, Olive A. *Over in the Meadow: A Counting Out Rhyme.* New York: Viking Kestrel, 1985.

Walker, Barbara K. *I Packed My Trunk.* Chicago and New York: Follett, 1969.

Watanabe, Shigeo. *How Do I Put It On?* New York and Cleveland: William Collins, 1977.

———. *Where's My Daddy?* New York: Philomel Books, 1979.

Welber, Robert. *Goodbye, Hello.* New York: Pantheon, 1974.

Wells, Rosemary. *A Lion for Lewis.* New York: Dial Press, 1982.

———. *Noisy Nora.* New York: Dial Press, 1973.

Westcott, Nadine B. *I Know an Old Lady Who Swallowed a Fly.* Boston: Little, Brown, 1980.

Wildsmith, Brian. *Cat on the Mat.* Oxford: Oxford University Press, 1982.

———. *The Twelve Days of Christmas*. New York: Franklin Watts, 1972.

Willard, Nancy. *Simple Pictures Are Best*. New York: Harcourt Brace Jovanovich, 1976.

Williams, Barbara. *Albert's Toothache*. New York: E. P. Dutton, 1974.

———. *If He's My Brother*. New York: Harvey House, 1976.

———. *Kevin's Grandma*. New York: E. P. Dutton, 1975.

Williams, Garth. *The Chicken Book*. New York: Delacorte Press, 1970.

Winter, Jeanette. *Hush Little Baby*. New York: Pantheon Books, 1984.

Wolcott, Patty. *Double-Decker, Double-Decker, Double-Decker Bus*. Reading, Mass.: Addison-Wesley, 1980.

———. *The Marvelous Mud Washing Machine*. New York: J. B. Lippincott, 1974.

———. *Pickle Pickle Pickle Juice*. Reading, Mass.: Addison-Wesley, 1975.

Wolkstein, Diane. *The Visit*. New York: Alfred A. Knopf, 1977.

Wondriska, William. *All the Animals Were Angry*. New York: Holt, Rinehart & Winston, 1970.

Wood, Audrey. *King Bidgood's in the Bathtub*. New York: Harcourt Brace Jovanovich, 1985.

———. *The Napping House*. New York: Harcourt Brace Jovanovich, 1984.

Wood, Leslie. *A Dog Called Mischief*. Oxford: Oxford University Press, 1985.

———. *The Frog and the Fly*. Oxford: Oxford University Press, 1985.

Yolen, Jane. *An Invitation to the Butterfly Ball*. New York: Parents' Magazine Press, 1976.

———. *It All Depends*. New York: Funk & Wagnalls, 1969.

Yulya (Julie Whitney). *Bears Are Sleeping*. New York: Charles Scribner's Sons, 1960.

Zaid, Barry. *Chicken Little*. New York: Random House, n.d.

Zemach, Harve. *The Judge*. New York: Farrar, Straus & Giroux, 1969.

———. *Mommy, Buy Me a China Doll*. New York: Follett, 1966.

Zemach, Margot. *The Fisherman and His Wife*. New York: Farrar, Straus & Giroux, 1980.

———. *Hush, Little Baby*. New York: E. P. Dutton, 1976.

———. *It Could Always Be Worse*. New York: Farrar, Straus & Giroux, 1976.

———. *The Teeny Tiny Woman*. New York: Scholastic, 1965.

Zolotow, Charlotte. *But Not Billy*. New York: Harper & Row, 1947.

———. *Do You Know What I'll Do?* New York: Harper & Row, 1958.

———. *The Hating Book*. New York: Harper & Row, 1969.

———. *If It Weren't for You*. New York: Harper & Row, 1966.

———. *It's Not Fair*. New York: Harper & Row, 1976.

———. *Mr. Rabbit and the Lovely Present*. New York: Harper & Row, 1962.

———. *Someday*. New York: Harper & Row, 1965.

———. *Summer Is . . .* New York: Thomas Y. Crowell, 1967.

Predictable books for middle-school children
Compiled by Margaret A. Atwell
California State University, San Bernadino

LIFE EXPERIENCE

PARENTS

Arundel, Honor. *Love Is a Blanket Word.* New York: Scholastic, 1976.

Babbitt, Natalie. *The Eye of Amarylis.* New York: Bantam, 1979.

Blume, Judy. *And Then Again, Maybe I Won't.* New York: Dell, 1979.

Colman, Hila. *Sometimes I Don't Love My Mother.* New York: Scholastic, 1979.

Cormier, Robert. *Eight Plus One.* New York: Bantam, 1982.

Danziger, Paula. *Can You Sue Your Parents for Malpractice?* New York: Dell, 1980.

Dixon, Paige. *Skipper.* New York: Antheneum, 1979.

Frantz, Evelyn. *A Bonnet for Virginia.* New York: Brethren, 1978.

Girion, Barbara. *A Tangle of Roots.* New York: Dell, 1979.

Hentoff, Nat. *This School Is Driving Me Crazy.* New York: Dell, 1978.

Hinton, S. E. *Tex.* New York: Dell, 1982.

Kerr, M. E. *Dinky Hocker Shoots Smack.* New York: Dell, 1973.

Klein, Norma. *Mom, the Wolfman, and Me.* New York: Avon, 1982.

Peck, Robert. *A Day No Pigs Would Die.* New York: Knopf, 1972.

Rockwood, Joyce. *Enoch's Place.* New York: Holt, Rinehart & Winston, 1980.

Samuels, Gertrude. *Adam's Daughter.* New York: Harper & Row, 1977.

Zindel, Bonnie, & Paul Zindel. *Star for the Latecomer.* New York: Harper & Row, 1980.

SIBLINGS

Blume, Judy. *Superfudge.* New York: Dell, 1981.

———. *Tales of a Fourth Grade Nothing.* New York: Dell, 1981.

Conford, Ellen. *The Luck of Pokey Bloom.* New York: Archway, 1977.

Peck, Ralph. *Father Figure.* New York: Viking, 1978.

PEERS

Blume, Judy. *Blubber*. New York: Dell, 1978.

———. *Freckle Juice*. New York: Dell, 1978.

Brancato, Robin. *Something Left to Lose*. New York: Bantam, 1979.

Conford, Ellen. *Anything for a Friend*. New York: Archway, 1981.

Greene, Constance. *Beat the Turtle Drum*. New York: Dell, 1979.

Myers, Walter. *The Young Landlords*. New York: Viking, 1979.

Pascal, Francine. *Hand-Me-Down Kid*. New York: Dell, 1980.

Rockwell, Thomas. *How to Eat Fried Worms*. New York: Dell, 1975.

GROWING UP

Blume, Judy. *Are You There God? It's Me, Margaret*. New York: Dell, 1974.

Broncato, Robin. *Come Alive at 505*. New York: Knopf, 1980.

Carris, Joan. *The Revolt of 10-X*. New York: Harcourt Brace Jovanovich, 1980.

Danziger, Paula. *There's a Bat in Bunk Five*. New York: Dell, 1982.

Holland, Isabelle. *Heads You Win, Tails I Lose*. New York: Harper & Row, 1973.

IDENTITY

Distad, Andre. *The Dream Runner*. New York: Harper & Row, 1978.

Klein, Norma. *Love Is One of the Choices*. New York: Fawcett, 1982.

ALTERNATE FORMS

Armstrong, William. *Sounder*. New York: Harper & Row, 1972.

Cebulash, Mel. *Herbie Rides Again*. New York: Scholastic, 1974.

Claro, Joe. *Herbie Goes Bananas*. New York: Scholastic, 1980.

Crume, Vic. *The Billion Dollar Hobo*. New York: Scholastic, 1979.

Farley, Walter. *The Black Stallion*. New York: Random House, 1982.

Gelman, Rita. *Benji at Work*. New York: Scholastic, 1980.

Gipson, Fred. *Old Yeller*. New York: Harper & Row, 1969.

Hamner, Earl. *Spencer's Mountain*. New York: Dell, 1973.

Head, Ann. *Mr. and Mrs. Bo Jo Jones*. New York: NAL, 1973.

Herz, Peggy. *The Mork and Mindy Story*. New York: Scholastic, 1979.

———. *Nancy Drew and the Hardy Boys*. New York: Scholastic, 1979.

———. *The Truth about Fonzie*. New York: Scholastic, 1977.

Kipling, Rudyard. *The Jungle Book*. New York: Putnam Publishing Group, 1950.

Lely, James. *Star Wars*. New York: Creative Editions, 1979.

Schultz, Charles. *You're the Greatest, Charlie Brown*. New York: Scholastic, 1980. (several titles)

Wilder, Laura Ingalls. *Little House on the Prairie*. New York: Harper & Row, 1975. (several titles)

BOOKS IN A SERIES

Alexander, Lloyd. *Taran Wanderer*. New York: Dell, 1980.

Blish, James. *StarTrek*. New York: Bantam, 1975.

Baum, Frank. *The Wizard of Oz*. London: J. M. Dent, 1975.

Cleary, Beverly. *Henry Huggins*. New York: Dell, 1979.

———. *Ramona Quimby, Age Eight*. New York: Dell, 1982.

Lewis, C. S. *Chronicles of Narnia*. New York: Macmillan, 1983.

Lindgren, Astrid. *Pippi Longstocking*. New York: Buccaneer Books, 1981.

McCloskey, Robert. *Homer Price*. New York: Penguin, 1976.

Tolkien, J. R. R. *The Hobbit*. New York: Balantine, 1982.

GUESSING BOOKS

Avallone, Michael. *Five-Minute Mysteries* New York: Scholastic, 1978.

Gelman, Rita. *Favorite Riddles, Knock Knocks and Nonsense*. New York: Scholastic, 1980.

Goldsweig, Beryl. *Artemus Flint: Detective*. New York: Scholastic, 1975.

Juster, Norton. *The Phantom Tollbooth*. New York: Random House, 1961.

Laycock, George. *Mysteries, Monsters and Untold Secrets*. New York: Doubleday, 1978.

McWhirter, Norris, and Ross McWhirter. *Guiness' Book of Young Recordbreakers*. New York: Bantam, 1976.

Packard, Edward. *Choose Your Own Adventure*. New York: Bantam, 1979.

Pearlroth, Norbert, ed. *Ripley's Believe It or Not*. New York: Pocketbook, 1984.

Piggin, Julia. *Mini-Mysteries*. New York: Scholastic, 1974.

Rockowitz, Murray, and Irwin Weiss. *The Arrow Book of Word Games*. New York: Scholastic, 1980.

Sobol, Donald. *Encyclopedia Brown: Boy Dectective*. New York: Bantam, 1978.

———. *Two-Minute Mysteries*. New York: Scholastic, 1969.

Zim, Herbert. *Codes and Secret Writing*. New York: Morrow, 1948.

References

Adams, P. 1973. *There was an old lady who swallowed a fly*. New York: Grosset and Dunlap.

Algozzine, B., et al. 1979. Toward defining discrepancies for learning disabilities: An analysis and alternatives. *Learning Disability Quarterly* 2:25–31.

Algozzine, B., J. E., Ysseldyke, and M. L. Shinn. 1982. Identifying children with learning disabilities: When is a discrepancy severe? *Journal of School Psychology* 20:299–305.

Allen, J., and J. Hansen. 1986. Satan joins a literate community. *Language Arts* 63:685–91.

Alley, G. and D. Deshler. 1979. *Teaching the learning disabled adolescent: Strategies and methods*. Denver, Colo.: Love Publishing Co.

Allington, R. 1975. Sustained approaches to reading and writing. *Language Arts* 52:813–15.

———. 1978. *Are good and poor readers taught differently? Is that why poor readers are poor readers?* Paper presented at the annual meeting of the American Educational Research Association, Toronto.

———. 1980. Poor readers don't get to read much in reading groups. *Language Arts* 57:872–76.

Alvarez, M. C. 1981. A cooperative reading plan starts from within, involves the entire school. *NAASP Bulletin* 65:67–74.

Alvermann, D. E. 1984. Helping the LD learner read in the content areas. *Topics in Learning and Learning Disabilities* 3:41–52.

Applebee, A. N., F. Lehr, and A. Auten. 1981. Learning to write in the secondary school: How and where. *English Journal* 70:78–82.

Aronson, E. 1978. *The jigsaw classroom*. Beverly Hills, Calif. Sage Publications.

Arter, J. A. and J. R. Jenkins. 1979. Differential diagnosis-prescriptive teaching: A critical appraisal. *Review of Educational Research* 49:517–55.

Astman, J. A. 1984. Special education as a moral enterprise. *Learning Disability Quarterly*, 7:299–308.

Atwell, M. A. 1980. The evolution of text: The interrelationship of reading and writing in the composing process. Doctoral dissertation, Indiana University.

———. 1987. Predictable books for the middle school child. In D. Watson (Ed.), *Ideas and insights: Teaching the English language arts, K–6*. Urbana, Ill.: National Council of Teachers of English.

Atwell, M. A., and L. K. Rhodes. 1984. Strategy lessons as alternatives to skills lessons in reading. *Journal of Reading* 27:700–705.

Atwell, N. 1982. Making the grade: Evaluating writing in conference. In T. Newkirk and N. Atwell (Eds.), *Understanding writing*, 137–44. Chelmsford, Mass.: Northeast Regional Exchange.

———. 1984. Having a writing conference with yourself. *Livewire*, December, 10–11.

Au, K. H. 1979. Using the experience-text-relationship method with minority children. *Reading Teacher* 32:677–79.

Auel, J. M. 1980. *Clan of the cave bear*. New York: Crown.

———. 1982. *Valley of the horses*. New York: Crown.

Balajthy, E. 1984. Using student-constructed questions to encourage active reading. *Journal of Reading* 27:408–11.

Barnard, D. P. and R. W. Hetzel. 1976. The principals' role in reading instruction. *Reading Teacher* 29:386–88.

Barrett, T. C. 1976. Taxonomy of reading comprehension. In R. Smith and T. C. Barrett (Eds.), *Teaching reading in the middle grades*. Reading, Mass.: Addison-Wesley.

Bartlett, R., J. Hall, and S. Neale. 1984. A parental involvement project in the primary schools of South Oxfordshire. *Reading* 18:173–77.

Bass, R. J., N. A. Jurenka, and E. G. Zirzow. 1981. Showing children the communicative nature of reading. *Reading Teacher* 34:926–31.

Bateman, B. D. 1965. An educator's view of a diagnostic approach to learning disorders. In J. Hallmuth (Ed.), *Learning Disorders*, vol. 1. Seattle, Wash.: Special Child Publications.

Bean, T. W. 1979. The miscue mini-form: Refining the informal reading inventory. *Reading World* 18:400–405.

Beck, I. L., E. S. McCaslin, and M. G. McKeown. 1981. Basal readers' purpose for story reading: Smoothly paving the road or setting up a detour? *Elementary School Journal* 81:156–61.

Beck, I. L., and M. G. McKeown. 1981. Developing questions that promote comprehension: The story map. *Language Arts* 58:913–17.

Beebe, M. J. 1980. The effect of different types of substitution miscues on reading. *Reading Research Quarterly* 15:324–36.

Beers, C., and J. Beers. 1977. Three assumptions about learning to spell. *Elementary School Journal* 19:238–42.

Beers, J. W. 1980. Developmental strategies of spelling competence in primary school children. In E. H. Henderson and J. W. Beers (Eds.), *Developmental and cognitive aspects of learning to spell*, 35–45. Newark, N.J.: International Reading Association.

Bergland, R. L. and J. L. Johns. 1983. A primer on uninterrupted sustained silent reading. *Reading Teacher* 36:534–39.

Bingham, A. 1982. Using writing folders to document student progress. In T. Newkirk and N. Atwell (Eds.), *Understanding writing*, 129–36. Chelmsford, Mass.: Northeast Regional Exchange.

Bissex, G. 1980. *GNYS AT WRK: A child learns to read and write*. Cambridge: Harvard University Press.

Bixby, M., et al. 1983. *Strategies that make sense: Invitations to literacy for secondary students*. Columbia, Mo.: Teachers Applying Whole Language.

Bond, S. J., and J. R. Hayes. 1984. Cues people use to paragraph text. *Research in the Teaching of English* 18:147–167.

Bonne, R., and A. Mills. 1961. *I know an old lady*. New York: Rand McNally.

Bookman, M. O. 1983. Spelling as a cognitive-linguistic developmental process: A study of two subgroups of learning disabled adults. Doctoral dissertation, University of Colorado at Boulder.

Bos, C. S. 1982. Getting past decoding: Assisted and repeated readings as remedial methods for learning disabled students. *Topics in Learning and Learning Disabilities* 1:51–75.

Bos, C. S., and D. Filip. 1984. Comprehension monitoring in learning disabled and average students. *Journal of Learning Disabilities* 17:229–33.

Braddock, R., R. Lloyd-Jones, and L. Schoer. 1963. *Research in written composition*. Urbana, Ill. National Council of Teachers of English.

Bransford, J. D., and M. K. Johnson. 1972. Contextual prerequisites for understanding: Some investigations of comprehension and recall. *Journal of Verbal Learning and Verbal Behavior* 11:717–26.

Brenneman, R. 1985. Debate to stretch. *Notes Plus* September, 2.

Bridge, C. 1979. Predictable materials for beginning readers. *Language Arts* 56:503–7.

Brieling, A. 1976. Using parents as teaching partners. *Reading Teacher* 30:187–92.

Brown, V. 1981. *Contemporary approaches to teaching spelling*. Paper presented at the annual conference of the Council for Learning Disabilities, October, Houston, Texas.

Bruce, B. 1978. What makes a good story? *Language Arts* 55:460–66.

Bruinsma, R. 1980. Should lip movements and sub-vocalization during silent reading be directly remediated? *Reading Teacher* 34:293–95.

Bryan, R. 1971. *When children speak.* San Rafael, Calif.: Academic Therapy, 1971.

Burke, C. L. 1980. Written conversation. In L. K. Crafton et al. (eds.), Language instruction: From theoretical abstractions to classroom implications. *Occasional papers in language and reading.* Bloomington, Ind.: Language Education Department, Indiana University.

———. 1982. Save the last word for me. In J. Newman (Ed.), *Whole language activites.* Halifax, N.S.: Dalhousie University.

———. 1985. Editors' table. In J. C. Harste, K. M. Pierce, and T. Cairney (Eds.), *The authoring cycle: A viewing guide* (69–75). Portsmouth, N.H.: Heinemann.

Burke, C. L. and J. C. Harste. 1978. Toward a socio-psycholinguistic model of reading comprehension. *Viewpoints in teaching and learning* 54:9–34.

Burns, J. and D. Swan. 1979. *Reading without books.* Belmont, Calif.: Fearon Pitman Publishers.

Buttery, T. J., and J. V. Powell. 1978. Teacher verbal feedback during primary basal reading instruction. *Reading Improvement* 15:183–89.

Cadieux, S. 1982. Letting children lead the way. In T. Newkirk and N. Atwell (eds.), *Understanding writing,* 63–67. Chelmsford. Mass.: Northeast Regional Exchange.

Calkins, L. M. 1983. *Lessons from a child.* Portsmouth, N.H.: Heinemann.

———. 1986. *The art of teaching writing.* Portsmouth, N.H.: Heinemann.

Cambourne, B. L., and P. D. Rousch. 1982. How do learning disabled children read? *Topics in Learning and Learning Disabilities* 1:59–68.

Carbo, M. 1978. Teaching reading with talking books. *Reading Teacher* 32:267–73.

———. 1981. Making books talk to children. *Reading Teacher* 35:186–89.

Carle, E. 1969. *The very hungry caterpillar.* New York: Philomel Books.

Carroll, L. 1960. *Alice's adventures in wonderland and through the looking glass.* New York: New American Library. First published in 1865.

Cassidy, J. 1981. Grey power in the reading program—a direction for the eighties. *Reading Teacher* 35:287–91.

———. 1984. The concept kit. *Reading Today* 1:9.

Catroppa, B.D. 1982. Working with writing is like working with clay. *Language Arts* 59:687–95.

Chase, M. L., and S. M. Pickert. 1978. Story retelling: An informal technique for evaluating children's language. *Reading Teacher* 31:528–31.

Chomsky, C. 1972. Stages in language development and reading exposure. *Harvard Educational Review* 42:1–33.

———. 1976. After decoding: What? *Language Arts* 53:288–96.

———. 1978. When you still can't read in third grade: After decoding, what? In S. J. Samuels (Ed.), *What research has to say about reading instruction.* Newark, Del.: IRA.

Clark, F. L., et al. 1984. Visual imagery and self-questioning: Strategies to improve comprehension of written material. *Journal of Learning Disabilities* 17:145–49.

Clay, M. 1987. *Writing begins at home.* Portsmouth, N.H.: Heinemann.

Clyde, J. A. 1981. Open-ended sentence questionnaire on writing. Elizabeth, Colo.: Elizabeth Elementary School.

Clymer, T., and P. M. Martin. 1980. The partridge and the fox. Lexington, Mass.: Ginn.

Cohen, R. 1983. Self-generated questions as an aid to reading comprehension. *Reading Teacher* 36:770–75.

Collier, J. L., and C. Collier. 1977. *My brother Sam is dead.* New York: Scholastic.

Cone, T. E. and Wilson, L. R. 1981. Quantifying a discrepancy: A critical analysis. *Learning Disability Quarterly* 4:359–71.

Cordeiro, P., M. E. Giacobbe, and C. Cazden. 1983. Apostrophes, quotation marks, and periods: Learning punctuation in the first grade. *Language Arts* 60:323–32.

Crafton, L. K. 1982. Comprehension before, during and after reading. *Reading Teacher* 36:293–97.

———. 1983. Learning from reading: What happens when students generate their own background information? *Journal of Reading* 26:585–92.

———. 1984. Framing. *Livewire* 1:6.

Crafton, L. K., et al. 1980. Language instruction: From theoretical abstractions to classroom implications. *Occasional Papers in Language and Reading*. Bloomington, Ind.: Language Education Department, Indiana University.

Cramer, R. L. 1978. *Writing, reading, and language growth*. Columbus, Ohio: Charles E. Merrill.

Criscuolo, N. P. 1978. Activities that help involve parents in reading. *Reading Teacher* 32:417–19.

Crocker, M. 1983a. Creating a vertical file. In J. Newman (Ed.), *Whole language: Translating theory into practice*, 150–61. Halifax, N.S.: Dalhousie University.

———. 1983b. On doing projects. In J. Newman (Ed.), *Whole language: Translating theory into practice*, 129–38. Halifax, N.S., Canada: Dalhousie University.

Cross, T. G. 1984. Habilitating the language-impaired child: Ideas from studies of parent child interaction. *Topics in Language Disorders* 4:1–14.

Cullinan, B., A. Jaggar, and D. Strickland. 1974. Oral language expansion in the primary grades. In B. Cullinan (Ed.), *Black dialects and reading*. Urbana, Ill. NCTE.

Cunningham, D., and S. Shablak. 1975. Selective reading guide-o-rama: The content area teacher's best friend. *Journal of Reading* 18:380–82.

Cunningham, P. 1978. "Mumble reading" for beginning readers. *Reading Teacher* 31:409–11.

D'Angelo, K. 1981. Wordless picture books and the young language-disabled child. *Teaching Exceptional Children* 14:34–37.

———. 1982. Correction behavior: Implications for instruction. *Reading Teacher* 35:395–99.

———. 1983. Precis writing: Promoting vocabulary development and compre-

hension. *Journal of Reading* 26:534–39.

Davey, B. 1983. Think aloud: Modeling the cognitive process of reading comprehension. *Journal of Reading* 27:44–47.

Davey, B., and S. M. Porter. 1982. Comprehension-rating: A procedure to assist poor comprehenders. *Journal of Reading* 26:197–201.

Davidson, J. L. 1982. The group mapping activity for instruction in reading and thinking. *Journal of Reading* 26:52–56.

Deardorff, B. 1982. Confessions of a skills teacher. *Learning* 11:42–43.

DeFord, D. E. 1981. Literacy: Reading, writing, and other essentials. *Language Arts* 58:652–58.

dePaola, T. 1978. *Pancakes for breakfast*. New York: Harcourt Brace Jovanovich.

Deshler, D. D., et al. 1980. *An epidemiological study of learning disabled adolescents in secondary schools: Social status, peer relationships, activities in and out of school, and time use* (Research Report no. 18). Lawrence, Kans.: University of Kansas Institute for Research in Learning Disabilities.

Deshler, D. D., et al. 1984. Academic and cognitive interventions for LD adolescents: Part II. *Journal of Learning Disabilities* 17:170–178.

DiMartini, S. 1987. *Teaching reading through Mother Goose*. Lakewood, Colo.: LINK.

Disney Productions 1977. *Pete's Dragon*. Racine, Wis.: Golden Press.

Dreher, M. J., and H. Singer. 1980. Story grammar instruction unnecessary for intermediate grade students. *Reading Teacher* 34:261–68.

Dudley-Marling, C. C. 1985. Perceptions of the usefulness of the IEP by teachers of learning disabled and emotionally disturbed children. *Psychology in the Schools* 22:65–67.

Dudley-Marling, C. C., N. J. Kaufman, and S. G. Tarver. 1981. WISC and WISC-R profiles of learning disabled children: A review. *Learning Disability Quarterly* 4:307–19.

Duggins, J., and T. Finn. 1976. The reading list: A thousand authors. In D. Fader (Ed.), *The New Hooked on Books*, 238–62. New York: Medalion Books.

Durr, W. K., et al. 1981. The little red

hen. In *Sunshine teacher's guide*. Boston: Houghton Mifflin.

Dyck, N. J., and L. Cox. 1981. Should LD students underline their texts? *Academic Therapy* 17:83−87.

Eckoff, B. 1983. How reading affects children's writing. *Language Arts* 60:607−16.

Edelsky, C. 1983. Segmentation and punctuation: Developmental data from young writers in a bilingual program. *Research in the Teaching of English* 17:135−56.

Edelsky, C. and K. Smith. 1984. Is that writing—Or are those marks just a figment of your curriculum? *Language Arts* 61:24−32.

Einsel, W. 1962. *Did you ever see?* New York: Scholastic.

Eisele, K. 1978. The telegram: Form and audience. In C. Koch and J. M. Brazil (Eds.), *Strategies for teaching the composition process*, 55−57. Urbana, Ill. National Council of Teachers of English.

Elbow, P. 1973. *Writing without teachers.* New York: Oxford University Press.

Elting, M., and M. Folsom. 1980. *Q is for duck.* New York: Ticknor and Fields.

Enstrom, E. A. 1968. Left-handedness: A cause for disability in writing. *Journal of Learning Disabilities*, 1:410−14.

Epps, D., J. E. Ysseldyke, and M. McGue. 1984. "I know one when I see one"—Differentiating LD and non-LD students. *Learning Disability Quarterly* 7:89−101.

Epps, S., M. McGue, and J. E. Ysseldyke. 1982. Inter-judge agreement in classifying students as learning disabled. *Psychology in the Schools* 19:209−20.

Fader, D. 1976. *The new hooked on books.* New York: Berkley Books.

Farley, C. 1983. *Korea: A land divided.* Minneapolis: Dillon Press.

Farnsworth, K. 1981. Storytelling in the classroom—not an impossible dream. *Language Arts* 58:162−67.

Farrell, E. 1982. SSR as the core of a junior high reading program. *Journal of Reading* 26:48−51.

Federal Register, December 29, 1977, 42 (163), p. 65083.

Feldman, C. F. 1977. Two functions of language. *Harvard Educational Review* 47:282−93.

Fish, S. 1980. *Is there a text in this class?* Cambridge: Harvard University Press.

Fisher, C. 1980. Grammar in the language arts program. In G. S. Pinnell, *Discovering language with children*, 60−64. Urbana, Ill.: National Council of Teachers of English.

Fitzgerald, J. 1983. Helping readers gain self-control over reading comprehension. *Reading Teacher* 37:249−53.

Fitzgerald, J., and D. L. Spiegel. 1983. Enhancing children's reading comprehension through instruction in narrative structure. *Journal of Reading Behavior* 15:1−18.

Forester, A. D. 1977. What teachers can learn from "natural readers." *Reading Teacher* 31:160−66.

Fowler, G. L. 1982. Developing comprehension skills in primary students through the use of story frames. *Reading Teacher* 36:176−79.

Freedman, B., and E. G. Reynolds, 1980. Enriching basal reader lessons with semantic webbing. *Reading Teacher* 33:677−84.

Friedman, M. I., and M. D. Rowls. 1980. *Teaching reading and thinking skills.* New York: Longman.

Fuhr, M. L. 1972. The typewriter and retarded readers. *Journal of Reading* 16:30−32.

Fulwiler, T. 1987. *The journal book.* Portsmouth, N.H.: Boynton/Cook.

Gagne, E. D., and D. Memory. 1978. Instructional events and comprehension: Generalization across passages. *Journal of Reading Behavior* 10:321−35.

Gale, J. 1975. *Neat and scruffy.* Toronto: Ashton Scholastic.

Gambrell, L. B. 1978. Getting started with sustained silent reading and keeping it going. *Reading Teacher* 32:328−31.

———. 1980. Think-time: Implications for reading instruction. *Reading Teacher* 34:143−146.

Gambrell, L. B. and C. Sokolski. 1983. Picture potency: Use Caldecott Award Books to develop children's language. *Reading Teacher* 36:868−71.

Ganschow, L. 1981. Discovering children's learning strategies for spelling through error pattern analysis. *Reading Teacher* 34:676−80.

Gaskins, I. W. 1982. A writing program for poor readers and writers and the rest of the class, too. *Language Arts* 59:854−61.

Gentry, J. R., and E. H. Henderson. 1978. Three steps to teaching beginning readers to spell. *Reading Teacher* 31:632−37.

Gerber, M. 1984. Orthographic problem-solving ability of learning disabled and normally achieving students. *Learning Disability Quarterly* 7:157−64.

Gerber, M., and R. Hall. 1981. Development of orthographic problem-solving in LD children (Technical Report no. 37). University of Virginia: Learning Disabilities Research Institute.

Giacobbe, M. E. 1986. Intensive writing workshop. Denver: Public Education Coalition.

Giermack, E. A. 1980. Reading to high school students: A painless method of improving language skills. *English Journal* 69:62−63.

Glass, G. V., and J. C. Stanley. 1970. *Statistical methods in education and psychology.* Englewood Cliffs. N.J.: Prentice-Hall.

Gold, P. C. 1984. Cognitive mapping. *Academic Therapy* 19:277−84.

Golden, J. M. 1984. Children's concept of story in reading and writing. *Reading Teacher* 37:578−84.

Gonzales, D. G. 1980. An author center for children. *Language Arts* 57:280−84.

Goodman, K. S. 1965. A linguistic study of cues and miscues in reading. *Elementary English* 42:639−43.

———. 1968. The psycholinguistic nature of the reading process. In K. S. Goodman (Ed.), *The psycholinguistic nature of the reading process.* Detroit, Mich.: Wayne State Press.

———. 1973. Miscues: Windows on the reading process. In K. S. Goodman (Ed.), *Miscue analysis: Applications to reading instruction.* Urbana, Ill. National Council of Teachers of English.

———. 1982. Revaluing readers and reading. *Topics in Learning and Learning Disabilities* 1:87−93.

———. 1986a. Basal readers: A call for action. *Language Arts* 63:358−63.

———. 1986b. *What's whole in whole language?* Portsmouth, N.H.: Heinemann.

Goodman, K. S. and C. L. Burke. 1973. *Theoretically based studies of patterns of miscues in oral reading performance.* U.S. Department of Health, Education, and Welfare, Final Report.

Goodman, K. S. and Y. M. Goodman. 1983. Reading and writing relationship: Pragmatic functions. *Language Arts* 60:590−99.

Goodman, Y. M. 1976. Developing reading proficiency. In P. D. Allen and D. J. Watson (Eds.), *Findings of research in miscue analysis: Classroom implications,* 113−28. Urbana, Ill.: National Council of Teachers of English.

———. 1978. Kidwatching: An alternative to testing. *National Elementary Principal* 57:41−45.

———. 1980. Test review: Concepts about print test. *Reading Teacher* 34:445−48.

———. 1982. Retellings of literature and the comprehension process. *Theory into Practice* 21:301−7.

Goodman, Y. M. and C. L. Burke. 1972. *Reading miscue inventory manual: Procedures for diagnosis and evaluation.* New York: Richard C. Owen.

———. 1980. *Reading strategies: Focus on comprehension.* New York: Holt, Rinehart and Winston.

Goodman, Y. M., D. J. Watson, and C. L. Burke. 1987. *Reading miscue inventory.* New York: Richard C. Owen.

Gordon, C. J. 1980. The effects of instruction in metacomprehension and inferencing on children's comprehension abilities. Doctoral dissertation, University of Minnesota, Minneapolis, Minn.

Gordon, C. J., and C. Braun. 1983. Using story schema as an aid to reading and writing. *Reading Teacher* 37:116−21.

Gourley, J. W. 1984. Discourse structure: Expectations of beginning readers and readability of text. *Journal of Reading Behavior* 16:169−88.

Granowsky, A., F. R. Middleton, and J. H. Mumford. 1979. Parents as partners in education. *Reading Teacher* 32:826−30.

Graves, D. H. 1977. Spelling texts and structural analysis methods. *Language Arts* 54:86−90.

———. 1978. Handwriting is for writing. *Language Arts* 55:393–99.

———. 1983. *Writing: Teachers and children at work.* Portsmouth, N.H.: Heinemann.

Graves, D. H., and J. Hansen. 1983. The author's chair. *Language Arts* 60:176–83.

Graves, D. H. and V. Stuart. 1985. *Write from the start.* New York: E. P. Dutton.

Graves, M. F., C. L. Cooke, and M. J. LaBerge. 1983. Effects of previewing difficult short stories on low ability junior high school students' comprehension, recall, and attitudes. *Reading Research Quarterly* 18:262–76.

Greene, F. 1979. Radio reading. In C. Pennock (Ed.), *Reading comprehension at four linguistic levels,* 104–7. Newark, Del.: International Reading Association.

Griffin, M. and K. Jongsma. 1980. Analyzing retelling and oral reading—Adaptations of the reading miscue inventory. In M. Griffin & K. Jongsma (Eds.), *Reading: Evaluative Teaching.* Toronto: Ginn.

Guszak, F. J. 1967. Teacher questioning and reading. *Reading Teacher* 21:227–34.

Hahn, A. L. 1985. Teaching remedial students to be strategic readers and better comprehenders. *Reading Teacher* 39:72–77.

Hallenbeck, M. J. 1983. A free reading journal for secondary LD students. *Academic Therapy* 18:479–85.

Halliday, M. A. K. 1978. *Language as social semiotic.* Baltimore: University Park Press.

Hammill, D. D., et al. 1981. A new definition of learning disabilities. *Learning Disability Quarterly* 4:336–42.

Hammond, W. D. 1982. The quality of reading miscues. In J. J. Pikulski and T. Shanahan (Eds.), *Approaches to the informal evaluation of reading,* 23–29. Newark, Del.: International Reading Association.

Hampton, D. W. 1984. Already-know time. *Livewire* 1:5.

Hansen, J. 1987. *When writers read.* Portsmouth, N.H.: Heinemann.

Harber, J. R. 1979. The effectiveness of selected perceptual and perceptual-motor tasks in differentiating between normal and learning disabled children. *Learning Disability Quarterly* 2:70–75.

Harber, J. R. 1982. Perceptual and perceptual-motor test scores are not a clue to reading achievement in second graders. *Reading Horizons* 22:207–10.

Hare, B. A. 1977. Perceptual deficits are not a cue to reading problems in second grade. *Reading Teacher* 31:624–27.

Harman, S. 1982. Are reversals a symptom of dyslexia? *Reading Teacher* 35:424–28.

Harste, J. 1982. Say something. In J. Newman (Ed.), *Whole language activities.* Halifax, N.S., Canada: Dalhousie University.

Harste, J., and C. Burke. 1978. Toward a socio-psycholinguistic model of reading comprehension. *Viewpoints in Teaching and Learning* 54:9–34.

———. 1980. Understanding the hypothesis: It's the teacher that makes the difference. In B. P. Farr and D. J. Strickler (Eds.), *Reading comprehension: Resource guide,* 111–23. Bloomington, Ind.: Indiana University Reading Programs.

Harste, J., C. Burke, and D. DeFord. 1976. An instructional development activity for teachers: Making whole language reading games. In J. Harste and M. A. Atwell (Eds.), *Mainstreaming, the special child, and the reading process,* 236–45. Bloomington, Ind.: Indiana University School of Education.

Harste, J., C. Burke, and V. Woodward. 1981. Children's language and world: Initial encounters with print. In J. Langer and M. Smith-Burke (Eds.), *Bridging the gap: Reader meets author.* Newark, Del.: International Reading Association.

Harste, J., K. M. Pierce, and T. Cairney. 1985. *The authoring cycle: A viewing guide.* Portsmouth, N.H.: Heinemann.

Harste, J., V. Woodward, and C. Burke. 1984. *Language stories and literacy lessons.* Portsmouth, N.H.: Heinemann.

Heibert, E. H. 1980. Peers as reading teachers. *Language Arts* 57:877–81.

Henderson, E. H., and J. W. Beers. 1980. *Developmental and cognitive aspects of learning to spell.* Newark, Del.: International Reading Association.

Henderson, L. C., and J. L. Shanker. 1978. The use of interpretive dramatics versus basal reader workbooks for developing comprehension skills. *Reading World* 17:239–43.

Hennings, D. G. 1982. A writing approach to reading comprehension—schema theory in action. *Language Arts* 59:8–17.

Henry, G. 1974. *Teaching reading as concept development: Emphasis on affective thinking.* Newark, Del.: International Reading Association.

Heshusius, L. 1982. At the heart of the advocacy dilemma: A mechanistic view of the world. *Exceptional Children* 49:6–11.

———. 1985. Why would they and I want to do it? A phenomenological view of special education. *Learning Disability Quarterly* 7:363–68.

Hess, J. B. 1968. There's more than talk to choral reading. *Grade Teacher* 85:107–9.

Hiebert, E. H. 1978. Preschool children's understanding of written language. *Child Development* 49:1231–34.

Hill, E. 1980. *Where's Spot?* New York: G. P. Putnam's Sons.

Hinshelwood, J. 1917. *Congenital word blindness.* London: Lewis.

Hinton, S. E. 1980. *The outsiders.* New York: Dell.

Hittleman, D. R. 1983. *Developmental reading, K–8.* Boston: Houghton Mifflin.

Hoffman, J. V. 1979. On providing feedback to reading miscues. *Reading World* 18:342–50.

———. 1981. Is there a legitimate place for oral reading instruction in a developmental reading program? *Elementary School Journal* 81:305–10.

Hoffman, J. V., and R. Clements. 1984. Reading miscues and teacher verbal feedback. *Elementary School Journal* 84:423–39.

Hoge, S. 1983. A comprehension-centered reading program using reader selected miscues. *Journal of Reading* 27:52–55.

Holdaway, D. 1979. Foundations of literacy. Portsmouth, N.H.: Heinemann.

Hollingsworth, P. M. 1970. An experiment with the impress method of teaching reading. *Reading Teacher* 24:112–14.

———. 1978. An experimental approach to the impress method of teaching. *Reading Teacher* 31:624–26.

Holmes, D., and R. Peper. 1977. An evaluation of spelling error analysis in the diagnosis of reading disability. *Child Development* 48:1709–11.

Holt, J. 1982. *The underachieving school.* Boston: Allyn & Bacon.

Hong, L. K. 1981. Modifying SSR for beginners. *Reading Teacher* 34:888–91.

Hoskisson, K., T. M. Sherman, and L. L. Smith. 1974. Assisted reading and parent involvement. *Reading Teacher* 27:710–14.

Howell, H. 1978. Write on, you sinistrals! *Language Arts* 55:852–56.

Huck, C. S. 1976. *Children's literature in the elementary school.* 3d ed. New York: Holt, Rinehart and Winston.

———. 1979. Literature for all reasons. *Language Arts* 56:354–55.

Hunt, L. 1970. The effect of self-selection, interest, and motivation upon independent instructional and frustrational levels. *Reading Teacher* 24:146–51.

Idol-Maestras, L. 1983. Getting ready to read: Guided probing for poor comprehenders. Unpublished paper.

Jackson, L. A. 1981. Whose skills system? Mine or Penny's? *Reading Teacher* 35:260–62.

Jaggar, A. 1980. Allowing for language differences. In G. S. Pinnell (Ed.), *Discovering language with children*, 25–28. Urbana, Ill.: National Council of Teachers of English.

Johns, J. L. 1975. Strategies for oral reading behavior. *Language Arts* 52:1104–1107.

———. 1982. Therapy for round robin oral reading. *Reading Horizons* 22:201–3.

Johnson, D. and H. R. Myklebust. 1967. *Learning disabilities: Educational principles and practices.* New York: Grune & Stratton.

Johnson, K. R. 1970. When should standard English be taught to speakers of nonstandard Negro dialect? *Language Learning* 20:19–30.

Johnson, R. J., K. L. Johnson, and J. F. Kerfoot. 1972. A massive oral decoding technique. *Reading Teacher* 25:421–23.

Johnston, P. H. 1983. *Reading comprehension assessment: A cognitive basis.* Newark, Del.: International Reading Association.

Jones, J. R. 1981. Advising parents on reading. *Reading* 15:27–30.

Jongsma, E. A. 1980. *Cloze instruction research*: *A second look*. Newark, Del.: International Reading Association.

Kaake, D. M. 1983. Teaching elementary age children touch typing as an aid to language arts instruction. *Reading Teacher* 36:640−44.

Kavale, K. A. 1980. Learning disability and cultural-economic disadvantage: The case for a relationship. *Learning Disability Quarterly* 3:97−112.

Kavale, K. A., and S. R. Forness. 1985. *The science of learning disabilities*. San Diego, Calif.: College-Hill Press.

Kavale, K. A., and C. Nye. 1981. Identification criteria for learning disabilities: A survey of the research literature. *Learning Disability Quarterly* 4:383−88.

Kettel, R. P. 1981. Reading road quiz: A literature game show that develops readers. *Reading Teacher* 34:815−17.

Kimmelman, L. 1981. Literacy ways toward enjoyable thinking. *Language Arts* 58:441−47.

Kingore, B. W. 1982. Storytelling: A bridge from the university to the elementary school to the home. *Language Arts* 59:28−32.

Kirby, D., and T. Liner. 1981. *Inside out*: *Developmental strategies for teaching writing*. Montclair, N.J.: Boynton/Cook.

Kirk, S. A. 1962. *Educating exceptional children*. Boston: Houghton-Mifflin.

Kitagawa, M. M. 1982. Improving discussions or how to get the students to ask the questions. *Reading Teacher* 36:42−45.

Krevisky, J., and J. L. Linfield. 1963. *The bad speller's dictionary*. New York: Random House.

Kucer, S. B., and L. K. Rhodes. 1986. Counterpart strategies: Fine tuning language with language. *Reading Teacher* 40:186−93.

Lamme, L. L. 1979. Song picture books— A maturing genre of children's literature. *Language Arts* 56:400−407.

———. 1981. Parents, volunteers, and aides: Human resources for a literature program. In L. Lamme (Ed.), *Learning to love literature*, 73−82. Urbana, Ill.: National Council of Teachers of English.

Lancaster, W., L. Nelson, and D. Morris. 1982. Invented spellings in Room 112: A writing program for low-reading second graders. *Reading Teacher* 35:906−11.

Landsberg, M. 1986. *Guide to children's books*. Markham, Ont.: Penguin Books.

Langer, J. A. 1981. From theory to practice: A prereading plan. *Journal of Reading* 25:152−56.

———. 1982. Facilitating text processing: The elaboration of prior knowledge. In J. A. Langer and M. T. Smith-Burke (Eds.), *Reader meets author*: *Bridging the gap*, 149−62. Newark, Del.: International Reading Association.

Larrick, N. 1982. *A parents' guide to children's reading*. Philadelphia: Westminster Press.

LaSasso, C. 1983. Using the National Enquirer with unmotivated or language-handicapped readers. *Journal of Reading* 26:546−48.

Lass, B. 1984. Do teachers individualize their responses to miscues? A study of feedback during oral reading. *Reading World* 23:242−54.

Lauritzen, C. 1982. A modification of repeated readings for group instruction. *Reading Teacher* 58:456−58.

Lehr, F. 1984. ERIC/RCS report: Student-teacher communication. *Language Arts* 61:200−203.

Lenski, L. 1942. *The Little Farm*. New York: H. Z. Walck.

———. 1949. *Cowboy Small*. New York: H. Z. Walck.

———. 1962. *Policeman Small*. New York: H. Z. Walck.

Lewis, M. E. B. 1982. Use of the thematic approach to curriculum development for learning disabled students: Assumptions and applications. *Learning Disabilities: An Interdisciplinary Journal* 1:25−33.

Lickteig, M. J., Sr. 1981. Research-based recommendations for teachers of writing. *Language Arts* 58:44−50.

Lindfors, J. W. 1980. *Children's language and learning*. Englewood Cliffs, N.J.: Prentice-Hall.

———. 1984. How children learn or how teachers teach? A profound confusion. *Language Arts* 61:600−614.

Lindquist, A. A. 1982. Applying Bloom's taxonomy in writing reading guides for literature. *Journal of Reading* 25:768−74.

Lipa, S. E. 1983. Reading disability: A new look at an old issue. *Journal of Learning Disabilities* 16:453−57.

Livo, N. J., and S. A. Rietz. 1985. *Storytelling: Process and practice*. Littleton, Colo.: Libraries Unlimited.

Maier, A. 1980. The effect of focusing on the cognitive processes of learning disabled children. *Journal of Learning Disabilities* 13:143−47.

Mandler, J. M., and N. S. Johnson. 1977. Remembrance of things parsed: Story structure and recall. *Cognitive Psychology* 9:111−57.

Manzo, A. 1969. The request procedure. *Journal of Reading* 12:123−26.

Maring, G. H. 1978. Matching remediation to miscues. *Reading Teacher* 31:887−91.

Marino, J. 1981. Spelling errors: From analysis to instruction. *Language Arts* 58:567−72.

Marshall, K. 1983. The reading problem: Some sensible solutions. *Learning* 12:50−60.

Martin, B., Jr. 1970a. *Brown bear, brown bear, what do you see?* New York: Holt, Rinehart & Winston.

———. 1970b. *Fire! Fire! Said Mrs. McGuire.* New York: Holt, Rinehart & Winston.

———. 1970c. *Instant Readers.* New York: Holt, Rinehart & Winston.

Martin, B., and P. Brogan. 1972. *Sounds of language readers.* New York: Holt, Rinehart & Winston.

Martin, R. J. 1981. Folk songs as a language experience. *Language Arts* 58:326−29.

Mason, G. E. 1981. High interest-low vocabulary books: Their past and future. *Journal of Reading* 24:603−7.

Meteja, J. 1982. Musical cloze: Background, purpose, and sample. *Reading Teacher* 35:444−48.

Mateja, J., and K. D. Wood. 1983. Adapting secondary level strategies for use in elementary classrooms. *Reading Teacher* 36:492−496.

Maya, A. Y. 1979. Write to read. Improving reading through creative writing. *Reading Teacher* 32:813−17.

Mayer, M. 1975. *Just for you.* New York: Golden Press.

McClintock, M. and F. Siebel. 1958. *A fly went by.* New York: Random House.

McClure, A. A. 1985. Predictable books: Another way to teach reading to learning disabled children. *Teaching Exceptional Children* 17:267−73.

McConaughy, S. H. 1980. Using story structure in the classroom. *Language Arts* 57:157−65.

McCormick, S. 1977. Should you read aloud to your children? *Language Arts* 54:139−43.

———. 1981. Assessment and the beginning reader. *Reading World* 2:29−39.

McCracken, R. A. 1971. Initiating sustained silent reading. *Journal of Reading* 14:521−24.

McCracken, R. A., and M. J. McCracken. 1978. Modeling is the key to sustained silent reading. *Reading Teacher* 31:406−8.

McGee, L. M., and G. E. Tompkins. 1983. Wordless picture books are for older readers, too. *Journal of Reading* 27:120−23.

McGee, M. M., and D. J. Richgels. 1985. Teaching expository text structure to elementary students. *Reading Teacher* 38:739−48.

McGovern, A. 1967. *Too much noise.* New York: Scholastic.

———. 1975. *The secret soldier: The story of Deborah Sampson.* New York: Scholastic.

McKenzie, G. R. 1979. Data charts: A crutch for helping pupils organize reports. *Language Arts* 56:784−88.

McLeod, J. 1983. Learning disability is for educators. *Journal of Learning Disabilities* 16:23−24.

McNaughton, S. 1981. The influence of immediate teacher correction on self-corrections and proficient oral reading. *Journal of Reading Behavior* 13:365−71.

Medway, P. 1981. *Finding a language: Autonomy and learning in school.* New York: Writers and Readers.

Mellon, J. C. 1975. *National assessment and the teaching of English.* Urbana, Ill.: National Council of Teachers of English.

Menosky, D. M. 1972. A psycholinguistic analysis of oral reading miscues generated during the reading of varying portions of text by selected readers from grades two, four, six and eight. Doctoral dissertation, Wayne State University. Ann Arbor, Mich.: University Microfilms, no. 72–14598.

Mercer, C. D., C. Hughes, and A. Mercer. 1985. Learning disabilities definitions used by state education departments. *Learning Disability Quarterly* 8:45–55.

Meyer, B. J., D. H. Brandt, and G. J. Bluth. 1980. Use of author's textual schema: Key for ninth-graders' comprehension. *Reading Research Quarterly* 16:72–103.

Meyer, B. J., and R. O. Freedle. 1979. Effects of discourse type on recall. Prose Learning Series Research Report no. 6. Tempe, Ariz.: Arizona State University.

Miccinati, J. L., and S. Phelps. 1980. Classroom drama from children's reading: From the page to the stage. *Reading Teacher* 34:269–72.

———. 1981. Use visual imagery to enhance recall of information. *Reading World* 21:139–43.

Miller, G. M., and G. E. Mason. 1983. Dramatic improvisation: risk-free role playing for improving reading performance. *Reading Teacher* 37:128–31.

Miramontes, O., L. Cheng, and H. T. Trueba. 1984. Teacher perceptions and observed outcomes: An ethnographic study of classroom interactions. *Learning Disability Quarterly* 7:349–57.

Moe, A. J., and C. J. Hopkins. 1978. Jingles, jokes, limericks, poems, proverbs, puns, puzzles and riddles: Fast reading for reluctant readers. *Language Arts* 55:957–65.

Moffett, J. 1968. *Teaching the universe of discourse.* Boston: Houghton Mifflin.

Moldofsky, P. B. 1983. Teaching students to determine the central story problem: A practical application of schema theory. *Reading Teacher* 36:740–45.

Moore, D. W. 1983. A case for naturalistic assessment of reading comprehension. *Language Arts* 60:957–68.

Moore, J. C., C. L. Jones, and D. G. Miller. 1980. What we know after a decade of sustained silent reading. *Reading Teacher* 33:445–50.

Moore, P. 1971. *The missing necklace.* Glenview, Ill.: Scott, Foresman.

Morey, W. 1965. *Gentle Ben.* New York: Avon Books.

Morris, J. 1987. *Create your own whole language games.* Lakewood, Colo.: LINK.

Morris, R. D. 1979. Some aspects of the interactional environment and learning to read. *Language Arts* 56:497–502.

Moss, J. F. 1978. Using the "focus unit" to enhance children's response to literature. *Language Arts* 55:482–88.

———. 1982. Reading and discussing fairy tales—old and new. *Reading Teacher* 35:656–60.

———. 1984. *Focus units in literature: A handbook for elementary school teachers.* Urbana, Ill.: National Council of Teachers of English.

Moss, J. F., and S. Oden. 1983. Children's story comprehension and social learning. *Reading Teacher* 36:784–89.

Moyer, S. B. 1982. Repeated reading. *Journal of Learning Disabilities* 15:619–23.

Murray, D. M. 1968. *A writer teaches writing.* Boston: Houghton Mifflin.

———. 1982. *Learning by teaching.* Montclair, N.J.: Boynton/Cook.

Name of the Tree. 1972. In *City sidewalks*, Bank Street College of Education. New York: Macmillan.

Neill, K. 1980. Turn kids on with repeated readings. *Teaching Exceptional Children* 13:63–64.

Nelson, H. 1980. Analysis of spelling errors in normal and dyslexic children. In U. Frith (Ed.), *Cognitive processes in spelling,* 475–93. New York: Academic Press.

Newman, J. 1978. Oral reading miscue analysis is good but not complete. *Reading Teacher* 31:883–85.

Newsom, S. D. 1979. Rock'n roll'n reading. *Journal of Reading* 22:726–30.

Nichols, J. 1978. Foiling students who'd rather fake it than read it or how to get students to read and report on books. *Journal of Reading* 22:245–47.

Norland, R. G. 1976. Sustained silent reading (SSR) as in let them read. *Reading Horizons* 16:157–59.

Norton, D. E. 1977. A web of interest. *Language Arts* 54:928–32.

————. 1982. Using a webbing process to develop children's literature units. *Language Arts* 59:348–56.

Nutter, N., and I. J. Safran. 1983. Sentence combining and the learning disabled student. ERIC Document no.: 252–94.

————. 1984. Improving writing with sentence combining exercises. *Academic Therapy* 19:449–55.

Ohanion, S. 1981. Smuggling reading into the reading program. *Learning* 10:45–47.

Olson, M. C., et al. 1982. *The writing process*. Boston: Allyn & Bacon.

Ontario Ministry of Education. 1980. *Curriculum ideas for teachers: Children with learning disabilities*. Toronto: Ontario Educational Communications Authority.

O'Rourke, W. J. 1979. Are parents an influence on adolescent reading habits? *Journal of Reading* 22:340–43.

Page, W. D., and G. S. Pinnel. 1979a. Developing purposes for reading. *Today's Education* 68:52–55.

————. 1979b. *Teaching reading comprehension*. Urbana, Ill.: National Council of Teachers of English.

Pearson, P. D., and M. C. Gallagher. 1983. The instruction of reading comprehension. *Contempory Educational Psychology* 8:317–44.

Pearson, P. D., J. Hansen, and C. Gordon. 1979. The effect of background knowledge on young children's comprension of explicit and implicit information. *Journal of Reading Behavior* 11:201–9.

Pearson, P. D., and D. D. Johnson. 1978. *Teaching reading comprehension*. New York: Holt, Rinehart & Winston.

Pearson, P. D., and R. Spiro. 1980. Toward a theory of reading comprehension instruction. *Language Disorders and Learning Disabilities* 71–88.

Perlmutter, B. F., and M. V. Parus. 1983. Identifying children with learning disabilities: A comparison of diagnostic procedures across school districts. *Learning Disability Quarterly* 6:321–28.

Pflaum, S. W., et al. 1980. The influence of pupil behaviors and pupil status factors on teacher behaviors during oral reading lessons. *Journal of Educational Research* 74:99–105.

Pflaum, S. W., and T. H. Bryan. 1982. Oral reading research and learning disabled children. *Topics in Learning and Learning Disabilities* 1:33–42.

Pitts, M. M. 1983. Comprehension monitoring: Definition and practice. *Journal of Reading* 26:516–22.

Pooley, R. C. 1974. *The teaching of English usage*. Urbana, Ill.: National Council of Teachers of English.

Poostay, E. J. 1984. Show me your underlines: A strategy to teach comprehension. *Reading Teacher* 37:828–30.

Poplin, M. S. 1983. *Learning disabilities at the crossroad*. Paper presented at the annual meeting of the Claremont Reading Conference. ERIC reproduction no. ED 229 958.

————. 1984a. Summary rationalizations, apologies and farewell: What we don't know about the learning disabled. *Learning Disability Quarterly* 7:130–34.

————. 1984b. Toward an holistic view of persons with learning disabilities. *Learning Disability Quarterly* 7:290–94.

Price, K., and M. Dequine. 1982. Peer tutoring: It builds skills and self-concept. *Academic Therapy* 17:365–71.

Quisenberry, N. L., C. Blakemore, and C. A. Warren. 1977. Involving parents in reading: An annotated bibliography. *Reading Teacher* 31:34–39.

Radebough, M. R. 1981. Using children's literature to teach mathematics. *Reading Teacher* 34:902–6.

Rand, M. K. 1984. Story schema: Theory, research and practice. *Reading Teacher* 37:377–82.

Rankin, E. F. 1974. *The measurement of reading flexibility*. Newark, Del.: International Reading Association.

Raphael, T. E. 1982. Question-answering strategies for children. *Reading Teacher* 36:186–90.

————. 1986. Teaching question answer relationships, revisited. *Reading Teacher* 39:516–23.

Raphael, T. E., and J. McKinney. 1983. An examination of 5th and 8th grade children's question-answering behavior: An instructional study in metacognition. *Journal of Reading Behavior* 15:67–86.

Raphael, T. E., and P. D. Pearson. 1982.

The effect of metacognitive awareness training on children's question answering behavior. Technical Report no. 238. Urbana, Ill.: Center for the Study of Reading.

Raphael, T. E., and C. A. Wonnacott. 1981. The effect of metacognitive training on question-answering behavior: Implementation in a fourth grade developmental reading program. Paper presented at the National Reading Conference, Dallas, Texas.

Rasmussen, C. 1962. *Let's say poetry together and have fun.* Minneapolis, Minn.: Burgess.

Rawls, W. 1974. *Where the red fern grows.* New York: Bantam.

Read, C. 1975. *Children's categorization of speech sounds in English.* Urbana, Ill.: National Council of Teachers of English.

Readence, J. E., T. W. Bean, and R. S. Baldwin. 1981. *Content area reading: An integrated approach.* Dubuque, Iowa: Kendall/Hunt.

Recht, D. R. 1976. The self-correction process in reading. *Reading Teacher* 29:632–36.

Reid, D. K., and W. P. Hresko. 1981. *A cognitive approach to learning disabilities.* New York: McGraw Hill.

Reid, D. K., W. P. Hresko, and D. D. Hammill. 1981. *Test of early reading ability.* Austin, Tex.: Pro-Ed.

Reynolds, R. E., and R. C. Anderson. 1982. Influence of questions on the allocation of attention during reading. *Journal of Educational Psychology* 74:623–32.

Rhodes, L. K. 1978. Making connections: I had a cat. *Language Arts* 58:772–74.

———. 1979. The interaction of beginning readers' strategies and texts displaying alternative models of predictability. Doctoral dissertation, Indiana University.

———. 1981. I can read! Predictable books as resources for reading and writing instruction. *Reading Teacher* 34:511–18.

———. 1983. Organizing the elementary classroom for effective language learning. In U. H. Hardt (Ed.), *Teaching reading with the other language arts,* 83–103. Newark, Del.: International Reading Association.

———. 1985. *Q is for duck: Activities and ideas.* Lakewood, Colo.: LINK.

Rhodes, L. K., and M. W. Hill. 1983. Home-school cooperation in integrated language arts program. In B. A. Bushching and J. I. Schwarz (Eds.), *Integrating the language arts in the elementary school,* 179–88. Urbana, Ill.: National Council of Teachers of English.

———. 1985. Supporting reading in the home naturally: Selected materials for parents. *Reading Teacher* 38:619–23.

Rhodes, L. K., and J. L. Shannon. 1982. Psycholinguistic principles in operation in a primary learning disabled classroom. *Topics in Learning and Learning Disabilities* 1:33–42.

Richardson, J. E. 1976. *A risky trip.* Beverly Hills, Calif.: Benziger.

Richgels, D. J., and R. Hansen. 1984. Gloss: Helping students apply both skills and strategies in reading content texts. *Journal of Reading* 27:312–17.

Richgels, D. J., and J. A. Mateja. 1984. Gloss II: Integrate content and process for independence. *Journal of Reading* 27:424–31.

Riley, J. D. 1979. Teachers' responses are as important as the questions they ask. *Reading Teacher* 32:534–37.

Robinson, F. P. 1961. Study skills for superior students in secondary schools. *Reading Teacher* 15:29–33.

Robinson, H. A. 1983. *Teaching reading, writing, and study strategies: The content areas.* Boston: Allyn & Bacon.

Rose, M. C., B. P. Cundick, and K. L. Higbie. 1983. Verbal rehearsal and visual imagery: Mnemonic aids for learning disabled children. *Journal of Learning Disabilities* 16:352–54.

Rosenblatt, L. M. 1978. *The reader, the text, the poem.* Carbondale Ill.: Southern Illinois University Press.

Ross, P. A. 1978. Getting books into those empty hands. *Reading Teacher* 31:397–99.

Rowe, J. L. 1959a. Readin', TYPIN', and 'rithmetic. *Business Education World* 39:9–12.

———. 1959b. Readin', TYPIN', and 'rithmetic. *Business Education World* 39:19–21.

———. 1959c. Readin', TYPIN', and 'rithmetic. *Business Education World* 39:19–22.

Rowe, M. B. 1974. Relation of wait-time and rewards to the development of language logic, and fate control: Part one—wait time. *Journal of Research in Science Teaching* 11:81−94.

———. 1986. Wait time: Slowing down may be a way of speeding up. *Journal of Teacher Education* 37:43−50.

Ruddell, R. B. 1978. Developing comprehension abilities: implications from research for an instructional framework. In S. J. Samuels (Ed.), *What research has to say about reading instruction.* Newark, Del: International Reading Association.

Rumelhart, D. E. 1975. Notes on a schema for stories. In D. G. Bobrow and A. Collins (Eds.), *Representations and understandings.* New York: Academic Press.

Ryan, E. G., and E. P. Torrance. 1967. Training in elaboration. *Journal of Reading* 11:27−32.

Sadoski, M. C. 1980. Ten years of uninterrupted sustained silent reading. *Reading Improvement* 17:153−56.

Sadow, M. 1980. The use of story grammar in the design of questions. *Reading Teacher* 35:518−23.

Samuels, S. J. 1979. The method of repeated readings. *Reading Teacher* 32:403−8.

Schaudt, B. A. 1983. ERIC/RCS: Another look at sustained silent reading. *Reading Teacher* 36:934−36.

Schiller, C. 1973. I'm OK, you're OK. Let's choral read. *English Journal* 62:791−94.

Schneeberg, H. 1977. Listening while reading: A four year study. *Reading Teacher* 30:629−35.

Schoof, R. N., Jr. 1978. Four-color words: Comic books in the classroom. *Language Arts* 55:821−27.

Schuck, A., F. Ulsh, and J. Platt. 1983. Parents encourage pupils (PEP): An innercity parent involvement reading program. *Reading Teacher* 36:524−27.

Schumaker, J., et al. 1982. Multipass: A learning strategy for improving reading comprehension. *Learning Disability Quarterly* 5:295−304.

Sebesta, S. L., J. W. Calder, and L. N. Cleland. 1982. A story grammar for the classroom. *Reading Teacher* 36:180−84.

Shanahan, T. 1980. The impact of writing instruction on learning to read. *Reading World* 19:357−66.

Shanklin, N. K. 1981. *Relating reading and writing; Developing a transactional theory of the writing process.* Bloomington, Ind.: Monographs in Teaching and Learning. School of Education, Indiana University.

Shaugnessy, M. D. 1977. *Errors and expectations: A guide for the teacher of basic writing.* New York: Oxford University Press.

Shuman, R. B. 1982. Reading with a purpose: Strategies to interest reluctant readers. *Journal of Reading* 25:725−30.

Siegel, M. G. 1984. Reading as signification. Doctoral dissertation, Indiana University.

Silverstein, S. 1974. *Where the sidewalk ends.* New York: Harper & Row.

———. 1981. *A light in the attic.* New York: Harper & Row.

Singer, H. 1978. Active comprehension: From answering to asking questions. *Reading Teacher* 31:901−8.

Singer, H., J. D. McNeil, and L. L. Furse. 1984. Relationship between curricular scope and reading achievement in elementary schools. *Reading Teacher* 37:608−12.

Sleeter, C. 1984. Why is there learning diabilities? A critical analysis of the birth of the field in its social context. Paper presented at the annual meeting of the American Educational Research Association, April 1, Chicago, Illinois.

Sloyer, S. 1982. *Readers' theatre: Story dramatization in the classroom.* Urbana, Ill.: National Council of Teachers of English.

Smith, C. F. 1978. Read a book in an hour. *Journal of Reading* 23:25−29.

Smith, F. 1973. *Psycholinguistics and reading.* New York: Holt, Rinehart & Winston.

———. 1981. Demonstrations, engagement, and sensitivity: The choice between people and programs. *Language Arts* 58:634−42.

——— 1982a. *Understanding reading.* New York: Holt, Rinehart & Winston.

———. 1982b. *Writing and the writer.* New York: Holt, Rinehart & Winston.

———. 1983. Reading like a writer. *Language Arts* 60:558−67.

Smith, L. B. 1982. Sixth graders write about reading literature. *Language Arts* 59:357−63.

Smith, S. L. 1979. *No easy answer: The LD*

child at home and at school. New York: Bantam Books.

Snow, C., et al. 1984. Therapy as a social interaction: Analyzing the contexts for language remediation. *Topics in Language Disorders* 4:72−85.

Spiegel, D. L., and C. Rogers. 1980. Teacher responses to miscues during oral reading by second-grade students. *Journal of Educational Research* 74:8−12.

Spier, P. 1961. *The fox went out on a chilly night.* Garden City, N.Y.: Doubleday.

Squire, J. R. 1983. Composing and comprehending: Two sides of the same basic process. *Language Arts* 60:581−89.

Stansell, J. C., and D. E. DeFord. 1981. When is a reading problem not a reading problem? *Journal of Reading* 25:14−20.

Stein, N. L., and C. G. Glenn, 1979. An analysis of story comprehension in elementary school children. In R. O. Freedle (Ed.), *New directions in discourse processing.* Norwood, N.J.: Ablex.

Steiner, B. 1980. *But not Stanleigh.* Chicago: Children's Book Press.

Stephens, D. 1985. Uncharted land: Reading comprehension research with the special education student. In A. Crismore (Ed.), *Landscapes: A state of the art assessment of reading comprehension research.* Final Report HUSDE-C-300-83-0130. Bloomington, Ind.: Language Education Department, Indiana University.

Stevens, K. 1982. Can we improve reading by teaching background information? *Journal of Reading* 25:326−29.

Stotsky, S. L. 1974. Sentence combining as a curricular activity: Its effect on written language development and reading comprehension. *Research in the Teaching of English* 8:30−71.

Stotsky, S. 1983. Research on reading/writing relationships: A synthesis and suggested directions. *Language Arts* 60:627−42.

Strickland, D. S. 1972. Black is beautiful vs. white is right. *Elementary English* 49:220−23.

Strom, L. 1980. Open to suggestion: Vocabulary game for the content areas. *Journal of Reading* 23:582−83.

Stubbs, M. 1982. Written language and society: Some particular cases and general observations. In M. Nystrand (Ed.),

What writers know: The language, process, and structure of written discourse, 31−55. New York: Academic Press.

Swaby, B. 1984. FAN out your facts on the board. *Reading Teacher* 37:914−16.

Taba, H., and F. F. Elzey. 1964. Teaching strategies and thought processes. *Teachers College Record* 65:524−43.

Tarver, S. G., and M. M. Dawson. 1978. Modality preference and the teaching of reading: A review. *Journal of Learning Disabilities* 11:5−17.

Tatham, S. M. 1978. Comprehension taxonomies: Their uses and abuses. *Reading Teacher* 32:190−94.

Taubenheim, B., and J. Christensen. 1978. Let's shoot "Cock Robin"! Alternatives to "round robin" reading. *Language Arts* 55:975−77.

Taylor, B. M. 1980. Children's memory for expository text after reading. *Reading Research Quarterly* 15:399−411.

Taylor, B. M., and R. W. Beach. 1984. The effects of text structure instruction on middle-grade students' comprehension and production of expository text. *Reading Research Quarterly* 19:134−46.

Taylor, B. M., and S. J. Samuels. 1983. Children's use of text structure in the recall of expository material. *American Educational Research Journal* 20:517−28.

Taylor, D. 1983. *Family literacy: Young children learning to read and write.* Portsmouth, N.H.: Heinemann.

Taylor, J. 1977. Making sense: The basic skill in reading. *Language Arts* 54:668−72.

Taylor, K. K. 1984. Teaching summarization skills. *Journal of Reading* 27:389−93.

Taylor, N. D., and O. Connor. 1982. Silent vs. oral reading: The rational instructional use of both processes. *Reading Teacher* 35:440−43.

Taylor, N. E., and J. M. Vawter. 1978. Helping children discover the functions of written language. *Language Arts* 55:941−45.

Teale, W. H. 1978. Positive environments for learning to read: What studies of early readers tell us. *Language Arts* 55:922−32.

Temple, C. A. and J. W. Gillet. 1984. *Language arts: Learning processes and teaching practices.* Boston: Little, Brown.

Temple, C. A., R. G. Nathan, and N. A.

Burris. 1982. *The beginnings of writing.* Boston: Allyn & Bacon.

Thorndyke, P. W. 1977. Cognitive structures in comprehension and memory of narrative discourse. *Cognitive Psychology* 9:77–110.

Thorpe, H. W., B. Chiang, and C. Darch. 1981. Individual and group feedback systems for improving oral reading accuracy in learning disabled and regular class children. *Journal of Learning Disabilities* 14:332–34.

Tierney, R. J., and J. LaZansky, 1980. The rights and responsibilities of readers and writers: A contractual agreement. *Language Arts* 57:606–13.

Tofler, A. 1980. *The third wave.* New York: Bantam Books.

Tolstoy, A. 1968. *The great big enormous turnip.* New York: Franklin Watts.

Tompkins, G. E., and L. M. McGee. 1983. Launching nonstandard speakers into standard English. *Language Arts* 60: 463–69.

Tortelli, J. P. 1976. Simplified psycholinguistic diagnosis. *Reading Teacher* 29:637–39.

Toth, M. 1982. We write for a reason. *Instructor* 91:38–40.

Tovey, D. R. 1979. Teachers' perceptions of children's reading miscues. *Reading Horizons* 19:302–7.

————. 1981. Children's perceptions of oral and silent reading. *Reading Horizons* 22:72–80.

Trelease, J. 1985. *The read-aloud handbook.* New York: Penguin Books.

True, J. 1979. Round robin reading is for the birds. *Language Arts* 56:918–21.

Turbill, J. 1983. *Now, we want to write!* Rozelle, N.S.W., Australia: Primary English Teaching Association (Heinemann, dist.).

Turnbull, A. P., J. A. Summers, and M. J. Brotherson. 1983. Family life cycle: Theoretical and empirical implications and future directions for families with mentally retarded members. Paper presented at the NICHD conference on "Research on families with retarded children."

Vacca, J. 1981. Reading with a sense of writer: Writing with a sense of reader. *Language Arts* 58:937–41.

Vacca, R. T. 1981. *Content area reading.* Boston: Little, Brown.

Vawter, J. M., and M. Vancil. 1980. Helping children discover reading through self-directed dramatization. *Reading Teacher* 34:320–23.

Vergason, E. L. 1974. Be your own Boswell. In P. A. Geuder, L. K. Harvey, D. Loyd, J. D. Wages (Eds.), *They really taught us to write*, 35–36. Urbana, Ill.: National Council of Teachers of English.

Vernon, M. D. 1957. *Backwardness in reading.* Cambridge: Cambridge University Press.

Vukelich, C. 1984. Parents' role in the reading process: A review of practical suggestions and ways to communicate with parents. *Reading Teacher* 37:472–77.

Vygotsky, L. 1986. *Thought and language,* ed. by A. Kozulin. Cambridge, Mass.: MIT Press.

Wardbaugh, R. 1969. *Reading: A linguistic perspective.* New York: Harcourt.

Watson, D. J. 1978a. Reader-selected miscues: Getting more from sustained silent reading. *English Education* 10:75–85.

————. 1978b. Recording, decoding, will the real reader stand up? Speech given at National Conference on the Language Arts in the Elementary school, Indianapolis, Ind.

————. In press. Skinny books. In D. J. Watson (ed.), *Language Arts Ideas for K–6.* Urbana, Ill.: National Council of Teachers of English.

Weaver, C. 1982. Welcoming errors as signs of growth. *Language Arts* 59:438–44.

Weener, P. 1981. On comparing learning disabled and regular classroom children. *Journal of Learning Disabilities* 14:227–32.

Weiderholt, J. L. 1974. Historical perspectives on the education of the learning disabled. In L. Mann & D. Sabatino (Eds.), *The second review of special education*, 103–52. Philadelphia: JSE Press.

Whaley, J. F. 1981. Story grammars and reading instruction. *Reading Teacher* 34:760–71.

Wilcox, L. M. 1977. Literature: The child's guide to creative writing. *Language Arts* 54:549–54.

Williams, F., R. Hopper, and D. S. Natalicio. 1977. *The sounds of children.* Englewood Cliffs, N.J.: Prentice-Hall.

Winkeljohann, R., and R. Gallant. 1979. Queries: Why oral reading? *Language Arts* 56:950−53.

Wixson, K. K. 1983. Questions about a text: What you ask about is what children learn. *Reading Teacher* 37:287−93.

Wong, B. 1985. Metacognition and learning disabilities. In T. G. Woller, T. Forest, and E. Mackinnon (Eds.), *Metacognition, cognition, and human performance*. New York: Academic Press.

Wong, B., and W. Jones. 1982. Increasing metacomprehension in learning disabled and normally achieving students through self-questioning training. *Learning Disability Quarterly* 5:228−40.

Wood, M. L. 1983. Shared reading. In J. Newman (Ed.), *Whole language activities*. Halifax, N.S.: Dalhousie University.

Yoakley, C. B. 1974. One approach to the process. In P. A. Geuder, L. K. Harvey, D. Lohd, and J. D. Wages (Eds.), *They really taught us how to write*, 46−49. Urbana, Ill.: National Council of Teachers of English.

Ysseldyke, J. E. and B. Algozzine, 1983. LD or not LD: That's not the question! *Journal of Learning Disabilities* 16:29−31.

Ysseldyke, J. E., B. Algozzine, and M. Thurlow. 1983. On interpreting institute research: A response to McKinney. *Exceptional Education Quarterly* 4:145−47.

Ysseldyke, J. E., et al. 1982. Similarities and differences between low achievers and students labeled learning disabled. *Journal of Special Education* 16:73−85.

Zutell, J. 1978. Some psycholinguistic perspectives on children's spelling. *Language Arts* 55:844−50.

Author index

Subject index